W9-BGX-114

MODERN ESSAYS
ON WRITING
AND STYLE

MODERN ESSAYS ON WRITING AND STYLE

second edition

Paul C. Wermuth
NORTHEASTERN UNIVERSITY

HOLT, RINEHART AND WINSTON, INC.

New York Chicago San Francisco Atlanta
Dallas Montreal Toronto London Sydney

Copyright © 1964, 1969 by Holt, Rinehart and Winston, Inc.
All Rights Reserved
Library of Congress Catalog Card Number: 69-15060
03-076565-X
Printed in the United States of America
1   2   3   4   5   6   7   8   9

TO BARBARA

PREFACE
to the Second Edition

The gratifying success of the first edition of this book seems to indicate a great interest in stylistic matters, and possibly some justification of the idea that a study of style can provide a fitting center on which to focus a writing course.

In this second edition I have eliminated six essays that did not seem to work well, or that were too dull or repetitious. However, I have added eleven new ones, making this version longer than the first. The greatest change has been to give more space to the linguists, who have dominated writing about style in recent years. Much linguistic writing on this topic, while not yet practically useful to the writer, is interesting and has helped greatly in the slow change of attitudes toward conventional usage. It holds great promise for the future, and demands the attention of those who care about writing.

The book has also been reorganized into what seems a more logical arrangement; and a section has been made of analyses of period and individual styles, to give the student some idea of the ways in which style can be talked about, and what value this might have. The object all along has been to make the book more useful for teaching, while leaving the individual teacher room for his own imagination. I hope it has been successful in this aim.

P. C. W.

Boston, Massachusetts
January 1969

PREFACE
to the First Edition

Santayana introduces his book, *Skepticism and Animal Faith,* by saying with gentle humor, "Here is one more system of philosophy"; he quickly adds, "If the reader is tempted to smile, I can assure him that I smile with him." Well, here is one more essay text purporting to teach something about writing. And I would like to add my agreeable and knowing smile to the reader's as evidence that I am aware many people think writing is unteachable. But I really cannot, because this book makes, I think, an unusual assertion: that it is possible to teach writing by concentrating on the matter of style.

There are many approaches to teaching writing: the grammatical approach, the rhetorical approach, and the reading approach, the last of which usually involves a set of essays on "current problems." Most college teachers have used all of these approaches at one time or another and know their virtues and short-comings. The particular virtues of concentrating on style, however, are not only that a discussion of style includes many of the most important concerns of rhetoric, but also that it makes writing itself the subject matter of the course. Furthermore, one could argue that style is the most important single factor to understand about writing. Who has not noticed—and been distressed by—the insensitivity of many modern students to writing style, their inability to distinguish one writer from another? If one could make style the center of their concern, make them more aware of style and more sensitive to it, one could create in them a new comprehension of what writing is all about—not to mention a new interest in developing their own writing.

For as any teacher of writing knows, each student does already have a style of his own, however primitive or embryonic it may be. It is one of the marvels of humanity that every person has a uniquely different spark that is himself, and that spark shows up in his writing. It ought to be the job of the teacher of writing to encourage that spark as much as possible, to make it into a real, developed style, which is one way—and the best way—of having the student realize himself.

This book's basic assumption is that style is a central concern of any writing course. The selections can be used for the whole or for a part of the traditional composition course; they can be used as supplementary reading for such a course; and they can be used as either text or supplementary reading for any course in advanced composition. The book brings together some of the best modern writing on the subject of style, or on aspects of the subject, though I have tried to avoid material which is too highly specialized and technical. The order of the material is, of course, somewhat artificial. Some attempt has been made to present different views on certain critical concerns of style without necessarily making a neat contrast of pairs. The essays are modern, mostly from the past three decades. The emphasis is on the modern not only because one would wish students to develop the style of their own time, but also because, in a way, the history of style is implied in modern style. The book deals with prose rather than verse, though of course much of it is applicable to verse; but not many people have written about verse style, and prose is the medium of our time. Finally, most of the authors represented here are writers and/or scholars, people who have made their living by use of the written language and most of whom have an individual and interesting style of their own.

The Appendix offers illustrative examples of many different modern styles for analysis. Many of these passages are from writers alluded to in the text, though many additional writers are quoted in the various essays; and, of course, many of the essays are themselves analyzable. Most of these passages are here to illustrate various stylistic possibilities; a few are supposed to be bad examples. A close and careful analysis of these passages by the teacher, in the light of the essays of the text, should prove highly effective in developing that understanding and appreciation of style which is the ultimate aim of the book.

P. C. W.

New Britain, Connecticut
November 1963

CONTENTS

III   ANALYSES OF STYLE

general or period styles

particular styles

Appendix: SAMPLE PASSAGES FOR ANALYSIS AND DISCUSSION 335

MODERN ESSAYS
ON WRITING
AND STYLE

1 THE BASES OF STYLE

THE FOUNDATION
OF STYLE—CHARACTER

F. L. Lucas

Most discussions of style seem to me to begin at the wrong end; like an architect who should disregard foundations, and give his mind only to superstructure and decoration. They plunge into the tricks of the trade —the choice of words, the employment of epithets, the build of paragraphs. Yet here their rules seem often arbitrary, their precepts often capricious; and I grow as bored and rebellious as, I take it, Laertes did while listening to the injunctions of Polonius (even though some of the injunctions are excellent, and Laertes himself shared only too fully his father's fondness for lecturing). I begin to damn all tricks of all trades; to forswear tricks of any sort; to wish I were away on a Scottish hillside, or among Greek peasants who have never heard of such coxcombries; in fact, to feel very like Samuel Butler . . .

A man may, and ought to take pains to write clearly, tersely and euphemistically:[1] he will write many a sentence three or four times over—to do much more than this is worse than not rewriting at all:

Reprinted with permission of Crowell-Collier and Macmillan, Inc. from Style *by F. L. Lucas. Copyright 1955 by F. L. Lucas. Reprinted also with permission of Cassell and Company, Ltd. Footnotes renumbered.*

[1] I suppose Butler meant, and perhaps wrote, "euphoniously"—few men have been less given than he to euphemism—that is, calling unpleasant things by pleasant names. (Quotation from *S. Butler's Note-Books,* ed. G. Keynes and B. Hill, 1951. [Ed.])

he will be at great pains to see that he does not repeat himself, to arrange his matter in the way that shall best enable the reader to master it, to cut out superfluous words and, even more, to eschew irrelevant matter: but in each case he will be thinking not of his own style but of his reader's convenience. Men like Newman and R. L. Stevenson seem to have taken pains to acquire what they called a style as a pre-liminary measure—as something they had to form before their writings could be of any value. I should like to put it on record that I never took the smallest pains with my style, have never thought about it, do not know nor want to know whether it is a style at all or whether it is not, as I believe and hope, just common, simple straightforwardness. I cannot conceive how any man can take thought for his style without loss to himself and his readers.

As I have already said, I suspect that Butler really knew he had an excellent style, but chose, aggressive creature, to misuse "style" to mean "elegant mannerism," in order then to damn it. But my point is this. Literary style is simply a means by which one personality moves others. The problems of style, therefore, are really problems of personality—of practical psychology. Therefore this psychological foundation should come first; for on it the rules of rhetoric are logically based. These are *not* (when they are sound) arbitrary or capricious. And when they are seen to be neither arbitrary nor capricious, but rational and logical, they may then cease to be irritating or boring.

The primary question, therefore, is how best to move and direct men's feelings. For even the most factual writing may involve feeling. Even the coldest biological monograph on the habits of flatworms, or the most detached piece of historical research into the price of eggs under Edward I, may be written so lucidly, argued so neatly, as to stir pleasure and admiration. Even mathematical solutions (though here I speak with trembling) can have aesthetic beauty.

Further, apart from the charm of neatness and lucidity, the influence of personality intrudes itself even into subjects where men try to be dispassionately judicial. You may have a new theory of trade-cycles; your evidence may be excellent; but, though the the truth may in the end prevail anyway, no matter how personally repellent its advocate, you are likely to make it prevail much more quickly if you know not only how to state, but how to state *persuasively*.

In less scientific and more literary forms of writing or speaking, the element of emotion becomes far larger, and so does the importance of persuasiveness.

A nation, for example, has to be persuaded that though Hitler is at Dunkirk, there can be no question of white flags (then, fortunately, little persuasion was needed); or a reader has to be persuaded that a skylark is not a bird, but "a blithe spirit" (to which, I own, I remain somewhat recalcitrant).

But persuasion, though it depends partly on the motives adduced for belief—how plausibly they are put, how compellingly they are worded —depends also, and sometimes depends still more, on the *personality* of the persuader. Just as, when we are advised in real life, we are often influenced as much by the character of the adviser as by the intrinsic merits of his advice.

Style, I repeat, is a means by which a human being gains contact with others; it is personality clothed in words, character embodied in speech. If handwriting reveals character, style reveals it still more—unless it is so colourless and lifeless as not really to be a style at all. The fundamental thing, therefore, is *not* technique, useful though that may be; if a writer's personality repels, it will not avail him to eschew split infinitives, to master the difference between "that" and "which," to have Fowler's *Modern English Usage* by heart. Soul is more than syntax. If your readers dislike you, they will dislike what you say. Indeed, such is human nature, unless they like you they will mostly deny you even justice.

Therefore, if you wish your writing to seem good, your character must seem at least partly so. And since in the long run deception is likely to be found out, your character had better not only *seem* good, but *be* it. Those who publish make themselves public in more ways than they sometimes realize. Authors may sell their books: but they give themselves away.

Does this, I wonder, seem very far-fetched? Yet it is not so new a view, after all. I find something not very different in that dry-minded person Aristotle (though he is talking, of course, only of oratory). "But since the art of speech aims at producing certain judgements . . . the speaker must not only look to his words, to see they are cogent and convincing, he must also present himself as a certain type of person and put those who judge him in a certain frame of mind. . . . For it makes all the difference to men's opinions whether they feel friendly or hostile, irritated or indulgent. . . . To carry conviction, a speaker needs three qualities—for there are three things that convince us, apart from actual proof—good sense, good character, and good will towards his hearers."[2] Such stress on sympathy and personality may seem to come a little strangely from the cold and detached Aristotle. But it is only the more telling for that.

Some three centuries later, the less prosaic "Longinus" glimpsed essentially the same truth (though I wish he had not mixed his metaphors): "Height of style is the echo of a great personality."[3] And when

---

[2] *Rhetoric*, II, 1.

[3] IX, 2. Compare the Roman definition of a good orator—'Vir bonus, dicendi peritus"—"A good man with practice in speech." Optimistic perhaps; but, in the long run, not without truth; and truer of literature, which has a longer run

the noble simplicity of Vauvenargues uttered its corollary as applied to the critic: "Il faut avoir de l'âme pour avoir du goût"; when Buffon penned his much quoted, and misquoted, "Le style est l'homme même",[4] when Yeats described style as "but high breeding in words and in argument," they were all restating this constantly forgotten point.

Napoleon was no sentimental aesthete. But even he, when asked to appoint some person to a post, replied, if I remember, "Has he written anything? Que je voie son style!"

The wisdom of China, indeed, realized this truth long ago. The *Book of Odes,* preserved for us by Confucius, includes popular ballads of the feudal states, which were periodically forwarded to the Son of Heaven so that, we are told, the Imperial Musicians might infer from them the moral state of the people. Plato would have approved. Confucius himself (says a fanciful tradition) thus studied a certain tune on his lute. After ten days he observed, "I have learned the tune, but I cannot get the rhythm"; after several days more, "I have the rhythm, but not the composer's intention"; after several days more, "I still cannot visualize his

---

than oratory. (This definition is said to be Cato the Elder's. See Seneca the rhetorician, *Controv.,* I, 9; Quintilian, XII, 1, 1.) Compare too Anatole France— "Les grands écrivains n'ont pas l'âme basse. Voilà, M. Brown, tout leur secret." (Though "tout" is too much.)

[4] Sometimes cited as "Le style, c'est l'homme"; sometimes in the form "le style est *de* l'homme." But it is weakened both by the addition of "de" and by the omission of "même." Needless difficulties, I think, have also been made over the meaning. Gosse, for example, (*s.v.* "Style" in *Encyclopædia Britannica,* 1910 edition) reminds us that Buffon was a biologist and that the sentence comes from his *Natural History;* therefore, he says, Buffon really meant that style "distinguished the language of man (*homo sapiens*) from the monotonous roar of the lion or the limited gamut of the bird. Buffon was engaged with biological, not with aesthetic ideas."

But I doubt if Buffon would have stooped to the platitude of telling us that man has style, birds not. It too much recalls *The Anti-Jacobin:*

> The feather'd tribes on pinions skim the air,
> Not so the mackerel, and still less the bear.

Actually, Buffon's phrase comes, not from his *Natural History,* but from his *Discours sur le Style,* his inaugural address to the French Academy. It seems to me not in the least "biological." And I take Buffon to be saying with classic calm very much what Victor Hugo proclaimed with romantic fervour:

> *Quinconque pense, illustre, obscur, sifflé, vainqueur,*
> *Grand ou petit, exprime en son livre son coeur.*
> *Ce que nous écrivons de nos plumes d'argile,*
> *Soit sur le livre d'or comme le doux Virgile,*
> *Soit comme Aligieri sur la bible de fer,*
> *Est notre propre flamme et notre propre chair.*

Or, as Gibbon put it, more briefly and clearly: "Style is the image of character" (*Autobiographies of E. Gibbon,* ed. J. Murray, 2nd ed. 1897, p. 353). The idea itself goes back far further. Socrates is credited with the saying: "As a man is, so is his speech"; similar maxims occur in Plato and Menander; and Seneca discusses it at length in *Epistle* 114.

person"; and finally, "Now I have seen one deep in thought gazing up to far heights, with intense longing. Now I see him—dark, tall, with whimsical eyes and the ambition of a world-ruler. Who could he be but King Wen the Civilized?"[5] Even in judging calligraphy and painting, according to Lin Yutang, "the highest criterion is not whether the artist shows good technique, but whether he has or has not *a high personality.*"[6]

All this may seem strangely remote from modern ideas. But it has a foundation of fact too often forgotten by most criticism; though Johnson and Sainte-Beuve kept it always in mind.

Return to Aristotle. The orator, he says, has to consider three things: the statements he utters; the attitude of his audience; the impression made by himself. This analysis can easily be extended from oratory to literature at large. Any literary writer is concerned with (A) statements, (B) feelings. (A) He makes his statements in a certain way. (B) (1) He arouses certain feelings in his audience[7] about his statements (a) intentionally, (b) unintentionally.

(2) He reveals certain feelings of his own (a) intentionally (unless he is deliberately impersonal), (b) unintentionally.

(3) He arouses certain feelings in his audience about himself and his feelings (a) intentionally, (b) unintentionally.

In short, a writer may be doing seven different things at once; four of them, consciously. Literature is complicated.

Consider, for example, Mark Antony's speech in the Forum. (A) Statements. Caesar has been killed by honourable men, who say he was ambitious.

(B) Feelings. (1) While pretending deference to the murderers, Antony rouses his hearers to rage against them.

(2) He reveals his own feelings. (a) (Intentionally): loyal resentment. (b) (Unintentionally): secret ambition.

(3) He arouses feelings in his audience towards himself. (a) (Intentionally): he poses as the moderate statesman, yet loyal friend. (b) (Unintentionally): he moves the more knowing theatre-audience to ironic amusement at his astuteness.

[5] Tsui Chi, *Short History of Chinese Civilization* (1942), p. 53.

[6] *Importance of Living* (1938), p. 384.

[7] In the most subjective forms of writing, such as the personal lyric, the writer's own feelings may become the main thing, and the audience may recede into the background. In Mill's phrase, the poet is less heard than overheard. Yet this convention contains a good deal of fiction. The poet may, indeed, proclaim as proudly as Hafiz:

> From the east to the west no man understands me—
> The happier I that confide to none but the wind!

Yet even modern poets, of whom the first of these lines would be far truer than of Hafiz, still seek publishers and read proofs. Whatever is published invites a public. And most prose-writers, at all events, are not much less conscious than the orator of addressing an audience.

The theatre-goer who knows the play, or Roman history, has Antony at a disadvantage. But even among Antony's audience in the Forum one can imagine a shrewd observer here and there seeing through his splendid rhetoric. For a writer, likewise, such shrewder minds are always there in wait. The readers who read between the lines, are the readers worth winning. But if the writer forgets them, if his mood in writing is mean or peevish or petty or vain or false, no cleverness and no technique are likely, in the end, to save him. That is why I repeat that the first thing in style is character. It is not easy to fool all one's readers all the time.

Consider side by side these two passages—letters to noble lords. (The first has become a lasting part of English Literature.)

Seven years, My Lord, have now past since I waited in your outward Rooms or was repulsed from your Door, during which time I have been pushing on my work through difficulties of which It is useless to complain, and have brought it at last to the verge of Publication without one Act of assistance, one word of encouragement, or one smile of favour. Such treatment I did not expect, for I never had a Patron before.

The Shepherd in Virgil grew at last acquainted with Love, and found him a native of the rocks.

Is not a Patron,[8] My Lord, one who looks with unconcern on a Man struggling for Life in the water and when he has reached ground encumbers him with help? The notice which you have been pleased to take of my Labours, had it been early, had been kind; but it has been delayed till I am indifferent and cannot enjoy it, till I am solitary and cannot impart it, till I am known, and do not want it.

I hope it is no very cynical asperity not to confess obligation where no benefit has been received, or to be unwilling that the Public should consider me as owing that to a Patron, which Providence has enabled me to do for myself.

Having carried on my work thus far with so little obligation to any Favourer of Learning I shall not be disappointed though I should conclude it, if less be possible, with less, for I have been long wakened from that Dream of hope, in which I once boasted myself with so much exultation,

My Lord,
Your Lordship's most humble,
Most Obedient Servant,
Sam: Johnson.

[8] Cf. the definition of "Patron" in Johnson's *Dictionary*—"commonly a wretch who supports with insolence, and is paid with flattery"; and the couplet in *The Vanity of Human Wishes:*

> There mark what ills the scholar's life assail,
> Toil, envy, want, the Patron, and the jail.

("The Patron" was substituted by Johnson, after his affray with Chesterfield, for "the garret" of the original version.)

And now for a different picture.

My Lord,

I feel that I am taking a liberty for which I shall have but small excuse and no justification to offer, if I am not fortunate enough to find one in your Lordship's approbation of my design; and unless you should condescend to regard the writer as addressing himself to your Genius rather than your Rank, and graciously permit me to forget my total inacquaintance with your Lordship personally in my familiarity with your other more permanent Self, to which your works have introduced me. If indeed I had not in *them* discovered that Balance of Thought and Feeling, of Submission and Mastery; that one sole unfleeting music which is never of yesterday, but still remaining reproduces *itself,* and powers akin to itself in the minds of other men:— believe me, my Lord! I not only could not have hazarded this Boldness, but my own sense of propriety would have precluded the very Wish. A sort of preestablished good will, like that with which the Swan instinctively takes up the weakling cygnet into the Hollow between its wings, I knew I might confidently look for from one who is indeed a Poet: were I but assured that your Lordship had ever thought of me as a fellow-laborer in the same vineyard, and as not otherwise unworthy your notice. And surely a fellow-laborer I *have* been, and a co-inheritor of the same Bequest, tho' of a smaller portion; and tho' your Lordship's ampler Lot is on the sunny side, while mine has lain upon the North, my *growing* Vines gnawed down by Asses, and my richest and raciest clusters carried off and spoilt by the plundering Fox. Excuse my Lord! the length and "petitionary" solemnity of this Preface, as attributable to the unquiet state of my spirits, under which I write this Letter and my fears as to its final reception. Anxiety makes us all ceremonious. . . .

The contrast is surely startling. One passage seems superb; the other, abject. Yet each is from the hand of genius.

Johnson's statement of fact is simple: Chesterfield is claiming grati-tude for helping him too little and too late. The feelings Johnson seeks to stir in his audience are also simple. (By "his audience" I do not mean Chesterfield, whom he merely wished to put in his place, but the public to whom, in fact, he is appealing against aristocratic arrogance. For his letter became "the talk of the town.") His readers are to feel anger towards a neglectful patron, and admiration for worth which no poverty could de-press. It is, in fine (much as Johnson would have disliked being compared to Americans or republicans) a Declaration of Independence in the re-public of letters.

As for Johnson's own feelings, what he reveals is the sturdy resent-ment of an honest man; and if one senses between the lines certain other feelings—satisfaction that Chesterfield's ill-treatment has relieved him of any obligations; pride, that he has accomplished his great work alone; triumph, that he can so trenchantly settle an old score—after all, these are perfectly human, and do him no discredit.

Therefore the letter as a whole is brilliantly effective. Full of art, it yet seems natural—for art has become second nature. Those balanced antitheses remains as much a part of Johnson as the majestic see-saw of his body when he perused a book; the irony vibrates; and the reader exults each time he reaches that sonorous Roman triplet—"cannot enjoy it . . . cannot impart it[9] . . . do not want it." It is hardly a very Christian letter, nor a very humble one; but it is the anger of a very honest man.

Only one note in it, to me, rings false. What is this shepherd doing here, who found Love a native of the rocks? What possessed Johnson, that contemner of *Lycidas,* that ceaseless mocker at the falsetto absurdities of the pastoral, to pose himself here with Arcadian pipe and crook? Drum and cudgel would have been more in *his* line. And Lord Chesterfield as a fickle Amaryllis?—Chesterfield, who looked more like a dwarf Cyclops!

But this false note, if false note it is, lasts only for one sentence. Contrast the second letter, written to Byron by Coleridge in March 1815.[10] Coleridge was, I suppose, as clever a man as Johnson—many would say cleverer; he was, at rare intervals, a finer poet; how could he here write so ill? So miscalculate his whole effect? For Byron, one imagines, must have read it with a pitying smile. No doubt it is easier to write with dignity letters refusing help than begging it. Yet it *can* be done. Read the appeal written—not in vain—by the despairing Crabbe to Burke. But this fulsome twaddle about weakling cygnets chirping for the hollow of his lordship's wings was surely not only feeble but also false and foolish.[11] Heep

---

[9] A reference to the death of his dear, queer Tetty.

[10] *Unpublished Letters,* ed. E. L. Griggs (1932), II, pp. 131–2. (Coleridge wanted Byron to recommend his poems to "some publisher" in the hope that Byron's influence would obtain him better terms.)

[11] In the margin of his *Pepys* (1825 edition) Coleridge expressed a franker opinion of Byron's work: "W. Wordsworth calls Lord Byron the mocking bird of our Parnassian ornithology, but the mocking bird, they say, has a very sweet song of his own, in true notes proper to himself. Now I cannot say I have ever heard any such in his Lordship's volumes of warbles; and in spite of Sir W. Scott, I dare predict that in less than a century, the Baronet's and the Baron's poems will lie on the same shelf of oblivion, Scott be read and remembered as a novelist and the founder of a new race of novels, and Byron not be remembered at all, except as a wicked lord who, from morbid and restless vanity, pretended to be ten times more wicked than he was."

So far from being "a swan," Byron had not "ever," apparently, seemed to Coleridge even so much as a mocking bird. It is rash to pass judgment on the animosities of authors; one never knows all the facts; though sometimes, as here, one may seem to know pretty well. At all events, in 1816 Coleridge had accepted £100 from Byron; in 1824, while Coleridge sat safe in Highgate, Byron had died for Greece in the marshes of Missolonghi. Coleridge's marginal note, like his letter, might have been better left unwritten.

and Pecksniff. Perhaps Coleridge dimly felt that, and was ashamed, and thereby grew demoralized in his style. Whether or no, my point is simply that this piece of writing is ruined, above all, by the personality behind— by Coleridge's weaker self. A good deal of difference between these two Samuels. No need to dwell on it—"look and pass."[12]

Naturally no fineness of character is likely to make an ungifted man write well (though I think that even this sometimes happens); but it can make a gifted one write far better. It is, I believe, personality above all that sets Virgil and Horace higher than Catullus and Ovid; Chaucer than Dryden,[13] Shakespeare than his contemporaries. Many Elizabethans could write at times blank verse as enchanting as his; but he alone could conceive a Hamlet or an Imogen. Or again we may read of Goldsmith's Vicar or Sterne's Uncle Toby with simple pleasure and amusement; but, if we stop to think, we must surely recognize also that, whatever faults or foibles Goldsmith and Sterne displayed in real life, yet they had characters fine enough to imagine these types of human nature at its most lovable. And it is for this above all that they are remembered.[14]

Again, though these are more questionable and more personal preferences, I find myself preferring Montaigne to Bacon, Flaubert and Hardy to Wilde and Shaw, as being fundamentally more honest characters; Sterne and Voltaire to Swift and Rousseau, as having more gaiety and good humour; Tennyson and Arnold to Browning and Meredith, as personalities more sensitive and more self-controlled. Or, to take a more recent example, amid the criticism of the last half-century, with all its acidulated sciolists and balderdashing decadents, dizzy with their own intellectual altitude, why is it, for me, such a relief to turn back to Desmond MacCarthy? Because his writing was not only witty and amusing, but also wise and good.

"And yet," you may exclaim, "think of the good writers who have been bad men—Villon, Rousseau, Byron, Baudelaire. . . ."

But I do not find this matter quite so simple. It is surely a little summary to dismiss a man in a monosyllable as "bad." No doubt Kingsley, when asked by one of his children who Heine was, is said to have replied, "A bad man, my dear, a bad man." And Carlyle, if I remember, dis-

---

[12] It is pleasant to contrast the refusal by Leconte de Lisle, though very poor, of a pension of 300 francs a month from Napoleon III on condition that he would dedicate his translations to the Prince Imperial. "Il serait sacrilège," he replied, "de dédier ces chefs d'oeuvre antiques à un enfant trop jeune pour les comprendre." To the honor of the Second Empire, Leconte de Lisle got his pension none the less.

[13] For a detailed comparison, from this point of view, between two typical passages of Chaucer and Dryden, see my *Decline and Fall of the Romantic Ideal* (1948 ed.), pp. 214–18.

[14] Cf. Goethe to Eckermann: "To Shakespeare, Sterne, and Goldsmith my debt has been infinite"—"Ich bin Shakespeare, Sterne, und Goldsmith unendliches schuldig gewesen."

missed Heine as "that blackguard." But do we take such judgements very seriously?

On ethics, as on aesthetics, men's judgements have varied wildly from age to age, without appearing any nearer to agreement. On certain points, indeed, there has been, since history began, surprising unanimity. Avarice, treachery, cowardice have had few admirers at any time. But in the Middle Ages, for instance, one of the deadliest sins was a refusal to believe certain abstruse theological details, hard to comprehend and impossible to establish; or to believe differently about them. Again in nineteenth-century England some people almost reduced sin to sex—a hazardous simplification, in reaction from which many of their grand-children made sex their only god. Therefore I should myself prefer to keep the term "bad" for moral qualities or actions that cause suffering to others without any justifying counter-balance of good.

Secondly, every man is many-sided—as Whitman said of himself, "I am large, I contain multitudes." Nor does this complicated blend of good and bad remain static. Character is not only a compound of ex-tremely various qualities, but the qualities themselves vary from year to year, even from hour to hour. The Spaniards will wisely say of a man, "He was brave *that day.*" We are all at war with ourselves; if an "indi-vidual" meant one literally "undivided," no such creature would exist.

Clearly Coleridge wrote *The Ancient Mariner* in a mood very dif-ferent from that in which he wrote his miserable letter to Byron (which Johnson, indeed, could not have written in any mood).

For all these reasons, judgements of character must remain extremely precarious. Yet it is often necessary to make them. A man with no sense of values is as crippled as a man cramped with prejudice.

Thirdly it has to be remembered in judging writers, that they often do—and indeed should—write with the best side of their character, and at their best moments. (It is indeed a commonplace that authors seem often less admirable and less interesting than their books.) Thus Mon-taigne confesses that his *Essays* kept him up to the mark in life, lest he should seem to live less uprightly than he wrote. Again, the Arabic poet al-Mutanabbi (d. 965), returning from Persia, was attacked near Kufa by the Beni Asad, and worsted; as he wheeled to flee, his slave said, "Never be it told that *you* turned in flight, you that wrote:

I am known to the horse-troop, the night, and the desert's expanse;
Not more to the paper and pen than the sword and the lance."

And al-Mutanabbi, shamed by his own verses, rode back into the battle, and fell. *Poésie oblige.*

No doubt a writer's worse qualities also are likely to get into his work—and to betray themselves there. But what still lives in Villon, ne'er-do-well as he may have been, is his bitter honesty of mind; his pity for his comrades swaying bird-pecked on the gallows, for his old mother shuddering before the fires of Hell, for the withered hags regretting their lost April, for the faded beauty of women dead long ago. What still lives in Rousseau, that walking museum of pathological curiosities—Narcissist, exhibitionist, and persecution-maniac—is his vivid sense for Nature, for simplicity, for the injustice and falsity of a decadent "civilization" riding on the necks of the poor. The histrionic melancholy and melodrama of Byron are long dead; but not the prose and verse he wrote in blazing scorn of shams and in detestation of tyranny. The carrion-side of Baudelaire is rotten; but not his tragic compassion for human waste and suffering and shame.

In short, where good writers have been commonly judged bad characters, one may sometimes answer that the code by which they were judged was narrow; or that the writers were better men in their studies than in the active world; or that they were better men at the moments when they wrote their best work.

On the other hand, when Croker in his review of Macaulay, as Rogers put it, "attempted murder and committed suicide," that was because the malicious feelings Croker betrayed in himself more than neutralized those that he tried to rouse in his readers. Well did Bentley say that no man was demolished but by himself; though unfortunately he also did his best to demonstrate it by his own edition of Milton.

In his *Commentaires*—"la Bible du Soldat" Henri IV called them— Blaise de Montluc (1502–77) describes his famous defence of Siena, against the forces of Charles the Fifth, in 1554–5, and the account he afterwards gave of it to Henri II. Montluc, a fiery Gascon famous for his choler, who might have been a ruder grandfather of d'Artagnan, and showed perhaps a touch of our own Montgomery, had yet astonished men by the patience and *finesse* with which, through those long months of famine and peril, he had steadied the Sienese to resist. How had he done it?

> I told the King that I had gone off one Saturday to the market, and in sight of everybody bought a bag, and a little cord to tie its mouth, together with a faggot, taking and shouldering them all in the public view; and when I reached my room, I asked for fire to kindle the faggot, then took the bag and stuffed into it all my ambition, all my avarice, my sensuality, my gluttony, my indolence, my partiality, my envy and my eccentricities, and all my Gascon humours—in short, everything that I thought might hinder me, in view of all I had to do in his service; then I

tightly tied the mouth of the bag with the cord, so that nothing should get out, and thrust it all in the fire. And thus I found myself clear of everything that could impede me in all I had to do for the service of His Majesty.[15]

A most vivid revelation of character; most graphically written. For, fire-eater as he was, Montluc knew the importance of being able to marshal words as well as troops. . . .

Yet I quoted this passage about the siege of Siena, not for its vivid style, but because it seems to me an admirable summary of what those who wish to attain style would be wise to do, each time they took pen in hand.

You may say that you came for a lecture, not a sermon. If so, I am sorry; but I speak the truth as I see it. The beginning of style is character. This discovery was not first made by me, but by others better able to judge; and since I made it, I have been surprised to find confirmation even where one might least have looked for it. None had believed more passionately than Flaubert in the vain cry of "Art for Art's sake"; yet at fifty-seven, the year before he died, he writes to Madame Sabatier: "Une théorie esthético-morale: le coeur est inséparable de l'esprit; ceux qui ont distingué l'un de l'autre n'avaient ni l'un ni l'autre."[16] And Samuel Butler, having begun by denying style, yet comes full circle before he ends: "I have also taken much pains, with what success I know not, to correct impatience, irritability and other like faults in my own character—and this not because I care two straws about my own character, but because I find the correction of such faults as I have been able to correct makes life easier, and saves me from getting into scrapes, and attaches nice people to me more readily. But I suppose this really is attending to style after all." It is, indeed.

My conclusion is: If you want to write decently, do not begin by reading up all about Synecdoche and Metonymy and the other pretty figures that dance in the rhetoricians' manuals—you can meet them later; but always remember the bag of Montluc.

"But," you may object, "you have said that the problem of style was concerned with the impact of one personality on many. You have gone on and on about the character of the writer. But what about the character of his public? Is that not also important?"

Yes, it is: sometimes to an unfortunate degree. One can sympathize with the anger of Schopenhauer, asking if ever man had so detestable a set of contemporaries as he; or with Flaubert's "Mon Dieu, dans quel âge

---

[15] Lucas gives this passage in the original French, then translates it in a footnote. I have here substituted the footnote for the original. [Ed. note]

[16] *Correspondence* (1926), VIII, p. 209 (February 1879).

m'avez-vous fait naître!" But the writers I most admire have not considered too much the tastes of their immediate public.

The arts of speaking or writing, like some sciences, can be either pure or applied. The applied form aims at some practical purpose—as in addressing a jury, canvassing a constituency, composing official memoranda or propaganda, writing for money. Here, obviously, a style is not good if it is not good for its audience. But the writer of pure literature hopes to be read by men whom he does not know—even by men unborn, whom he cannot know. He must therefore write more to please himself, trusting so to please others; or he may write for an ideal audience, of the kind that he values—for *les âmes amies*. He may—I think he should—show this unknown audience the courtesy due to any audience, of communicating as clearly as he can what he thinks and feels; but he may well consider that to set about satisfying tastes not his own would be a betrayal and a prostitution.

No doubt great writers have sometimes acted otherwise. Shakespeare seems to have contrived to serve both God and Mammon, both his own ideals and popular taste—though not, to judge from some bitter phrases in the *Sonnets,* without moments of revulsion and shame. Dryden, again (in contrast to the inflexible Milton) offers a striking instance of the terrible pull exerted by public taste, or lack of it. If much Restoration Drama is poor, or worse, that could hardly have been otherwise with the type of audience whose tone was set by the Whitehall of Charles II—men and women who were largely rakes, or brutes, or both, thinly veneered with French polish and Spanish rhodomontade—as shallowly cynical as the bright young of the nineteen-twenties, yet at moments as foolishly romantic as the intoxicated young of the eighteen-twenties. The surprising thing, then, is not that *All for Love* should be shallower than *Antony and Cleopatra,* but that it contains as fine things as it does. Dryden can here be praised for not being more subdued than he was, to what he worked in.

And then there is Scott, who, never making an idol of literature as compared with still more important things in life, felt no hesitation about consulting his sales-returns to see what the public liked.

But though in judging past writers it is vital to remember the character of their audiences, I confess that my preference in this matter is for those who have never given in to the world—who have remained as proud as Lucifer, as unbending as Coriolanus. When Wordsworth, or Hopkins, follows his own crotchets to the limit, Wordsworth seems to me at times rather stupid, and Hopkins downright silly; but I respect their independence. I like the aloofness of Landor, and Stendhal's acceptance of being unappreciated for half a century to come, and Flaubert's disdain for both critics and public. And when Ibsen said that, if *Peer Gynt* were not the

Norwegian idea of poetry, then it was going to become so, this seems finely consistent with his brave contempt for all "compact majorities."

In fine, I think the author of character will not bow too much to the character of his audience. Courtesy is better than deference. Confucius, as so often, hit the mark, when he said that the gentleman is courteous, but not pliable; the common man pliable, but not courteous.

But if character is important for style, what characteristics are most important? There are, I think, several human qualities that, despite all the variations in ethics from time to time and place to place, men have generally agreed to value; and have especially valued, whether consciously or not, in writers or speakers. I mean such things as good manners and courtesy towards readers, like Goldsmith's; good humour and gaiety, like Sterne's; good health and vitality, like Macaulay's; good sense and sincerity, like Johnson's. These are the opposites of some of the failings Montluc burnt in his bag. . . .

LITERATURE AND THE SCHOOLMA'M

H. L. Mencken

With precious few exceptions, all the books on style in English are by writers quite unable to write. The subject, indeed, seems to exercise a special and dreadful fascination over schoolma'ms, bucolic college professors, and other such pseudo-literates. One never hears of treatises on it by George Moore or James Branch Cabell, but the pedagogues, male and female, are at it all the time. In a thousand texts they set forth their depressing ideas about it, and millions of suffering high-school pupils have to study what they say. Their central aim, of course, is to reduce the whole thing to a series of simple rules—the overmastering passion of their melancholy order, at all times and everywhere. They aspire to teach it as bridge whist, the American Legion flag drill and double-entry bookkeeping are taught. They fail as ignominiously as that Athenian of legend who essayed to train a regiment of grasshoppers in the goose-step.

For the essence of a sound style is that it cannot be reduced to rules—that it is a living and breathing thing, with something of the devilish in it—that it fits its proprietor tightly and yet ever so loosely, as his skin fits him. It is, in fact, quite as securely an integral part of him as that skin is. It hardens as his arteries harden. It has *Katzenjammer* on the days succeeding his indiscretions. It is gaudy when he is young and gathers decorum when he grows old. On the day after he makes a mash on a new

From Prejudices, Fifth Series, *by H. L. Mencken. Copyright 1926 by Alfred A. Knopf, Inc. and renewed 1954 by H. L. Mencken. Reprinted by permission of the publisher.*

17

girl it glows and glitters. If he has fed well, it is mellow. If he has gastritis it is bitter. In brief, a style is always the outward and visible symbol of a man, and it cannot be anything else. To attempt to teach it is as silly as to set up courses in making love. The man who makes love out of a book is not making love at all; he is simply imitating someone else making love. God help him if, in love or literary composition, his preceptor be a pedagogue!

The schoolma'm theory that the writing of English may be taught is based upon a faulty inference from a sound observation. The sound observation is that the great majority of American high-school pupils, when they attempt to put their thoughts upon paper, produce only a mass of confused and puerile nonsense—that they express themselves so clumsily that it is often quite impossible to understand them at all. The faulty inference is to the effect that what ails them is a defective technical equipment—that they can be trained to write clearly as a dog may be trained to walk on its hind legs. This is all wrong. What ails them is not a defective technical equipment but a defective natural equipment. They write badly simply because they cannot think clearly. They cannot think clearly because they lack the brains. Trying to teach them is as hopeless as trying to teach a dog with only one hind leg. Any human being who can speak English understandably has all the materials necessary to write English clearly, and even beautifully. There is nothing mysterious about the written language; it is precisely the same, in essence, as the spoken language. If a man can think in English at all, he can find words enough to express his ideas. The fact is proved abundantly by the excellent writing that often comes from so-called ignorant men. It is proved anew by the even better writing that is done on higher levels by persons of great simplicity, for example, Abraham Lincoln. Such writing commonly arouses little enthusiasm among pedagogues. Its transparency excites their professional disdain, and they are offended by its use of homely words and phrases. They prefer something more ornate and complex—something, as they would probably put it, demanding more thought. But the thought they yearn for is the kind, alas, that they secrete themselves—the muddled, highfalutin, vapid thought that one finds in their own text-books.

I do not denounce them because they write so badly; I merely record the fact in a sad, scientific spirit. Even in such twilight regions of the intellect the style remains the man. What is in the head infallibly oozes out of the nub of the pen. If it is sparkling Burgundy the writing is full of life and charm. If it is mush the writing is mush too. The Late Dr. Harding, twenty-ninth President of the Federal Union, was a highly self-conscious stylist. He practiced prose composition assiduously, and was regarded by the pedagogues of Marion, Ohio, and vicinity as a very talented fellow. But when he sent a message to Congress it was so muddled in style that even the late Henry Cabot Lodge, a professional literary man, could not understand it. Why? Simply because Dr. Harding's thoughts, on the high and grave subjects he discussed, were so muddled that he couldn't understand them himself. But on matters within his range of customary meditation he was clear and even charming, as all of us are. I once heard him deliver a brief address upon the ideals of the Elks. It was a topic close to his heart, and he had thought about it at length and *con amore*. The result was an excellent speech—clear, logical, forceful, and with a touch of wild, romantic beauty. His sentences hung together. He employed simple words, and put them together with skill. But when, at a public meeting in Washington, he essayed to deliver an oration on the subject of the late Dante Alighieri, he quickly became so obscure and absurd that even the Diplomatic Corps began to snicker. The cause was plain: he knew no more about Dante than a Tennessee county judge knows about the Institutes of Justinian. Trying to formulate ideas upon the topic, he could get together only a few disjected fragments and ghosts of ideas—here an ear, there a section of tibia; beyond a puff of soul substance or other gas. The resultant speech was thus enigmatical, cacophonous, and awful stuff. It sounded precisely like a lecture by a college professor on style.

A pedagogue, confronted by Dr. Harding in class, would have set him to the business of what is called improving his vocabulary—that is, to the business of making his writing even worse than it was. Dr. Harding, in point of fact, had all the vocabulary that he needed, and a great deal more. Any idea that he could formulate clearly he could convey clearly. Any idea that genuinely moved him he could invest with charm—which is to say, with what the pedagogues call style. I believe that this capacity is possessed by all literate persons above the age of fourteen. It is not acquired by studying text-books; it is acquired by learning how to think. Children even younger often show it. I have a niece, now eleven years old, who already has an excellent style. When she writes to me about things that interest her—in other words, about the things she is capable of thinking about—she puts her thoughts into clear, dignified, and admirable English. Her vocabulary, so far, is unspoiled by schoolma'ms. She doesn't try to knock me out by bombarding me with hard words, and phrases filched from Addison. She is unaffected and hence her writing is charming. But if she essayed to send me a communication on the subject, say, of Balkan politics or government ownership, her style would descend instantly to the level of that of Dr. Harding's state papers.

To sum up, style cannot go beyond the ideas which lie at the heart of it. If they are clear, it too will be clear. If they are held passionately, it will be eloquent. Trying to teach it to persons who cannot think, especially when the business is attempted by persons who also cannot think, is a great waste of time, and an immoral imposition upon the taxpayers of the nation. It would be far more logical to devote all the energy to teaching, not writing, but logic—and probably just as useless. For I doubt that the art of thinking can be taught at all—at any rate, by school-teachers. It is not acquired, but congenital. Some persons are born with it. Their ideas flow in straight channels; they are capable of lucid reasoning; when they say anything it is instantly understandable; when they write anything it is clear and persuasive. They constitute, I should say, about one-eighth of one per cent, of the human race. The rest of God's children are just as incapable of logical thought as they are incapable of jumping over the moon. Trying to teach them to think is as vain an enterprise as trying to teach a streptococcus the principles of Americanism. The only thing to do with them is to make Ph.D.'s of them, and set them to writing handbooks on style.

ON DEFINING STYLE

Nils   Enkvist

"A discussion of the word Style," said John Middleton Murry, "if it were pursued with only a fraction of the rigour of a scientific investigation, would inevitably cover the whole of literary aesthetics and the theory of criticism. Six books would not suffice for the attempt: much less would six lectures."[1] All the same, an analysis of some four or five score definitions of style culled from critical works, linguistic studies, dictionaries, and encyclopedias of different periods shows that such definitions can, allowing for much overlapping, be classified under a limited number of major headings.[2]

One way to classify definitions of style is by the basic stages of the communication process. First there are definitions based on the point of

From "On Defining Style" by Nils Erik Enkvist included in Linguistics and Style *published by Oxford University Press. Footnotes renumbered.*

[1] *The Problem of Style,* Oxford Paperbacks, 1960, p. 3.
[2] It is necesary to point out that these definitions are here quoted in their barest form, without all the conceptual frames, qualifications, and explanations with which they may be surrounded in their complete, original context. I am of course not criticizing individual works but commenting on different major approaches to style. In addition to the works quoted in the notes, helpful sources include William T. Brewster, *Representative Essays on the Theory of Style,* New York, 1913, and the introductory section of Pierre Naert, *Stilen i Vilhelm Ekelunds aforismer och essäer,* Malmö, 1949.

view of the writer,[3] such as Goethe's in *Einfache Nachahmung der Natur, Manier, Stil.*[4] Here Goethe regards style as a higher, active principle of composition by which the writer penetrates and reveals the inner form of his subject. Style is opposed to a passive imitation of nature or to the facile application of mannerisms to the subject. Secondly, there are definitions that deal with characteristics of the text itself, attempting analysis of style entirely in terms of objective investigation of textual features. Thirdly, there are definitions based on the impressions of the reader. They are extremely common in most works of literary criticism and literary history that characterize individual or group styles. Often a definition is composed of more than one of these three kinds of *dicta*. Examples of all three kinds will appear in the following.

Another distinction can be made between statements on style that are objectively verifiable and those that are subjectively impressionistic. Presumably a foreign-language teacher is best served by a definition of style making possible stylistic analyses that are operationally concrete. They should be based on those linguistic features that each student, at his particular level of progress, can verify on his own. This requirement immediately disqualifies a host of definitions, including those which merely identify style with existence or thought[5] and those which state that style involves saying the right thing in the most effective way.[6] Of the remaining approaches, six will be mentioned in the following: style as a shell surrounding a pre-existing core of thought or expression; as the choice between alternative expressions; as a set of individual characteristics; as deviations from a norm; as a set of collective characteristics; and as those

---

[3] As the main concern of the present chapter is with written texts, I shall use the simple 'writer' and 'reader' even where the observations are equally valid for spoken language.

[4] Discussed and quoted by Emil Ermatinger in *Das dichterische Kunstwerk*, Leipzig and Berlin, 1921, p. 199.

[5] e.g., "Le style est pour nous une disposition de l'existence, une manière d'être." (Henri Morier, *La Psychologie des styles*, Genève, 1959, p. 7.) [To us, style is a disposition of existence, a way of being.] "Style, indeed, is not really a mere invisible transparent medium, it is not really a garment but, as Gourmont said, the very thought itself. It is the miraculous transubstantiation of a spiritual body, given to us in the only form in which we may receive and absorb that body . . ." (Havelock Ellis in "The Art of Writing", *The Dance of Life*, London, 1923, p. 163.)

[6] e.g., Kenneth Burke in *Permanence and Change*, Los Altos, Calif., 1954, p. 50. "In its simplest manifestation, style is ingratiation. It is an attempt to gain favor by the hypnotic or suggestive process of 'saying the right thing'." And Sir Arthur Quiller-Couch, *On the Art of Writing*, Cambridge, 1920, p. 248: "This then is Style. As technically manifested in Literature it is the power to touch with ease, grace, precision, any note in the gamut of human thought and emotion. But essentially it resembles good manners."

relations among linguistic entities that are statable in terms of wider spans of text than the sentence.

First, then, some examples of definitions that regard style as an addition to a central core of thought or expression:

> Style consists in adding to a given thought all the circumstances calculated to produce the whole effect that the thought ought to produce.[7]

Here Stendhal apparently took for granted the existence of the "given thought" *per se* before its final verbalization. To him, style was an addition whose function was defined not in terms of beauty but more inclusively in terms of expediency and effect.

Once style is regarded as an addition, it becomes possible to conceive of utterances that have no style. In *Counter-Statement,* Kenneth Burke thus regards manner and style as characteristic only of eloquent works, not of uneloquent ones, though presumably even the latter build on thought:

> In so far as a work becomes eloquent, it manifests either manner or style. Here again the distinction is quantitative, manner being a greater confinement of formal resources and Symbolic ramifications. . . . Manner obviously has the virtue of "power," with the danger of monotony (Wilde's *Salome* may illustrate both). Style has the virtue of "complexity," with the danger of diffusion. (The later prose of James Joyce is a good instance of style impaired by diffusion.)[8]

Such a distinction between uneloquent statements, manner and style would be impossible to establish merely by linguistic description. Another, somewhat similar, frame is set up by Paul Goodman in *The Structure of Literature:*

> Mostly in the sonnets of Milton there is no style; it is the speech of earnestness personally involved and calls all attention to the thought and feeling. Given a similar theme treated by Donne, for instance, much would have to be said about the style; or, in speaking of *Paradise Lost* or *Lycidas,* we should say independent things about the style, as we did in discussing the verses of Catullus. We can speak of "no style" in three

---

[7] Quoted from Joseph T. Shipley, ed., *Dictionary of World Literary Terms,* London, 1955, p. 398.

[8] Los Altos, Calif., 1953, pp. 166–7.

senses: the sense of Milton's sonnets, where a powerful diction is artistically neutralized in the interest of the thought and feeling, and this neutralizing itself is then expressive of attitude; the sense of a nonliterary writing, where the writer has never gotten into contact with his speech—this is "no style" absolutely; and the sense of poor poetry, where "no style" is a confusion of styles.[9]

To say that Milton had no style when writing sonnets and that in non-literary writing poor writers never get into contact with their speech will of course necessitate a very personal, complex definition of style, writing and speech. Mr. Goodman is hardly helpful when he defines style in his Glossary (p. 276 as "character of implications." It is easier to follow De Quincey, who insisted in his essay on language that style may have an independent value apart from the content, and that it may perform either an absolute or a ministerial function:

> It is certain that style, or (to speak by the most general expression) the management of language, ranks amongst the fine arts, and is able therefore to yield a separate intellectual pleasure quite apart from the interest of the subject treated . . . [10]

In separating an outer halo of style from an inner core of thought, content or styleless language, and in thus postulating the existence of prelinguistic thought or prestylistic expression, these definitions recall the classic distinction between logic and rhetoric. They also build on the Platonic critics' view of style as a quality that need not be present in every utterance. However, to a student of language, such attempts at defining style are awkward on at least two counts. As the complete, finished text usually is the only reliable means we have of getting at a writer's thought, there seems to be no way of separating the original thought or nascent, underlying expression from its final verbal garb. Also it becomes impossible to distinguish between utterances that have a style and utterances that do not without employing either completely arbitrary criteria or complex, predominantly subjective ones of a kind that a linguist tries to avoid.

Definitions of style as an addition can be further subgrouped according to which effect of the addition is stressed in each definition. Like many rhetoricians, Stendhal regarded style as effective presentation. Others have more explicitly opposed style to a dry and scholarly recapitulation of

---

[9] Chicago, 1954, p. 215.

[10] M, X, 260, quoted by John E. Jordan in *Thomas De Quincey, Literary Critic,* Berkeley and Los Angeles, 1952, p. 36.

facts. Charles Bally's famous theory of style identifies it with a layer of affective elements. According to Bally, stylistics studies

> . . . the affective value of the features of organized language and the reciprocal action of the expressive features that together form the system of the means of expression of a language.—[*My translation. N.E.E.*][11]

To Bally, language is a set of means of expression which are simultaneous with thought. A speaker can give his thoughts an objective, intellectual form which conforms to reality as closely as possible. More often, however, he chooses to add various affective elements that partly reflect his ego and partly the social forces he is subject to.[12] The task of stylistics is to examine these *caractères affectifs,* to study the means by which language expresses them and their mutual relations, and to analyse the total *système expressif* of which they are parts:

> Consequently, stylistics studies the features of organized language from the point of view of their affective content, that is, the expression of sensibility through language and the effect of language on sensibility. —[*My translation. N.E.E.*][13]

Bally further distinguishes between internal stylistics, which studies the balance and contrast of affective *versus* intellectual elements within one and the same language, and external or comparative stylistics, which compares such features of one language with those of another.[14]

To Bally, then, the origin of style is the addition of a *contenu affectif* to expression. If we substitute emotional content, *Gemüthaftigkeit,* for Bally's affective content, and start from the reader rather than from the writer, we arrive at the definition proposed by Herbert Seidler in *Allgemeine Stilistik:*

> Style is a definite emotional effect achieved by linguistic means in a text. —[*My approximate translation. N.E.E.*][15]

Seidler distinguishes between *Sachdarstellung* and *Sprachkunst,* the latter being characterized by *Gemüthaftigkeit* and thus by style. He admits that style can be present also in *Sachdarstellung,* but only when *das Gemüthafte,* the emotional factor, forms the structural core (*Strukturkern*) of a

---

[11] *Traité de stylistique française,* Heidelberg, 1921, I, 1.
[12] *Ibid.,* I, 12.
[13] *Ibid.,* I, 16.
[14] *Le language et la vie,* Paris, 1926, p. 88.
[15] Göttingen, 1953, p. 61.

work can we speak of *Sprachkunstwerke*. Stylistics thus become "die Wissenschaft vom Stil oder von den Gemütskräften der Sprache."[16]

A modern version of the very frequent view of style as choice is that of Cleanth Brooks and Robert Penn Warren: ". . . in this book [*Understanding Fiction*], style is used merely to refer to the selection and ordering of language."[17] Less sophisticated definitions of this type may fall into the same trap as those which regard style as an addition by referring more explicitly to prelinguistic thought. To speak about selection readily leads to an undesirable emphasis on the mental processes of the writer. By the time the reader sees the text, the process of selection is a *fait accompli* only accessible through textual analysis. If the use of "selection" is merely a roundabout way of referring to features actually present in the text, we might as well try to describe these features directly. And if by "selection" we are only implying that no writer can use all the resources of his language at the same time, the argument is, at this level of study, trivial. The "ordering" of language, on the other hand, involves grammatical and literary considerations as well as stylistic ones, and therefore seems too inclusive.

Even if we approve of the idea of style as choice, if we define "selection and ordering" only with reference to a given text, and thus escape undue emphasis on the mental processes of the writer, we must still accept the onus of distinguishing between different types of choice that are manifested in language. This is a fundamental point sometimes overlooked. One such type is exemplified in the choice between, say, *to eat* and *John* for *x* in *x loves Mary*. Such a choice is primarily grammatical: *to eat loves Mary* is not English, that is, it does not conform to the patterns occurring in materials that grammarians approve as a basis for descriptions of Eng-

---

[16] *Ibid.*, p. 65. When I quoted this passage in a lecture, a learned German listener volunteered the wry comment that the virtue of *Gemüthaftigkeit* lies in its being a *Gummiwort:* it stretches without breaking!

[17] New York, 1943, p. 605. The definition in *Understanding Poetry*, New York, 1960, p. 640, will do better justice to the views held by the authors: "This term [style] is usually used with reference to the poet's manner of choosing, ordering, and arranging his words. But, of course, when one asks on what grounds certain words are chosen and ordered, one is raising the whole problem of form. Style, in its larger sense, is essentially the same thing as form." A large collection of definitions of style as choice can be readily compiled. See e.g. J. Marouzeau, *Précis de stylistique française*, Paris, 1946, p. 10: "Language would thus be a catalogue of linguistic symbols and of their connexions with things-meant, represented by the inventory furnished by the dictionary, and by the systematization that is given by grammar. It is a repertory of possibilities, a common stock at the disposition of the users, who use it according to their needs of expression in making the choice—that is, style—within the limits granted to them by the laws of language."—[*My translation. N.E.E.*]

lish structure.[18] In Marouzeau's words, it is not permitted by the laws of the language. Another type may be illustrated by the choice between *Peter and John* in *x loves Mary,* or between *drizzling* and *pouring* in *it was x. Peter loves Mary, John loves Mary, it was drizzling* and *it was pouring* are all grammatically possible, but presumably the speaker will, on extra-linguistic grounds of truth, prefer one to the other in a given situation. Such a choice will here be called non-stylistic. A third type of selection appears in the choice between *fine man* and *nice chap* in *he is a x.* Both are grammatically possible, even idiomatic; and both have a certain range of frames and referents in common. This type of choice may be labelled as stylistic. It is important to note that stylistic choice exists on a number of different levels, not only in the lexis. It may involve phonetic features (special voice quality, speech rate, &c.), phonemes (*singing/singin'*), morphemes (*sings/singeth*), words, phrases, clauses, sentences, and larger units.

It is, then, necessary for a definition of style as choice to distinguish between these three types of selection: grammatical, non-stylistic, and stylistic. The boundary between grammatical choice and the two other types need here give us little trouble.[19] Briefly, grammar distinguishes between the possible and the impossible, whereas non-stylistic and stylistic choice both involve grammatically optional selection in that they choose between different, grammatically permissible alternatives. The foreign-language teacher bent on giving his pupils a sense for the style of set texts may assume that these texts are grammatical. Otherwise they would not have been selected for teaching. Besides, in some classroom situations it does not much matter whether a given construction is commented on under the express heading of style or of grammar, as long as the teacher knows exactly what he is doing. Indeed, traditional grammar of the

---

[18] I am here very crudely cutting a Gordian knot. In applied linguistics, such rough operational procedures are justifiable; there are other areas in which the question of grammaticalness must be approached with great care. For those working with generative grammar, "grammaticality" is a crucial problem probably best solved in terms of different levels of grammaticalness. See Noam Chomsky, *Syntactic Structures,* 's-Gravenhage, 1957, 2.2–4; Thomas A. Sebeok, ed., *Style in Language,* Boston, Mass., New York, and London, 1960, pp. 84–85, 91–92, and 340; Archibald A. Hill, "Grammaticality," *Word,* XVII, 1961, 1–10; and Chomsky, "Some Methodological Remarks on Generative Grammar," *Word,* XVII, 1961, 219–39.

[19] In many countries, schoolteachers notoriously spend much time in deciding whether a given mistake in a student's paper should be penalized more severely as a grammatical mistake, or less severely as an unidiomatic or awkward construction. The solution usually has more to do with the details of the particular syllabus than with questions of linguistic principle: what goes against the recommendations of the grammar-book in use is by definition regarded as a grammatical mistake. Such a scholastic procedure often puzzles the detached outsider who has a better mastery of the foreign language than of local grammar-books.

normative kind is full of overlaps between stylistic and grammatical considerations. Friedrich Kainz has labelled this overlap as an example of the general principle of multiple precautions:

> In the sense of Fechner's principle of association, serious violations of linguistic correctness always seem ugly, and—except for occasional instances of poetic licence—an utterance that claims to be beautiful must also satisfy the demands of correctness. The distinction between these two evaluation principles and norm fields is made unclear only by the fact that popular stylistics constantly works with shifts in values. Thus utterances that are aesthetically indifferent and trespass merely against logical clarity are described as ugly, whereas violations of definite aesthetic requirements (such as variation) are additionally penalized by setting up a grammatical rule *ad hoc* and by describing the aesthetically deficient violation as a mistake as well. The principle of multiple precautions is of course also known from other fields.—[*My translation. N.E.E.*][20]

The borderline between non-stylistic and stylistic selection is much harder to draw, both being in a sense optional. As an example of choice involving larger units I might quote a text I saw in an Edinburgh hotel-room. The meter that swallowed coins for the electric fire bore a small metal plaque inscribed SHILLINGS ONLY. On the wall there was another plaque giving the management's version: "Visitors are respectfully informed that the coin required for this meter is 1/-. No other coin is suitable." Now contemplation of the three types of choice may suggest that the selection between SHILLINGS ONLY and the management's elaborate, but no more informative, politeness is an instance of stylistic choice. It cannot be grammatical, as both utterances satisfy the patterns of English structure, and it cannot be non-stylistic because both utterances exhort the visitor to do, and to abstain from, the same things in the same situation. Stylistic choice, then, at first sight seems to be a choice between items that mean roughly the same, whereas non-stylistic choice involves selection between different meanings. In fact, definitions of style have been based on this observation:

> Good style, it seems to me, consists in choosing the appropriate symbolization of the experience you wish to convey, from among a number of words whose meaning-area is roughly, but only roughly, the same (by saying *cat*, for example, rather than *pussy*).[21]

[20] *Psychologie der Sprache,* **IV**, Stuttgart, 1956, 344.

[21] Jeremy Warburg, "Some Aspects of Style" in Randolph Quirk and A. H. Smith, eds., *The Teaching of English.* Studies in Communication 3, London, 1959, p. 50. However, style does not only involve words but other linguistic units as well.

Or, if the choice is tacitly transferred from the writer to the reader, and the reader is given the job of deciding what utterances mean roughly the same:

> Roughly speaking, two utterances in the same language which convey approximately the same information, but which are different in their linguistic structure, can be said to differ in style.[22]

Such definitions are highly useful and help to clarify an important point. But there is, unfortunately, no simple way of measuring whether the information carried by two different utterances is approximately the same or not. To me, Professor Hockett's examples *Sir, I have the honor to inform you* and *Jeez, boss, get a load of dis* immediately evoke two so different situations and contexts that I should hesitate before regarding their information as approximately the same. (The situations evoked by these two linguistic stimuli must be regarded as part of the information they carry.) A "meaning-area" is also difficult to determine. Even if we do so by semantic-field techniques, we must in practice start by listing all the contexts in which the items involved occur. It would therefore be simpler to focus directly on context than to appeal to meaning. And if we approach meaning through referents or things-meant, we are again moving from rigorous linguistics into extralinguistic territory. Several types of context are easier to define and classify than things-meant.

Altogether, even if we allow that roughly the same information can be transmitted by different selections of language, we shall find it hard to decide when the information of two utterances is sufficiently similar to permit our labelling the difference between these utterances as stylistic. What about *It is pouring* and *It is raining cats and dogs?* Do they mean the same or not? To what extent a writer is free to choose between grammatically optional elements, and to what extent the same meaning can be conveyed by different linguistic structures readily turn into metaphysical problems beyond the reach of simple and rigorous methods. Indeed Flaubert and many others, including the New Critics, have maintained that there is only one *mot juste*. If this is so, style becomes part of meaning, and two stylistically different utterances can never mean exactly the same. Deciding whether they mean more or less the same is hardly a satisfactory basic operation in investigations of style.

The definition of style as choice, then, leads to problems whose stringent resolution is difficult. I shall return to this question later.

---

[22] Charles W. Hockett, *A Course in Modern Linguistics,* New York, 1958, p. 556.

Le style, c'est l'homme meme, said Buffon. The epigrammatic elegance of his definition has contributed to its vogue, even at the expense of the finer distinctions and qualifications he made in the same Academy Address in 1753. This emphasis on the individual element of style is, of course, very important, and must be allowed for in all stylistic analysis. As everybody knows, many writers, including a host of great ones, have arrived at the kind of individuality that makes it possible for an experienced reader to identify their writings. Sometimes scholars succeed in doing so by objective means, for example by statistical counts of frequencies of linguistic features in limited contexts.[23] Usually we do so more or less intuitively with the aid of a complex of criteria enclosed in what a scientist might call a black box. The contents of this black box may at first glance defy simple operational description.

The same insistence on the individual quality of style can be found in a vast number of definitions. Here is one of Rémy de Gourmont's:

> Having a style means that in the midst of the language shared with others one speaks a particular, unique and inimitable dialect, which is at the same time everybody's language and the language of a single individual.—[*My translation. N.E.E.*][24]

A related concept is that of *Pierre Naert,*[25] who ascribes style to the Saussurian level of *parole,* not *langue,* just as de Gourmont contrasts *le langage d'un seul* with *le langage de tous.* In Professor Naert's frame, stylistics is, very elegantly, *la linguistique de la parole* as opposed to *la linguistique de la langue.*

Such definitions are useful enough in the study of styles of individual writers. Still, the identification of style with individual expression leads to two difficulties. First, some features generally labelled as stylistic are not individual at all. They are shared by groups of varying size. Indeed the lack of individual features may serve as a hallmark of some style categories. In officialese and scientific writing, for instance, the writer often

---

[23] See for instance G. Udny Yule, "On Sentence-Length as a Statistical Characteristic of Style in Prose," *Biometrika,* XXX, 1939, 363–90, and *The Statistical Study of Literary Vocabulary,* Cambridge, 1944; Gustav Herdan, *Language as Choice and Chance,* Groningen, 1956 and *Type-Token Mathematics,* 's-Gravenhage,, 1960; Alvar Ellegård, *A Statistical Method for Determining Authorship,* Gothenburg Studies in English 13, Gothenburg, 1962 and *Who Was Junius?* Stockholm &c., 1962; Pierre Guiraud, *Les Caractères statistiques du vocabulaire,* Paris, 1954, and Guiraud *et al., Bibliographie critique de la statistique linguistique,* Utrecht, 1954.

[24] *La culture des idées,* Paris, 1916, p. 9.

[25] *Stilen i Vilhelm Ekelunds essayer och aforismer,* Lund, 1949.

aims at, and succeeds in, complete self-effacement. In a general theory of style—as opposed to the *ad hoc* study of an individual writer—it would run counter to established usage and linguistic expediency to exclude group styles from the heading of style. Such group styles are hard to fit exclusively under *parole* in its basic sense of a specific linguistic act of one individual; they could, it seems, with some justification be included under *langue* as well, and perhaps best within the Hjelmslevian subsection of *usage.*

Secondly, how are we to separate the "unique and inimitable" features of a given style from among all the other features necessarily present in our text? In Saussurian terms, as *langue* can only be approached through *parole,* what corpus of *parole* should we use in setting up that model of *langue* against which our text is to be matched? Such a matching is inevitable as long as we define stylistics as the study of individual expression or as the linguistics of *parole:* unless we compare *la linguistique de la parole* with *la linguistique de la langue* we cannot define what features only occur in the former, and thus what features are characteristic of style. Obviously, to get at style, the investigator must begin with the laborious task of setting up a corpus of reference to find the norm or norms from which a given text differs. To establish such frames of reference is one of the basic aims of all linguistic and literary education. Many critics seem to take it for granted, thanks to the noiseless workings of their black box. But in the study of a foreign language, and even of our own, we must have much experience before we can safely assert that a given text has a style different from that of a range of other texts. In brief: individual modes of expression form a category too special to give us a general basis for an ideally powerful style definition. The identification of style with the individual element of language tacitly presupposes the setting up of norms of comparison.

With this, we have already entered upon definitions of style as a deviation from a norm, which inevitably overlap the definitions based on individual traits of expression. I need only quote one example:

> Style, in the linguistic sense, usually signifies every special usage clearly contrasted against the general. More closely, style could be defined as that way of presenting a subject which differs more or less from the average and which is motivated by the character of the subject, the purpose of the presentation, the reader's qualifications and the writer's personality.—[*My translation. N.E.E.*][26]

[26] Erik Wellander, *Riktig svenska*, Stockholm, 1948, p. 18.

Such definitions are also very useful, especially if they succeed in defining both the norm and the deviations in concrete, operational terms. However, we must again emphasize what was hinted at in the last paragraph. When defining style, we cannot take for granted a norm defined with the aid of style. If we do so, we are merely moving in a circle.[27] Breaking the circularity by contrasting a given style with the language as a whole is impracticable as well as theoretically undesirable.[28] If the norm is to be defined in operationally meaningful terms, it must be carefully circumscribed. But drawing its boundaries is a crucial step which will determine the results of the comparison. To give a crudely obvious instance: if a poet's style is compared with that of an engineering handbook, we are bound to arrive at statements relevant to the difference between poetry and technical prose, not at an assessment of the poet's individuality in terms of the difference between his poems and those of other poets.

Altogether, it seems advisable first to define the norm against which the individuality of a given text is measured, not as the language as a whole but as that part of language which is significantly related to the passage we are analysing. Given the means, we may later return to more ambitious comparisons with a wider range of norms. In the above definition, the subject, the writer's aims, the reader, and the writer's personality were obviously mentioned for this very reason.

Now some norms can be defined with perfect rigor, either by linguistic criteria ("literature in Northumbrian Old English," "poems written in fourteeners") or with the air of extra-linguistic context ("third leaders in *The Times* during 1960"). As long as we define the norm so that it yields a meaningful background for the text and feature under analysis, and as long as we limit it with operationally unambiguous procedures, definitions of style as deviations from a norm give us a good first basis for stylistic comparison. In fact the critic's black box was designed precisely to compare the linguistic features of a new text with relevant past experiences of the occurrence of similar linguistic features in related contexts. The crucial point is that limitations of the norm are based on criteria which can be labelled as contextual.

In working towards an increased precision of definitions of style as deviations from a norm, linguists and others have rightly begun to make explicit the rôle of frequencies and of statistical analysis. This enables us to formalize the difference between the usual and the unusual, and between the text and the norm:

[27] See further Sol Saporta, "The Application of Linguistics to the Study of Poetic Language" in Thomas A. Sebeok, ed., *Style in Language,* Boston, Mass., New York, and London, 1960, especially pp. 82–85.

[28] Besides, the language as a whole includes the text under investigation. This may lead to complications in the selection of distributional and statistical criteria for analysis.

The style of a discourse is the message carried by the frequency distributions and transitional probabilities of its linguistic features, especially as they differ from those of the same features in the language as a whole.[29]

Style is defined as an individual's deviation from norms for the situations in which he is encoding, these deviations being in the statistical properties of those structural features for which there exists some degree of choice in his code.[30]

The first of these two definitions again gives us the formidable, and theoretically objectionable, task of using the entire language as a norm. The second involves us in the difficulties inherent in the use of choice as a basis of style.[31] Nevertheless, it seems that if we can only combine the emphasis on frequencies and probabilities with a more precise relationship between text and norm, we shall be on the right track. There is, of course, no risk of the statistician's putting the linguist and the literary critic out of business: in practice, only the linguist and the critic can tell the statistician what features are worth counting in the first place.

As style can be defined as a deviation from a norm, the question arises whether it could be defined positively, in terms of a norm rather than in terms of deviations. We can of course always say that two texts which differ in the same way from a given norm are in the same style. The question is rather, can we do without the norm? We must also distinguish between the definition of style in general and the description of specific style categories. At first sight, the latter seem to yield readily to norm-bound definition, and every literate person is prepared to distinguish a host of norm-defining features in a number of styles. Such features may be stated in terms of metre ("heroic couplets"), time ("Elizabethan style"), place ("Yankee humour"), language, dialect, writer ("Byronic style") or literary work ("Euphuism"), school of writers ("romantic style"), genre ("poetic style, journalese"), social situation ("Sergeant-Major of the Guards addressing recruit"), and so forth. Again, all such norms seem to be roughly circumscribed by context, including time, place and situation. And all of them tacitly presuppose definition of a norm. Here, the emphasis is put on similarities, not differences, between the given text and the norm; otherwise this approach is identical with that described above as comparison of the text with a contextually related corpus.

[29] Bernard Block, "Linguistic Structure and Linguistic Analysis," in Archibald A. Hill, ed., *Report on the Fourth Annual Round Table Meeting on Linguistics and Language Teaching,* Washington, 1953, pp. 40–44.

[30] Charles E. Osgood, "Some Effects of Motivation of Style of Encoding," in Sebeok, ed., *Style in Language,* p. 293.

[31] See pp. 26–29 above.

To define style in general in the positive terms of a norm is more difficult. Such attempts have often contained a strongly arbitrary element, and they easily lead to statements such as that quoted on pages 23–4 above, denying Milton's sonnets the privilege of style.

Starting out from Professor Trager's distinction between microlinguistics, viz. the area beginning with phonemes and ending with sentences, and macrolinguistics, concerned with units beyond the sentence, Professor Hill has defined stylistics as concerning

> all those relations among linguistic entities which are statable, or may be statable, in terms of wider spans than those which fall within the limits of the sentence.[32]

This definition neither conflicts with the view of style as choice or as tabulation of alternatives, nor rules out the study of frequencies and probabilities as style determinants. Yet it seems to need some explanatory corollaries. Even in phonemic analysis the search for certain types of contrasts may involve spans wider than a sentence: if, for instance, a speaker marks what in writing would be the end of a paragraph with a deeper fall of intonation and a longer pause than the end of a sentence, we may ask whether such devices qualify as entirely stylistic. Also some matters of intersentence concord or selection (*My brother is eight. He/ she/it goes to school every day.*) involve spans longer than the sentence, but are nevertheless not stylistic but grammatical. Conversely, there are stylistic matters that are statable within the sentence span (*They said singin', which we found ugly, because we had been taught to say singing*), though here admittedly the morphemics of *singin'/singing* only acquire stylistic significance when viewed in the light of a norm longer than one sentence. If, then, the definition could be amended so as to point out that the longer-than-sentence span concerns the norm rather than the individual stylistic feature under analysis, these explanatory corollaries might perhaps be dispensed with.

---

[32] Archibald A. Hill, *Introduction to Linguistic Structures*, New York, 1958, pp. 406–9.

STYLE AS MEANING

William K. Wimsatt

"Betwixt the formation of words and that of thought there is this difference," said Cicero, "that that of the words is destroyed if you change them, that of the thoughts remains, whatever words you think proper to use."[1] This is a clear statement of the view of style and meaning which today may be conveniently called "the ornamental." The ancient rhetoricians all seem to have something like this in mind.[2] They may stress the need of meaning, or may in their metaphysics insist on the interdependence of matter and form, but when they reach the surface of meaning, the plane of most detailed organization, they are not able to speak so as to connect this with meaning. It is as if, when all is said for meaning, there remains an irreducible something that is superficial, a kind of scum—which they call style. One may consult as representative the whole treatment of rhetorical figures in Quintilian's *Institute*.

There is the opposite theory of style, one that has been growing on us since the seventeenth century. "So many *things,* almost in an equal

From The Prose Style of Samuel Johnson, *by W. K. Wimsatt, Jr., Copyright* © *1941 by Yale University Press.*

[1] *De Oratore,* III, lii, in *Cicero on Oratory and Orators,* ed. J. S. Watson (New York, 1890), p. 252.
[2] Cf. Benedetto Croce, *Aesthetic as Science of Expression and General Linguistic,* trans. Douglas Ainslee (London, 1929), pp. 422–9.

number of *words,"* says Sprat.[3] And Pascal, "La vraie éloquence se moque de l'éloquence."[4] And somewhat later Swift, "Proper words in proper places, make the true definition of a style";[5] and Buffon, "Style is simply the order and movement one gives to one's thoughts."[6] By the nineteenth century the doctrine is proclaimed on every hand—very explicitly, for example, by Cardinal Newman:

> Thought and speech are inseparable from each other. Matter and expression are parts of one: style is a thinking out into language. . . . When we can separate light and illumination, life and motion, the convex and the concave of a curve . . . then will it be conceivable that the . . . intellect should renounce its own double.[7]

In one of the best books on style to appear in our own day, Mr. Middleton Murry has said:

> Style is not an isolable quality of writing; it is writing itself.[8]

[3] Thomas Sprat, *History of the Royal Society* (London, 1702), p. 113. Cf. Richard F. Jones, "Science and English Prose Style in the Third Quarter of the Seventeenth Century," *PMLA*, XLV (1930), 977–1009.

[4] *Pensées*, VII, 34, ed. Ernest Havet (Paris, 1866), Vol. I, p. 106; cf. VII, 28, *op. cit.,* Vol. I, p. 105.

[5] *A Letter to a Young Clergyman, Lately Entered into Holy Orders,* 1721, *Prose Works,* ed. Temple Scott (London, 1898), III, 200–01.

[6] *An Address Delivered Before the French Academy* [generally known as the *Discours sur le Style*], 1753, in Lane Cooper, *Theories of Style* (New York, 1907), p. 171. This, rather than the too-often-quoted "The style is the man," is Buffon's real definition of style—a point well taken by W. C. Brownell, *The Genius of Style* (New York, 1924), p. 46.

[7] "Literature, a Lecture in the School of Philosophy and Letters," 1858, in *The Idea of a University* (London, 1907), pp. 276–7. In Lane Cooper's *Theories of Style* one may conveniently find similar expressions by Coleridge, Wackernagel, De Quincey, Schopenhauer, Lewes, Pater, and Brunetière (esp. pp. 10, 207, 222–223, 252, 320, 391, 399, 401, 422). See also *Pensées de J. Joubert,* ed. Paul Raynal (Paris, 1888), II, 275–8, Titre XXII, paragraphs IX–XXV; August Boeckh, *Encyklopädie und Methodologie der Philologischen Wissenschaften* (Leipzig, 1886), p. 128.

For the opposite way of thinking, see William Minto, *Manual of English Prose Literature* (Edinburgh and London, 1881) (first published in 1872), Introduction, pp. 14–15; George Saintsbury, "Modern English Prose," 1876, in *Miscellaneous Essays* (London, 1892), pp. 83, 84, 99.

[8] J. Middleton Murry, *The Problem of Style* (Oxford, 1922), p. 77; cf. pp. 16, 71. Cf. Walter Raleigh, *Style* (London, 1897), esp. p. 62; Herbert Read, *English Prose Style* (London, 1932), *passim.* Mr. Logan Pearsall Smith would probably admit that the rich and poetic prose for which he pleads is as much a matter of expression as the plainest (*S.P.E. Tract no. XLVI, Fine Writing* [Oxford, 1936], esp. pp. 203, 220). For a cross-section of opinion from modern professional writers, see Burges Johnson, *Good Writing* (Syracuse University, 1932).

It is hardly necessary to adduce proof that the doctrine of identity of style and meaning is today firmly established. This doctrine is, I take it, one from which a modern theorist hardly can escape, or hardly wishes to.

The chief difficulty with the modern doctrine of style lies in its application to rhetorical study. The difficulty appears in two ways: partly in the implicit abandonment of the doctrine when rhetorical study is attempted, but more largely in a wide, silent rejection of the whole system of rhetoric. "We have done with the theory of style," proclaims an eminent critic in Crocean vein, "with metaphor, simile, and all the paraphernalia of Graeco-Roman rhetoric."[9] Now it must be contended that we have not done with "metaphor"—that we still have an important use for the term.[10] But for scarcely any other term of rhetoric have we better than a shrug. We no longer are willing to take seriously a set of terms which once—for centuries—were taken seriously, and which must, no matter how unhappy their use, have stood for something. In throwing away the terms it is even possible we have thrown away all definite concept of the things they once stood for. The realities of antithesis and climax, for example, are perhaps less and less a part of our consciousness. But literary history without these old realities and their old terms is impossible; without an evaluation of them it is superficial. The fact is that Cicero used "figures" of this and that sort—moreover, he wrote criticism about them. Hooker and Donne and Johnson used such figures too. And the old terms when used to describe these old writings do mean something. We cannot avoid admitting that we recognize certain things as denoted by the terms, that we know the nominal definitions. Furthermore, we are not ready to call Cicero and the rest simply bad writers. We may insist, and properly, that the accounts they give of their devices, their theories of rhetoric, are insufficient —even baneful as guides to composition; as for the living use they made of what they called "devices," their actual saying of things, in this we see that their intuition was better than their theory.

Any discourse about a definition of "style" is fruitless if it concerns itself too simply with protesting: style *is this* or *is that*. Definitions are impervious to the "lie direct," mere "intrenchant air" for the sword of evidence. The only reason a term *should* mean something is the history of its application, the fact that it *has* meant something. We may say that dubious terms have a kind of repertoire of related meanings. But the meaning of a term in a given instance is what any man decides to make it, and if I dislike what he makes it, I may not tell him he is mistaken.

Nevertheless I may dislike it, and justly. This is the problem in facing definitions—that they do often bother us as bad definitions and make us

---

[9] J. E. Spingarn, *Creative Criticism* (New York, 1917), p. 30.
[10] Cf. *post* p. 45.

wish vehemently to reject them. The basis for our uneasiness is ultimately one of relevance, relevance of a definition to the principles of the whole science of which the term is accepted as a part. If there is not a fixed real meaning for a term, there is at least an ideal one, a something to which the term *should* refer if it is to be used in its science without producing nonsense. It is the purpose of definition to determine *what* is referred to, and the business of him who formulates a definition to determine what *should be* referred to, as most relevant to the presiding science. The first step toward forming a definition, a theory, of "style" must be taken in the science of literary esthetics, more specifically in a consideration of the nature of words as esthetic medium.

It is the nature of words to mean. To consider words only as sounds, like drum taps, or to consider written letters as patterned objects, as in alphabet soup, is the same as to consider a Stradivarius as material for kindling wood. There is, to be sure, a certain truth in the contention that it is useless to speak of the limits of each art. If a painter of abstractions succeeded in conveying a concept which he described as rhythmic, it would be pointless to contend that such a concept should properly be expressed in music. Insofar as the painting did succeed as an expression, there would simply be *that* expression. On the other hand, even Croce will admit that different artistic intuitions need different media for their "externalization."[11] Even when the various media are considered as forming a continuum, a spectrum, one point in the spectrum is not another point. Red is not green. Stone is not B flat. Stone can be used for a statue; B flat cannot. Words can be used to "mean" in a way that nothing else can. In various senses the other arts may be called expressive or communicative. But it is not in any such senses that words are expressive. When Maritain says that "music *imitates* with sound and rhythms . . . the movements of the soul,"[12] and when Dewey says that architecture " 'expresses' . . . enduring values of collective human life,"[13] they are speaking of the kind of representation we should speak of if we said that the images of autumn, nightfall, and a dying fire in Shakespeare's sonnet stand for his sense of mortality, or if we said that the whole poem is a symbol of his sense of mortality. While the music and the architecture *are* the symbols of what they represent, the words of a writing must *express* a meaning

[11] Benedetto Croce, *op. cit.*, pp. 114–16. Cf. C. K. Ogden *et al.*, *The Foundations of Aesthetics* (London, 1925), p. 28; David Daiches, *The Place of Meaning in Poetry* (Edinburgh, 1935), esp. pp. 30, 61–3.

[12] Jacques Maritain, *Art and Scholasticism*, trans. J. F. Scanlan (London, 1930), p. 58.

[13] John Dewey, *Art as Experience* (New York, 1934), p. 221. Cf. Gilbert Murray, "An Essay on the Theory of Poetry," *Yale Review*, X (1921), 484; Theodore M. Greene, *The Arts and the Art of Criticism* (Princeton, 1940), esp. p. 108.

which *is* a symbol. "A poem should not mean But be," writes Mr. Archibald MacLeish. But a poem cannot *be* in the simple sense that a statue or a piece of Venetian glass *is*. For each thing insofar as it *is,* must *be,* have *being,* according to its nature. The nature of words is to mean, and a poem *is* through its meaning.

There are such things as the Caroline shape poems, the winged or altar shapes of Herbert or Quarles; there are the typographical oddities of E. E. Cummings. There are illuminated manuscripts or illustrated books, Gothic books of Gospels, arabesque texts of the Koran on mosque walls. And people may even have wondered what they ought to think of Cummings. But nobody thinks that the Gospel suffers when not read in the Book of Kells. It is clear that in the case of illuminations and illustrations of a text there is not a single art expression, but two running side by side. Words, music, costume, and stage may make one expression in an opera; the poetry of Vachel Lindsay read aloud and the accompanying dance may have made one expression; it may be possible to conceive a text so referred to and interrelated with a series of pictures that the two make one expression.[14] Yet it remains true that what we call literature, whether prose or poetry, has not been a graphic medium. It has not been possible or worth while to employ words in this way.

But language is spoken before it is written; even after it is written it is implicitly spoken; and language as sound has potentialities far beyond those of language as written or visual.[15] Sound is in some sense the medium of literature, no matter how words are considered as expressive. What is more questionable is how near this medium ever can come to being that of music. Sound in its conventional semantic value is certainly not a musical medium. Further it is not musical in its whole complex of suggestive or directly imitative values, onomatopoeia, and all the more mysteriously felt shades of sound propriety.[16]

A more difficult problem of sound in literature is that of meter and such associates as rhyme and alliteration. But it is usual to insist that these elements of verse are in some way expressive. They express the

[14] Mr. Archibald MacLeish's *Land of the Free* (New York, 1938) is "a book of photographs illustrated by a poem. . . . The original purpose had been to write some sort of text to which these photographs might serve as commentary. But so great was the power and the stubborn inward livingness of these vivid American documents that the result was a reversal of that plan" (p. 89).

[15] Cf. Otto Jespersen, *Language, Its Nature, Development and Origin* (London, 1922), *passim;* D. W. Prall, *Aesthetic Judgment* (New York, 1929), pp. 289–90.

[16] Many of these values, as a matter of fact, are not, as has been commonly thought, due to any direct expressiveness of sounds but rather to linguistic analogies as ancient as the roots of language (Leonard Bloomfield, *Language* [New York, 1933], pp. 244–5; I. A. Richards, *The Philosophy of Rhetoric* [New York, 1936], pp. 63–5). For a treatment of word sounds as suggestive of or appropriate to meaning, see Otto Jespersen, *Language* (London, 1922), pp. 396–406.

emotion of poetic experience; or, by inducing in us a pattern of expectancy and playing against that the surprise of variation, they make us realize more intensely both sense and emotion.[17] Or, the verse of a whole poem may be considered as a form, an aspect or way of being known, which gives unity and particularity to the whole—makes it the special poetic symbol that it is.[18] It may be possible to say that this second kind of expressiveness is on the same level as that of music and architecture mentioned above, a direct symbol of experience. But in this case it will be necessary to remember that the expression of the verse coalesces with and is in effect the same as that of the words in their semantic function.

Here we might let the question of language as sound medium rest were it not for the persistent appearance of the mysterious critical term "prose rhythm." From what has been said of verse it is plain that a prose rhythm is conceivable—that is, some alternation of sounds akin to meter, though more variable. If such a succession of sounds could be detected with certainty in any body of prose, and if one had no sense that this was unconnected with the meaning or detracted from it, then it would have to be admitted that in the given case a prose rhythm as an expressive medium did exist. The general question, then, is not whether there *can* be a prose rhythm but whether there *is*. And a particular question, such as that concerning English literature, is but the general question narrowed— whether there *is*. Certain things may be asserted: I. The rhetoricians of antiquity found in Greek and Latin oratory a rhythm which they analyzed almost as definitely as verse meter, particularly in the sequence of syllables ending clauses, the cursus.[19] II. The cursus was also a part of Medieval Latin prose.[20] III. There are some who hold that variations of the cursus occur in English prose.[21] IV. There is, however, no agreement, but the widest divergence of opinion, among those who have made extended studies of the nature of rhythm in English prose. Their number is not

[17] Cf. I. A. Richards, *Principles of Literary Criticism* (New York, 1934), "Rhythm and Metre," pp. 137–42. It may be too that meter has a hypnotic function. See Edward D. Snyder, *Hypnotic Poetry* (Philadelphia, 1930), pp. 19, 39ff.

[18] Cf. Lascelles Abercrombie, *Principles of English Prosody* (London, 1923), pp. 15–18, 31; *The Theory of Poetry* (New York, 1926), pp. 70, 95, 138, 140–6.

[19] See, for example, John W. Sandys, *A Companion to Latin Studies* (Cambridge, 1921), p. 655. François Novotny, *État Actuel des Études sur le Rhythme de la Prose Latine* (Livów, 1929), sees "un bel avenir dans notre science," but confesses: "Ces essais et leur résultats dépendent bien souvent du sentiment esthétique subjectif de l'observateur" (p. 33).

[20] See, for example, Karl Strecker, *Introduction à l'Étude du Latin Médiéval*, trad. par Paul van der Woestijne (Gand, 1933), pp. 51–3; Edouard Norden, *Die Antike Kunstprosa* (Leipzig, 1898), II, 950–1.

[21] See, for example, Oliver Elton, "English Prose Numbers," *Essays and Studies by Members of the English Association*, IV (Oxford, 1913), 29–54; Morris W. Croll, "The Cadence of English Oratorical Prose," *Studies in Philology*, XVI (1919), 1–55.

small (and each is at odds in some respect with almost all the others):
those who would scan, or make meter; those who are interested in some
vaguer kind of periodicity, time measurement; those who rely on the
cursus; and those who find rhythm in the movement of phrases.[22]

It would be within the province only of a very special investigation
to dare say what English prose rhythm *is*. And I have admitted above that
the question is not whether there *can* be a prose rhythm. Yet there are
some things that can be said about the possibilities of prose rhythm. If
it is a quality of sound, it is either expressive of something or not. If not
(if, say, it is like the number of times the letter "t" occurs on a given
page), it is not a medium of art and therefore claims no interest; it is not
in fact prose rhythm at all. Secondly, if it is expressive, it expresses either
the same meaning as the words do otherwise, or it does not. If it expresses
the same meaning, it may, like meter, expresses perhaps from the same
level as words do otherwise, perhaps from a level more like that of music.
These possibilities are admissible.[23] But thirdly, if it expresses other than
the same meaning, then it must express some meaning which is proper to
nonverbal sounds—some kind of musical meaning. This is perhaps conceivable, that words should do two separate things, convey their language
meaning, and at the same time be a nonlinguistic tune—perhaps even
harmonious with the language meaning. This, however, seems improbable
in view of the limited musical value of spoken word sounds. It is, like the
pictorial value of print in typographical poems, very slight.[24] Music is not
written in words, but in tones and time.

The notion of a separate music is further crippled if we consider
that it is impossible for any system of sound in prose to be unconnected

[22] Cf. John Hubert Scott, *Rhythmic Prose,* "University of Iowa Humanistic
Studies," Vol. III, No. 1 (Iowa City, 1925), p. 11. Norton R. Tempest, a more
recent writer, is a scanner and at the same time belongs to the cursus school
(*The Rhythm of English Prose* [Cambridge University Press, 1930], p. 134).
André Classe is a timer with a kymograph, who proposes "only . . . to investigate
the question of rhythm from the phonetic point of view" (*The Rhythm of English
Prose* [Oxford, 1939], pp. 1, 4, 135). Such investigation doubtless does discover
physical facts, but just as phoneticians distinguish between the gross acoustic
quality of words and that part of the acoustic quality which has semantic value,
so literary students may distinguish between the gross discoverable physical facts
about "rhythm" and that part of the facts which relates to expression. Professor
Sapir has distinguished between the phonetic and the esthetic analysis of rhythm
("The Musical Foundations of Verse," *Journal of English and Germanic Philology,* xx [1921], 223–4).

[23] Under this head, rather than under what follows, should be considered
meter in prose, in Dickens, for example. Here there is a linguistic expressiveness,
just as in poetry, but not a coalescence, as in poetry, with the rest of the meaning
meter in prose, see H. W. and F. G. Fowler, *The King's English* (Oxford, 1906),
p. 295.

[24] Cf. D. W. Prall, *Aesthetic Judgment* (New York, 1929), pp. 289, 295;
Aesthetic Analysis (New York, 1936), pp. 105–6.

with its meaning—that is, neither contribute to it nor detract from it. Suppose a man to be writing a double composition, both prose and music; then in the use of any given piece of language he must, consciously or unconsciously, choose for the meaning or for the music. (It is impossible that two such disconnected effects should often coincide.) Or, to change the sense of "must," he must choose for the meaning and sacrifice the music, for the meaning of words is their nature, while the music of words is negligible. "In the vast majority of those words which can be said to have an independent musical value," says Mr. Middleton Murry, "the musical suggestion is at odds with the meaning. When the musical suggestion is allowed to predominate, decadence of style has begun."[25]

Let me close this part of the discussion by indicating my own notion of what ought to be called prose rhythm—if something must be called that. The notion has been well expressed by H. W. Fowler: "A sentence or a passage is rhythmical if, when said aloud, it falls naturally into groups of words each well fitted by its length & intonation for its place in the whole & its relation to its neighbors. Rhythm is not a matter of counting syllables & measuring the distance between accents."[26] Prose rhythm is a matter of emphasis; it is putting the important words where they sound important. It is a matter of coherence; it is putting the right idea in the right place.[27]

"Rhythm" as applied to prose is a metaphor. "Rhythm," when used literally, means "measure" or "regularity," and since the movement of good prose is precisely *not* regular but varied with the sense, the union of the terms "prose" and "rhythm" has been none the happiest.

A first step toward a theory of style might be the reflection that one may say different things about the same topic—or different things which are very much alike.[28] A rose and a poppy are different, but both are

[25] J. Middleton Murry, *The Problem of Style* (Oxford, 1922), p. 86. And it seems to me that this is also true of criticism: when the musical suggestion predominates, decadence has begun. The authors of books on prose rhythm are aware of their danger but they cannot save themselves. See, for example, William M. Patterson, *The Rhythm of Prose* (New York, 1916), p. 84; John Hubert Scott, *op cit.*, pp. 24, 36–7, 127, 133.

[26] *A Dictionary of Modern English Usage* (Oxford, 1927), "Rhythm," p. 504.

[27] Mr. Ezra Pound says: "The attainment of a style consists in so knowing words that one will communicate the various parts of what one says with the various degrees and weights of importance which one wishes" (*Guide to Kulchur,* quoted in *Times Literary Supplement,* xxxvii [1938], p. 489).

For a detailed study of inversion of subject and predicate and position of adverbs in English according to sense, see August Western, *On Sentence-Rhythm and Word-Order in Modern English* (Christiania, 1908), esp. p. 9. Cf. *post* pp. 69–71. P. Fijn van Draat, "The Place of the Adverb, A Study in Rhythm," *Neophilologus,* vi (1921), 56–88, esp. 62, 87, admits Western's general principle but would connect certain variations not with sense but with "rhythmic formulas."

[28] Cf. A. C. Bradley, *Poetry for Poetry's Sake* (Oxford, 1901), pp. 12–13.

flowers. Sidney writes, "Come, sleep! O sleep, the certain knot of peace, etc." Shakespeare writes, "O sleep, O gentle sleep, Nature's soft nurse, etc.," and again, "Sleep that knits up the ravell'd sleave of care, etc." It is not that these writers have had the same meaning and have "dressed" it, or expressed it, differently. Rather they have had the same subject, the benefits of sleep, or beneficent sleep, but have had different thoughts, different meanings, which have found expression in different language. They have expressed different, if similar, meanings. Even Betterton, when he recasts one of Shakespeare's passages on sleep, has not merely reëxpressed the same meaning; he has actually changed the meaning. Different words make different meanings.

It is true that meaning is not identical with words.[29] Meaning is the psychic entity, the something in the mind—for which material is not adequate. In the language of the scholastics: *Voces referuntur ad res significandas mediante conceptione intellectus.*[30] Nevertheless, words do determine meanings relentlessly. To come at it another way, meanings vary persistently with variations of words.[31] It may be well to recall one of Newman's figures, "the convex and the concave of a curve." The convex is not the concave, but if we conceive the curve as a line, then every change in the concave produces a corresponding change in the convex. There is that much truth in the contention of Croce: "Language is a perpetual creation. What has been linguistically expressed is not repeated. . . . Language is not an arsenal of arms already made, and it is not a *vocabulary,* a collection of abstractions, or a cemetery of corpses more or less well embalmed."[32]

We may be tempted to believe that we have at length distilled words

[29] Cf. Alfred North Whitehead, *Modes of Thought* (New York, 1938). pp. 48–9; Alan H. Gardiner, *The Theory of Speech and Language* (Oxford, 1932), p. 70; Edward Sapir, *Language* (New York, 1921), pp. 14, 238; I. A. Richards, *The Philosophy of Rhetoric* (New York, 1936), p. 13; Louis H. Gray, *Foundations of Language* (New York, 1939), pp. 88, 93–4.

[30] St. Thomas Aquinas, *Summa Theologica,* I, q. 13, a. 1, quoted by Désiré Cardinal Mercier, *A Manual of Modern Scholastic Philosophy* (London, 1919), II, 154.
Cf. Alan H. Gardiner, *op cit.,* pp. 44 ff., 70 ff., 102–3.

[31] The term "meaning" as I am using it may be taken to include all that Ogden and Richards have divided into different kinds of language meaning—the really referential, symbolic, intellectual meaning, and the group of emotive meanings (C. K. Ogden and I. A. Richards, *The Meaning of Meaning* [New York, 1936], pp. 11–12, 126, 186–7, 224–30). Obviously if such is the meaning to which we refer, if we are thinking of works of literature, not treatises of mathematics or philosophy, it is much easier to see how meaning depends on the very words in which it is cast. I choose not to emphasize this, however, because, as will be seen shortly, some of the effects of style in which I am interested are very slightly if at all dependent on emotive meaning.

[32] *Op. cit.,* pp. 150–1; cf. p. 68, on translation. Cf. Leone Vivante, *Intelligence in Expression* (London, 1925), pp. 2–3.

or style away from meaning when we think of *bad* style. It might be plausible and would probably be useful to formulate some rule like this: Style occurs in isolation only when it is bad, when it fails to coincide with meaning.[33] This might be almost the truth where writing is so bad that it is meaningless—for example, in errors of expression made by one unfamiliar with a language, matters of syntax and elementary vocabulary. But poor expression in the wider sense cannot be reduced to this. The nature of words is against it—their constant tendency to mean. It is not as if we could forget or fail to put meaning in words. They persist in meaning, no matter what we intend or are conscious of. We may fail to say what we intend, but we can scarcely fail to say something.

Bad style is not a deviation of words from meaning, but a deviation of meaning from meaning. Of what meaning from what meaning? Of the actually conveyed meaning (what a reader receives) from the meaning an author intended or ought to have intended. This is true even of those cases where we might be most tempted to say that the fault of style is mere "awkwardness," since the meaning is conveyed completely. In such cases, the awkwardness consists in some absence of meaning (usually but implicit) or in some contrary or irrelevant meaning, which we disregarded, inferring the writer's real meaning, at least so far as it would be explicit. We must do this so continually for most writing—seek out the meaning, put the most relevant construction on every word and phrase, disregard what tries to say the wrong thing—that we fail to sense any lack of meaning and dub the cause of our annoyance metaphorically and conveniently "awkwardness."

The question what the author ought to have said is the true difficulty in judging style. *Ut jam nunc dicat,* says Horace, *jam nunc debentia dici.* It is the only difficulty, for it is the only question, and it is one we implicitly answer every time we judge style. We do it by our sense, more or less definite, of what the author intends to say as a whole, of his central and presiding purpose. The only consideration that can determine an author in a given detail is the adequacy of the detail to his whole purpose.[34] It does not follow that when we are sure this or that phrase or passage is bad style we shall always refer our judgment precisely to our impression

---

[33] Frederick Schlegel has said: "Although, in strict application and rigid expression, thought and speech always are, and always must be regarded as two things metaphysically distinct,—yet there only can we find these two elements in disunion, where one or both have been employed imperfectly or amiss" (*Lectures on the History of Literature* [New York, 1841], pp. 7–8).

[34] H. B. Lathrop, in arguing that emphasis is an aspect of coherence, and coherence an aspect of unity, has shown admirably how the school-book terms may be squared with this philosophy of style ("Unity, Coherence, and Emphasis," *University of Wisconsin Studies in Language and Literature,* No. 2, *Studies by Members of the Department of English* [Madison, 1918], pp. 77–98).

of the whole.[35] The steps in subordination are too complicated. Furthermore, a fault in one whole can have something in common with a fault in another whole; whence arises the classification of faults of style and a tendency to refer individual faults only to the class definition.[36] The whole is usually forgotten.

From the foregoing one may begin to infer that a detailed study of style can be fruitful—even in the hands of those who least connect style with meaning. If faults can be classed, so to some extent can merits. That which has for centuries been called style differs from the rest of writing only in that it is one plane or level of the organization of meaning; it would not be happy to call it the outer cover or the last layer; rather it is the furthest elaboration of the one concept that is the center. As such it can be considered. The terms of rhetoric, spurned by Croce and other moderns, did have a value for the ancients, even though they failed to connect all of rhetoric with meaning. To give the terms of rhetoric a value in modern criticism it would be necessary only to determine the expressiveness of the things in language to which the terms refer. This has been done for metaphor, which used to be an ornament, but has now been made "the unique expression of a writer's individual vision" or "the result of the search for a precise epithet."[37] Mr. Empson has spoken ingeniously of that highly "artificial" figure the zeugma.[38] Mr. Bateson has praised a hypallage.[39]

The greatest obstacle to recognizing the expressive value of rhetorical devices is the fact that they recur. One notices that Cicero uses a *litotes* or a *praeteritio* several times in a few pages, or so many hundreds of balances are counted in the *Ramblers* of Johnson. This suggests play with words, disregard of meaning. One is likely to reflect: if these devices express something, then the author must be expressing, or saying, much the same thing over and over—which is useless; therefore the author is really not trying to say anything; he is using words viciously, for an inexpressive purpose.

[35] For small faults of inconsistency and irrelevancy in a composition largely good, one would have to examine only a short section of the surrounding text. At the other extreme might be a composition by a schoolboy, where one could guess the central meaning only from the title or from what the schoolboy said when asked, or where there might not be any at all.

[36] An operation essential to the economy of thinking, but one which can lead to error when the reason for considering the class as faulty is forgotten, and faults of one type of whole are referred to another—for example, when what would be a fault in a poem of heroic couplets is adduced against the verse of *Christabel.*

[37] J. Middleton Murry, *The Problem of Style* (Oxford, 1922), pp. 133, 83.

[38] William Empson, *Seven Types of Ambiguity* (New York, 1931), pp. 89–90.

[39] F. W. Bateson, *English Poetry and the English Language* (Oxford, 1934), p. 22.

Such an attitude would not have been possible if the theoretical rhetoricians had not thrust forward the repertory of devices so as to throw them out of focus and conceal their nature as part of language. No one thinks, for example, that sentences because they recur are artificial, that they say the same thing over or say nothing. This is the key to what our attitude toward devices ought to be. Sentences are expressive; so also are declensions, and conjugations; they are expressive forms.[40] They express, not ideas like "grass" or "green," but relations. The so-called "devices," really no more devices than a sentence is a device, express more special forms of meaning, not so common to thinking that they cannot be avoided, like the sentence, but common enough to reappear frequently in certain types of thinking and hence to characterize the thinking, or the style. They express a kind of meaning[41] which may be discussed as legitimately as the more obvious kinds such as what a man writes about—the vanity of human wishes or the River Duddon.

It might be better if the term "device" were never used, for its use leads almost immediately to the carelessness of thinking of words as separable practicably from meaning. That is, we think of a given meaning as if it may be weakly expressed in one way but more forcefully in another. The latter is the device—the language applied, like a jack or clamp, or any dead thing, to the meaning, which itself remains static and unchanged, whether or not the device succeeds in expressing it. There is some convenience in this way of thinking, but more philosophy in steadily realizing that each change of words changes the meaning actually expressed. It is better to think of the "weak" expression and the "strong" expression as two quite different expressions, or, elliptically, two different meanings, of which one is farther from, one nearer to, what the author ought to say, or what he intends to say. The whole matter of emphasis, which is the real truth behind Herbert Spencer's wooden theory of economy in words, seems to be best considered in this light. (To keep the mind from being fatigued while receiving ideas—this is Spencer's function for style.[42] One may object that the most important thing about the mind is not that it

[40] Cf. Alan H. Gardiner, *The Theory of Speech and Language* (Oxford, 1932), pp. 130–4, 158–61.

[41] The better modern treatments of rhetoric have recognized this. See, for example, Alexander Bain, *English Composition and Rhetoric* (New York, 1886), esp. pp. 20–64, though it is hard to think the doctrine of expressiveness is an abiding principle when he says that one of the functions of metaphor is to "give an agreeable surprise" (pp. 30–1). For a treatment of figures as common elements of speech, see James B. Greenough and George L. Kittredge, *Words and Their Ways in English Speech* (New York, 1901), pp. 14–17.

[42] "The Philosophy of Style," in Lane Cooper's *Theories of Style* (New York, 1907), pp. 273–4. What if a passage were read twice or pondered at length? Would it not lose most of its force—through being relieved of the duty of preventing our misconceptions? Spencer's essay appeared first in the *Westminster Review* of 1852.

can be fatigued—but that it can entertain splendid, though often difficult and fatiguing, conceptions.) If a word is to be placed here or there in a sentence in order to be effective, to have due weight, this ought to be thought of not as a juggling of words round a meaning to give the meaning emphatic expression, but as a choice of a more emphatic rather than a less emphatic meaning, or, strictly, the choice of the meaning needed, for meaning exists through emphasis; a change of emphasis is a change of meaning. We must preserve a notion of words, even in their most purely suggestive functions, as something transparently intellectual, not intervening between us and the meaning but luminous and full of their meaning and as if conscious of it.

The expressiveness of the rhetorical device is not always so easily analyzed as that of the sentence or declension—frequently it is a form of implicit expressiveness, one which is certainly present but not simply in virtue of meanings of words or of syntax or of morphology. For example, one of the most frequent forms of implicit expressiveness, or meaning, is that of equality or likeness—with its opposite, inequality or unlikeness. Any succession of words, phrases, or sentences must in any given degree be either like or unlike, and appropriately or inappropriately so in accordance with whether the successive explicit meanings are like or unlike. The "jingles" collected by H. W. and F. G. Fowler[43] are admirable illustrations of the fault which consists in a likeness of word sounds and hence of implicit meaning where there is no corresponding explicit meaning to be sustained. "To read his tales is a baptism of optimism," they quote from the *Times.* Here there is a nasty jingle of "ptism," "ptimism"—nasty just because the two combinations so nearly alike strive to make these words parallel, whereas they are not; one qualifies the other. The case is even plainer if we take an example of the common "ly" jingle, "He lived practically exclusively on milk," and set beside it something like this: "We are swallowed up, irreparably, irrevocably, irrecoverably, irremediably."[44] In the second we are not conscious of the repeated "ly" as a jingle, any more than of the repeated "irre." The reason is that behind each of these parallel sounds (implicit parallel meanings) there is a parallel explicit meaning. So far as we advert to the sounds as sounds at all it is with a sense of their concordance with the structure of meaning. Such is perhaps the most frequently underlying reason why expressions are approved of or objected to as "euphonious" or "cacophonous," "harmonious" or "inharmonious."

---

[43] *The King's English* (Oxford, 1906), p. 291. Cf. H. W. Fowler, *A Dictionary of Modern English Usage* (Oxford, 1927), "Jingles," pp. 308–9.

[44] The first is from E. F. Benson, quoted in *The King's English,* p. 292; the second, from John Donne, Sermon LXVI, in *Donne's Sermons,* ed. Logan Pearsall Smith (Oxford, 1919), p. 10.

And matters of sound are not the only ones to which the principle of equality and inequality applies. Even so basically wrong a thing as parataxis, the monotony of a schoolboy's writing, consists just in that he is using the same form of meaning in successive clauses and hence fails to relate his meanings, that is, fails to express the really different meanings which lurk dimly in his mind as his real intention or are at least what he should intend. Hypotaxis, the rare-sounding opposite of parataxis, but no other than all modulated writing, consists in the use of different forms of meaning to sustain the sequence of the complex whole meaning. The author whose style is the subject of this study offers on every page emphatic demonstrations of implicit meaning through equality; and it will be one of the purposes of the study to show that what is sometimes called cumbrousness or pompousness in Johnson is but the exaggeration into more rigid lines of an expressive principle that lies in the very warp of all verbal discourse.

METAPHYSICAL CRITICISM OF STYLE

Louis Milic

No wonder style interests so many—such interesting things have been said about it. Buffon, of course, is always mentioned: "Le style est l'homme même." Swift's famous aphorism is in the same category: "Proper words in proper places makes the true definition of a style." Alfred North Whitehead has told us that "style is the ultimate morality of mind." Who can resist Jean Cocteau's formulation, however oblique it may seem: "Style is not a dance: it is an overture"? And is there anyone who does not feel better informed when he learns what Hemingway has said about his own style: "In stating as fully as I could how things really were, it was often very difficult and I wrote awkwardly and the awkwardness is that they called my style."[1]

These statements are among the best-known or the best-formulated of the hundreds of axioms, aphorisms and apothegms on style, but they are fully typical in two respects. They all seem to mean something, some-

Address delivered at the Conference on College Composition and Communication, March 25, 1966, Denver, Colorado. With revisions, April, 1966. Reprinted by permission of the author.

[1] Buffon, "Discours sur le style," *Oeuvres Philosophiques,* ed. Jean Piveteau (Paris, 1954), p. 500; Swift, "A Letter to a Young Gentleman," *Irish Tracts and Sermons,* ed. Herbert Davis (Oxford, 1948), p. 65; Whitehead, *The Organisation of Thought* (London, 1917), p. 25; Cocteau, *Oeuvres Completes* (Geneva, 1950), X, 355 ["Le style n'est pas une danse, c'est une demarche,"]; A. E. Hotchner, "Hemingway Talks to American Youth," *This Week,* Oct. 18, 1959, p. 11.

thing that we ought to find instructive. And they strive by wit, paradox and imagery, to express the ineffable. The struggle with the reluctant medium of words is concealed, though it can be sensed in the high density of such statements. But when we examine the propositional content of these sayings and find it tautological, obvious, contradictory or simply absent, we realize that they do not really contribute to our understanding of the problem of style, however much they may enlighten us about the feelings of those who said them. For words, if they are arranged in a certain way (even by a random sentence-generator), have a constant tendency to mean, in Professor Wimsatt's phrase. But this kind of haphazard meaning is incomplete and leads to the metaphysical.[2]

Everyone who has tried to say something about an author's style has probably committed this kind of fault. He has read, let us say, a very impressive writer, and he is full of the desire to say what possessed him and what fascinated him about the writer's language, but he has nothing to fall back on except burning intensity and the tendency of sentences to mean something. Professor Trilling has truly said: "It is notoriously difficult to dispute about style in *some* way."[3]

The reader of these disputes must make allowances, for he has no means of judging the criticism of style. In this department of literary study, there seems to be no generally accepted method. Though biography is not a science, some canons of historical description obtain there, and biographical writing is judged by those standards. Bibliography has stated requirements and textual criticism is even more particular. It should be noted that no aphorisms are extant of the type "Bibliography is the order of the cosmos" or "Textual criticism is not a grave minuet, but a marathon upon all fours."

Stylistics, however, has for most scholars still no method beyond the method of impressionistic description and a vague use of rhetoric. But even those who describe the style of a writer in terms of the impression they have received scarcely seem to be aware of the nature of such descriptions. A description of style, when it is not quantitative, can only be figurative. Such a description tends to rely on comparisons, analogies and similarly crude approximations. Of course, even impressionistic descriptions can be responsible and verifiable, e.g., "Swift depends on seriation" or "Johnson is given to antithetic parallel clauses." But few impressionistic critics are satisfied with such tame accounts of their responses. They have their eyes on the empyrean.

I became most keenly aware of this when I was studying the style

---

[2] The term *metaphysical* is used in two ways in this paper: loosely, to describe any criticism of style that is not usefully quantitative; and strictly, to describe any statement not verifiable even in principle. The details of my classification are set out schematically in the outline provided in the Appendix.

[3] Lionel Trilling, "The Two Environments: Reflections on the Study of English," *Encounter*, XXV (1965), 9.

of Jonathan Swift.[4] Nearly all critics have praised it and some have tried to describe it. When all these descriptions are placed side by side, they amount to little more than a glossary of adjectives: *charming, clear, common, concise, correct, direct, elaborate, elegant, energetic, graceful, hard-round-crystalline, homely, lucid, manly, masculine, muscular, nervous, ornamented, perfect, plain, poor, proper, pure, salty, simple, sinewy, sonorous, vigorous.* This is far from a complete list, but it suggests some of the shortcomings of this method of description.

Though *clear* may seem to refer specifically to the writing process, it actually describes the response of the reader. What is clear to one may not be to another. Similarly, with *lucid, simple, plain;* the attention is on the reader, not on the writing. *Simple* describes nothing in the writing, unless it is specified as referring to particular predicates of simplicity, such as sentence structure, choice of word, modification, sentence order, for example. Absolutes like *pure* and *perfect* describe nothing at all, but are merely assertions by the critic that the writer is without flaw. Such terms as *muscular, nervous, sinewy,* drawing as they do from various parts of the writer's anatomy, reveal the critic's desire to move from the style to the man, or to use the man to describe the style.

The difficulties of description are clearly great enough to drive a man to desperation. For example, F. L. Lucas in the space of two pages describes Swift as "a lean gray wolf, with white fangs bared" and says he is like a Pennine moorland not like the Highlands.[5] Somerset Maugham presses the landscape analogy even harder, calling Swift's style a placid French canal whereas Dryden's is a cheerful English river.[6]

Any critic is capable of a far-fetched or outrageous metaphor on occasion, but descriptions of style pullulate with this kind of thing. In part this is the result of a certain confusion of terms, which reflects a theoretical disorganization in this field of criticism. The very meaning of the term *style* is in question. In common speech, style is always *somehow, somewhat* or *in a manner* whatever it is: "His style was somehow reminiscent of a tight steel spring." Or it is joined to another term roughly synonymous: *his style and manner, his style and outlook, his style and tone.* And the term is always modified, usually by adjectives: *a lapidary, an elegant, a personal, a drab, a breathless, a mannered* or *an affected style.*

Implicit in all these usages is a nebulous sense that style is what distinguishes individuals from one another, especially in their linguistic behavior. But the efficacy of the technical term has been compromised by its use as a word of all work, expressing a mere *je-ne-sais-quoi* of dis-

[4] See my forthcoming, *A Quantitative Approach to the Style of Jonathan Swift* (The Hague, in press).

[5] *Style* (London, 1955), pp. 210, 126.

[6] *The Summing-Up* (New York, 1957), pp. 20–21.

tinctiveness. This slipshod kind of definition leads to metaphysical stylistics, which does nothing to advance understanding and a good deal to retard progress in the method and the practice of criticism.

To be studied effectively, style must be defined in such a way that its boundary with content can be clearly distinguished. Whether it is considered the sum of a writer's deviations from the linguistic norm or his characteristic features of expression is not material. Both imply the same requirements for effective study: a knowledge of the background against which he is trying to stand out and a means of stating his degree of distinctiveness. A feature of style, whether it be a favored area of the vocabulary, a preference in imagery, a rhetorical habit or tendency to have recourse to certain syntactical patterns, must be described in concrete and verifiable terms, which finally means, in quantitative terms.

It is precisely this understandable reluctance to deal in quantities, in *parameters* of style, which has forced reputable scholars into gross errors and primitive distortions. Any statistician will point out that sampling is crucial in statistical demonstration. In dealing with a large corpus of any kind, if we cannot examine all of it, we must content ourselves with a sample. Most scholars proceed as if all samples, regardless how drawn, were equivalent in quality, which is the same as saying that any part is typical of the whole and that any part typifies every part. This is plainly not so, yet it is implicit in much scholarly work concerned with style.

An interesting example is found in the question of Henry James's later prose. Around 1905, when he began to prepare the New York edition of his works, he extensively revised the language of his novels. His early novel *Roderick Hudson* was first published in 1876 and in a revised version a few years later. When it emerged from the final revision, it was considerably changed. In 1924, Helene Harvitt asserted, in a published paper, that James's revisions had disfigured his work, making it "labored, heavy, ambiguous and sometimes almost impenetrable."[7] She illustrated this thesis with examples drawn from the versions of *Roderick Hudson*.[8] In his book on Henry James, F. O. Matthiessen undertook to refute this charge, claiming that James's revisions had generally resulted in improvements. But he conducted his refutation by examining the revisions of a different book, *The Portrait of a Lady*.[9]

The suggestion that the study of style must be pursued by rigorous means derived from linguistics and the quantitative sciences is likely to

[7] "How Henry James Revised *Roderick Hudson:* A Study in Style," *PMLA,* XXIX (1924), 203–227.

[8] Raymond D. Havens has noted that Helene Harvitt's "first" edition was really the thoroughly-revised second ("The Revision of *Roderick Hudson,*" *PMLA,* XL [1925], 433).

[9] Appendix: "The Painter's Sponge and Varnish Bottle," in *Henry James: The Major Phase* (New York, 1963), pp. 152–186.

find no favor among literary scholars. Nonetheless, it seems to be the inevitable direction such work must take. Intuitive impressionism cannot often lead to productive results. I shall not illustrate this contention by citing the naive attempts to attribute works to an author by internal evidence, which consist mainly of claiming that some lexical items are present in large numbers (unstated) and that no one but X could therefore have written Y.

No, the kind of thing I have in mind is exemplified by the following comment:

> When we call Newman's prose concrete and particular, we do not, I think, mean to suggest that it is . . . particularly attentive to the minute surface details of experience. . . . an examination of the *Apologia* suggests that the particular and concrete rarely appear except as internal impression transmuted from thing into idea or feeling. And this leads to the problem of how Newman's style appears to create a living felt reality while at the same time it remains largely abstract, one might almost say eighteenth-century, not only in its rhythms and diction but in the generalizing force of its language.[10]

The writer casts his impression—that Newman's prose is concrete—in the teeth of the fact that he knows it is abstract. His struggle consists of trying to find a way to join these opposites by violence together. This is truly metaphysical, both in Johnson's sense of the term and in the common sense, as belonging to a different order of reality, one in which the ordinary rules of evidence do not apply.

That this kind of defective criticism is not merely a chance aberration but a regular aspect of reputable scholarship can be amply documented. Here for instance is a comment on the style of C. P. Snow, part of a critical biography:

> Snow's prose, as well, is marked by plainness, an innocuous prose that rarely does more than indicate essentials. His style is, as it were, virtually an absence of style when we use the word to signify something distinctive. There is, also, a curious lack of development in his power of expression from first novel to last, as though Snow refused to tamper with something that he considered adequate.[11]

A bit further on, the writer says that the prose calls for parody and that Snow uses the word *diffident* in the same way in passages written twenty

---

[10] George Levine, "The Prose of the *Apologia Pro Vita Sua*," *Victorian Newsletter,* No. 27 (Spring 1965), p. 5.

[11] Frederick R. Karl, *C. P. Snow: The Politics of Conscience* (Carbondale, Ill., 1963), p. 9.

years apart. The first sentence of the quotation says the prose is plain, an assertion verifiable only in principle, for we have no sure criteria of plainness. The claim that Snow has no style is a hackneyed paradox belied by the writer's own evidence, for parody can deal only with the distinctive feature. The claim that Snow's style lacks development reveals merely that Snow's critic does not admire Snow's style.

My third example has a peculiar interest because of the height to which it builds on sand:

> Wordsworth's prose is admirable. It is seldom magnificent. "It does not sparkle," said Nowell C. Smith justly. As a prose stylist, Wordsworth lacks the clarity of Dryden, the force of Hazlitt, the passion of Milton, the metaphorical daring of Coleridge, the simultaneous levels of either Swift or Lamb, and the opulence of an admirer who borrowed power from Wordsworth, De Quincey. And yet Wordsworth practiced to a viable degree clarity, force, passion, strength of metaphor, levels at least of scorn, and richness if not opulence. He achieved what he most wanted, the signature of personal conviction.[12]

The first two sentences alone would not puzzle anyone: Wordsworth's prose is worthy to be admired, though it lacks the quality of magnificence (or sparkle). But when the passage goes on with its list of abstractions assigned to other writers, it surely requires us to know what these abstractions stand for, which is questionable. Anyway, how is *force* to be told from *passion, richness* from *opulence*? And are "levels of scorn" an aspect of style? When, finally, the writer says that Wordsworth had in some vague degree these vague qualities, he has not greatly added to our knowledge. His conclusion, to the extent that we can decipher it, is either metaphysical or not about style at all.

Though it would be valuable to be able to infer the mental processes of an author from his style, no means exist for doing so. A claim of that sort often passes unnoticed, possibly because statements about style are not taken very seriously anyway, but it would be good to know how such a conclusion as this one could be validated:

> For all its quietness, however, the prose of *Dombey and Son* is consistently hard, compact and unsparing. Its economy comes from the fact that Dickens knew at each moment just what he wanted to say and said it without hesitation.

[12] Carl R. Woodring, *Wordsworth* (Boston, 1965), p. 133.
[13] Steven Marcus, *Dickens: From Pickwick to Dombey* (New York, 1965), p. 293.

Passing over the adjectives as mere decoration, we can wonder how the critic knew what he asserts to be a fact about Dickens, even granting that the "economy" of the style could be derived from it.

Another type of questionable assertion is made in this discussion of the style of Ruskin:

> Ruskin had a painful story to tell and evolved a style which enabled the telling to be both ingratiating and true. The writing is remarkably colloquial, yet taut with ironies which he directs at his parents or himself. What appears to be an ingenuous ecstasy of pure presentation was the product of a lifelong effort to suppress all evidence of laboriousness, to substitute the suppleness of speech for the formalities of rhetoric. Through a triumph of style, Ruskin made his most sophisticated prose on his most complex subject read as if it were mere artless causerie.[14]

If we take "mere artless causerie" to be a synonym for "colloquial writing," we are faced with an incredible paradox, achieved through a "triumph of style." Ruskin perhaps labored to make his prose informal. The exaggerated assertion that he succeeded must be laid to the critic's inability wholly to believe this and therefore to convey it demonstratively. Such a statement about Ruskin requires some demonstration.

Writers about style usually do not trouble to demonstrate anything, except by single instances. Consider the difficulties of demonstrating the assertion in the following encomium of Henry James:

> On the whole, for richness, for subtlety, for attention to concords of sense and sound, James's later style was the most remarkable style in English since the 17th century. With all its artifices, there is something elemental about it. Unlike the virtuoso styles, admirable though they are, of a Stevenson or a Swinburne, that of James refers us back, not to the eloquence of the author, but to the resources of the language.[15]

Though we may differ about the meaning of *remarkable*, we can agree that over 250 years have elapsed since the seventeenth century. We are surely not asked to believe that the critic has examined all the remarkable styles in those centuries and has declared James the winner. No, like most such claims it is hyperbole and does not refer to anything, any more than *elemental* does or the reference to Stevenson and Swinburne or the resources of the language. It is all metaphysics, demonstrable in principle,

---

[14] John D. Rosenberg, *The Darkening Glass* (New York, 1961), pp. 218–219.
[15] F. W. Dupee, *Henry James* (New York, 1951), pp. 195–196.

but not on earth, and is just a form of praise disguised as a description.
My last exhibit is from Lionel Trilling:

> As for the style of the book, it is not less than definitive in American
> literature. The prose of *Huckleberry Finn* established for written prose
> the virtues of American colloquial spech. This has nothing to do with
> pronunciation or grammar. It has something to do with the structure of
> the sentence, which is simple, direct, and fluent, maintaining the rhythm
> of the word-groups of speech and the intonations of the speaking
> voice.
> Out of his knowledge of the actual speech of America Mark Twain
> forged a classic prose. The adjective may seem a strange one, yet it is
> apt. Forget the misspellings and the faults of grammar, and the prose
> will be seen to move with the greatest simplicity, directness, lucidity and
> grace.[16]

The prose of *Huckleberry Finn* is colloquial. But why this eminent critic
should wish to say that Mark Twain accomplished this effect without
grammar is not easy to understand. Take out the grammar and the mis-
spellings and do you have the same prose, the same Huck Finn? This
curious reluctance to be specific and concrete, to admit that style is first
of all made up of certain kinds of linguistic units betrays a distrust of
available methods of discussing style.

It is all rather dispiriting; from Morris Croll to Spitzer, Ullman,
Josephine Miles and Herdan, there is a bulky literature of stylistics, with
something for every taste. And yet the great majority of scholars are
without any knowledge of it. They write about style in a Rhetoric of Metaphysics, whose main components are remoteness from the facts of language, a reluctance to believe that style can be concretely described and
romantic exaggeration.

It is my impression that some of this disorder may derive from the
debilitating belief that style and content are inseparable and the resulting
unwillingness to attempt anything that might seem to show trust in their
disjunction. The organic theory of Croce seems to have given special impe-
tus to metaphysical discussion of style because of Croce's explicit distrust
of anything smacking of the technical, especially rhetoric. Yet this ancient
discipline, whatever its deficiencies in an age that has abandoned formal
studies, did furnish a method for both the study of literature and the teaching of composition.

The perpetuation of this corrupt traditon of commentary about style
is productive of a number of evil effects. In the study of literature, where

16 "Huckleberry Finn," in *The Liberal Imagination* (New York, 1950), pp.
115–116, 117.

the habit of precise and responsible thinking is highly desirable, it en-
courages habits of slipshod and haphazard thinking which undermine the
whole process. Large and vague generalizations, conclusions without
evidence, atypical examples, paradoxes and contradictions, words used
without understanding and sheer nonsense embellish the pages of our
students' critical essays. These defects are surely related to the criticism I
have described.

An even more immediate consequence of this same criticism is manifested in the teaching of composition. Here, especially in the correction of
essays, stylistic criticism is the foremost means of instruction. If it has
no sounder basis than metaphysics, how can the student learn? To improve,
he must know what his mistakes are and how to correct them. These tasks
require commentary with a high degree of specificity. The summarizing
comment which lurks malevolently at the end of a student's paper usually
announces its consanguinity to the literary examples I cited earlier. This
quotation from a well-known textbook betrays its metaphysical ancestry:
"This is the style you've been working for: not too big, not too little,
sensible, clear, on its toes. You are touching the concrete beautifully."[17]
The student may gather that he has done something right, but how can he
discover what it was, unless it be concerned with gymnastics?

What is to be done? A great deal of skepticism about such euphonious vacuities as I have quoted is evidently necessary. Metaphysical stylistics is a rewarding study for the skeptic, and the evidence of its defects
can be gathered by anyone who can read, count and reason. It is also
obvious that sane and useful criticism of style can no longer proceed without technical knowledge of the language and of rhetoric or without reference to available systems of stylistic analysis.

Unlike the critics I have cited, Aristotle did not allow his Metaphysics
to contaminate his Poetics. In fact, his *Poetics* contains three technical
chapters (on parts of speech, figurative words, and word-choice) which
we are always being urged to ignore. We should be foolish to do so, for
analysis cannot proceed without technical detail or it becomes metaphysical
by default.

APPENDIX

A RHETORIC OF METAPHYSICAL STYLISTICS
Outline of a Classification

I.   Statements *not* really about style
II. Statements about style

[17] Sheridan Baker, *The Practical Stylist* (New York, 1962), p. 133.

A. Pure Metaphysical (referring to a different order of reality)
B. Verifiable
   1. Only in principle
   2. In practice
      a. Erroneous in fact
      b. Correct
         (1) Useless
            (a) Obvious
            (b) Tautological
         (2) Useful
            (a) Possibly: Impressionistic
            (b) Generally: Quantitative*

2 THE ELEMENTS OF STYLE

grammar

GRAMMAR AND STYLE

Hugh Sykes Davies

The main problems of style centre round the gap which exists between the spoken and written versions of the same language. This gap is not always of the same size. Written English, for example, is now much more different from spoken English than it was in Shakespeare's time, and critics are generally agreed that our literature is the worse for it. Ever since Wordsworth urged that poetry should be written in a "selection of the language really used by men" it has been generally agreed that the gap should be narrowed again, and the best modern writers and authorities on style repeat the Wordsworthian view in one form or another, generally without acknowledgement.

But while it is certainly true that written English would be all the better if it approached spoken English more closely than it does, it would be impossible to close the gap completely, and foolish even to try. The fact is that a speaker commands resources of expression far richer than those of a writer. He can reinforce particular points by giving special emphasis of voice and intonation to them; he can make use of facial gesture, "Nods and Becks and wreathed Smiles," or their opposites. He can play tricks with his hands and fingers, opening and shutting them, waving them up and down and sideways. If he is near enough to his victim, he can even nudge him to drive home a specially important sally, although modern ideas of good manners tend to look on this practice as low-bred.

Reprinted from Grammar Without Tears *by Hugh Sykes Davies by permission of The John Day Company, Inc., publisher, and The Bodley Head, Ltd. Copyright 1951.*

Sometimes these oratorical and conversational tricks are more than mere adornments and graces of style. The first especially, vocal emphasis, is often a part of the meaning itself; if it is altered, the meaning alters with it. Victorian church-goers seem to have solaced themselves largely for the rigors of their religious duties by collecting examples of this kind of emphasis, the more misplaced the better. For example, a passage from *Samuel,* describing how Saul was finally persuaded to eat after long fasting, was once rendered like this: "And the woman had a fat calf in the house; and she hasted, and killed it, and took the flour, and kneaded it, and did bake unleavened bread thereof; and she brought it before Saul, and before his servants; and they *did eat."* On another occasion, a passage in the first *Book of Kings* was spoken thus: "He spake to his sons, saying, 'Saddle me the ass.' And they saddled *him."*

The same kind of modulation of meaning is very common in ordinary social intercourse. A hostess, for example, welcoming some guests might say "I'm very glad you've come" in at least three different ways. First, with a fairly even accent throughout, she would imply nothing more than a conventional greeting. Second, she might accent the sentence like this: "I'm very glad *you've* come," and so indicate that she was particularly pleased with the arrival of these guests rather than any of the others. And thirdly, she might accent it thus: "I'm very glad you've *come,"* which would mean that there had been some doubt of their ability to be at the party, and that she was relieved to know that the obstacles had been overcome.

A very rich example of the same kind is the phrase "It's no use asking her to change her mind," which can be given at least five quite different meanings by means of vocal accent:

> It's *no use* asking her to change her mind.
> It's no use *asking* her to change her mind.
> It's no use asking *her* to change her mind.
> It's no use asking her to *change* her mind.
> It's no use asking her to change her *mind.*[1]

Compared with this luxuriance of variation and modulation, the resources at the command of the writer are indeed limited. The words on the page are as dead as butterflies in a museum case; they have no life and glitter and movement; and one cannot be made to spring to notice before the others, or more than the others, by being uttered more loudly. Many of the special qualities of a written as opposed to a spoken version

[1] I owe this admirable example to Mr. Walter de la Mare, who gave it in a lecture some years ago.

of the same language arise from the necessity to overcome this deadness in the word on the page, and to give life and emphasis to it by other means.

The simplest and most direct of these other means is the use of *italics* in print or underlining in manuscript. But for some reason not clearly explained by its exponents, modern taste is against these devices. Underlining is generally described as "feminine," by which it is to be inferred that no real man would make use of it, for fear of being thought womanly, while no real woman would use it either, because it is unmanly. Italics have suffered a similar discouragement, and it is likely that printers have reinforced it because they feel that their art is displayed in an entirely uniform, ultra-tidy page. It is true, of course, that both underlining and italics are liable to abuse, especially in the hands of the young, who are inclined to make use of them for escaping from linguistic tight corners they never should have got into. But the danger of abuse is no good reason for avoiding the use of these devices altogether, and it would probably be a means of enlivening modern English style if they were more freely allowed. Coleridge and De Quincey would afford good models of their effective use.

But a revival of italics alone would go only a short way to solving the special problems of the writer. It is the simplest resource for pointing emphasis in writing or print; and for that reason, one of the least effective and most quickly exhausted of its full force by frequent use. Other resources must be understood and used as well, and the more of them the better. The most obvious and important is to bring into play a far wider vocabulary than is generally used in speaking. This enables the writer to make his most emphatic words do their own shouting, as it were—to impinge sharply on the consciousness of his readers by their unfamiliarity and inherent force. The first variation of the last sentence quoted above, for example, "It's *no use* asking her to change her mind," might be rendered in writing by doing away with the commonplace phrase *no use,* and putting in its place some word such as *futile* or *otiose*. But since this is not a book on the use of the English vocabulary, it is enough to observe the existence of this second way of marking emphasis, without illustrating it further.

A third way of doing the same thing, not so generally known, at any rate consciously, but hardly less important, is the proper management of word-order. A good deal has been said about this already, in its relation to various grammatical problems. But it fully deserves further consideration here, because it is the main contribution that grammatical studies can make to good style in the positive sense—to liveliness and force of language.

We have seen that in an ordinary English sentence (excluding questions and certain other special orders of words) the positions of greatest emphasis will be found at the end and at the beginning. There is, of course, nothing absolute about this rule, and in particular instances the fall of the emphasis will be altered greatly by the shape of the sentences that have come before, or those that come after. But as a rough general guide it can probably be accepted. Here are two examples of it:

> The true aspect of the place, especially of the house in which he lived as a child, the fashion of its doors, its hearths, its windows, the very scent upon the air of it, was with him in sleep for a season; only, with tints more musically blent on wall and floor, and some finer light and shadow running in and out, along its curves and angles, and with all its little carvings daintier (Walter Pater, *Emerald Uthwart*).

> Patrons are respectfully requested not to use the plates and saucers as ash-trays, as not being of china these will burn.

No other orders of words would have given Pater just this degree of emphasis on "daintier," or the proprietor of the cafe where the second sentence hangs such an effective advertisement of the inflammable nature of his crockery.

Very nearly the same force of emphasis can be gained by making good use of the beginning of a sentence, and this is particularly effective when there is some approach to an inversion, or obvious departure from the normal order. There is in English a special device for bringing about this type of emphasis, in the use of the phrase "It is . . ." For example, "Man shall not live by bread alone" can be made substantially more emphatic by being written: "It is not by bread alone that man shall live."

But these examples of variation of emphasis by means of word-order are only the simplest part of the writer's special problem. Except for a few specialists in epigrams and apothegms, literary composition does not consist of the contruction of single sentences; it is made up of the far more difficult process of stringing sentences together in such a way that they link up with one another naturally and easily, carrying the attention of the reader along with them in a sequence that corresponds as closely as possible with the development of the meaning itself. This process has been well described, and its importance rightly estimated, by one of the greatest masters of it, De Quincey:

> The two capital secrets of prose are these: first, the philosophy of transition and connexion, or the art by which one step in the evolution of thoughts is made to arise out of another: all fluent and effective composition depends on the connexions; secondly, the way in which sentences are made to modify each other; for the most powerful effects in written eloquence arise out of this reverberation, as it were, from each other in a rapid succession of sentences . . .

Although De Quincey did not say it himself, it is obvious that one of the most important ways of securing ease of transition and connection, and of enabling sentences to "reverberate," is by arranging the words in them in suitable orders.

One of the most obvious ways of securing these benefits is by the various forms of parallelism in word-order. Mrs. Micawber, for example, shows a real grasp of the principles of prose, as well as of her husband's character, when she says: "Talent, Mr. Micawber has; capital, Mr. Micawber has not." On a much more elaborate scale, Dr. Johnson was a regular employer of the same device, and one of his choicest examples of it is his comment on Pope's famous grotto at Twickenham: "Pope's excavation was requisite as an entrance to his garden, and as some men try to be proud of their defects, he extracted an ornament from an inconvenience, and vanity created a grotto where necessity enforced a passage." Another variant of the same device is Peacock's account of a young nobleman whose hobbies included breaking-in wild horses and designing patent safety-carriages: "The grooms said they wouldn't drive any horse in that carriage, nor that horse in any carriage."

But parallelism, though very useful for special effects of this kind, and for witty and ironic expression generally, is perhaps too sparkling and conscious a device for the ordinary, day-to-day business of plain prose. For this, a less obtrusive way of linking sentences together is needed: one which allows the thoughts to "arise out of one another" naturally and easily, without obtruding itself on the reader's conscious attention. A very good and workmanlike example of this type of connection is this set of sentences from Dr. Johnson again:

> The metaphysical poets were men of *learning,* and to *show* their *learning* was their whole endeavour; but unluckily resolving to *show* it in *rhyme,* instead of writing poetry, they only wrote *verses,* and very often such *verses* as stood the trial of the finger better than of the ear; for the modulation was so imperfect, that they were only found to be *verses* by counting the syllables. (*Life of Cowley.* The italics are mine.)

Here the thought is carried on by a careful and very skilful repetition of words, and even more by ensuring that the order of the words in each sentence provides, as it were, a hook at the beginning and an eye at the end, so that they make an unbroken, closely linked chain. How aptly the hooks and eyes fit together can best be seen by disturbing their order, so that hooks are next to hooks and eyes to eyes, in this way:

> The metaphysical poets were men of *learning,* and their whole endeavour was to show their *learning;* but unluckily, instead of *writing*

poetry, they only *wrote* verses, having resolved to *show* it in rhyme; and very often it was rather by the trial of the finger than by the ear that they were *verses* at all.

Perhaps to the average modern taste, there is something a little cumbrous in Dr. Johnson's repetition of the nouns and verbs intact, instead of putting pronouns and "pro-verbs" in their places. But the fundamental soundness of his word-placing allows this substitution to be made very easily:

> The metaphysical poets were men of learning, and their whole endeavour was to show it; but unluckily resolving to do so in rhyme, instead of writing poetry, they only wrote verses, which very often stood the trial of the finger better than the ear, for the modulation was so imperfect that they were only found to be verses by counting the syllables.

This runs more naturally, at any rate to the modern eye; but the trick of repeating the words entire, as in the original, is well worth the notice of the modern prose-writer. If it is used with tact, and not too constantly, it can be of great help in securing firm connections between one sentence and another. And if a warning is needed of the results of its abuse, it is ready to hand in the works of Matthew Arnold.

A somewhat more elaborate and subtle method of linking thoughts and sentences together is often found in Burke, who was generally regarded by Coleridge and De Quincey as the greatest exponent of "reverberation" and the mutual modification of sentences. Here is the content of one of his admirably constructed periods, expressed in hack-English:

> Opinions exert a strong influence on men's actions, because they are often combined with strong feelings. Sometimes they even produce strong feelings. It is the duty of a government, in its own interest, to pay much attention to opinions. And therefore a government has the right to do so.

This is logical enough in the order of presentation, but in the actual manner of expression, flat, feebly orchestrated, unlikely to seize upon the attention of any but the most willing listener. This is what Burke makes of it:

> It is the interest, and it is the duty, and because it is the interest and the duty, it is the right, of government to attend much to opinions; because, as opinions soon combine with passions, even when they do not produce them, they have much influence on actions.

There is a richly varied and significant order of words and structure of sentences, presenting the thoughts with the greatest possible impact and interweaving of their necessary connections. It is essentially clearer than the other version, not because it is more logical, but because it treats its reader as a human being, liable to be weary or blunted in his faculties and capacity for attention; it does far more work for him, in the psychological sense, and is far more likely to be understoood. And it depends ultimately upon the good management of word-order, on a highly developed sense of the possible varieties of one and the same expression.

The possibility of variation in word order, then, is the greatest single contribution that grammar, as distinct from vocabulary, can make to solving the fundamental problems of written English, and to supplying resources for the variation of emphasis to take the place of those which are restricted to the spoken language. And therefore the real English grammarian will make it his business to preserve these possibilities of variation so far as possible, and to avoid making rules about word-order for purely grammatical purposes unless they are absolutely unavoidable. He should not, for example, make rules for the order and placing of words such as those which have been made in the past for the placing of prepositions and adverbs with the infinitive. They are unnecessary from the point of view of pure grammar. And they are far better left to the general guidance of the over-all rule that the words should be placed in the order which makes the meaning most clearly and forcibly.

The teacher of grammar—not necessarily quite the same person as the grammarian—should pay careful attention to developing in his pupils a sense of the possibilities of variation in sentence structure. This would be a far more direct contribution to the formation of a good, lively style than any amount of parsing and analysis, and it is not very difficult to devise interesting exercises for the purpose. One such exercise, indeed, often used to appear in the older books of grammar, and is still retained, on a small scale, in some modern ones. It was thus described, very sensibly, in one of the later supplements to that grammar by Lindley Murray that was one of the great forgotten formative books of the Victorian age:

The practice of transposing the members of sentences, is an exercise so useful to young persons, that it requires a more particular explanation, than could have been properly given in the preceding work. A few of the various modes in which the parts of a sentence may be arranged, have, therefore, been collected. By examining them attentively, the student will perceive, in some degree, the nature and effect of transposition: and, by being frequently exercised in showing its variety in other sentences, he will obtain a facility in the operation; and a dexterity in discovering and applying, on all occasions, the clearest and most forcible arrangement.

By this practice, he will also be able more readily to penetrate the meaning of such sentences, as are rendered obscure and perplexing to most readers, by the irregular disposition of their parts.

These remarks, sensible in themselves as they are pawky in expression, are followed by a series of examples in the same tradition of English prose. This is one of them:

> That greatness of mind which shows itself in dangers and labours, if it wants justice, is blamable.
> If that greatness of mind, which shows itself in dangers and labours, is void of justice, it is blamable.
> That greatness of mind is blamable, which shows itself in dangers and labours, if it wants justice.
> If that greatness of mind is void of justice, which shows itself in dangers and labours, it is blamable.
> That greatness of mind is blamable, if it is void of justice, which shows itself in dangers and labours.
> If it wants justice, that greatness of mind, which shows itself in dangers and labours, is blamable.

This example, like all the others in the same book, would be altogether unsuitable for modern use. Indeed, if we bear in mind the fruit that it bore in so much Victorian prose, we can hardly escape the conclusion that it was very unsuitable for use a century and a half ago. But although this particular sentence is intolerably heavy and cumbrous, the principle that it illustrates is a sound one. It ought not to be difficult to devise sentences on the same grammatical principle, but much lighter in tone, and more interesting in matter, upon which modern learners of English could exercise themselves with real profit, and with at any rate a little amusement. Certainly with more amusement (and therefore generally more profit too) than they can ever be expected to derive from most of the grammatical exercises now in use. It would open a path to the teaching of grammar, not in the abstract, as a business of formal classifications of words and phrases (subject, predicate, and so forth), but concretely, in the process of molding and remolding meaningful sentences in such a way as to explore and modify their meaning. It would, incidentally, provide a basis for a more realistic education in the use of the comma; for it would be a rough working rule that commas should come before and after the blocks of words that could be transferred from one place to another in such a sentence, but never in the middle of a block. And this, rough though it may be, would be preferable to the seventeen or eighteen different rules that are generally necessary to cover its use. The whole problem of punctuation, in fact, would be greatly simplified by this kind of training, for most errors of punctuation arise from ill-designed, badly shaped sentences, and from the attempt to make them work by means of violent tricks with commas and colons and such like. If sentence structure were more malleable, most difficulties over punctuation would disappear of themselves.

Above all, this kind of exercise would come a little nearer to the modern conception of an education based on activity and construction, rather than on static memory work or supine submission to rules laid down in a vacuum. It would give children some encouragement to feel that language is something which can be manipulated with as much pleasure as plasticine or bricks, with something to show at the end of the exercise, something created, if not wholly original. It would go some way towards abolishing the idea that English is merely something that you generally get wrong and that gives you no fun even if you get it right.

POETRY AND GRAMMAR

Gertrude Stein

What is poetry and if you know what poetry is what is prose.

There is no use in telling more than you know, no not even if you do not know it.

But do you do you know what prose is and do you know what poetry is.

I have said that the words in plays written in poetry are more lively than the same words written by the same poet in other kinds of poetry. It undoubtedly was true of Shakespeare, is it inevitably true of everybody. That is one thing to think about. I said that the words in a play written in prose are not as lively words as the words written in other prose by the same writer. This is true of Goldsmith and I imagine it is true of almost any writer.

There again there is something to know.

One of the things that is a very interesting thing to know is how you are feeling inside you to the words that are coming out to be outside of you.

Do you always have the same kind of feeling in relation to the sounds as the words come out of you or do you not. All this has so much to do with grammar and with poetry and with prose.

Words have to do everything in poetry and prose and some writers

From Lectures in America *by Gertrude Stein. Copyright 1935 and renewed 1963 by Alice B. Toklas. Reprinted by permission of Random House, Inc.*

write more in articles and prepositions and some say you should write in nouns, and of course one has to think of everything.

A noun is a name of anything, why after a thing is named write about it. A name is adequate or it is not. If it is adequate then why go on calling it, if it is not then calling it by its name does no good.

People if you like to believe it can be made by their names. Call anybody Paul and they get to be a Paul call anybody Alice and they get to be an Alice perhaps yes perhaps no, there is something in that, but generally speaking, things once they are named the name does not go on doing anything to them and so why write in nouns. Nouns are the name of anything and just naming names is alright when you want to call a roll but is it any good for anything else. To be sure in many places in Europe as in America they do like to call rolls.

As I say a noun is a name of a thing, and therefore slowly if you feel what is inside that thing you do not call it by the name by which it is known. Everybody knows that by the way they do when they are in love and a writer should always have that intensity of emotion about whatever is the object about which he writes. And therefore and I say it again more and more one does not use nouns.

Now what other things are there beside nouns, there are a lot of other things beside nouns.

When you are at school and learn grammar grammar is very exciting. I really do not know that anything has ever been more exciting than diagraming sentences. I suppose other things may be more exciting to others when they are at school but to me undoubtedly when I was at school the really completely exciting thing was diagraming sentences and that has been to me ever since the one thing that has been completely exciting and completely completing. I like the feeling the everlasting feeling of sentences as they diagram themselves.

In that way one is completely possessing something and incidentally one's self. Now in that diagraming of the sentences of course there are articles and prepositions and as I say there are nouns but nouns as I say even by definition are completely not interesting, the same thing is true of adjectives. Adjectives are not really and truly interesting. In a way anybody can know always has known that, because after all adjectives affect nouns and as nouns are not really interesting the thing that affects a not too interesting thing is of necessity not interesting. In a way as I say anybody knows that because of course the first thing that anybody takes out of anybody's writing are the adjectives. You see of yourself how true it is that which I have just said.

Beside the nouns and the adjectives there are verbs and adverbs. Verbs and adverbs are more interesting. In the first place they have one very nice quality and that is that they can be so mistaken. It is wonderful the number of mistakes a verb can make and that is equally true of its adverb. Nouns and adjectives never can make mistakes can never be mistaken but verbs can be so endlessly, both as to what they do and how they agree or disagree with whatever they do. The same is true of adverbs.

In that way any one can see that verbs and adverbs are more interesting than nouns and adjectives.

Beside being able to be mistaken and to make mistakes verbs can change to look like themselves or to look like something else, they are, so to speak on the move and adverbs move with them and each of them find themselves not at all annoying but very often much mistaken. That is the reason any one can like what verbs can do. Then comes the thing that can of all things be most mistaken and they are prepositions. Prepositions can live one long life being really being nothing but absolutely nothing but mistaken and that makes them irritating if you feel that way about mistakes but certainly something that you can be continuously using and everlastingly enjoying. I like prepositions the best of all, and pretty soon we will go more completely into that.

Then there are articles. Articles are interesting just as nouns and adjectives are not. And why are they interesting just as nouns and adjectives are not. They are interesting because they do what a noun might do if a noun was not so unfortunately so completely unfortunately the name of something. Articles please, a and an and the please as the name that follows cannot please. They the names that is the nouns cannot please, because after all you know well after all that is what Shakespeare meant when he talked about a rose by any other name.

I hope now no one can have any illusion about a noun or about the adjective that goes with the noun.

But an article an article remains as a delicate and a varied something and any one who wants to write with articles and knows how to use them will always have the pleasure that using something that is varied and alive can give. That is what articles are.

Beside that there are conjunctions, and a conjunction is not varied but it has a force that need not make any one feel that they are dull. Conjunctions have made themselves live by their work. They work and as they work they live and even when they do not work and in these days they do not always live by work still nevertheless they do live.

So you see why I like to write with prepositions and conjunctions and articles and verbs and adverbs but not with nouns and adjectives. If you read my writing you will you do see what I mean.

Of course then there are pronouns. Pronouns are not as bad as nouns because in the first place practically they cannot have adjectives go with them. That already makes them better than nouns.

Then beside not being able to have adjectives go with them, they of course are not really the name of anything. They represent some one but they are not its or his name. In not being his or its or her name they already have a greater possibility of being something than if they were as a noun is the name of anything. Now actual given names of people are more lively than nouns which are the name of anything and I suppose that this is because after all the name is only given to that person when they are born, there is at least the element of choice even the element of change and anybody can be pretty well able to do what they like, they may be born Walter and become Hub, in such a way they are not like a noun. A noun has been the name of something for such a very long time.

That is the reason that slang exists it is to change the nouns which have been names for so long. I say again. Verbs and adverbs and articles and conjunctions and prepositions are lively because they all do something and as long as anything does something it keeps alive.

One might have in one's list added interjections but really interjections have nothing to do with anything not even with themselves. There so much for that. And now to go into the question of punctuation.

There are some punctuations that are interesting and there are some punctuations that are not. Let us begin with the punctuations that are not. Of these the one but the first and the most the completely most uninteresting is the question mark. The question mark is alright when it is all alone when it is used as a brand on cattle or when it could be used in decoration but connected with writing it is completely entirely completely uninteresting. It is evident that if you ask a question you ask a question but anybody who can read at all knows when a question is a question as it is written in writing. Therefore I ask you therefore wherefore should one use it the question mark. Beside it does not in its form go with ordinary printing and so it pleases neither the eye nor the ear and it is therefore like a noun, just an unnecessary name of something. A question is a question, anybody can know that a question is a question and so why add to it the question mark when it is already there when the question is already there in the writing. Therefore I never could bring myself to use a question mark, I always found it positively revolting, and now very few do use it. Exclamation marks have the same difficulty and also quotation marks, they are unnecessary, they are ugly, they spoil the line of the writing or the printing and anyway what is the use, if you do not know that a question is a question what is the use of its being a question. The same thing is true of an exclamation. And the same thing is true of a quotation. When I first began writing I found it simply impossible to use question marks and quotation marks and exclamation points and now anybody sees it that way. Perhaps some day they will see it some other way but now at any rate anybody can and does see it that way.

So there are the uninteresting things in punctuation uninteresting in a way that is perfectly obvious, and so we do not have to go any farther into that. There are besides dashes and dots, and these might be interesting spaces might be interesting. They might if one felt that way about them.

One other little punctuation mark one can have feelings about and that is the apostrophe for possession. Well feel as you like about that, I can see and I do see that for many that for some the possessive case apostrophe has a gentle tender insinuation that makes it very difficult to definitely decide to do without it. One does do without it, I do, I mostly always do, but I cannot deny that from time to time I feel myself having regrets and from time to time I put it in to make the possessive case. I absolutely do not like it all alone when it is outside the word when the word is a plural, no then positively and definitely no, I do not like it and in leaving it out I feel no regret, there it is unnecessary and not ornamental but inside a word and its s well perhaps, perhaps it does appeal by its weakness to your weakness. At least at any rate from time to time I do find myself letting it alone if it has come in and sometimes it has come in. I cannot positively deny but that I do from time to time let it come in.

So now to come to the real question of punctuation, periods, commas, colons, semi-colons and capitals and small letters.

I have had a long and complicated life with all these.

Let us begin with these I use the least first and these are colons and semi-colons, one might add to these commas.

When I first began writing, I felt that writing should go on, I still do feel that it should go on but when I first began writing I was completely possessed by the necessity that writing should go on and if writing should go on what had colons and semi-colons to do with it, what had commas to do with it, what had periods to do with it what had small letters and capitals to do with it to do with writing going on which was at that time the most profound need I had in connection with writing. What had colons and semi-colons to do with it what had commas to do with it what had periods to do with it.

What had periods to do with it. Inevitably no matter how completely I had to have writing go on, physically one had to again and again stop sometime and if one had to again and again stop some time then periods had to exist. Beside I had always liked the look of periods and I liked what they did. Stopping sometime did not really keep one from going on, it was nothing that interfered, it was only something that happened, and as it happened as a perfectly natural happening, I did believe in periods and I used them. I really never stopped using them.

Beside that periods might later come to have a life of their own to commence breaking up things in arbitrary ways, that has happened lately with me in a poem I have written called Winning His Way, later I will read you a little of it. By the time I had written this poem about three years ago periods had come to have for me completely a life of their own. They could begin to act as they thought best and one might interrupt one's writing with them that is not really interrupt one's writing with them but one could come to stop arbitrarily stop at times in one's writing and so they could be used and you could use them. Periods could come to exist in this way and they could come in this way to have a life of their own. They did not serve you in any servile way as commas and colons and semi-colons do. Yes you do feel what I mean.

Periods have a life of their own a necessity of their own a feeling of their own a time of their own. And that feeling that life that necessity that time can express itself in an infinite variety that is the reason that I have always remained true to periods so much so that as I say recently I have felt that one could need them more than one had ever needed them.

You can see what an entirely different thing a period is from a comma, a colon or a semi-colon.

There are two different ways of thinking about colons and semi-colons you can think of them as commas and as such they are purely servile or you can think of them as periods and then using them can make you feel adventurous. I can see that one might feel about them as periods but I myself never have, I began unfortunately to feel them as a comma and commas are servile they have no life of their own they are dependent upon use and convenience and they are put there just for practical purposes. Semi-colons and colons had for me from the first completely this character the character that a comma has and not the character that a period has and therefore and definitely I have never used them. But now dimly and definitely I do see that they might well possibly they might have in them something of the character of the period and so it might have been an adventure to use them. I really do not think so. I think however lively they are or disguised they are they are definitely more comma than period and so really I cannot regret not having used them. They are more powerful more imposing more pretentious than a comma but they are a comma all the same. They really have within them deeply within them fundamentally within them the comma nature. And now what does a comma do and what has it to do and why do I feel as I do about them.

What does a comma do.

I have refused them so often and left them out so much and did without them so continually that I have come finally to be indifferent to them. I do not now care whether you put them in or not but for a long time I felt very definitely about them and would have nothing to do with them.

As I say commas are servile and they have no life of their own, and their use is not a use, it is a way of replacing one's own interest and I do decidedly like to like my own interest my own interest in what I am doing. A comma by helping you along holding your coat for you and putting on your shoes keeps you from living your life as actively as you should lead it and to me for many years and I still do feel that way about it only now I do not pay as much as much attention to them, the use of them was positively degrading. Let me tell you what I feel and what I mean and what I felt and what I meant.

When I was writing those long sentences of The Making of Americans, verbs active present verbs with long dependent adverbial clauses became a passion with me. I have told you that I recognize verbs and adverbs aided by prepositions and conjunctions with pronouns as possessing the whole of the active life of writing.

Complications make eventually for simplicity and therefore I have always liked dependent adverbial clauses. I have liked dependent adverbial clauses because of their variety of dependence and independence. You can see how loving the intensity of complication of these things that commas would be degrading. Why if you want the pleasure of concentrating on the final simplicity of excessive complication would you want any artificial aid to bring about that simplicity. Do you see now why I feel about the comma as I did and as I do.

Think about anything you really like to do and you will see what I mean.

When it gets really difficult you want to disentangle rather than to cut the knot, at least so anybody feels who is working with any thread, so anybody feels who is working with any tool so anybody feels who is writing any sentence or reading it after it has been written. And what does a comma do, a comma does nothing but make easy a thing that if you like it enough is easy enough without the comma. A long complicated sentence should force itself upon you, make you know yourself knowing it and the comma, well at the most a comma is a poor period that it lets you stop and take a breath but if you want to take a breath you ought to know yourself that you want to take a breath. It is not like stopping altogether which is what a period does stopping altogether has something to do with going on, but taking a breath well you are always taking a breath and why emphasize one breath rather than another breath. Anyway that is the way I felt about it and I felt that about it very very strongly. And so I almost never used a comma. The longer, the more complicated the sentence the greater the number of the same kinds of words I had following one after another, the more the very many more I had of them the more I felt the passionate need of their taking care of themselves by themselves and not helping them, and thereby enfeebling them by putting in a comma.

So that is the way I felt punctuation in prose, in poetry it is a little different but more so and later I will go into that. But that is the way I felt about punctuation in prose. . . .

REDUNDANCY AND AMBIGUITY

H. A. Gleason

REDUNDANCY

It is said that a composition teacher once commented that a paper was "redundant, tautologous, and pleonastic." Obviously, this was not intended as a compliment. Redundancy is commonly considered one of the great errors in writing. Yet all writing, and all speech, is redundant. This must not be considered a fault, but a very necessary quality of language if it is to be successful as an instrument of communication. What the composition teacher decries is not redundancy as such, but an excess, or a crude handling, of redundancy.

Redundancy is familiarly defined as saying something more than once. It is only the grosser instances that are noticed and condemned; the subtler types escape interdiction.

Consider a sentence such as the following:

> The ducks quacked at the top of their voices.   (1)

Almost every bit of information conveyed by the verb stem *quack* is duplicated elsewhere in the sentence. This can be seen by deleting it, leaving:

From Chapter 19 from Linguistics and English Grammar *by H. A. Gleason, Jr. Copyright © 1965 by Holt, Rinehart and Winston, Inc. Copyright © 1963, 1965 by H. A. Gleason, Jr. Reprinted by permission of Holt, Rinehart and Winston, Inc.*

The ducks_____-ed at the top of their voices.　　　　　　　　(2)

Only *quack* can be inserted easily and naturally into the blank. There are a number of verbs that will fit well with *ducks* as their subject: *swim, sleep, waddle,* and so on. Likewise there are many that are compatible with *at the top of their voices: bark, howl, sing,* and so on. To fit in sentence (2) a word must belong to both these lists. *Quack* is alone or almost alone. It fits because it means something like "make a vocal noise like a duck," that is, because its meaning includes information already given in the sentence by *voice* and by *duck. Quack* in (1) is nearly one hundred percent redundant.

We have just seen that redundancy in sentence (1) is associated with the fact that *ducks* as a subject imposes restrictions on the possible verbs while *at the top of their voices* does likewise. Any sort of restriction on occurrences is equivalent to redundancy. Grammar consists of restrictions on possible structures. It must therefore produce redundancy. In a few instances it is easy to see that this is so since it produces actual duplication of a very evident sort. For example, a phrase like *these stones* is marked as plural twice, only by *-s* and once by *these* rather than *this.* If this phrase is the subject of a sentence, the number may be marked a third time by the verb form, perhaps *are* rather than *is.* In a sentence such as:

The wisdom of Solomon was unparalleled.　　　　　　　　(3)

the word *wisdom* is known to be a noun from its form. In addition, we expect *the* to be followed by a noun; *of* is more often than not preceded by a noun; and *wisdom* is in the subject position, a place by no means restricted to nouns, but nevertheless most often filled by nouns. At least four indications point to the same fact; this constitutes high redundancy.

Throughout the remainder of this chapter, we will use "redundancy" in the technical sense suggested in the last two paragraphs. It is a measure of excess of linguistic signals above the minimum that could carry the message. Equivalently, it is a measure of the extent to which each element is predictable from the context.

One way to estimate redundancy is by the "cloze" technique. Words are systematically deleted from a text. Then it is determined how much damage this does to the intelligibility. The more redundant, the more words can be taken out without serious difficulty. In the following passage[1] decreasing portions—indicated by a fraction at the left—have been removed:

---

[1] The opening paragraph and part of the second from Edward Gibbon, *The Decline and Fall of the Roman Empire,* 1776.

1/2   In . . . . . second . . . . . of . . . . . Christian . . . . ., the . . . . . of
      . . . . . comprehended . . . . . fairest . . . . . of . . . . . earth, ... the
      . . . . . civilized . . . . . of . . . . . The . . . . . of . . . . . extensive . . . . .

1/3   were guarded . . . . . ancient renown . . . . . disciplined valour.
      . . . . . gentle but . . . . . influence of . . . . . and manners . . . . .
      gradually cemented . . . . . union of . . . . . provinces. Their

1/4   peaceful . . . . . enjoyed and abused . . . . . advantages of wealth
      . . . . . luxury. The image . . . . . a free constitution . . . . . was
      preserved with . . . . reverence: the Roman . . . . . appeared to

1/6   possess the sovereign . . . . ., and devolved on the emperors . . . . .
      the executive powers of government. . . . . . a happy period of
      more . . . . . fourscore years, the public administration . . . .

1/8   conducted by the virtues and abilities of . . . . ., Trajan,
      Hadrian, and the two Antonines. It . . . . . the design of this,
      and of the two . . . . . chapters, to describe the prosperous

1/10   condition of their empire; . . . . . afterwards, from the death
      of Marcus Antoninus, to deduce . . . . . most important
      circumstances of its decline and fall; a . . . . . which will

1/12   ever be remembered, and is still felt by the . . . . . of the
      earth. The principal conquests of the Romans were
      achieved . . . . . the republic; and the emperors, for the most
      part, were satisfied . . . . . preserving those dominions
      which had been acquired by the policy of . . . . . senate,
      the active emulation of the consuls, and the martial
      enthusiasm . . . . . the people.   (4)

The intelligibility is very poor when one half of the words are omitted, but increases until in the last section, with only one word in twelve
missing, there is little difficulty for a competent reader of English.

Actual reading is more like the cloze technique than it might at first
appear. Almost every text contains some vocabulary items which will be
unknown to some of the intended readers. A small number of unfamiliar
words will cause a good reader no trouble; he will merely determine their
meaning from the context and go on. That is, he will treat them more or
less like blanks in the last section of passage (4).

Moreover, everyone has a much larger recognition vocabulary than
his active vocabulary. This means, simply, that there are many words
which he reads without difficulty but does not himself use in speaking or
writing. Many of these he is unable to recall at will. Some of them he cannot recognize at all out of context. In a sense, he only partly knows these
words. That they give him no trouble in reading is largely because this par-
tial understanding is supplemented or confirmed by the context in which
he finds them—that is, by redundancy. They might be compared to items
that are partly removed in a cloze experiment.

Nor is this the end of the matter. Any dictionary will show that all common words, and even many of the rarer, have two or more meanings, often quite distinct. It is virtually impossible to understand language by merely knowing, however thoroughly or precisely, the meanings of words. We must have at our command the ability to select the correct meaning for the passage at hand. Thus, even with perfectly familiar items, it is imperative that we use contextual redundancy. The model, then, is not a cloze experiment with blanks, but something much the same with multiple choices.

Intelligible writing, therefore, must have enough of the right sort of redundancy to meet the needs of the intended readers—to enable them to guess meanings of words new to them, to assist their recall of words only partly known, and to help them select the right meaning for words with two or more. How much redundancy there will be depends on many factors, including the nature of the subject matter, the way in which it is to be read, the importance of correct understanding, and the ability of the readers.[2] On the other hand, excessive rebundancy is not only wasteful of paper and of the reader's time and effort but also very annoying. The proper CONTROL of redundancy, then, is an important responsibility of the writer.

> If what going to a clearly not very adequately staffed school really means is little appreciated, we should be concerned. (5)

> We should be concerned, if there is little appreciation of what it really means to go to a school that clearly is not very adequately staffed. (6)

Various choices affect the redundancy of a passage, including many of those which figure in other aspects of style. For example, sentence (5) contained twenty words. It was altered by a series of operations which do not affect meaning. The result was sentence (6) with twenty-six, an increase of thirty percent.[3] An improvement in clarity was achieved at the cost of additional redundancy. We may judge that this was a reasonable price in this case. There are times, however, when clarity must be balanced against redundancy and where a compromise must be reached.

Choice among agnate constructions may affect redundancy more or less, but the use or nonuse of modifiers is usually more important. Many people would consider that both sentence (5) and sentence (6) would be improved by simply deleting *really, clearly,* and *very.* That such a change

---

[2] The ability to make efficient use of redundancy is one of the characteristics of a good command of language. For this reason, the cloze technique is an excellent device to measure reading ability in either a first or a second language.

[3] We must not assume that thirty percent is a measure of the redundancy in sentence (6). Sentence (5) had appreciable redundancy to start with.

can even be considered is a consequence of the high redundancy in these words. That is to say, they contribute so little to the sentence that their removal hardly alters the meaning. Their function is largely stylistic, and most would judge their value to be negative.

Comparison of two closely parallel versions will often show places where one has material lacking in the other, but where the meaning is effectively the same. For example, the Revised Standard Version and the New English Bible differ in this way in Acts 27:13:

RSV: they...   sailed along   Crete
NEB: ...they sailed along the coast of Crete   (7)

If, as seems quite certain to me, these two mean very nearly the same, then *the coast of* is almost wholly redundant. Part of the meaning of these words is contained in that of *sailed along* and the remainder in *Crete*.

How highly redundant modifiers can be is easily seen by experimenting with a set of contrasting adjectives—the eleven basic color terms (*red, orange, yellow, green, blue, purple, brown, pink, black, gray, white*) are excellent. The possible combinations of these with a suitable set of nouns may be examined. It will be found that some combinations are very likely, others highly improbable. *Red rose* or *blue lupine* is much more likely than *blue rose* or *red lupine*.[4] This reflects redundancy. In a cloze experiment, *red* is an excellent guess for. . . . .*rose,* whereas *blue* is a very poor one.

If, then, in a sentence about roses, the word *red* is added, there is an increase in redundancy. The same effect is obtained by adding to a sentence containing *red* the phrase *as a rose*. Many of these similes are quite standard—that is, highly redundant—and their usefulness is determined by that fact, for example, *black as coal, white as snow, green as grass, gray as ashes*. They must be avoided in texts where redundancy is not needed, but are useful in certain special situations where it is needed.

AMBIGUITY

It is a commonplace that everything we say or write is open, somehow, to misinterpretation. This cannot be charged simply to the careless-

---

[4] One might object that at this point I am talking about facts of nature rather than facts of language. We speak more often of red roses than of blue simple because the former are common and familiar, the latter rare, unknown, or freakish. Yet it is still redundancy. It has the linguistic function (a linguistic origin is not necessary) of helping a reader over rough spots in a text, or a hearer to fill in words that have been masked by noise. Moreover, some comparable combinations are not so easily laid at the door of nature: *blue Monday, purple prose*. These are also highly redundant.

ness of the reader; the greatest skill and care cannot always abstract from the text the meaning the writer intended. Nor is it wholly the shortcoming of the author; feasible techniques for forestalling misunderstanding are not always available to him. The problem lies, in part at least, within language itself. There is no way in which words can be selected or constructed into sentences that will automatically assure a single unambiguous meaning. The best that is ordinarily possible is to make one meaning so overwhelmingly more likely than any other that the lesser alternatives can be safely disregarded. Even this is not always easy, and may, indeed, entail a cost that the writer cannot assume.

Ambiguity, like redundancy, is a characteristic of language. It is less easy to show that it is a useful feature, but much easier to show that it is pervasive. While the popular view of redundancy is too narrow, that of ambiguity is too broad. A very disparate collection of phenomena is often gathered together under this heading. Any muddy thinking or any poor phrasing is sure to be called "ambiguity" by someone. The extremes aside, "ambiguity" is used of two quite different things.

One is a matter of what is NOT said. Consider a very prosaic sentence:

He looked at the table.   (8)

This might refer to a large dinner table or a small coffee table, to one with chrome legs and a plastic top or to one of hand-carved cherry wood. Many quite different things may be referred to, but this sentence applies equally well to all. If the writer had judged it to be worthwhile, he might have added any specification he desired. A good writer fills out no more of the details than suit his purpose.

There is a second kind of ambiguity which lies WITHIN what is actually said. Reading sentence (8), one person may visualize a piece of furniture. Another may imagine a page in a mathematics book. (Whether he thinks of logarithms, trigonometric functions, or multiplication facts is an instance of the first type of ambiguity.) In each case there are additional details that might have been given. But whether the sentence is interpreted as referring to a piece of furniture or an array of data is on a different level. *Table* has two (at least) basic meanings, not apparently connected in any way except that they are expressible by the same word. Only one of these can, ordinarily, apply in any one sentence. In (8) nothing tells the reader which the author had in mind.

We will restrict the term "ambiguity," for this discussion, to the second phenomenon. So limited, it can be given a reasonably precise meaning in terms of the lexical, grammatical, or other systems of the language. It is a basic feature that must be taken account of in the study of language, or of any single system within language. Moreover, it is a crucial matter in literature. Genres differ in the ways that they either exploit, tolerate, or seek to avoid ambiguity. Types of ambiguity differ in the values that are put on them in literature. These questions, however, are outside our scope here. Rather, we are concerned with the language basis for ambiguities, their resolution and control. Three types might be distinguished:

The first and most familiar is a matter of vocabulary, already illustrated in sentence (8). Many words, including almost all the common ones, have two or more distinct meanings. The combinations, taking any of the available meanings for each word in a sentence, may be extremely numerous. Actually most of these are ruled out, one way or another. A sentence is said to be ambiguous when there is nothing that will make one set of meanings for its components—hence one meaning for the sentence as a whole—definitely preferable to all others.

A second kind of ambiguity rests not in the vocabulary but in the grammar. A syntactic construction is more than a mere sequence of words or morphemes. There must be some identifiable relationship between the elements. It is possible, therefore, to have the same words in the same order but representing two quite different constructions. Any such sequence is ambiguous—each construction suggests a different meaning or list of meanings. Several classic examples have been mentioned in earlier chapters —*old men and women, flying planes, Virginia ham packer.*

A third kind of ambiguity is also grammatical, but rests not in the syntactic relations of elements, but in the identification of elements. Probably the most elaborate and familiar short example is the ambiguity in speech between: *The sons raise meat,* and *The sun's rays meet.*

RESOLUTION OF AMBIGUITY

The reader or hearer must have some mechanism by which to resolve ambiguities, that is, to select the most likely interpretation for a sentence or longer sample.

In the resolution of vocabulary ambiguities, one important factor is grammatical structure. It is easy to create sentences, as the examples above, which are unresolvably ambiguous on the basis of the two meanings of *table,* "article of furniture" and "array of information." It is more difficult to find one where the ambiguity is between one of these and a third meaning "to postpone discussion." The reason is obvious: the first two are meanings of *table* as a noun, the third as a verb. Nouns and verbs usually occur in quite different places in the sentence. The grammatical context, therefore, prevents some pairs of meanings being confused except in very rare instances.

A second factor often resolving ambiguity is redundancy between words in the sentence. A set of examples will show something of how this operates. For simplicity, we will consider that each of the words which are our central concern has only two meanings:

> *table:* "article of furniture," "array of data"
> *chair:* "article of furniture," "endowment for a professorship"
> *scholarship:* "endowment for student aid," "academic performance"

Abbreviating still further, we will list these glosses under the words concerned:

> He gave the university a table and a chair. (9)
> "furniture" ↔ "furniture"
> "data" "endowment"
> He gave the university a chair and a scholarship. (10)
> "furniture" → "endowment"
> "endowment" ← "performance"

Table potentially brings both its meanings to sentence (9) as does *chair.* The similarity in meanings expressed by glossing each as "article of furniture" strengthens the probability for that meaning in each case. An arrow has been added to point out the redundant relationship between the two words. Similarly, in (10) the common meaning "endowment" is strengthened in each word by the possibility of such a meaning in the other.

But this effect can be overridden if a conflicting pattern of redundancy is present:

> He gave the university a very valuable hand-carved antique table
> and a chair in the history of furniture design. (11)

The way this works is best seen by considering the result if certain parts of the sentence are omitted or altered.

> He gave the university a very valuable hand-carved antique table
> and a chair. (12)

Table is marked as meaning "article of furniture" not only by the context *and a chair* as in (9) but also by the modifiers *antique* and *hand-carved.* In turn *table and* seems to determine the meaning of *chair* even more strongly than in (9). Conflict arises when *in the history of furniture design* is added. This points to the meaning "endowment for a professorship" for *chair*. In turn, this is strengthend by *university,* as may be seen by substituting *his wife:*

> He gave his wife a very valuable hand-carved antique table and a
> chair in the history of furniture design.   (13)

The conflict remains, but it cannot now be so easily resolved and the sentence seems nonsensical—the kind where we automatically start searching for a typographical error. Moreover, in (11) the redundancy between *antique* and *history* strengthens the interpretation—try omitting all the modifiers of *table:*

> He gave the university a table and a chair in the history of furni-
> ture design.   (14)

Or again, try the following:

> He gave the university a table and a chair in history.   (15)

Such experiments—and many more could be performed with this same sentence as a starting point—demonstrate that very many of the words in the sentence figure in the context determining the correct meaning for *table* or for *chair.* When there are conflicts, one bit of context pulling in one direction and one in another, there seems to be something about their places in the structure of the sentence which determines which has the greater effect.[5]

The reader's problem in working out the meaning of a passage seems much like that of the writer in attempting to achieve a balanced style. In the latter case, every choice of construction or vocabulary item weights the probabilities at the remaining points where a choice must be made. Conflicts arise and must be resolved, sometimes by seeking an additional more elaborate option which had not been considered before. In reading, the words are given but each presents a choice among its meanings. Each choice of a meaning affects all others nearby. Alternatives become weighted. Weightings cumulate in a favorable circumstance until one mean-

[5] To state in detail how this operates would be to give a large part of a full theory of semantics, a thing which we cannot, at present, do. Perhaps the most important effort in this direction in recent times is Jerrold J. Katz and Jerry A. Fodor, *The Structure of a Semantic Theory,* 1963, Language 39:170–210. This is based on a transformational-generative view of grammar.

ing for each word seems far more probable than any other. In this case, the sentence may be considered unambiguous.

A third factor involved in resolution of ambiguity may be called "unity of the discourse." The reader or listener must assume, unless there is clear evidence to the contrary, that any given word carries the same meaning throughout the passage. In good writing, it generally does. Thus we would avoid using a sentence like:

> He got up from his chair and announced that he had given a chair
> to the university. (16)

Instead:

> He got up from his seat and announced that he had given a chair
> to the university. (17)

Paronomasia must be clearly signaled.

The resolution of potential grammatical ambiguities is more complex. The same principles of vocabulary redundancy and unity of discourse operate, however, though in an opposite way. Consider *old men and women* and *old men and children*. The first is ambiguous, the second not. One reason is that there is a meaning for *old* which is compatible with both *men* and *women,* but none which is easily compatible with both *men* and *children.*

Or consider the following:

> He is a Virginia ham packer from North Carolina. (18)

The phrase *Virginia ham packer* is, by itself ambiguous. The most likely interpretation for the structure *Virginia (ham packer)* is "ham packer from Virginia." This is not compatible with *from North Carolina,* and so is ruled out. For the structure *(Virginia ham) packer,* the most probable interpretation is "packer of a certain type of hams." This is compatible with the rest of (18), and the hearer or reader will generally select this analysis. Much the opposite argument and conclusion apply in the following:

> He is a Virginia ham packer specializing in sugar-cured meats. (19)

Something much like vocabulary redundancy resolves the structural ambiguity.

Probably the most complex operation in reading is the resolution of potential ambiguities. It is the writer's responsibility to provide the necessary help and to control ambiguity. This does not necessarily mean simply to avoid it, or even to minimize it. Ambiguity may be deliberately used for some special purpose, as in much poetry, belletristic prose, advertising copy, or humor, but this must be done with care. If there is too much, if it is of an inappropriate kind, or if it is badly handled, the desired effect may be spoiled. In other kinds of writing, straightforward exposition for example, ambiguity should be minimized.

This can be done in several ways. One is the careful choice of vocabulary. A word with fewer meanings might be selected in preference to one with more. But there are limitations. Often the less ambiguous words are little known. It may be necessary to increase redundancy to insure that they will be understood. Too many such words will interfere with readability for many audiences. Often the most precise words are to be found in specialized terminologies, but if these are used they will give a highly technical cast to the whole, and this may be undesirable.

Often a more satisfactory strategy is to focus attention on the contexts rather than the words themselves. Even the most polysemous words may be unambiguous if they can be used in the right environments. The trick is to see that they are provided, at their first appearance, with sharply defining contexts. Often this is best done by careful selection of modifiers—words so closely related syntactically that they are clearly relevant context, and semantically compatible with only the desired meaning. *Hand-carved* in sentence (11) is an example; even if the writer had no interest in the details of the table, this might be added to assist in making the noun unambiguous.

Careful attention to grammatical constructions is as important as vocabulary selection. But the two are not independent. The sentence pattern determines how the context applies, and hence whether individual words are ambiguous or not. Similarly, the words inserted in a sentence pattern determine whether it is grammatically ambiguous or not.

We can illustrate this by considering the following sentence which has a grammatically ambiguous phrase for a subject:

The killing of the lion was a wanton act. (20)

At least four ways are available to render this sentence unambiguous: First, we can replace the phrase by an agnate phrase which has only one meaning:

To kill the lion was a wanton act. (21)

Second, we may replace a word in the phrase by a near synonym which will fit into only one of the two possible constructions:

The shooting of the lion was a wanton act. (22)

Third, we may replace a word remote from the point of ambiguity but significant as context:

The killing of the lion was an illegal act. (23)

Finally, we may add a largely redundant expression of some kind:

The killing of the lion was a wanton act and the hunter should not
have done it. (24)

These and other techniques may reduce ambiguity very materially, but they never wholly eliminate it. Beyond a certain point, further reduction is only at a cost, most often in the form of excessive redundancy and diminished clarity. This mounts steeply, and may soon become prohibitive. How soon depends on the purposes behind the writing. Extreme examples can often be seen in legal documents. The following example shows this:

Ordered, that six months from the 2nd day of July, 1964, be and the same are limited and allowed for the presentation of all claims against the said estate to the executor thereof and said executor is directed to cite all creditors of said decedent to bring in their claims within said time allowed by publishing the same once in some newspaper having a circulation in said Probate District within thirty days from the date of this order.[6] (25)

From any point of view, this is highly redundant. It is by no means easy reading. Yet it cannot properly be considered bad writing. It does

[6] This formula is repeated day after day, with only a change of date, in every notice of this kind in the state of Connecticut. The specific example was found in the *Hartford Times,* July 7, 1964, where there were three such notices. The fact that these notices are so highly standardized means that from some broader point of view the whole formula is entirely redundant. A regular reader of probate notices (say, a lawyer) never bothers to read the formula at all; he already knows exactly what is in it. Moreover, he knows exactly what it means as it has been interpreted through years of judicial consideration and legal practice. The relevant context is not contained in the notice, but in many volumes of legal decisions. These make it ALMOST completely unambiguous.

precisely what it is designed to do in the most effective way known to do it. Ambiguity is cut to a minimum; high redundancy and poor clarity are the price. For its purpose, however, such a cost is bearable. Legal proceedings can tolerate almost any feature of language more readily than ambiguity. In this context, we are willing to put up with great difficulty in reading, provided, once the meaning is made out, it will be certain and precise. To insure this, we leave both the writing and the reading of contracts to specialists. A lawyer has more than one function, but not the least is simply to handle the special kind of language required to avoid costly misunderstandings.

For other purposes, such a price cannot be paid. The relative values of artistry, clarity, brevity, and unambiguousness may vary from one kind of writing to another. In each situation an appropriate compromise must be found between the several conflicting demands. To write well, one needs a feel for the proper balance, as well as an understanding of the devices available to effect the best possible resolution of the tensions.

NOMINAL AND VERBAL STYLE

Rulon Wells

DESCRIPTION AND EVALUATION

Pronouncements about style are of two sorts, descriptive and evaluative. Description is logically prior to evaluation, in that a reasoned description is possible without evaluation whereas a reasoned evaluation is not possible without description. Some who do descriptive stylistics do it in deliberate abstraction from evaluation, that is, without the intention of proceeding to evaluate; others do the description primarily for the sake of the evaluation which they regard as the end to which description is a means.

What should be a mere distinction is widely regarded as an opposition; a division that should only divide subject from subject too often divides man from man. There is a reason for this. It is not the case, in practice, that the "describers" and the "appraisers" study the same things from different points of view. For the two intents—sheer description, on the one hand, and description conjoined with evaluation—lead to different selections. In principle the appraiser evaluates or appraises all texts, but in practice, in addition to the obvious specialties (texts in French, or English texts of the Elizabethan period, or Latin poetry), he tends to select for study the texts that he will evaluate *favorably*.[1] In particular, he

Reprinted from Style in Language, *edited by T. Sebeok, by permission of the M.I.T. Press, Cambridge, Massachusetts.*

[1] At least to the extent of finding them interesting. A critic may pronounce the style of some poem or essay a failure but add that it is a distinguished failure, or a significant experiment, or the like.

is likely to shy away from spending his efforts on the meaner texts, those that do not even purport to be literature, and to concentrate on belles-lettres, which more vigorously exercise his powers. And equally, the sheer describer, who in principle describes all texts, tends in practice to focus on less pretentious texts precisely because they are less complicated. Experimentalists and statisticians, in particular, are likely to regard belles-lettres as too complicated for fruitful study. The time may come when this limitation is passed beyond, but I am speaking of the present day.

In general, then, appraiser and sheer describer tend to study mutually exclusive phenomena or aspects. But there are exceptions. One of these is the degree to which nouns and verbs are used in various styles. Here is a variable of style at once simple and interesting. Nominal (nominalizing) style, the tendency to use nouns in preference to verbs, and the opposite verbal or verbalizing style, which tends to use verbs rather than nouns, are two features that are fairly easy to describe yet are of great interest to appraisers. Those who appraise at all mostly appraise nominal style as inferior to verbal. And yet it crops up again and again, defended on the ground that it is adapted to its purpose.

NOMINAL AND VERBAL STYLE

In this and the next two sections I shall confine my discussion to English, and to written English. The advice to shun the nominal style is sometimes put this way: "Don't use nouns where you could use verbs; don't shrink from the use of verbs." This way of putting it takes two things for granted: first, that nominality and verbality are matters of continuous degree, and second, that the continuum is characterized by the proportion of nouns to verbs in a given text. These presumptions, in turn, seem to indicate a "quantization" (quantitative measure) of our variable, by defining it as a ratio—the sort of thing that might be dubbed the Noun-Verb Quotient (NVQ). Before this indication can be precise, however, three points need to be settled.

1.   What is a noun? (*a*) Shall we count pronouns and adjectives as nouns? They share many of the characters that distinguish nouns from verbs. (*b*) Shall a noun phrase count as a single noun? For example, shall "the foot of the mountain" be reckoned as containing one noun or two?

2.   What is a verb? (*a*) Do nonfinite forms (infinitives, gerunds, participles) count as verbs, as nouns, as both, or as neither? (*b*) Shall a periphrastic verb like "will do" count as one verb or as two? (*c*) Shall the verb "to be" count the same as other verbs? (The feeling is sometimes expressed that the copula is not a true verb, since it has a purely logical function. On the other hand, it has person, tense, etc., like other verbs. Thus a discrepancy between its form and its meaning is felt. We might

recognize this discrepancy by counting occurrences of forms of "to be" one-half, rather than one; or we might take the view that there is no quantitative way of recognizing the peculiar nature of the copula.)

3.   The advice might be formulated a little differently. "Keep the proportion of nouns low and of verbs high." An index that would show whether this advice was being followed would have two parts: a Noun-Word Quotient (NWQ) *and* a Verb-Word Quotient (VWQ). For any given text the sum of these two quotients cannot exceed 1.0 and will only equal 1.0 if there are no other parts of speech in the text, but beyond that there is no necessary connection between the two quotients. It would be interesting to determine experimentally whether there is a consistent inverse relation between them.

The problem of quantizing nominality will not be pursued further here. It might well turn out that some of the questions raised are insignificant, for example, that the NVQ of scientific writers differs markedly from that of literary writers, no matter how noun and verb are delimited. But of course these facts could only be determined by experiment, for which reflections such as those of the present paper are a necessary preamble but no substitute.

There is a further consideration of which any treatment, quantitative or otherwise, should take account. Style is understood to be optional like vocabulary, as contrasted with grammar. So far as the writer of English has a choice, what he writes is *his* diction and *his* style; so far as he has none, it is the *English* language. A treatment that respects this optionality will somehow take account of whether, and in how many ways, a sentence with a certain degree of nominality could be replaced by one with a different degree, for example, a highly nominal by a highly verbal sentence. And of course it is understood that mere variation of style is made not to alter the substance or content of what is expressed but only the way of expressing it; underlying the very notion of style is a postulate of *independence of matter from manner*. If a given matter dictates a particular manner, that manner should not be called a style, at least not in the sense that I have been speaking of. But this postulate does not preclude that a certain matter shall favor or "call for" a certain manner—the so-called fitness of manner to matter, or consonance with it.

CONSEQUENCES OF NOMINALITY

The advice to prefer verbs to nouns makes it sound as though it were a simple substitution, like the choice of familiar words in preference to rare ones, or of short words in preference to long ones. Occasionally this is so, but not in the usual case. In the more nominal phrase "the doctrine of the immortality of the human soul," the particles are different from those in the more verbal phrase "the doctrine that the human soul is immortal"; the one uses prepositions, the other a conjunction. In changing the verb of "He began to study it thoroughly" into the noun of "He began a thorough study of it," we must follow through by a corresponding change of adverb to adjective. The elementary fact of syntax that prepositions and adjectives go with nouns, conjunctions and adverbs with verbs, prevents the contrast of nominality and verbality from being *minimal*.

This fact has two consequences. (1) When nominality is evaluated good or bad, the ground may lie in whole or in part in features entailed by nominality, although distinct from it. (2) And so the nominal-verbal contrast is not a *pure dimension* of style, that is, it is not a variable which can vary without variation in the other basic factors of style.

The aforementioned consequences are necessary ones. Another class must be acknowledged, the probable consequences. From the statistical point of view, necessary consequences appear as those whose probability is 1.0, impossible consequence as those with probability .00, and the less or more probable consequences as those having intermediate probability values.

Even an impressionistic study can estimate some of these probabilities. To facilitate discussion, let us pretend—what is false, but not grossly false—that nominalizing and verbalizing sentences can be paired, so that we can speak of *the* nominal counterpart of such and such a verbal sentence and of the verbal counterpart of a given nominal sentence. The intent of this fiction is to concentrate our discussion on differences as near to minimal as is syntactically possible.

A nominal sentence is likely to be longer, in letters and in syllables, than its verbal counterpart. The greater length in the diction of those writers who favor nominal style results from the fact that the noun corresponding to verb is likely to be longer than the verb—usually because it is derived from the verb stem by suffixes—and the entailed changes (loss of verb endings, replacement of conjunctions by prepositions, etc.) are not likely to compensate. Compare "when we arrive" with "at the time of our arrival"—fourteen letters (including word spaces) replaced by twenty-six, four syllables by eight.

Another likelihood is that the average number of clauses per sentence tends to decrease (the minimum being 1.0), for nominalization replaces conjunctions by prepositions. The sentence "If he does that, he will be sorry" has two clauses; its nominal counterpart "In the event of his doing that, he will be sorry" has only one.

A third likelihood, entailed by the second and also somewhat likely even in the absence of the second condition, is that the number of distinct sentence patterns will decrease. Compound sentences (both with coordinating and with subordinating conjunctions) tend to disappear, so that only simple (subject-predicate) sentences, more or less swollen by parentheses and modifiers, will be left.

EVALUATION OF NOMINALITY

Nominality is judged bad by some, good by others.

1. Those who judge nominal style bad judge it so for one or more of the following reasons:

a. Nouns are more static, less vivid than verbs. Sometimes this view is defended on deep philosophical grounds. For example, Étienne Gilson[2] sees in Aristotle's remark (*De interpretatione* 3.16b19) that "verbs in and by themselves are substantival" a revealing clue to his philosophy; not Aristotle but Thomas Aquinas is the one who gives to "is," to existence *in actu exercito,* its full due. And to the argument that the traditional, semantical definitions of noun and verb are of no avail because what one language considers an action, another may treat as a state, the rejoinder might be made that this is just the point: the contrast of action and state varies with the point of view, and one that does not reduce all actions to states is to be recommended. Something like this seems to be intended by Peter Hartmann, to whom I shall refer in the next section.

b. Longer sentences are (on the whole) less vivid and less comprehensible than shorter ones.

c. A text whose sentences are all or mostly of one basic pattern will usually be monotonous. Verbal style allows more diversity, and a good style will exploit the genius of its language.

2. Those who judge nominal style good do so implicitly, for the most part; nominal style is practiced more than preached. The implicit reasons in its favor appear to be these:

a. It is easier to write. Thus it is natural for those who are more concerned with what they say than with how they say it to choose this style, or to drift into it.

b. It helps impersonality. In scientific writing ("scientific" in the broadest sense, including philosophy, and as contrasted with artistic and literary writing), expressions of personality are frowned upon. Now personality can be avoided in various ways. One is the use of the passive voice. Where the seventeenth and eighteenth centuries would have been

---

[2] *Being And Some Philosophers,* Toronto, Second Edn., 1952, p. 199. On quite different grounds some philosopher mentioned but not named by Aristotle (*Physics* 1.2.185b28) proposed to replace, for example, "The man is white" by "The man whites," coining a verb for the purpose if need be.

anecdotal—"I collected sea anemones at low tide"—the nineteenth and twentieth centuries would cast the reporting subject into the shadow of implicitness: "Sea anemones were collected at low tide." Another way to avoid personality is to avoid finite verbs altogether, by nominalizing.

c. Nominality offers another advantage to the scientific writer. The finite verb has not only person but also number and (as does the participle) tense. Of these three dimensions tense is widely felt to be the most fundamental; similarly Aristotle distinguishing the Greek verb from the Greek noun does it on the basis of having or lacking tense (*De interpretatione* 2.16a19, 3.16b6). Now to the extent that a writer can avoid finite verbs and participles (including forms of the verb "to be"), he can avoid commitments as to tense. Indeed, it is partly because of this fact that the pairing of nominalizing and verbalizing sentences is a fiction. "At the time of our arrival" has not one verbal counterpart but two, "when we arrived" and "when we arrive."

d. The very fact that nominality is contrary to conversational style has its value. It sets off the writing as esoteric, specialized, technical. Nominal style in English can be used to play the role (although much less conspicuously and effectively) that Latin played until several hundred years ago.

Certain neutral remarks can be made about these judgments. Those who approve nominal style and those who disapprove it are not in utter disagreement. Its advocates do not claim that it is graceful or elegant, and its critics do not deny that it achieves impersonality and the rest. But after the mutual concessions, a residue of disagreement remains. It is admitted by all that verbal style is harder to write than nominal style; it is *worth* the trouble? This would raise the broader question whether good style is being urged for its own sake (i.e., as an end), or as a means to some other end, or on both grounds. Advocates of nominal style usually defend it as a means to an end; its attackers might argue that it does not achieve its end, and that for the very same end verbal style is more effective. In that case, verbal style would be preferable to nominal both as an end and as a means.

sentences

THE SENTENCE

Herbert Read

The sentence as a unit in prose style is best approached from the evolutionary standpoint suggested by Jespersen. The further back we go in the history of known languages, the more we find that the sentence was one indissoluble whole in which those elements we are accustomed to think of as single words were not yet separated.[1] Jespersen says too, that we must think of primitive language "as consisting (chiefly at least) of very long words, full of difficult sounds, and sung rather than spoke."

This supports the view I wish to advance as to the function of the sentence in prose writing. The sentence is a single cry. It is a unit of expression, and its various qualities—length, rhythm and structure—are determined by a right sense of this unity.

The process by which the various parts of speech became differentiated is of great interest, but must not concern us here. We will only note that in all probability the sentence, as distinct from the primitive indissoluble sound suggested by Jespersen, arose when it first became possible to distinguish between action and objects—between things in themselves and the mobile properties of those things. For then the verb became dis-

From English Prose Style *by Herbert Read, copyright 1952 by Herbert Read. Reprinted by permission of Pantheon Books, a Division of Random House, Inc., and G. Bell & Sons, Ltd.*

[1] *Language,* p. 421. Cf. Piaget, *Language and Thought of the Child* (Humanities Press): "The line of development of language, as of perception, is from the whole to the part, from syncretism to analysis, and not vice versa."

tinct from the substantive, and these two parts of speech give us the essentials of a sentence.

A substantive may stand alone as a sentence, and sometimes does, effectively. But the verb is always understood, or some construction including a verb. When a verb stands alone it usually has the previous sentence, or the subject of the previous sentence, as a latent subject or predicate. Such isolation of a noun or a verb is merely a device of punctuation: to gain vividness (though the gain be only typographical) the word in question is as it were framed between two full stops. The following passages illustrate the deliberate use of this manner of composition, and it is a mannerism less liable to abuse than many since it tends to concision rather than verbosity. It has the vitality of directly transmitted thought, of the "interior monologue" which takes place in each thinking mind. On the other hand, it lends itself to false dramaticism and a sham "poetic" atmosphere:

> The day was beginning to break as they walked along together. The light shot up from the east, filling the sky with a warm tinge of soft half-light. And it grew and grew till suddenly the broad, clear light fell upon them.
>
> It was day. How quiet looked the town in the full, soft clearness. The houses seemed to sleep in the middle of strange, soft, thrilling sound. The wonderful first flush of the day. It fell on the outcasts as they walked on. Through the quietness of the streets they could hear the low, deep sound of the waters of the Gulf beating on the beach.
>
> Day. It had come after darkness. It was shining for these nameless and homeless men just as it was shining for kings or for those whose names rang greatly through the world.
>
> Two straying passing figures coming from nowhere and going nowhere.
>
> Day had come for them.
>
> *Bart Kennedy,* A Sailor Tramp[2]

> On the steps of the Paris Stock Exchange the gold-skinned men quoting prices on their gemmed fingers. Gabble of geese. They swarmed loud, uncouth about the temple, their heads thickplotting under maladroit silk hats. Not theirs: these clothes, this speech, these gestures. Their full slow eyes belied the words, the gestures eager and unoffending, but knew the rancours massed about them and knew their zeal was vain. Vain patience to heap and hoard. Time surely would scatter all. A hoard heaped by the roadside: plundered and passing on. Their eyes knew the years of wandering, and, patient, knew the dishonours of their flesh.
>
> *James Joyce,* Ulysses[3]

[2] Grant Richards.
[3] Random House.

Sometimes the verb is omitted from a sentence as unessential to its meaning:

> No matins here of birds; not a rock partridge-cock, calling with bithesome chuckle over the extreme waterless desolation.
> *C. M. Doughty,* Arabia Deserta, *i.*[4]

Again, the device suggests poetry rather than prose. "The moment we use the copula, the moment we express subjective inclusions, poetry evaporates" (Fenollosa). But as Fenollosa makes clear, in prose it is not so much the presence or absence of the verb that matters, but the choice between a transitive and an intransitive verb. The great strength of the English language, he points out, "lies in its splendid array of transitive verbs, drawn both from Anglo-Saxon and from Latin sources. . . . Their power lies in their recognition of nature as a vast storehouse of forces . . . I had to discover for myself why Shakespeare's English was so immeasurably superior to all others. I found that it was his persistent, natural, and magnificent use of hundreds of transitive verbs. Rarely will you find an 'is' in his sentences. . . . A study of Shakespeare's verbs should underline all exercises in style."

Sentences in their variety run from simplicity to complexity, a progress not necessarily reflected in length: a long sentence may be extremely simple in construction—indeed, *must be* simple if it is to convey its sense easily.

Other things being equal, a series of short sentences will convey an impression of speed, and are therefore suited to the narration of action or historical events; whilst longer sentences give an air of solemnity and deliberation to writing. In the first of the following passages, the great variety in the length of the sentences gives animation to a serious subject; whilst in the second passage a more trivial subject is, by the grandeur and dignity of the sentences, endowed with a fictitious seriousness:

> France, by the perfidy of her leaders, has utterly disgraced the tone of lenient council in the cabinets of princes, and disarmed it of its most potent topics. She has sanctified the dark suspicious maxims of tyrannous distrust; and taught kings to tremble at (what will hereafter be called) the delusive plausibilities of moral politicians. Sovereigns will consider those who advise them to place an unlimited confidence in their people as subverters of their thrones; as traitors who aim at their destruction, by leading their easy good nature, under specious pretences, to admit combinations of bold and faithless men into a participation of their power. This alone, if there were nothing else, is an irreparable

[4] Jonathan Cape, Ltd.

calamity to you and to mankind. Remember that your parliament of Paris told your king, that in calling the states together, he had nothing to fear but the prodigal excess of their zeal in providing for the support of the throne. It is right that these men should hide their heads. It is right that they should bear their part in the ruin which their counsel has brought on their sovereign and their country. Such sanguine declarations tend to lull authority asleep; to encourage it rashly to engage in perilous adventures of untried policy; to neglect those provisions, preparations and precautions, which distinguish benevolence from imbecility; and without which no man can answer for the salutary effect of any abstract plan of government or of freedom. For want of these, they have seen the French rebel against a mild and lawful monarch, with more fury, outrage and insult, than ever any people has been known to raise against the most illegal usurper, or the most sanguinary tyrant. Their resistance was made to concession; their revolt was from protection; their blow was aimed at a hand holding out graces, favours, and immunities.

This was unnatural. The rest is in order. They have found their punishment in their success. Laws overturned; tribunals subverted; industry without vigour; commerce expiring; the revenue unpaid, yet the people impoverished; a church pillaged, and a state not relieved; civil and military anarchy made the constitution of the kingdom; everything human and divine sacrificed to the idol of public credit, and national bankruptcy the consequence; and to crown all, the paper securities of new, precarious, tottering power, the discredited paper securities of impoverished fraud, and beggared rapine, held out as a currency for the support of an empire, in lieu of the two great recognised species that represent the lasting conventional credit of mankind, which disappeared and hid themselves in the earth from whence they came, when the principle of property, whose creatures and representatives they are, was systematically subverted.

Were all these dreadful things necessary? Were they the inevitable results of the desperate struggle of determined patriots, compelled to wade through blood and tumult, to the quiet shore of a tranquil and prosperous liberty? No! nothing like it. The fresh ruins of France, which shock our feelings wherever we can turn our eyes, are not the devastation of civil war; they are the sad, but instructive monuments of rash and ignorant counsel in time of profound peace. They are the display of inconsiderate and presumptuous, because unresisted and irresistible, authority.

The persons who have thus squandered away the precious treasure of their crimes, the persons who have made this prodigal and wild waste of public evils (the last stake reserved for the ultimate ransom of the state) have met in their progress with little, or rather with no opposition at all. Their whole march was more like a triumphal procession than the progress of a war. Their pioneers have gone before them, and demolished and laid everything level at their feet. Not one drop of their blood have they shed in the cause of the country they have ruined. They have made no sacrifices to their projects of greater consequence than their shoe-buckles, whilst they were imprisoning their king, murdering their fellow-citizens, and bathing in tears, and plunging in poverty and distress, thousands of worthy men and worthy families. Their cruelty has not even been the base result of fear. It has been the effect of their sense of perfect safety, in authorizing treasons, robberies, rapes, assassinations, slaughters and burnings throughout their harassed land. But the cause of all was plain from the beginning.

Edmund Burke, Reflections on the Revolution in France

Nothing is more destructive, either in regard to the health, or the vigilance and industry of the poor than the infamous liquor, the name of which, derived from Juniper in *Dutch,* is now by frequent use and the laconick spirit of the nation, from a word of middling length shrunk into a monosyllable, intoxicating gin, that charms the unactive, the desperate and crazy of either sex, and makes the starving sot behold his rags and nakedness with stupid indolence, or banter both in senseless laughter, and more insipid jests; it is a fiery lake that sets the brain in flame, burns up the entrails, and scorches every part within; and at the same time a *Lethe* of oblivion, in which the wretch immersed drowns his most pinching cares, and, with his reason all anxious reflections on brats that cry for food, hard winter's frosts, and horrid empty home.

In hot and adust tempers it makes men quarrelsome, renders 'em brutes and savages, sets 'em on to fight for nothing, and has often been the cause of murder. It has broke and destroyed the strongest constitutions, thrown 'em into consumptions, and been the fatal and immediate occasion of apoplexies, phrensies, and sudden death. But as these latter mischiefs happen but seldom, they might be overlooked and connived at, but this cannot be said of the many diseases that are familiar to the liquor, and which are daily and hourly produced by it; such as loss of appetite, fevers, black and yellow jaundice, convulsions, stone and gravel, dropsies and leucophlegmacies.

Among the doating admirers of this liquid poison, many of the meanest rank, from a sincere affection to the commodity itself, become dealers in it, and take delight to help others to what they love themselves, as whores commence bawds to make the profits of one trade subservient to the pleasures of the other. But as these starvelings commonly drink more than their gains, they seldom by selling mend the wretchedness of condition they laboured under whilst they were only buyers. In the fag-end and out-skirts of the town, and all places of the vilest resort, it's sold in some part or other of almost every house, frequently in cellars and sometimes in the garret. The petty traders in this *Stygian* comfort are supplied by others in somewhat higher station, that keep professed brandy shops, and are as little to be envied as the former; and among the middling people, I know not a more miserable shift for a livelihood than their calling; whoever would thrive in it must in the first place be of a watchful and suspicious, as well as a bold and resolute temper, that he may not be imposed upon by cheats and sharpers, nor out-bully'd by the oaths and imprecations of hackney coachmen and foot-soldiers; in the second, he ought to be a dabster at gross jokes and loud laughter, and have all the winning ways to allure customers and draw out their money, and be well versed in the low jests and ralleries the mob make use of to banter prudence and frugality. He must be affable and obsequious to the most despicable; always ready and officious to help down a porter with his load, shake hands with a basket-woman, pull off his hat to an oyster wench, and be familiar with a beggar; with patience and good humour he must be able to endure the filthy actions and viler language of nasty drabs, and lewdest rake-hells, and without a frown or the least aversion bear with all the stench and squalor, noise and impertinence that the utmost indigence, laziness and ebriety can produce in the most shameless and abandoned vulgar.

The vast number of the shops I speak of throughout the city and suburbs, are an astonishing evidence of the many seducers that, in a lawful occupation are accessory to the introduction and increase of all the sloth, sottishness, want and misery which the abuse of strong waters is the immediate cause of, to lift above mediocrity perhaps half a dozen men that deal in the same commodity by wholesale; whilst among the retailers, though qualify'd as I required, a much greater number are broke and ruined, for not abstaining from the *Circean* cup they hold out to others; and the more fortunates are their whole lifetime obliged to take the uncommon pains, endure the hardships, and swallow all the ungrateful and shocking things I named, for little or nothing beyond a bare sustenance, and their daily bread.

Bernard de Mandeville, Fable of the Bees *(Remark G.)*

The simple clause may be varied only in the order of its words: "Cold was the night" for "The night was cold"; and here all that is gained is an unusual emphasis on the word *cold*. But in compound sentences there is scope for much greater variety—words within clauses, and clauses within the sentence. Everything must depend on the required emphasis, and the emphasis is secured by the rhythm, and the rhythm by the necessities of expression. Let us therefore proceed straight to the examination of such sentences.

Pleasant, as the fiery heat of the desert daylight is done, is our homely evening fire. The sun gone down upon a highland steppe of Arabia, whose common altitude is above three thousand feet, the thin dry air is presently refreshed, the sand is soon cold; wherein yet at three fingers' depth is left a sunny warmth of the past day's heat until the new sunrise. After a half hour it is the blue night, and clear hoary starlight in which there shines the girdle of the milky way, with a marvellous clarity.

As the sun is setting, the nomad housewife brings in a truss of sticks and dry bushes, which she has pulled or hoed with a mattock (a tool they have seldom) in the wilderness; she casts down this provision by our hearthside, for the sweet-smelling evening fire. But to Hirfa, his sheykhly young wife, Zeyd had given a little Beduin maid to help her. The housewife has upon her woman's side an hearth apart, which is the cooking-fire. Commonly Hirfa baked then, under the ashes, a bread-cake for the stranger: Zeyd her husband, who is miserable, or for other cause, eats not yet, but only near midnight, as he is come again from the mejlis and would go in to sleep.

C. M. Doughty, Arabia Deserta, *i.*[5]

In this passage the arrangement of clauses, and of words within clauses, is, as always in Doughty's writing, very deliberate. The paragraph begins with an inversion, to bring into prominence the word "pleasant," which word is the keynote of the passage. The subject of the first sentence, "our homely evening fire," is reserved to the end, not only to suspend "pleasant" in a still more marked isolation, but to give the subject itself an emphasis, by placing it where we should least expect it. In the next sentence clauses are treated in much the same way as words in the first sentence. The purpose is to describe the effect of the going down of the sun, and the direct way would be to use adverbial phrases, as, for example, *"when* the sun has gone down." But direct statements are more vivid, and in this particular case permit, without confusion of syntax, the insertion of qualifying clauses like "whose common altitude is above three thousand feet." But the main object is the compact accretion of details of observation. The third sentence is again remarkable for its careful disposition of emphasis, and the rest of the paragraph eases its rhythm to permit a relaxed observation; it is now not so much direct visualization, as comment. The retardation of the rhythm, towards the end of the paragraph, until it ends with a sense of inevitability on the word "sleep," is also a deliberate effect.

When it is desired to contrast opposing ideas, this is most effectively done by confining them within a single sentence. The two ideas are placed in *antithesis,* which is a balance or opposition of sense:

They went down to the camp in black, but they came back to the town in white; they went down to the camp in ropes, they came back in chains of gold; they went down to the camp with their feet in fetters, but came back with their steps enlarged under them; they went also to the camp looking for death, but they came back from thence with

[5] Jonathan Cape, Ltd.

assurance of life; they went down to the camp with heavy hearts, but
came back with pipe and tabor playing before them,

John Bunyan, Life and Death of Mr. Badman

Antithesis has been a very popular device with self-conscious writers,
and particularly with the Eighteenth Century school, from Bolingbroke to
Gibbon. Used with discretion it adds point and vivacity to expression; but
when abused it becomes tedious and artificial.

If by a more noble and more adequate conception, that be considered as wit which is at once natural and new, that which, though not
obvious, is, upon its first production, acknowledged to be just; if it be that
which he that never found it, wonders how he missed; to wit of this kind
the metaphysical poets have seldom risen. Their thoughts are often new,
but seldom natural; they are not obvious, but neither are they just; and
the reader, far from wondering that he missed them, wonders more
frequently by what perverseness of industry they were ever found.

Samuel Johnson, Life of Cowley

Mr. Wimsatt, in his book on Johnson's prose style, distinguishes three
ways of binding groups of words, viz. (1) by the use of conjunctive or
disjunctive words, (2) by the syntax of words, and (3) by the repetition
of identical words. What he calls *parallelism* or *balance* is achieved by the
simple pairing of words ("faults and follies"), by two elements in each
member ("unnatural thoughts and rugged numbers"), by three elements
("Examples of national calamities and scenes of extensive misery"), and
even by four elements ("the various forms of connubial felicity, the unexpected causes of lasting discord")—all examples from Johnson. There
is in addition the device of antithetical parallels, e.g. "a state too high
for contempt and too low for envy." Such antithetical clauses have been
compared "to the false handles and keyholes with which furniture is
decorated."[6]

But Hazlitt gave the most effective criticism of such mannerisms in
his essay on "Edmund Burke":

Burke was not a verbose writer. If he sometimes multiplies words,
it is not for want of ideas, but because there are no words that fully
express his ideas, and he tries to do it as well as he can by different ones.
He had nothing of the *set* or formal style, the measured cadence, and

[6] Quoted by Wimsatt, *The Prose Style of Samuel Johnson,* p. 49, from
Whately's *Elements of Rhetoric,* 1828, which does not give the source of the
comparison.

stately phraseology of Johnson, and most of our modern writers. This style, which is what we understand by the *artificial,* is all in one key. It selects a certain set of words to represent all ideas whatever, as the most dignified and elegant, and excludes all others as low and vulgar. The words are not fitted to the things, but the things to the words. Everything is seen through a false medium. It is putting a mask on the face of nature, which may indeed hide some specks and blemishes, but takes away all beauty, delicacy, and variety. It destroys all dignity or elevation, because nothing can be raised where all is on a level, and completely destroys all force, expression, truth, and character, by arbitrarily confounding the differences of things, and reducing everything to the same insipid standard. To suppose that this stiff uniformity can add anything to real grace or dignity, is like supposing that the human body in order to be perfectly graceful, should never deviate from its upright posture. Another mischief of this method is, that it confounds all ranks in literature. Where there is no room or variety, no discrimination, no nicety to be shewn in matching the idea with its proper word, there can be no room for taste or elegance. A man must easily learn the art of writing, when every sentence is to be cast in the same mould: where he is only allowed the use of one word, he cannot choose wrong, nor will he be in much danger of making himself ridiculous by affectation or false glitter, when, whatever subject he treats of, he must treat of it in the same way. This indeed is to wear golden chains for the sake of ornament.

William Hazlitt, Essay on Edmund Burke

Compare also Coleridge:

The style of Junius is a sort of metre, the law of which is a balance of thesis and antithesis. When he gets out of this aphorismic metre into a sentence of five or six lines long, nothing can exceed the slovenliness of the English. Horne Tooke and a long sentence seem the only two antagonists that were too much for him. Still the antithesis of Junius is a real antithesis of images or thought; but the antithesis of Johnson is rarely more than verbal.

Table Talk, *July 3, 1833 (Oxford edn., 1917) p. 255.*

Antithesis operates by a tension or suspense between two ideas; the sentence becomes a balance between equal but opposite forces. A similar kind of suspense is maintained in the *period* proper. A period is a complex sentence of which the meaning remains in suspense until the completion of the sentence. The main sentence of the following passage from Wordsworth's *Covention of Cintra* is an extreme example:

But it is a belief propagated in books, and which passes currently among talking men as part of their familiar wisdom, that the hearts of the many *are* constitutionally weak; that they *do* languish; and are slow to answer to the requisition of things. I entreat those who are in this delusion, to look behind them and about them for the evidence of experience. Now this, rightly understood, not only gives no support to any such belief; but proves that the truth is in direct opposition to it. The history of all ages; tumults after tumults; wars, foreign or civil, with short, or with no breathing-spaces, from generation to generation; wars —why and wherefore? yet with courage, with perseverance, with self-sacrifice, with enthusiasm—with cruelty driving forward the cruel man from its own terrible nakedness, and attracting the more benign by the accompaniment of some shadow which seems to sanctify it; the senseless weaving and interweaving of factions—vanishing and reviving and piercing each other like the Northern Lights; public commotions, and those in the bosom of the individual; the long calenture, to which the Lover is subject; the blast, like the blast of the desert, which sweeps perennially through a frightful solitude of its own making in the mind of the Gamester; the slow quickening but ever quickening descent of appetite down which the Miser is propelled; the agony and cleaving oppression of grief; the ghost-like hauntings of shame; the incubus of revenge; the life-distemper of ambition;—these inward existences, and the visible and familiar occurrences of daily life in every town and village; the patient curiosity and contagious acclamations of the multitude in the streets of the city and within the walls of the theatre; a procession, or a rural dance; a hunting, or a horse-race; a flood, or a fire; rejoicing and ringing of bells for an unexpected gift of good fortune, or the coming of a foolish heir to his estate;—these demonstrate incontestably that the passions of men (I mean, the soul of sensibility in the heart of man)—in all quarrels, in all delights, in all employments which are either sought by men or thrust upon them—do immeasurably transcend their objects. The true sorrow of humanity consists in this; —not that the mind of man fails; but that the course and demands of action and of life so rarely correspond with the dignity and intensity of human desires; and hence that, which is slow to languish, is too easily turned aside and abused.

William Wordsworth, Convention of Cintra

Most periods can be analysed into subject, verb and predicate, the subject or verb being in the nature of an extensive catalogue. Wordsworth's sentence is really of this nature, though somewhat disguised by its eloquence. The following sentence of Burke's has a more obvious catalogue-subject:

To be bred in a place of estimation; to see nothing low and sordid from one's infancy; to be taught to respect one's self; to be habituated to the censorial inspection of the public eye; to look early to public opinion; to stand upon such elevated ground as to be enabled to take a large view of the widespread and infinitely diversified combinations of men and affairs in a large society; to have leisure to read, to reflect, to converse; to be enabled to draw the court and attention of the wise and learned wherever they are to be found;—to be habituated in armies to command and to obey; to be taught to despise danger in the pursuit of honour and duty; to be formed to the greatest degree of vigilance, foresight, and circumspection, in a state of things in which no fault is committed with impunity, and the slightest mistakes draw on the most ruinous consequences—to be led to a guarded and regulated conduct, from a sense that you are considered as an instructor of your fellow-citizens in their highest concerns, and that you act as a reconciler between God and man—to be employed as an administrator of law and justice, and to be thereby amongst the first benefactors of mankind—to be a professor of high science or of liberal and ingenuous art—to be amongst rich traders, who from their success are presumed to have sharp and vigorous understandings, and to possess the virtues of diligence, order, constancy, and regularity, and to have cultivated an habitual regard to commutative justice —these are the circumstances of men, that form what I should call a *natural* aristocracy, without which there is no nation.

Burke, Appeal from the New to the Old Whigs

A truer period is one in which the suspense is created by a complexity of clauses, as in the following example:

Corruption could not spread with so much success, though reduced into a system, and though some ministers, with equal impudence and folly, avowed it by themselves and their advocates, to be the principal expedient by which they governed; if a long and almost unobserved progression of causes and effects did not prepare the conjuncture.

Bolingbroke, Spirit of Patriotism

Not all long and complex sentences have the architectural harmony of the period. Many such sentences are often in the nature of an agglomeration of inconsistent and unrelated clauses, and should really be split up into several sentences. There is an extreme example in a letter of Swift's, which shows that Swift could on occasion write like a servant girl:

Last year a paper was brought here from England, called a Dialogue between the Archbishop of Canterbury and Mr. Higgins, which we ordered to be burnt by the common hangman, as it well deserved, though we have no more to do with his Grace of Canterbury, than you have with the Archbishop of Dublin, whom you suffer to be abused openly, and by name, by that paltry rascal of an observator; and lately upon an affair, wherein he had no concern; I mean, the business of the missionary

of Drogheda, wherein our excellent primate was engaged, and did nothing
but according to law and discretion.

Jonathan Swift, Letter concerning the Sacramental Test

Such a sentence betrays itself, if by nothing else, by its rhythm; it
jerks along like a car in distress; and this is because we so often come to
a point which completes the sense of a possible sentence within the sentence. There is no suspense from beginning to end, but only an inorganic
aggregation of phrases.

The danger with all long and complex sentences is that they may
lack *balance*. The sense may be logically clear, the rhythm may be easy,
but still they try our patience or offend our sensibilities. There is a want
of proportion between the subject and the predicate, or between either
of these and the verb—not so much a proportion of sense, which would
result in humour, but a proportion of structure, the simple against the
complicated, the devious against the direct.

As sentences increase in complexity, the use of punctuation becomes
more complicated and more worthy of attention. At least three methods
of punctuation have been used in English prose writing, these being determined respectively by structure, respiration and rhythm.

Punctuation by structure is logical: it serves to indicate and help the
sense of what is being said. It marks off the processes of thought, outlines
the steps of the argument; in fact, orders and controls the expression in
the interests of meaning:

Concerning faith, the principal object whereof is that eternal verity
which hath discovered the creatures of hidden wisdom in Christ; concerning hope, the highest object whereof is that everlasting goodness
which in Christ doth quicken the dead; concerning charity, the final
object whereof is that incomprehensible beauty which shineth in the
countenance of Christ the Son of the living God: concerning these virtues, the first of which beginning here with a weak apprehension of
things not seen, endeth with the intuitive vision of God in the world
to come; the second beginning here with a trembling expectation of
things far removed and as yet but only heard of, endeth with real and
actual fruition of that which no tongue can express; the third beginning
here with a weak inclination of heart towards him unto whom we are
not able to approach, endeth with endless union, the mystery whereof is
higher than the reach of the thoughts of men; concerning that faith,
hope, and charity, without which there can be no salvation, was there
ever any mention made saving only in that law which God himself hath
from heaven revealed?

Richard Hooker, Of the Laws of Ecclesiastical Polity,
I. *xi. 6.*

The logic of this passage is not entirely controlled by punctuation; there enter into its structure repetitions such as that of the word "concerning," and enumeration, and rhythm. But the structure is perfectly reflected in the punctuation, and is determined by it.

Punctuation by "respiration" is determined by physical ease; it is assumed that what is read is really spoken, however unconsciously; and that since our natural speech is punctuated by the physical limits of respiration, our silent or imaginary speech should conform to similar laws. Each stop—comma, semi-colon, full-stop—represents a degree of pause; it has a certain time-value and is inserted to represent a proportionate duration. This type of punctuation is perhaps the one most commonly in use, and almost any passage of colloquial prose will illustrate it:

His loose entertainments in this stage were, as usual with gentlemen cadets of noble families in the country, sporting on horseback; for which there was opportunity enough at his grandfather's house (at Kirtling), where was a very large and well-stocked deer park: and at least twice a week in the season there was killing of deer. The method then was for the keeper with a large cross bow and arrow to wound the deer, and two or three disciplined hounds pursued till he dropped. There was most of the country sports used there for diverting a large family, as setting, coursing, bowling; and he was in it all; and, within doors, backgammon and cards with his fraternity and others; wherein his parts did not fail him for he was an expert gamester. He used to please himself with raillery, as he found any that by minority of age or majority of folly and self-conceit were exposed to be so practised upon. I could give instances enough of this sort and not unpleasant, if such trifles were to be indulged in a design such as mine is. His most solemn entertainment was music, in which he was not only master, but doctor. This for the country; where, to make good his exhibition, he was contented (though in truth forced) to pass the greater part of his time. But in town, he had his select of friends and acquaintance; and with them he passed his time merrily and profitably for he was as brisk at every diversion as the best. Even after his purse flowed sufficiently a petit supper and a bottle always pleased him. But he fell into no course of excess or vice; and whenever he was a little overtaken it was a warning to him to take better care afterwards: and against women his modesty was an effectual guard, though he was as much inclined as any man which made him desirous to marry. And that made his continence a positive virtue; for who may not be good that is not inclined to evil? The virtue of goodness is where a contrary inclination is strove with and conquered. He was in town a noted hunter of music meetings; and very often the fancy prevailed to go about town and see trades work; which is a very diverting and instructive entertainment. There was not anything extraordinary which he did not, if he might visit, for his information as well

as diversion; as engines, shows, lectures, and even so low as to hear Hugh Peters preach.
> *Roger North,* Life of the Rt. Hon. Francis North,
> Baron Guildford.

Punctuation, whether logical or mechanical, should always be subordinate to the general sense of rhythm but may also itself determine rhythm. But this use of punctuation is artificial and rare; it is the mark of the conscious artist, of Donne and Browne, of Milton and Ruskin, and of Pater. It is raised to great complexity and effectiveness by Doughty, to whom punctuation is almost a system of rhythmical notation, to be deliberately observed by the reader, and given due weight. This famous speech from Landor illustrates the more obvious qualities of such a mode of punctuation:

> Laodameia died; Helen died; Leda, the beloved of Jupiter, went before. It is better to repose in the earth betimes than to sit up late; better than to cling pertinaciously to what we feel crumbling under us, and to protract an inevitable fall. We may enjoy the present while we are insensible of infirmity and decay: but the present, like a note in music, is nothing but as it appertains to what is past and what is to come. There are no fields of amaranth on this side of the grave: there are no voices, O Rhodopé, that are not soon mute, however tuneful: there is no name, with whatever emphasis of passionate love repeated, of which the echo is not faint at last.
> *W. S. Landor,* Aesop and Rhodopé

The rhythm of this passage is controlled by the subtle distinction in value made between the colon and semi-colon. The semi-colon seems to mark a carrying over of an even beat; the colon, the recovery of an initial emphasis. In Doughty, however, the poor company of stops is made to serve a score of uses:

> Here passing, in my former journeys, we saw Arab horsemen which approached us; we being too many for them, they came but to beg insolently a handful of tobacco. In their camps such would be kind hosts; but had we fallen into their hands in the desert we should have found them fiends, they would have stripped us, and perchance in a savage wantonness have cut some of our throats. These were three long-haired Beduins that bid us *salaam* (peace); and a fourth shock-haired cyclops of the desert, whom the fleetness of their mares had outstripped, trotted in after them, uncouthly seated upon the rawbone narrow withers of his dromedary, without saddle, without bridle, and only as an herdsman

driving her with his voice and the camel-stick. His fellows rode with naked legs and unshod upon their beautiful mares' bare backs, the halter in one hand, and the long balanced lance, wavering upon the shoulder, in the other. We should think them sprawling riders; for a boast or war-like exercise, in the presence of our armed company, they let us view how fairly they could ride a career and turn: striking back heels and seated low, with pressed thighs, they parted at a hand-galop, made a tourney or two easily upon the plain; and now wheeling wide, they betook themselves down in the desert, every man bearing and handling his spear as at point to strike a foeman; so fetching a compass and we marching, they a little out of breath came gallantly again. Under the most ragged of these riders was a very perfect young and startling chestnut mare,—so shapely there are only few among them. Never combed by her rude master, but all shining beautiful and gentle of herself, she seemed a darling life upon that savage soil not worthy of her gracious pasterns: the strutting tail flowed down even to the ground, and the mane (*orfa*) was shed by the loving nurture of her mother Nature.

Charles M. Doughty, Travels in Arabia Deserta, *i.*[7]

Though the sentence is the unit of rhythm, it is not the whole of rhythm. Rhythm, as I shall attempt to show in the next chapter, is an affair of the paragraph, and rhythmically the sentence is subordinate to the paragraph. A sentence must be isolated to stand secure in its rhythm, and this is one of the requisites of an aphorism—that it is complete in its own rhythm.

The hours of folly are measur'd by the clock; but of wisdom, no clock can measure.

No bird soars too high, if he soars with his own wings.

The roaring of lions, the howling of wolves, the raging of the stormy sea, and the destructive sword, are portions of eternity, too great for the eye of man.

William Blake, The Marriage of Heaven and Hell

The following marginal note from the *Ancient Mariner* is a perfect example of the independent sentence:

In his loneliness and fixedness he yearneth toward the journeying Moon, and the stars that still sojourn, yet still move onward; and every where the blue sky belongs to them, and is their appointed rest, and

[7] Reprinted by permission of Jonathan Cape, Ltd.

their native country and their own natural homes, which they enter unannounced, as lords that are certainly expected and yet there is a silent joy at their arrival.

In a sentence the rhythm keeps close to the inner necessities of expression; it is determined in the act of creation. It is the natural modulation of the single cry. Only in the paragraph does it become modified in the interests of a larger unity. We might, therefore, expect to find authors who though perfect in the formation of their sentences, neglect the paragraph and its wider, all-embracing sweep. And this indeed is the case, and may be the explanation of some stylistic defect which at first we find hard to analyse. Writers of foreign extraction, in whom the idiom of a language is not perfectly engrained, are particularly liable to this fault —as we find in Joseph Conrad and George Santayana. In the case of Santayana in particular the individual sentences may be rhythmical enough, but they do not form part of a more sustained rhythm; they follow in a series of minute percussions; they are like stepping-stones that finally weary the strained attention of the reader:

True love, it used to be said, is love at first sight. Manners have much to do with such incidents, and the race which happens to set at a given time the fashion in literature makes its temperament public and exercises a sort of contagion over all men's fancies. If women are rarely seen and ordinarily not to be spoken to; if all imagination has to build upon is a furtive glance or casual motion, people fall in love at first sight. For they must fall in love somehow, and any stimulus is enough if none more powerful is forthcoming. When society, on the contrary, allows constant and easy intercourse between the sexes, a first impression, if not reinforced, will soon be hidden and obliterated by others. Acquaintance becomes necessary for love when it is necessary for memory. But what makes true love is not the information conveyed by acquaintance, not any circumstantial charms that may be therein discovered: it is still a deep and dumb instinctive affinity, an inexplicable emotion seizing the heart, an influence organizing the world, like a luminous crystal, about one magic point. So that although love seldom springs up suddenly in these days into anything like a full-blown passion, it is sight, it is presence, that makes in time a conquest over the heart; for all virtues, sympathies, confidences will fail to move a man to tenderness and to worship unless a poignant effluence from the object envelops him, so that he begins to walk, as it were, in a dream.

Not to believe in love is a great sign of dullness. There are some people so indirect and lumbering that they think all real affection must rest on circumstantial evidence. But a finely constituted being is sensitive to its deepest affinities. This is precisely what refinement consists in, that we may feel in things immediate and infinitesimal a sure premonition of things ultimate and important. Fine senses vibrate at once to harmonies which it may take long to verify; so sight is finer than touch, and thought than sensation. Well-bred instinct meets reason halfway, and is prepared for the consonances that may follow. Beautiful things, when taste is formed, are obviously and unaccountably beautiful. The grounds we may bring ourselves to assign for our preferences are discovered by analysing those preferences, and articulate judgments follow upon emotions which they ought to express, but which they sometimes sophisticate. So too the reasons we give for love either express what it feels or else are insincere, attempting to justify at the bar of reason and convention something which is far more primitive than they and underlies them both.

George Santayana[1]

But foreigners are not the only writers who practise this fatal, lapidary style. Emerson may be quoted as an example of an author who was so concerned with the aphoristic quality of his sentences that he forgot the rhythmical life of his paragraphs.[9]

We have a great deal more kindness than is ever spoken. Maugre all the selfishness that chills like east winds the world, the whole human family is bathed with an element of love like a fine ether. How many persons we meet in houses, whom we scarcely speak to, whom yet we honour, and who honour us! How many we see in the street, or sit with in church, whom, though silently, we warmly rejoice to be with! Read the language of these wandering eye-beams. The heart knoweth.

Ralph Waldo Emerson, Essay on Friendship

In the passage from Santayana we feel in each sentence the force of the same even and impassive mood. The rhythms are consequently too uniform. In the case of Emerson the sentences do not seem to belong to each other; the transitions are mostly abrupt; there is no carrying-over of the rhythm from one sentence to another.

It is in such transitions of sense and rhythm that conjunctions play their part; and the appropriate use of conjunctions is, indeed, one of the marks of a good style. "Of all the parts of speech," wrote George Campbell,[10] "the conjunctions are the most unfriendly to vivacity." And he quotes Exodus xv. 9, 10, as an example of vigor due to simplicity of phrasing:

[8] From *Reason in Society,* by George Santayana. Reprinted by permission of Charles Scribner's Sons. Copyright 1905.

[9] His essays were actually composed by grouping together sentences which he had separately entered into a journal.

[10] *Philosophy of Rhetoric,* iii. 3.

The enemy said, I will pursue; I will overtake; I will divide the spoil; my revenge shall be satiated upon them: I will draw my sword; my hand shall destroy them: thou blewest with thy breath; the sea covered them; they sank as lead in the mighty waters.

But here, as Campbell notes, "the natural connection of the particulars mentioned is both close and manifest; and it is this consideration which entirely supersedes the artificial signs of that connection, such as conjunctions and relatives." The whole verse is actually suspended in one animation, in one breath, as it were. But where this natural connection is lacking, the result of dispensing with rhythmical transitions is exacting to the attention and ultimately wearying. Coleridge made the best comment on the use of conjunctions:

A close reasoner and a good writer in general may be known by his pertinent use of *connectives*. Read that page of Johnson (the Whig— author of *A humble and hearty Address to all English Protestants in the present Army,* 1686.); you cannot alter one conjuction without spoiling the sense. It is a linked strain throughout. In your modern books, for the most part, the sentences in a page have the same connexion with each other that marbles have with a bag; they touch without adhering.

Table Talk, *May 15, 1833.*

MODIFICATION AND
SHIFT OF EMPHASIS

Harold Whitehall

The complements of a predicate restrict the range of application of the verb. Thus, in a very real sense, they are *modifiers*. But the modification of sentence elements does not stop short with the complements. Neither human communication nor the life occurrences it reflects are often uncomplicated, and any key word in a fixed word-order slot may need to carry its own modification. This may be accomplished by the use of single word modifiers, or word-group modifiers, or both.

In positions 1, 3, and 4, within the sentence, *individual* words used as word modifiers, whether singly or in series, tend to occur before the word that they modify. Such modifiers, therefore, build up noun word-groups of which the modified word is the head:

1	**2**	**3**	**4**
A handsome reporter	*gave*	a young lady	valuable presents.

1   **2**   **3**

All the young reporters   *gave*   a most charming young lady

4

certain very valuable books.

In word-order position 2, the specialized modifiers called auxiliaries (verbal helpers) always precede the modified verb, building up verb word-groups of which the verb is the head:

From Structural Essentials of English *by Harold Whitehall, copyright, 1954,* © *1956, by Harcourt, Brace & World, Inc., and reprinted with their permission.*

1	2	3	4
A reporter	*had been giving*	*a lady*	*the books.*

1	2	3	4
A reporter	*had been about to give*	*a lady*	*the books.*

Word-groups used as word modifiers follow the word that they modify:

1	2	3
A reporter on the News	*gave*	*the* lady I have mentioned

4

books of accumulated press clippings.

1	2	3
The reporter I have been consulting	*gave*	*the* lady from Duluth

4

the books I have just mentioned.

1	2
A reporter persuaded of his own irresistible charm	*gave*

3	4
a lady convinced of hers	*various* books of verse.

1	2
The reporter, a very charming person,	*gave*

3	4
this lady, a young debutante,	various books of verse.

Although word-group modifiers are usually of the non-headed types, headed groups, as can be seen above, are not infrequent in positions 1, 3, and 4. In speech, noun groups (*appositives,* repeaters) are separated from the word they modify by the internal grammatical juncture; in writing, by the comma that is its symbol. The presence of this juncture between the word modified and the modifying word-group marks the latter as *non-restrictive;* its absence marks it as *restrictive.* As used in modification, noun groups seem always to be non-restrictive; modifier and subject-predicate groups may be either restrictive or non-restrictive; prepositional groups are usually—not always—restrictive. But today a new factor seems to be entering the situation: the use of such groups as (*the man*) *I have just mentioned,* (*the girl*) *I was speaking about,* (*the reporter*) *persuaded of his own charm* instead of the older and fuller forms (*the man*) *whom I have just mentioned,* (*the girl*) *about whom I was speaking,* (*the reporter*) *who was persuaded of his own charms.* Among certain modern writers, groups with *who(m), which, that,* seem to be used as automatically non-restrictive when immediately following the word modified, those without *who(m), which, that* being automatically restrictive. A new method of expressing the grammatical distinction of restriction may be arising.

[Earlier,] the first major grammatical device was stated:

In the subject-predicate sentence, the subject, the verb, any inner complement, and any outer complement occur in a fixed 1, 2, 3, 4 order. To this we may add a second device, almost equally important:

Single word modifiers normally precede, and word-group modifiers normally follow, the words they modify.

In these two simple principles is embodied the essential core of English grammatical structure. To understand them and to make practical use of them is to take the first long stride towards mastery of effective written English. Once they are thoroughly understood, the structure of a sentence even as badly complicated and undesirably over-modified as the following will become immediately transparent:

1

Very nearly all of the many fine young reporters I spoke to in the offices

1

of the News at Duluth, a group of energetic young men,

2   **3**

had been going to give   the very pretty little debutante girl from

3

Indianapolis, who was more than a little persuaded of her own

4

charms,   magnificent presents of orchids from Java.

So far we have been concerned with the *must* elements of sentences. In addition to these, many English sentences possess less essential elements —a kind of linguistic envelope for the *must* elements—which provide a spatial, temporal, emotional, and intensity setting appropriate to the sentence situation. These are often thought of as *adverbial modifiers,* considered as reacting on the verb and its expansions. From the standpoint of word order, the important thing about them is that their positions are relatively unfixed; they are the only really movable elements that English sentences possess. Thus they exemplify to a remarkable degree the basic principle already mentioned:

The essential elements occupy fixed positions; less essential elements tend to be movable.

Since the important thing about these modifiers is that they *are* movable, and since the term *adverb* is commonly used to cover several classes of words quite different in function, we shall call these modifiers *movable modifiers.*

Movable modifiers include single words, headed groups, and non-headed groups. According to the positions in which they may be inserted, they may be further classified as follows:

a. **Directives** (spatial adverbs), such as *in, out, under, over, back, home,* etc., normally occur *after* the verb. When only a single complement is present, they may occur immediately after the verb or immediately after the complement (i.e., after positions 2 or 3):

	2	3	
The reporter	gave	*back*	the books.

	2	3	
The reporter	gave	the books	*back.*

When an inner and an outer complement are present in a sentence, *directives* may occur either before them, or between them, or immediately after the outer complement (i.e., after positions 2, 3 or 4):

	2	3	4
The reporter	gave *back*	the lady	her books.

	2	3	4
The reporter	gave	the lady *back*	her books.

	2	3	4
The reporter	gave	the lady	her books *back.*

That *directives* are very intimately linked with their verbs is proved by the noun compounds into which they enter: *cutback* (v. *cut back*), *come-on* (v. *come on*), *breakthrough* (v. *break through*), etc.[1] Consequently, they precede all other movable modifiers placed after the verb:

	1	2	3	4
The reporter	gave	the lady	her books	

back at noon today.

b. **Qualifiers** (qualifying adverbs), which include modifiers ending in *-ly,* and such other words as *here, now, then, there, next, often, later, still, almost, sometimes,* differ from directives in that they can be inserted before the verb as well as after it. If the verb is a single word they may be placed before the subject or between the subject and the verb (that is, before position 1 or between positions 1 and 2):

	1	2	3	4
Presumably the	reporter	gave	the lady	books.

	1	2	3	4
Next the	reporter	gave	the lady	books.

[1] If directives could not shift in position after the verb, another type of word group, verb plus directive (complex verb), might be established.

```
          1                      2        3          4
The reporter presumably       gave    the lady    books.
          1              2       3         4
The reporter next      gave   the lady   books.
```

In speech, but more rarely in writing, they are often placed at the end of the sentence:

```
          1            2          3         4
The reporter         gave     the lady   books presumably.
          1            2          3         4
The reporter         gave     the lady   books then.
```

If position 2 (the verb position) is filled by a verb-headed word-group qualifiers may either precede it or be placed after its first element:

```
          1                         2         3         4
The reporter presumably        was giving   a lady    books.
          1                 2           3        4
The reporter         was presumably giving   a lady   books.
          1                 2                    3        4
The reporter         had still been about to give   a lady    books.
```

    c. **Group qualifiers** commonly appear at the end of the sentence, but they may precede position 1 or be placed between positions 1 and 2:

```
          1            2         3         4
The reporter         gave    the lady   books on the way home.
          1            2         3         4
The reporter         gave    the lady   books to show appreciation.
          1            2         3         4
The reporter         gave    the lady   books when he returned.

On the way home      ⎫          1            2         3
                     ⎬  the reporter      gave      the lady
To show appreciation, ⎭          4
                        books.

          1                               2         3         4
The reporter, when he returned,         gave    the lady   books.
```

Needless to say, any sentence may contain various kinds of movable modifiers in any or all of the available positions:

```
                              1                   2
When he returned, the reporter       had presumably given
              3            4
         the lady     these books back in that Italian garden.
```

The tremendous flexibility of the English sentence is largely made possible by the various positions open to the movable modifiers.

The fixed patterns of word order in English have one practical disadvantage: they limit the opportunity to shift the emphasis from one part of a sentence to another merely by changing the order of the words. Few writers of modern prose would be daring enough to follow the example set by Dickens' famous sentence:

> **3**   **1**   **2**   **3**   **1**   **2**
> Talent, Mr. Micawber has; money, Mr. Micawber has not.

Even such milder inversions of the normal order as *Came the dawn!* and *Had she been there, she would have been safe* (.) are felt to be strange, the former as a Hollywood cliché and the latter as belonging to the nineteenth rather than to the twentieth century. In expository writing, however, occasional use of the inverted complement marks the continuity of thought in contiguous sentences:

> **1**   **2**   **3**
> *Certain persons* resisted his military regime.
> **3**   **1** **2**   **4**
> *Those persons* he called "pseudo-internationalists."

Similarly, for purposes of enumeration, a qualifier is sometimes placed at the beginning of the sentence with the verb immediately following:

> **2**   **1**
> *Next* comes the logical figure termed the syllogism.

In story-telling technique, a directive and verb sometimes occur in this same order:

> **2**   **1**
> *Back* ran the bear to his mother.

Yet, in general, sentence emphasis is now varied not by changing the order of the words but by using special constructions. Just as we possess a grammatical device of fixed word order, we also possess devices for shifting emphasis from one element of the standard written sentence to another.

Special emphasis may be thrown upon the subject (position 1) by placing before it either of the two introductory formulae *it is* (*was*), *there is* (*are, was, were*) and by turning the following part of the sentence into a modifying subject-predicate group preceded by the linking words *who*(*m*), *which* or *that:*

> *It was* the reporter *who* gave the lady books.
>
> *There was* a reporter *that* gave the lady books.

In all fairness, we should note that this is only one of the astonishing array of *it is, there is* constructions in English.

Special emphasis may be thrown upon the words forming the inner and outer complements of the standard sentence (positions 3 and 4) by the use of the so-called *passive construction.* In this, the words to be emphasized are moved to position 1, the verb is transformed into a word group introduced by parts to *be, become,* and *get,* and the original subject (position 1) is hooked onto the end of the sentence by means of the preposition *by* (occasionally, *through*):

1	2	3	4
The reporter	gave	the lady	books.

1	2	3
The lady	*was* given	books *by the reporter.*

1	2	3
Books	*were* given	the lady *by the reporter.*

Notice, however, that the use of this device is greatly restricted by the kinds of expressions found in the complements:

a. When either complement can be put into the passive construction, the inner complement is an *indirect object,* the outer complement is a *direct object.*

b. When only the inner complement can be put into the passive construction, the inner complement is a *direct object,* the outer complement an *objective complement.*

c. When only a single complement occurs, it is a *direct object* if it can be put into the passive construction, a *subjective complement* (*predicate complement, attributive complement*) if it cannot.

For a native speaker of English, these restrictions are of minor importance. His sense of the language is sufficient to guide him. For the grammarian, however, who can be seriously troubled by such so-called idioms as *She looked daggers*(.) or *We talked dogs*(.), the use of the passive construction as a test of the kinds of complements present in the standard 1, 2 ,3, 4 construction is of major importance.

The inner complement (position 3) is remarkable in that it can be *de*-emphasized as well as emphasized. To accomplish this result, it is transformed into a prepositional word-group by the addition of *to* or *for:*

1	2	3	4
The reporter	gave	the lady	books.

1	2	3
The reporter	gave	books *to the lady*.

1	2
Books	were given *to the lady* by the reporter.

In the first example, the group *the lady* is a *must* element of the sentence; in the other examples, it has been demoted in function to the role of a movable modifier by the introduction of the preposition *to:*

1	2	3
The reporter	gave	books *to the lady*.

1	2	4
To the lady, the reporter	gave	books.

It should be noticed that *to the lady* is neither more elegant nor more explicit in these constructions than *the lady* in the other construction:

1	2	3	4
The reporter	gave	*the lady*	books.

It is simply a different type of word-group (prepositional versus noun) which relegates *the lady* to a secondary role among the constituents of the sentence.

Like the fixed 1, 2, 3, 4 order of the standard English sentence, the fixed order of modification tends to limit emphatic variation. Yet even here, especially in writing of a frankly literary quality, English is by no means lacking in resources. The language possesses a number of fossil constructions, chiefly drawn from medieval and legal French, in which single word modifiers occurring *after* the word they modify carry the principal stress of the word-group:

heirs *male*

the body *politic*

God Almighty

devil *incarnate*

chapter *ten*

Similarly:

s
Edward the *First*

s
John the *Baptist*

s
William the *Conqueror*

s
St. John the *Martyr*

By analogy with these, we can reverse many other modifiers to bring them under the principal stress and hence make them emphatic:

s
soldiers *three*

s
water *enough*

s
the day *following*

s
the journey *inland*

A skillful writer can make use of such reversed modifiers to great stylistic advantage, particularly when he places them under emphatic stress:

s   s
The clown *absolute* differs from the actor *droll*.

In estimating the emphatic effects of reversal, however, we should not forget that certain modifiers invariably follow the word that they modify. These include (1) the space pointing words *here* and *there;* (2) two- and three-syllable words normally used as adverbs and space-prepositions (*after, before, behind, ahead, around, beneath, between, beyond, under, across, within, underneath,* etc.); and (3) past participle forms:

this man *here*
that man *there*
my brother *alone*
the ground *beneath*
the space *within*
the space *around*
the money *obtained*
the song *sung*

Because overuse spoils their effectiveness, the various devices for securing variations of sentence emphasis should be sparingly and carefully employed. They are not, as teachers often intimate, inherently weaker than the usual constructions. Proper use of the "passive," the *it is, there is* formulae, and the reversed modifiers can be a valuable aid in writing. On the other hand, too frequent use of these devices is to be avoided because it robs them of their emphatic function. Where everything is emphatic, nothing is emphatic.

COORDINATION (FAULTY) AND SUBORDINATION (UPSIDE-DOWN)

James Sledd

(This paper attributes certain opinions to "the linguist," a fictitious in-dividual whose authority I find it convenient to cite for opinions of my own, and certain others to "the traditionalist," a hollow man who is never allowed to talk back. For these innocent inventions, perhaps no actual linguist living or dead would care to be responsible).

The first and most important way in which linguistics can serve us as teachers of composition is that it can help us see what we have to do and how we can best do it. The teacher who knows some linguistics sees the composition course in the light of his knowledge; and if he does not fool-ishly conclude that linguistics is a panacea, his introduction to linguistic science may be part of a general reorientation which is more valuable than any one specific use of linguistic methods or materials. Linguistics can teach us something about the relations between speech and writing —for example, that speech comes first in time and in importance, that writing is an incomplete but partially independent secondary representa-tion of speech, that the kinds of speech which we normally write are very different from plain talk, and that mastering these differences is a large part of our students' job. Linguistics can teach us something about the nature of style as choice; and when we are dealing with style in language,

From College Composition and Communication, *Vol. 7. (December, 1956), pp. 181–187. Reprinted with the permission of the National Council of Teachers of English and James Sledd.*

it can give us the necessary terms and distinctions to describe the choices that are open. Linguistics can teach us that grammatical structure is stylistically no less important than vocabulary and that structure must be described systematically, *as* a system and as a *formal* system, whose categories cannot be adequately defined in terms of meaning. And linguistics has already taught us that when we have specified the choices which the student can make in speech and writing, we should not ruin our work by upholding some silly standard of mechanical correctness. A good linguist is no *enemy* of standards, but he does believe that we should know what is before we try to say what ought to be. He can therefore help us, I think, to set higher ideals than we have often been contented with—and to reach them, too.

If this faith that is in me is more than the faith of an apprentice witch-doctor in a new and blacker magic, I must welcome the demand that the linguist and his converts put up or shut up. I do welcome it, and happily accept my share in the burden of proof that the principles of linguistics are directly relevant to problems of writing. Such proof, in one small area, is what I am here to offer.

A grammatical system, the linguist says, is a formal structure whose categories must be formally defined. His reason is not only that it is difficult to deal precisely and objectively with meaning. Grammatical and logical categories, he argues, do not always coincide; even if they did, the logical or semantic categories which would have to be recognized in the description of a particular language would still be determined by the number and nature of the formal distinctions in that language; and if grammar is to be a means of interpretation, the grammarian must start with the forms in order to avoid circularity. It is only by way of the forms that we can get at the meanings.

These propositions, if they are true, have the most immediate and far-reaching consequences for the teaching of composition. Both our descriptions and our prescriptions will have to be revised. With at least some of the necessary changes in description all of us are familiar. The conservative himself is now a little uneasy when he tells a class that a noun is the name of a person, place, or thing, that the subject of a sentence is what the sentence is about, or that a sentence itself is a group of words that expresses a complete thought. The junior witch-doctor, like me, is more than just uneasy. He begins his definition of the English noun by describing its inflections; he goes on to note the main positions which nouns occupy in phrases and sentences; he says something about the derivational patterns in which nouns occur; and he strictly subordinates his semantic descriptions to these matters of form. Happily or unhappily witch-hunters and witch-doctors both recognize that in description a revolution has begun.

Perhaps we have not yet recognized so clearly that the changes in grammatical description which have been forced upon us will force us also to change our statements of what is good and what is bad in our students' speech and writing. Ultimately, we cannot escape that recognition. If we accept the linguist's doctrines, we will find that our whole treatment of diction must be modified, and modified at every level of our teaching, from the freshman classroom to the graduate seminar. A good example is our classification of clauses and our instructions for the use of coordination and subordination.

Our usual teaching about clauses rests, I think, on the false assumption that grammatical and semantic categories do coincide. Having made that assumption, we quite logically tell our students to put their main ideas into main clauses and their subordinate ideas into subordinate clauses. Principal clauses, we tell them, express principal ideas, so that compound sentences, consisting of two or more such clauses, give equal emphasis to equal thoughts but weaken unity or coherence. Between the clauses of a compound sentence, which we say are related just as separate sentences are related, there is then no logical advance; two ideas, or two expressions of the same idea (if two are possible), are merely juxtaposed. With complex sentences, we say, the case is altered. Since subordinate clauses express subordinate ideas, complex sentences rank and relate our thoughts in the order of their importance. The primary thought services primary emphasis, and complex sentences are therefore more unified and more coherent than compound sentences.

I have been careful not to misrepresent the traditional theory of clauses, which I have found in learned histories of prose style as well as a variety of handbooks; and I think I am equally fair in saying that to a linguist, this theory seems to rest on a series of bad puns, the old confusion of grammatical and logical terms. Subordinate clauses, the linguist tells us, are grammatically subordinate; that is, they are used like single nouns, adjectives, or adverbs, often to expand smaller constructions. Just as we can say, for example, "The man is my uncle," so we can expand the nominal construction *the man* with a subordinate clause and say, "The man *whom you met is* my uncle." In this grammatical sense, *whom you met* is subordinate, precisely as we might say that *big* is subordinate in the sentence, "The big man is my nephew," or that *there* is subordinate in "The boy there is my nephew." Similarly, according to the linguist, independent or principal clauses are *grammatically* independent; they are subject-predicate combinations which do not expand smaller constructions and whose only *grammatical* equivalents are similar combinations. It does *not* follow that the same state of affairs *must* always be symbolized or *should* always be symbolized by the same clause-pattern. Principal clauses can and sometimes should express subordinate ideas, which need not be expressed by grammatical subordination; and the clauses of a compound sentence may be as unified and coherent and as precisely related as the clauses of a *complex* sentence. The traditional theory of clauses is simply untenable. When we teach it, we are teaching a rhetoric that is bad because we have confused our grammar with our logic.

The most obviously false statement in the traditional theory is the least generally accepted, that compound sentences, by comparison with complex sentences, lack unity, coherence, and precise articulation. I will not laboriously disprove this statement, either by analyzing the meanings of words like *and* or *but* or by citing the logician's rules for the transformation of propositions from one form to another; our everyday experience is ample refutation of an obvious absurdity.

Other propositions in the traditional theory turn out to be less clear, but more dangerous, because more plausible and more widely believed. One version might be summed up in the ambiguous platitude that form and meaning are inseparable. Thus when he lays down his rules about clauses, the traditionalist may mean that in their use we have no stylistic choice, because it is impossible to say the same thing in two different clause-patterns; "the writer's meaning *is* his language, and his language *is* his meaning."[1] We should therefore tell our students, when their use of subordination or coordination displeases us, only that they should re-think their material and say what they really mean.

If this is what the traditonalist intends, his theory is easily reduced to absurdity, for it denies the possibility of translation, paraphrase, summary, accurate indirect quotation, and deductive logic. Indeed, if there were no synonymous expressions, language and communication themselves would be impossible, since meanings would be inseparably bound to particular sequences of phones or graphs. If we asked a man what he meant, he could only repeat what he had said before, and if we did not understand him, he could give no further explanation.

The second step in the refutation of this wild notion is again the appeal to the logician's transformation-rules, which guarantee the possibility of expressing the same content in clauses of different form. So if we say, "Either it's not raining, or the streets are wet," we have uttered a compound sentence; but that compound sentence may be exactly translated by the *complex* sentence, "If it's raining, the streets are wet." Such transformations are the stock in trade of the logician, who puts his propositions into the form that best suits his purpose; and we do precisely the same thing unless we have lost our senses by reading the New Critics. Consider the following pairs of sentences:

[1] This quotation is genuine, but no good purpose would be served by identifying its authors, who must have written it in their sleep.

(1) Though he was tired, he still worked hard.
He was tired, but he still worked hard.
(2) Language would be impossible, since meanings would be inseparably
bound to particular phones.
Language would be impossible, for meanings would be inseparably
bound to particular phones.
(3) I won't write you, since I wouldn't have anything to say.
^{2}I won't ^{3}write you^2 | ^{2}I wouldn't have anything to ^{3}say^1#

The members of each pair, though one sentence is complex and the other
compound, are the same in meaning.

To my examples it may be objected that although two sentences may
say the same thing, they say it with different emphases—that main clauses
are by nature more emphatic than subordinate clauses. Such an objection
would embody the traditional theory in its most limited but clearest, most
persuasive, and most generally accepted form. For all that, I answer that
the objection is preposterous; and the form of my answer proves that the
answer is correct. The sentence "I answer that the objection is preposterous" does not emphasize the mere fact that I am meeting an objection,
though that fact is stated in the main clause. Rather the emphasis is on
the subordinate clause, "that the objection is preposterous," and as far as
I can tell the sentence would not be improved by reversing this arrangement.

Better examples than my own are of course a dime a dozen. Turning
the pages of Kruisinga's big grammar,[2] I quickly find numbers of good
sentences in which a nominal clause is more emphatic than the main
clause that it depends on:

It was generally discovered that the maker of these splendid books
was himself a splendid old man.

The fact was that Yeobright's fame had spread to an awkward
extent before he left home.

A good deal of its importance consists in this, that it is minute and
detailed.

As for adjectival clauses, Kruisinga actually sets up a special class among
them, defined as giving additional information "which is not subordinate
to the rest of the sentence but of equal weight." From his discussion, one
can gather many convincing specimens:

She was much attracted by the novels of Kingsley, between whose
genius and his faults she drew a drastic contrast.

[2] E. Kruisinga, *A Handbook of Present-Day English,* Part II, Vol. 3 (5th ed.,
Groningen, 1932), pp. 367, 373, 375, 376, 379, 381, etc.

Eustacia was indoors in the dining-room, which was really more like a kitchen, having a stone floor and a gaping chimney-corner.
It is a point that we must exert our imaginations a little to understand.

To complete the roll call of cause-types, I will here just mention certain kinds of sentence where the main idea almost has to go in an adverbial clause in order to avoid absurdity:

As the years passed, I grew wiser. When Lincoln was assassinated, my father was a young man.
Before the war began, Joe went to America.

In most contexts it would be plain silly to write, "As I grew wiser, the year passed"; yet the passage of time is certainly more important than any individual's increase in wisdom. The traditionalist will have to say, when he is faced with these sentences, that coordination and subordination need not reflect the intrinsic importance of ideas, but only their importance to the writer.

The evasion will not save him from the ultimate necessity of junking his theory, deliberately writing bad sentences, or deliberately wrecking good ones: the most telling of all the instances in which the traditional theory fails to account for the facts are those where it would require damaging revision. Consistency would require the traditionalist, for example, to revise the following neat sentence from Kruisinga's collection:

The noise echoed terribly through the building, and then there was a silence that was even more terrible.

To my mind, that sentence emphasizes the fact that the silence was more terrible than the noise, and I assume that the professional who wrote it knew and wrote what he intended; but the traditionalist must spoil the sentence because he cannot leave the main idea in a subordinate clause. He will have to write something awful, like this:

The noise echoed terribly through the building, and then the silence was even more terrible.

In the same way, he will have to ruin my next example, where again an empty clause actually contributes to emphasis:

It is not everybody that cares for early Staffordshire pottery.

The edge would be quite taken off of that admirable generalization if it were revised:

> Not everybody cares for early Staffordshire pottery.

And so it goes, in sentence after sentence. The traditionalist, however, is determined to uphold standards even though he has none worth upholding. It is thus that he promotes vice in the name of virtue.

I suggest, then, in summarizing the critical part of this paper, that the linguist's general insistence on the formal nature of grammatical categories will force us to delete specific sections from our handbooks—namely all instructions to put main ideas in main clauses and subordinate ideas in subordinate clauses. "Determine the most important idea of the sentence," the typical handbook says, "and express it in the main clause. Put lesser ideas in subordinate clauses, phrases, or words."[3] I think I have shown that that rule will do more harm than good; and if I am right, the demonstration has positive value and cannot be dismissed as merely negative. I am still not content with the mere deletion of a bad rule. We will have to put something in its place if we are able to teach the student anything about the use of principal and subordinate clauses; and I should like to offer some modest suggestions, centering on the analysis of a few sentences such as we typically use for horrible examples.

If grammatical and logical terms cannot be equated and if we can say the same thing in different clause-patterns, then the student must regularly face stylistic choices which cannot be made mechanically. He must learn that writing is purposeful, that good writing is writing that serves its purpose well, and that the real abnegation of standards is the assumption that a single kind of writing is the only correct kind for all purposes. He may then grasp the possibility of reasoned choice by various criteria, one of which, in the matter of clauses, is proper emphasis. An idea may be emphasized by making a separate sentence of the clause which expresses it, by giving that clause a certain position within a larger sentence, by balancing or contrasting its structure with that of other clauses, or in some cases (as my examples have shown) by subordinating the important clause. Sometimes different clause-patterns will be equally emphatic, and the choice of *for,* or *since, though* or *but, who* or *and he* will have to be made by some other standard—variety, rhythm, ease in transition, or the like.

Since stylistic choices are so complicated, and since we cannot trust the traditional rules to decide them, we will have to replace the old rules of thumb with a more detailed analysis, both formal and semantic, of the patterns of clause-connection and sentence-connection in English; and we

---

[3] This quotation is also genuine, but too familiar to need identification.

must try to invent exercises which will turn the student's theoretical knowledge into active control of the resources of his language. For example, *but* and *though* may be synonymous; often they both indicate that the simultaneous truth of the two propositions which they connect is for some reason not to be expected or out of the ordinary. The differences between *but* and *though* are largely formal: *though*-clauses are grammatically subordinate and rather freely movable, while *but*-clauses are grammatically independent and must follow a *preceding* independent clause. These facts could easily be impressed on the student's mind by asking him to observe the effects of replacing *but* by *though* in a collection of sentences or throughout a single long passage.

I would add, however, that a great deal of our trouble with subordination and coordination is not grammatical at all, but logical or rhetorical; and here I come to my analysis of horrible examples: In the following sentence, all of us would object to the faulty coordination:

> The barometer's falling, and those clouds have wind in them, and we'd better put into harbor at once.

Certainly the sentence is bad, but not because it contains three independent clauses; we would not object to sentences like the following:

> He laughed, and he laughed, and he laughed.
>
> Fox singled, and Minoso doubled, and the game was won.
>
> In that one morning it rained, and it hailed, and it snowed.

Since the difference between the accepted and rejected sentences is not in their clause-patterns, which are identical, we must look for it elsewhere; and it is easy to see that by the label "faulty coordination" we actually mean, in this instance, a failure in logic. In the sentence about the barometer, the suggested relation of premise and conclusion, situation and consequence, is not made clear; and any rewriting will be acceptable if it introduces the needed clarity. A first rewriting changes the one sentence into two and makes their relation clear by inference from their relative positions.

> The barometer's falling, and those clouds have wind in them. We'd better put into harbor at once.

Two other rewritings make the relation explicit, but in notably different patterns of coordination and subordination:

> We'd better put into harbor at once; for the barometer's falling, and those clouds have wind in them.
>
> Since the barometer's falling and those clouds have wind in them, we'd better put into harbor at once.

Unless the original sentence were placed in a determining context, there would be little to choose, for all their differences in clause-patterns, among the three corrections.

Of my next example, the usual criticism would be "upside-down subordination":

> He had almost reached Gainesville when he saw the tornado that struck the town and killed two hundred people.

One man's arrival in town, most of us would say, is not so important as the death of two hundred people—which is no doubt true, but irrelevant to the judgment of the sentence. The sentence is bad because its first two clauses state that two things happened about the same time, while the third clause has nothing to do with this temporal relation; and the fault will remain if the unimportant first clause is subordinated and the important third clause is made independent and coordinate with the second:

> When he had almost reached Gainesville, he saw the tornado, and it struck the town and killed two hundred people.

As a matter of fact, it is almost indifferent which of the first two clauses is introduced by *when,* but in either case the third clause must be made a separate sentence:

> When he had almost reached Gainesville, he saw the tornado. It struck the town and killed two hundred people.
>
> He had almost reached Gainesville when he saw the tornado. It struck the town and killed two hundred people.

The really applicable rule would not be to avoid upside-down subordination, but to talk about one thing at a time.

I would conclude, from my two horrible examples, that when we have given a student a theoretical and practical knowledge of English clause-patterns, the best general advice that we can next give him is to use both coordination and subordination in such a way that the natural or logical relations in his material will be clear. When he puts one sentence after another, when he puts two clauses together in a single sentence, or when he chooses a conjunction or a pair of intonation-patterns to connect his clauses, he is building, at the same time, a pattern of meaning. Neither we nor the linguist can decide for the student what he wants that pattern to be; but we *can* show him any formal indications of contradiction or confusion in his finished product. We can insist that he talk sense; and though when we do so we have quite properly left the realm of grammar for those of logic and rhetoric, our insistence will be more effective if our grammar has been sensible—that is, if we have abandoned, among other delusions, the identification of main and subordinate ideas with main and subordinate clauses.

RHYTHM IN THE SENTENCE

Paull F. Baum

There is a simple repetition in Poor Richard's "God helps them that help themselves," in Thomas Paine's "These are the times that try men's souls," and in St. Paul's (*an.* 1611) "Whatsoever a man soweth, that shall he also reap." These are rhythms, if they are properly to be called such, of sound not of syntax. Yet if to the second we improvise a companion sentence: "These are the days that build character," and if we add the rest of what Paul wrote to the Galatians (7:7,8)—

> Be not deceived: God is not mocked: for whatsoever a man soweth, that shall be also reap. For he that soweth to his flesh shall of the flesh reap corruption; but he that soweth to the Spirit shall of the Spirit reap life everlasting.—

then we see a rhetorical balance of similar syntactic arrangements which is plainly enough a rhythmic phenomenon. Such parallelisms appear both in phrases and in clauses—in Ben Jonson's "There was ever more in him to be praised than to be pardoned," and in Disraeli's "It is much easier to be critical than to be correct"; and, expanded, in Sir Thomas Browne's "Man is a noble animal, splendid in ashes and pompous in the grave," or Jeremy Taylor's "He that is choice of his time will also be choice of his company, and choice of his actions"; or simply, in Sidney's "There is no

From The Other Harmony of Prose *by Paull F. Baum. Reprinted by permission of the Duke University Press. Copyright 1952.*

man suddenly either excellently good or extremely evil"; or more elaborately in Taylor's

> For we must remember that we have a great work to do, many enemies to conquer, many evils to prevent, much danger to be run through, many difficulties to be mastered, many necessities to serve, and much good to do, many children to provide for, or many friends to support, or many poor to relieve, or many diseases to cure, besides the needs of nature and of relation, our private and our public cares, and duties of the world, which necessity and the providence of God hath adopted into the family of religion.

As with phrases, so with clauses, ranging from the simple "Youth is a blunder; manhood a struggle; old age a regret" (Disraeli) and "A witty woman is a treasure; a witty beauty is a power" (Meredith)— through the slightly different, though still simple "Kings will be tyrants from policy when subjects are rebels from principle" (Burke) and "The figure of a man may be a monster, but he is a solid monster. The figure of God may be a mistake, but it is an unmistakable mistake" (Chesterton) and "The Puritans hated bearbaiting, not because it gave pain to the bear, but because it gave pleasure to the spectators" (Macaulay)—to the longer and more complex:

> The fact disclosed by a survey of the past that majorities have been wrong must not blind us to the complementary fact that majorities have usually not been entirely wrong.
>
> *Spencer*
>
> Whenever literature consoles sorrow or assuages pain; wherever it brings gladness to eyes which fail with wakefulness and tears, and ache for the dark house and the long sleep, there is exhibited in its noblest form the immortal influence of Athens.
>
> *Macaulay*
>
> He often expressed his commiseration of Dryden's poverty, and his indignation at the age which suffered him to write for bread; he repeated with rapture the first lines of *All for Love*, but wondered at the corruption of taste which could bear anything so unnatural as rhyming tragedies.
>
> *Johnson*

In a favorite form of this parallelism the final member is expanded. This is, at its simplest, what Saintsbury (not too happily, but the name may stand in lieu of a better) called "gradation"; as in "Where is the wise?

where is the scribe? where is the disputer of this world?" (I Cor. 1:20) or Landor's "Laodameia died; Helen died; Leda, the beloved of Jupiter, went before." The effect may be observed by comparing the illustrations; in the example from Disraeli there is something sharp and staccato, appropriate to the intention of the epigram, but not so pleasing to the ear as the protracted ending of the others, like the lengthened notes of a musical cadence. Or for a contrasting effect the third member may be shorter:

Softly beautiful are the tremulous shadows of leaves on the sunned sand; and the scent of flowers comes thinly sweet with every waft of tepid air; and there is a humming of bees.

Lafcadio Hearn

Or there may be a cumulative series, in which the long last member is itself divided, as in Addison's essay on Westminster Abbey:

When I look upon the tombs of the great, every emotion of envy dies in me: when I read the epitaphs of the beautiful, every inordinate desire goes out: when I meet with the grief of parents upon a tombstone, my heart melts with compassion: when I see the tombs of the parents themselves, I consider the vanity of grieving for those whom we must quickly follow: when I see kings lying by those who deposed them, when I consider rival wits placed side by side, or the holy men that divided the world with their contests and disputes, I reflect with sorrow and astonishment on the little competitions, factions, and debates of mankind.

These gradations show some other interesting varieties, in which the obvious rhythm is as it were veiled. These of Dryden's (on Chaucer) and Swift's (on Garrick) are simple:

All his pilgrims are severally distinguished from each other; and not only in their inclinations but in their very physiognomies and persons.

His death eclipsed the gayety of nations, and impoverished the public stock of harmless pleasure.

In this of Bishop South's both subject and object in the last clause are expanded by a phrase, and in the second clause the negative is put into a suffix:

Study was not then a duty, night-watchings were needless: the light of reason wanted not the assistance of a candle.

This from William Lloyd Garrison (a common oratorical form) expands the third member by a clause:

> With reasonable men, I will reason; with humane men I will plead; but to tyrants I will give no quarter, nor waste arguments where they will certainly be lost.

In this from Burke the subject of the verb is graduated: "The cheap defence of nations, the nurse of manly sentiment and heroic enterprise, is gone." In this from Carlyle it is the verb itself: "Every noble crown is, and on earth will for ever be, a crown of thorns." In this from Lytton Strachey there are three sections in each member, with graduated variations:

> The sisters were never separated for the whole of their long lives. Agnes was cheerful, but of little value in the head; she painted. Old Mr. Berry was cheerful, but quite incompetent; he did nothing at all. Mary was intelligent, with enough character for three at the very least; and she did everything that had to be done, with consummate ease.

Finally, in this from Ezekiel observe how curiously the four short clauses (the third itself graduated *up,* and the fourth *down* again) are balanced by the two short, or shorter, clauses, strengthened and lengthened with "behold" and "lo."

> The hand of the Lord was upon me, and carried me out in the spirit of the Lord, and set me down in the midst of the valley which was full of bones, and caused me to pass by them round about, and behold, there were very many in the open valley, and lo, they were very dry.

All varieties of anaphora and similar figures, moreover, are sources of rhythmic effect, though not all in the same degree, for in some the repetition may be accompanied by such different matter that the feeling of the unit is lost. Macaulay has an interesting variation:

> The Life of Johnson is assuredly a great—a very great work. Homer is not more decidedly the first of heroic poets, Shakespeare is not more decidedly the first of dramatists, Demosthenes is not more decidedly the first of orators, than Boswell is the first of biographers. He has no second. He has distanced all his competitors so decidedly that it is not worth while to place them. Eclipse is first, and the rest nowhere.

To illustrate more fully—perhaps more fully than need be—the different kinds of balance and parallelism I submit the following specimens, with this observation (partly illustrative itself) from Ruskin:

> In all perfectly beautiful objects there is found the opposition of one part to another and a reciprocal balance obtained. . . . Absolute equality is not required, still less absolute similarity. A mass of subdued colour may be balanced by a point of a powerful one, and a long and latent line overpowered by a short and conspicuous one.
>
> Modern Painters

This from Donne is tripartite, with gradation in the first member of each section, but the third member shortened by way of compensation:

> One dieth at his full strength, being wholly at ease, and in quiet; and another dies in the bitterness of his soul and never eats with pleasure; but they all lie down alike in the dust and the worm covers them.

These two from Johnson need no comment, but the second is of interest as showing an appreciation of simplicity on the part of one who so often overplayed "the rhetorician's brass instrument":

> All the other powers of literature are coy and haughty, they must long be courted, and at last are not always gained; but Criticism is a goddess easy of access, and forward of advance, who will meet the slow and encourage the timorous; the want of meaning she supplies with words, and the want of spirit she recompenses with malignity.
>
> Idler, *"Dick Minim the Critic."*

> Criticism, either didactic or defensive, occupies almost all his [Dryden's] prose, except those pages which he has devoted to his patrons; but none of his prefaces were ever thought tedious. They have not the formality of a settled style, in which the first half of the sentence betrays the other. The clauses are never balanced, nor the periods modelled: every word seems to drop by chance, though it falls into its proper place. Nothing is cold or languid; the whole is airy, animated, and vigorous; what is little is gay; what is great is splendid. He may be thought to mention himself too frequently; but while he forces himself upon our esteem, we cannot refuse him to stand high in his own. Everything is excused by the play of images and the spriteliness of expression. Though all is easy, nothing is feeble; though all seems careless, there is nothing harsh; and though since his earlier works more than a century has passed, they have nothing yet uncouth or obsolete.
>
> *"Life of Dryden"*

The next illustration, from Landor's "Æsop and Rhodopé," is more subtly woven, the members are more varied; but the balance is carefully observed.

Laodameia died; Helen died; Leda, the beloved of Jupiter, went before. It is better to repose in the earth betimes than to sit up late; better, than to cling pertinaciously to what we feel crumbling under us, and to protract an inevitable fall. We may enjoy the present, while we are insensible of infirmity and decay: but the present, like a note in music, is nothing but as it appertains to what is past and what is to come. There are no fields of amaranth on this side of the grave: there are no voices, O Rhodopé, that are not soon mute, however tuneful: there is no name, with whatever emphasis of passionate love repeated, of which the echo is not faint at last.

This opens with a simple gradation (already quoted). The next sentence turns on "better . . . than," the latter part of the comparison being protracted by additional modifiers. The third sentence has simple balance ("enjoy the present . . . insensible of decay") varied by the extra phrase "of infirmity"; then "the present" is repeated, precisely "like a note in music." The final sentence comprises the threefold anaphora, with considerable expansion like the gradation of the first sentence. From such a sentence—and in order not to anticipate, the metrical adjuncts are passed over in silence—one can see what Landor meant when he wrote: "Good prose, to say nothing of the original thought it conveys, may be infinitely varied in modulation. It is only an extension of metres, and amplification of harmonies, of which even the best and most varied poetry admits but few."

Three further illustrations will more than suffice: a simple one (from Washington Irving), a more complex one, with inversions (from Vaughan), and a flamboyant one (from Macaulay)—

How many bright eyes grow dim—how many soft cheeks grow pale— how many lovely forms fade away into the tomb, and none can tell the cause of their blighted loveliness.

O pitiful and astonishing transformations. All is gone, all is dust, deformity and desolation. Their bones are scattered in the pit, and instead of well-set hair, there is baldness, and loathsomeness instead of beauty. This the state of their bodies, and (O blessed Jesus) who knows the state of their souls?

Death is there associated, not, as in Westminster Abbey and Saint Paul's, with genius and virtue, with public veneration and with imperishable renown; not, as in our humblest churches and churchyards, with everything that is most endearing in social and domestic charities; but with whatever is darkest in human nature and in human destiny, the savage triumph of implacable enemies, with the inconstancy, the ingratitude, the cowardice of friends, with all the miseries of fallen greatness and blighted fame.

It should be clear now that the repetition of syntactic parallelisms is a form of rhythm. However the parallel units may vary among themselves, however the content may differ provided the form is parallel, the repetition, so long as it is recognizable, is potential rhythm. Other rhythmic elements may complicate the picture, . . . but the sole point I wish to make here is that parallel construction, recognizably repeated, is the simple beginning of prose rhythm. . . .

diction

SYNONYMS: AND THE "PERFECT WORD"

Walter Raleigh

Let the truth be said outright: there are no synonyms, and the same statement can never be repeated in a changed form of words. Where the ignorance of one writer has introduced an unnecessary word into the language, to fill a place already occupied, the quicker apprehension of others will fasten upon it, drag it apart from its fellows, and find new work for it to do. Where a dull eye sees nothing but sameness, the trained faculty of observation will discern a hundred differences worthy of scrupulous expression. The old foresters had different names for a buck during each successive year of its life, distinguishing the fawn from the pricket, the pricket from the sore, and so forth, as its age increased. Thus it is also in that illimitable but not trackless forest of moral distinctions, language halts far behind the truth of things, and only a drowsy perception can fail to devise a use for some new implement of description. Every strange word that makes its way into a language spins for itself a web of usage and circumstance, relating itself from whatsoever centre to fresh points in the circumference. No two words ever coincide throughout their whole extent. If sometimes good writers are found adding epithet to epithet for the same quality, and name to name for the same thing, it is because they despair of capturing their meaning at a venture, and so practise to get near it by a maze of approximations. Or, it may be, the generous breadth of their purpose scorns the minuter differences of related terms, and in-

From Style *by Walter Raleigh. Reprinted by permission of Edward Arnold (Publishers) Ltd. Copyright 1897.*

cludes all of one affinity, fearing only lest they be found too few and too weak to cover the ground effectively. Of this sort are the so-called synonyms of the Prayer-Book, wherein we "acknowledge and confess" the sins we are forbidden to "dissemble or cloke"; and the beadroll of the lawyer, who huddles together "give, devise, and bequeath," lest the cunning of litigants should evade any single verb. The works of the poets yield still better instances. When Milton praises the *Virtuous Young Lady* of his sonnet in that the spleen of her detractors moves her only to "pity and ruth," it is not for the idle filling of the line that he joins the second of these nouns to the first. Rather he is careful to enlarge and intensify his meaning by drawing on the stores of two nations, the one civilised, the other barbarous; and ruth is a quality as much more instinctive and elemental than pity as pitilessness is keener, harder, and more deliberate than the inborn savagery of ruthlessness.

It is not chiefly, however, for the purposes of this accumulated and varied emphasis that the need of synonyms is felt. There is no more curious problem in the philosophy of style than that afforded by the stubborn reluctance of writers, the good as well as the bad, to repeat a word or phrase. When the thing is, they may be willing to abide by the old rule and say the word, but when the thing repeats itself they will seldom allow the word to follow suit. A kind of interdict, not removed until the memory of the first occurrence has faded, lies on a once used word. The causes of this anxiety for a varied expression are manifold. Where there is merely a column to fill, poverty of thought drives the hackney author into an illicit fulness, until the trick of verbiage passes from his practice into his creed, and makes him the dupe of his own puppets. A commonplace book, a dictionary of synonyms, and another of phrase and fable equip him for his task; if he be called upon to marshall his ideas on the question whether oysters breed typhoid, he will acquit himself voluminously, with only one allusion (it is a point of pride) to the oyster by name. He will compare the succulent bivalve to Pandora's box, and lament that it should harbour one of the direst of ills that flesh is heir to. He will find a paradox and an epigram in the notion that the darling of Apicius should suffer neglect under the frowns of Æsculapius. Question, hypothesis, lamentation, and platitude dance their allotted round and fill the ordained space, while Ignorance masquerades in the garb of criticism, and Folly proffers her ancient epilogue of chastened hope. When all is said, nothing is said; and Montaigne's *Que sçais-je,* besides being briefer and wittier, was infinitely more informng.

But we dwell too long wth disease; the writer nourished on thought, whose nerves are braced and his loins girt to struggle with a real meaning, is not subject to these tympanies. He feels no idolatrous dread of repetition when the theme requires it, and is urged by no necessity of concealing real identity under a show of change. Nevertheless he, too, is hedged about by conditions that compel him, now and again, to resort to what seems a synonym. The chief of these is the indispensable law of euphony, which governs the sequence not only of words, but also of phrases. In proportion as a phrase is memorable, the words that compose it become mutually adhesive, losing for a time something of their individual scope, bringing with them, if they be torn away too quickly, some cumbrous fragments of their recent association. That he may avoid this a sensitive writer is often put to his shifts, and extorts, if he be fortunate, a triumph from the accident of his encumbrance. By a slight stress laid on the difference of usage the unshapeliness may be done away with, and a new grace found where none was sought. Addison and Landor accuse Milton, with reason, of too great a fondness for the pun, yet surely there is something to please the mind, as well as the ear, in the description of the heavenly judgment,

That brought into this world a word of woe.

Where words are not fitted with a single hard definition, rigidly observed, all repetition is a kind of delicate punning, bringing slight differences of application into clear relief. The practice has its dangers for the weak-minded lover of ornament, yet even so it may be preferable to the flat stupidity of one identical intention for a word or phrase in twenty several contexts. For the law of incessant change is not so much a counsel of perfection to be held up before the apprentice, as a fundamental condition of all writing whatsoever; if the change be not ordered by art it will order itself in default of art. The same statement can never be repeated even in the same form of words, and it is not the old question that is propounded at the third time of asking. Repetition, that is to say, is the strongest generator of emphasis known to language. Take the exquisite repetitions in these few lines:—

Bitter constraint and sad occasion dear
Compels me to disturb your season due;
For Lycidas is dead, dead ere his prime,
Young Lycidas, and hath not left his peer.

Here the tenderness of affection returns again to the loved name, and the grief of the mourner repeats the word "dead." But this monotony of sorrow is the least part of the effect, which lies rather in the prominence given by either repetition to the most moving circumstance of all—the youthfulness of the dead poet. The attention of the discursive intellect, impatient of reiteration, is concentrated on the idea which these repeated and exhausted words throw into relief. Rhetoric is content to borrow force from simpler methods; a good orator will often bring his hammer down, at the end of successive periods, on the same phrase; and the mirthless refrain of a comic song, or the catchword of a buffoon, will raise laughter at last by its brazen importunity. Some modern writers, admiring the easy power of the device, have indulged themselves with too free a use of it; Matthew Arnold particularly, in his prose essays, falls to crying his text like a hawker:

> Beating it in upon our weary brains,
> As tho' it were the burden of a song.

clattering upon the iron of the Philistine giant in the effort to bring him to reason. These are the ostentatious violences of a missionary, who would fain save his enemy alive, where a grimmer purpose is glad to employ a more silent weapon and strike but once. The callousness of a thick-witted auditory lays the need for coarse method on the gentlest soul resolved to stir them. But he whose message is for minds attuned and tempered will beware of needless reiteration, as the noisiest way of emphasis. Is the same word wanted again, he will examine carefully whether the altered incidence does not justify and require an altered term, which the world is quick to call a synonym. The right dictionary of synonyms would give the context of each variant in the usage of the best authors. To enumerate all the names applied by Milton to the hero of *Paradise Lost,* without reference to the passages in which they occur, would be a foolish labour; with such reference, the task is made a sovereign lesson in style. At Hell gates, where he dallies in speech with his leman Sin to gain a passage from the lower World, Satan is "the subtle Fiend," in the garden of Paradise he is "the Tempter" and "the Enemy of Mankind," putting his fraud upon Eve he is "the wily Adder," leading her in full course to the tree he is "the dire Snake," springing to his natural height before the astonished gaze of the cherubs he is "the grisly King." Every fresh designation elaborates his character and history, emphasises the situation, and saves a sentence. So it is with all variable appellations of concrete objects; and even in the stricter and more conventional region of abstract ideas the same law runs. Let a word be changed or repeated, it brings in either case its contribution of emphasis, and must be carefully chosen for the part it is to play, lest it should upset the business of the piece by irrelevant clownage in the midst of high matter, saying more or less than is set down for it in the author's purpose.

*　　　*　　　*　　　*　　　*

Enough has been said of change; it remains to speak of one more of those illusions of fixity wherein writers seek exemption from the general lot. Language, it has been shown, is to be fitted to thought; and, further, there are no synonyms. What more natural conclusion could be drawn by the enthusiasm of the artist than that there is some kind of preordained harmony between words and things, whereby expression and thought tally exactly, like the halves of a puzzle? This illusion, called in France the doctrine of the *mot propre,* is a will o' the wisp which has kept many an artist dancing on its trail. That there is one, and only one way of expressing one thing has been the belief of other writers besides Gustave Flaubert, inspiriting them to a desperate and fruitful industry. It is an amiable fancy, like the dream of Michael Angelo, who loved to imagine that the statue existed already in the block of marble, and had only to be stripped of its superfluous wrappings, or like the indolent fallacy of those economic soothsayers to whom Malthus brought rough awakening, that population and the means of subsistence move side by side in harmonious progress. But hunger does not imply food, and there may hover in the restless heads of poets, as themselves testify—

> One thought, one grace, one wonder, at the least,
> Which into words no virtue can digest.

Matter and form are not so separable as the popular philosophy would have them; indeed, the very antithesis between them is a cardinal instance of how language reacts on thought, modifying and fixing a cloudy truth. The idea pursues form not only that it may be known to others, but that it may know itself, and the body in which it becomes incarnate is not to be distinguished from the informing soul. It is recorded of a famous Latin historian how he declared that he would have made Pompey win the battle of Pharsalia had the effective turn of the sentence required it. He may stand for the true type of the literary artist. The business of letters, howsoever simple it may seem to those who think truth-telling a gift of nature, is in reality two-fold, to find words for a meaning, and to find a meaning for words. Now it is the words that refuse to yield, and now the meaning, so that he who attempts to wed them is at the same time altering his words to suit his meaning, and modifying and shaping his meaning to satisfy the requirements of his words. The humblest processes of thought have had their first education from language long before they took shape in literature. So subtle is the connexion between the two that it is equally possible to call language the form given to the matter of thought, or, inverting the application of the figure, to speak of thought as the formal principle that shapes the raw material of language. It is not until the two become one that they can be known for two. The idea to be expressed is a kind of mutual recognition between thought and language, which here meet and claim each other for the first time, just as in the first glance exchanged by lovers, the unborn child opens its eyes on the world, and pleads for life. But thought, although it may indulge itself with the fancy of a predestined affiance, is not confined to one mate, but roves free and is the father of many children. A belief in the inevitable word is the last refuge of that stubborn mechanical theory of the universe which has been slowly driven from science, politics, and history. Amidst so much that is undulating, it has pleased writers to imagine that truth persists and is provided by heavenly munificence with an imperishable garb of language. But this also is vanity, there is one end appointed alike to all, fact goes the way of fiction, and what is known is no more perdurable than what is made. Not words nor works, but only that which is formless endures, the vitality that is another name for change, the breath that fills and shatters the bubbles of good and evil, of beauty and deformity, of truth and untruth.

No art is easy, least of all the art of letters. Apply the musical analogy once more to the instrument whereon literature performs its voluntaries. With a living keyboard of notes which are all incessantly changing in value, so that what rang true under Dr. Johnson's hand may sound flat or sharp now, with a range of a myriad strings, some falling mute and others being added from day to day, with numberless permutations and combinations, each of which alters the tone and pitch of the units that compose it, with fluid ideas that never have an outlined existence until they have found their phrases and the improvisation is complete, is it to be wondered at that the art of style is eternally elusive, and that the attempt to reduce it to rule is the forlorn hope of academic infatuation?

POLITICS AND THE ENGLISH LANGUAGE

George Orwell

Most people who bother with the matter at all would admit that the English language is in a bad way, but it is generally assumed that we cannot by conscious action do anything about it. Our civilization is decadent and our language—so the argument runs—must inevitably share in the general collapse. It follows that any struggle against the abuse of language is a sentimental archaism, like preferring candles to electric light or hansom cabs to aeroplanes. Underneath this lies the half-conscious belief that language is a natural growth and not an instrument which we shape for our own purposes.

Now, it is clear that the decline of a language must ultimately have political and economic causes: it is not due simply to the bad influence of this or that individual writer. But an effect can become a cause, reinforcing the original cause and producing the same effect in an intensified form, and so on indefinitely. A man may take to drink because he feels himself to be a failure, and then fail all the more completely because he drinks. It is rather the same thing that is happening to the English language. It becomes ugly and inaccurate because our thoughts are foolish, but the slovenliness of our language makes it easier for us to have foolish thoughts. The point is that the process is reversible. Modern English, especially written English, is full of bad habits which spread by imitation

From Shooting an Elephant and Other Essays *by George Orwell, copyright, 1945, 1946, 1949, 1950, by Sonia Brownell Orwell. Reprinted by permission of Harcourt, Brace & World, Inc., and Martin Secker & Warburg, Ltd.*

and which can be avoided if one is willing to take the necessary trouble. If one gets rid of these habits one can think more clearly, and to think clearly is a necessary first step towards political regeneration: so that the fight against bad English is not frivolous and is not the exclusive concern of professional writers. I will come back to this presently, and I hope that by that time the meaning of what I have said here will have become clearer. Meanwhile, here are five specimens of the English language as it is now habitually written.

These five passages have not been picked out because they are especially bad—I could have quoted far worse if I had chosen—but because they illustrate various of the mental vices from which we now suffer. They are a little below the average, but are fairly representative samples. I number them so that I can refer back to them when necessary:

(1) I am not, indeed, sure whether it is not true to say that the Milton who once seemed not unlike a seventeenth-century Shelley had not become, out of an experience ever more bitter in each year, more alien [*sic*] to the founder of that Jesuit sect which nothing could induce him to tolerate.

Professor Harold Laski, Essay in Freedom of Expression

(2) Above all, we cannot play ducks and drakes with a native battery of idioms which prescribes such egregious collocations of vocables as the Basic *put up with* for *tolerate* or *put at a loss* for *bewilder.*

Professor Lancelot Hogben, Interglossa

(3) On the one side we have the free personality: by definition it is not neurotic, for it has neither conflict nor dream. Its desires, such as they are, are transparent, for they are just what institutional approval keeps in the forefront of consciousness; another institutional pattern would alter their number and intensity; there is little in them that is natural, irreducible, or culturally dangerous. But *on the other side,* the social bond itself is nothing but the mutual reflection of these self-secure integrities. Recall the definition of love. Is not this the very picture of a small academic? Where is there a place in this hall of mirrors for either personality or fraternity?

Essay on psychology in Politics *(New York)*

(4) All the "best people" from the gentlemen's clubs, and all the frantic fascist captains, united in common hatred of Socialism and bestial horror of the rising tide of the mass revolutionary movement, have turned to acts of provocation, to foul incendiarism, to medieval legends of poisoned wells, to legalize their own destruction of proletarian organizations, and rouse the agitated petty-bourgeoisie to chauvinistic fervour on behalf of the fight against the revolutionary way out of the crisis.

Communist pamphlet

(5) If a new spirit *is* to be infused into this old country, there is one thorny and contentious reform which must be tackled, and that is the humanization and galvanization of the B.B.C. Timidity here will bespeak canker and atrophy of the soul. The heart of Britain may be sound and of strong beat, for instance, but the British lion's roar at present is like that of Bottom in Shakespeare's *Midsummer Night's Dream*—as gentle as any sucking dove. A virile new Britain cannot continue indefinitely to be traduced in the eyes or rather ears, of the world by the effete lauguors of Langham Place, brazenly masquerading as "standard English." When the Voice of Britain is heard at nine o'clock, better far and infinitely less ludicrous to hear aitches honestly dropped than the present priggish, inflated, inhibited, school-ma'amish arch braying of blameless bashful mewing maidens!

Letter in Tribune

Each of these passages has faults of its own, but, quite apart from avoidable ugliness, two qualities are common to all of them. The first is staleness of imagery: the other is lack of precision. The writer either has a meaning and cannot express it, or he inadvertently says something else, or he is almost indifferent as to whether his words mean anything or not. This mixture of vagueness and sheer incompetence is the most marked characteristic of modern English prose, and especially of any kind of political writing. As soon as certain topics are raised, the concrete melts into the abstract and no one seems able to think of turns of speech that are not hackneyed: prose consists less and less of *words* chosen for the sake of their meaning, and more and more of *phrases* tacked together like the sections of a prefabricated hen-house. I list below, with notes and examples, various of the tricks by means of which the work of prose-construction is habitually dodged:

Dying Metaphors. A newly invented metaphor assists thought by evoking a visual image, while on the other hand a metaphor which is technically "dead" e.g. (*iron resolution*) has in effect reverted to being an ordinary word and can generally be used without loss of vividness. But in between these two classes there is a huge dump of worn-out metaphors which have lost all evocative power and are merely used because they save people the trouble of inventing phrases for themselves. Examples are: *Ring the changes on, take up the cudgels for, toe the line, ride roughshod over, stand shoulder to shoulder with, play into the hands of, no axe to grind, grist to the mill, fishing in troubled waters, on the order of the day, Achilles' heel, swan song, hotbed.* Many of these are used without knowledge of their meaning (what is a "rift," for instance?), and incompatible metaphors are frequently mixed, a sure sign that the writer is not interested in what he is saying. Some metaphors now current have been twisted out of their original meaning without those who use them even being aware of the fact. For example, *toe the line* is sometimes written *tow the line*. Another example is *the hammer and the anvil*, now always used with the implication that the anvil gets the worst of it. In real life it is always the anvil that breaks the hammer, never the other way about: a writer who stopped to think what he was saying would be aware of this, and would avoid perverting the original phrase.

Operators or *verbal false limbs*. These save the trouble of picking out appropriate verbs and nouns, and at the same time pad each sentence with extra syllables which give it an appearance of symmetry. Characteristic phrases are: *render inoperative, militate against, make contact with, be subjected to, give rise to, give grounds for, have the effect of, play a leading part* (role) *in, make itself felt, take effect, exhibit a tendency to, serve the purpose of, etc., etc.* The keynote is the elimination of simple verbs. Instead of being a single word, such as *break, stop, spoil, mend, kill*, a verb becomes a *phrase*, made up of a noun or adjective tacked on to some general-purposes verb such as *prove, serve, form, play, render.* In addition, the passive voice is wherever possible used in preference to the active, and noun constructions are used instead of gerunds (*by examination of* instead of *by examining*). The range of verbs is further cut down by means of the *-ize* and *de-* formations, and the banal statements are given an appearance of profundity by means of the *not un-* formation. Simple conjunctions and prepositions are replaced by such phrases as *with respect to, having regard to, the fact that, by dint of, in view of, in the interests of, on the hypothesis that;* and the ends of sentences are saved from anticlimax by such resounding commonplaces as *greatly to be desired, cannot be left out of account, a development to be expected in the near future, deserving of serious consideration, brought to a satisfactory conclusion*, and so on and so forth.

Pretentious diction. Words like *phenomenon, element, individual* (as noun), *objective, categorical, effective, virtual, basic, primary, promote, constitute, exhibit, exploit, utilize, eliminate, liquidate*, are used to dress up simple statement and give an air of scientific impartiality to biased judgments. Adjectives like *epoch-making, epic, historic, unforgettable, triumphant, age-old, inevitable, inexorable, veritable*, are used to dignify the sordid processes of international politics, while writing that aims at glorifying war usually takes on an archaic colour, its characteristic words being: *realm, throne, chariot, mailed fist, trident, sword, shield, buckler, banner, jackboot, clarion.* Foreign words and expressions such as *cul de sac, ancien régime, deus ex machina, mutatis mutandis, status quo, gleichschaltung, weltanschauung*, are used to give an air of culture and elegance. Except for the useful abbreviations *i.e., e.g.,* and *etc.*, there is no real need for any of the hundreds of foreign phrases now current in English. Bad writers, and especially scientific, political and sociological writers, are nearly always haunted by the notion that Latin or Greek words are grander than Saxon ones, and unnecessary words like *expedite, ameliorate, predict, extraneous, deracinated, clandestine, subaqueous* and hundreds of others constantly gain ground from their Anglo-Saxon opposite numbers.[1] The jargon peculiar to Marxist writing (*hyena, hangman, cannibal, petty bourgeois, these gentry, lacquey, flunkey, mad dog, White Guard,* etc.) consists largely of words and phrases translated from Russian, German or French; but the normal way of coining a new word is to use a Latin or Greek root with the appropriate affix and, where necessary, the -ize formation. It is often easier to make up words of this kind (*deregionalize, impermissible, extramarital, non-fragmentatory* and so forth) than to think up the English words that will cover one's meaning. The result, in general, is an increase in slovenliness and vagueness.

Meaningless words. In certain kinds of writing, particularly in art criticism and literary criticism, it is normal to come across long passages which are almost completely lacking in meaning.[2] Words like *romantic, plastic, values, human, dead, sentimental, natural, vitality,* as used in art criticism, are strictly meaningless, in the sense that they not only do not point to any discoverable object, but are hardly ever expected to do so by the reader. When one critic writes, "The outstanding feature of Mr. X's work is its living quality," while another writes, "The immediately striking thing about Mr. X's work is its peculiar deadness," the reader accepts this as a simple difference of opinion. If words like *black* and *white* were involved, instead of the jargon words *dead* and *living,* he would see at once that language was being used in an improper way. Many political words are similarly abused. The word *Fascism* has now no meaning except in so far as it signifies "something not desirable." The words *democracy, socialism, freedom, patriotic, realistic, justice,* have each of them several different meanings which cannot be reconciled with one another. In the case of a word like *democracy,* not only is there no agreed definition, but the attempt to make one is resisted from all sides. It is almost universally felt that when we call a country democratic we are praising it: consequently the defenders of every kind of régime claim that

[1] An interesting illustration of this is the way in which the English flower names which were in use till very recently are being ousted by Greek ones, *snapdragon* becoming *antirrhinum, forget-me-not* becoming *myosotis,* etc. It is hard to see any practical reason for this change of fashion: it is probably due to an instinctive turning-away from the more homely word and a vague feeling that the Greek word is scientific.

[2] Example: "Comfort's catholicity of perception and image, strangely Whitmanesque in range, almost the exact opposite in aesthetic compulsion, continues to evoke that trembling atmospheric accumulative hinting at a cruel, an inexorably serene timelessness . . . Wrey Gardiner scores by aiming at simple bull's-eyes with precision. Only they are not so simple, and through this contented sadness runs more than the surface bitter-sweet of resignation." (*Poetry Quarterly.*)

it is a democracy, and fear that they might have to stop using the word if it were tied down to any one meaning. Words of this kind are often used in a consciously dishonest way. That is, the person who uses them has his own private definition, but allows his hearer to think he means something quite different. Statements like *Marshal Pétain was a true patriot, The Soviet Press is the freest in the world, The Catholic Church is opposed to persecution,* are almost always made with intent to deceive. Other words used in variable meanings, in most cases more or less dishonestly, are: *class, totalitarian, science, progressive, reactionary, bourgeois, equality.*

Now that I have made this catalogue of swindles and perversions, let me give another example of the kind of writing that they lead to. This time it must of its nature be an imaginary one. I am going to translate a passage of good English into modern English of the worst sort. Here is a well-known verse from *Ecclesiastes:*

"I returned and saw under the sun, that the race is not to the swift, nor the battle to the strong, neither yet bread to the wise, nor yet riches to men of understanding, nor yet favour to men of skill; but time and chance happeneth to them all."

Here it is in modern English:

"Objective consideration of contemporary phenomena compels the conclusion that success or failure in competitive activities exhibits no tendency to be commensurate with innate capacity, but that a considerable element of the unpredictable must invariably be taken into account."

This is a parody, but not a very gross one. Exhibit (3), above, for instance, contains several patches of the same kind of English. It will be seen that I have not made a full translation. The beginning and ending of the sentence follow the original meaning fairly closely, but in the middle the concrete illustrations—race, battle, bread—dissolve into the vague phrase "success or failure in competitive activities." This had to be so, because no modern writer of the kind I am discussing—no one capable of using phrases like "objective consideration of contemporary phenomena" —would ever tabulate his thoughts in that precise and detailed way. The whole tendency of modern prose is away from concreteness. Now analyse these two sentences a little more closely. The first contains forty-nine words but only sixty syllables, and all its words are those of everyday life. The second contains thirty-eight words of ninety syllables: eighteen of its words are from Latin roots, and one from Greek. The first sentence contains six vivid images, and only one phrase ("time and chance") that could be called vague. The second contains not a single fresh, arresting phrase, and in spite of its ninety syllables it gives only a shortened version of the meaning contained in the first. Yet without a doubt it is the second kind of sentence that is gaining ground in modern English. I do not want to exaggerate. This kind of writing is not yet universal, and outcrops of simplicity will occur here and there in the worst-written page. Still, if you or I were told to write a few lines on the uncertainty of human fortunes, we should probably come much nearer to my imaginary sentence than to the one from *Ecclesiastes.*

As I have tried to show, modern writing at its worst does not consist in picking out words for the sake of their meaning and inventing images in order to make the meaning clearer. It consists in gumming together long strips of words which have already been set in order by someone else, and making the results presentable by sheer humbug. The attraction of this way of writing is that it is easy. It is easier—even quicker, once you have the habit—to say *In my opinion it is a not unjustifiable assumption that* than to say *I think.* If you use ready-made phrases, you not only don't have to hunt about for words; you also don't have to bother with the rhythms of your sentences, since these phrases are generally so arranged as to be more or less euphonious. When you are composing in a hurry—when you are dictating to a stenographer, for instance, or making a public speech—it is natural to fall into a pretentious, Latinized style. Tags like *a consideration which we should do well to bear in mind* or *a conclusion to which all of us would readily assent* will save many a sentence from coming down with a bump. By using stale metaphors, similes and idioms, you save much mental effort, at the cost of leaving your meaning vague, not only for your reader but for yourself. This is the significance of mixed metaphors. The sole aim of a metaphor is to call up a visual image. When these images clash—as in *The Fascist octopus has sung its swan song, the jackboot is thrown into the melting pot*—it can be taken as certain that the writer is not seeing a mental image of the objects he is naming; in other words he is not really thinking. Look again at the examples I gave at the beginning of this essay. Professor Laski (1) uses five negatives in fifty-three words. One of these is superfluous, making nonsense of the whole passage, and in addition there is the slip *alien* for akin, making further nonsense, and several avoidable pieces of clumsiness which increase the general vagueness. Professor Hogben (2) plays ducks and drakes with a battery which is able to write prescriptions, and, while disapproving of the everyday phrase *put up with,* is unwilling to look *egregious* up in the dictionary and see what it means. (3), if one takes an uncharitable attitude towards it, is simply meaningless: probably one could work out its intended meaning by reading the whole of the article in which it occurs. In (4), the writer knows more or less what he wants to say, but an accumulation of stale phrases chokes him like tea leaves blocking a sink. In (5), words and meaning have almost parted company. People who write in this manner usually have a general emotional meaning—they dislike one thing and want to express solidarity with another—

but they are not interested in the detail of what they are saying. A scrupulous writer, in every sentence that he writes, will ask himself at least four questions, thus: What am I trying to say? What words will express it? What image or idiom will make it clearer? Is this image fresh enough to have an effect? And he will probably ask himself two more: Could I put it more shortly? Have I said anything that is avoidably ugly? But you are not obliged to go to all this trouble. You can shirk it by simply throwing your mind open and letting the ready-made phrases come crowding in. They will construct your sentences for you—even think your thoughts for you, to a certain extent—and at need they will perform the important service of partially concealing your meaning even from yourself. It is at this point that the special connection between politics and the debasement of language becomes clear.

In our time it is broadly true that political writing is bad writing. Where it is not true, it will generally be found that the writer is some kind of rebel, expressing his private opinions and not a "party line." Orthodoxy, of whatever colour, seems to demand a lifeless, imitative style. The political dialects to be found in pamphlets, leading articles, manifestos, White Papers and the speeches of under-secretaries do, of course, vary from party to party, but they are all alike in that one almost never finds in them a fresh, vivid, home-made turn of speech. When one watches some tired hack on the platform mechanically repeating the familiar phrases—*bestial atrocities, iron heel, bloodstained tyranny, free peoples of the world, stand shoulder to shoulder*—one often has a curious feeling that one is not watching a live human being but some kind of dummy: a feeling which suddenly becomes stronger at moments when the light catches the speaker's spectacles and turns them into blank discs which seem to have no eyes behind them. And this is not altogether fanciful. A speaker who uses that kind of phraseology has gone some distance towards turning himself into a machine. The appropriate noises are coming out of his larynx, but his brain is not involved as it would be if he were choosing his words for himself. If the speech he is making is one that he is accustomed to make over and over again, he may be almost unconscious of what he is saying, as one is when one utters the responses in church. And this reduced state of consciousness, if not indispensable, is at any rate favourable to political conformity.

In our time, political speech and writing are largely the defense of the indefensible. Things like the continuance of British rule in India, the Russian purges and deportations, the dropping of the atom bombs on Japan, can indeed be defended, but only by arguments which are too brutal for most people to face, and which do not square with the professed aims of political parties. Thus political language has to consist largely of euphemism, question-begging and sheer cloudy vagueness. Defenseless villages are bombarded from the air, the inhabitants driven out into the countryside, the cattle machine-gunned, the huts set on fire with incendiary bullets: this is called *pacification*. Millions of peasants are robbed of their farms and sent trudging along the roads with no more than they can carry: this is called *transfer of population* or *rectification of frontiers*. People are imprisoned for years without trial, or shot in the back of the neck or sent to die of scurvy in Arctic lumber camps: this is called *elimination of unreliable elements*. Such phraseology is needed if one wants to name things without calling up mental pictures of them. Consider for instance some comfortable English professor defending Russian totalitarianism. He cannot say outright, "I believe in killing off your opponents when you can get good results by doing so," Probably, therefore, he will say something like this:

"While freely conceding that the Soviet régime exhibits certain features which the humanitarian may be inclined to deplore, we must, I think, agree that a certain curtailment of the right to political opposition is an unavoidable concomitant of transitional periods, and that the rigours which the Russian people have been called upon to undergo have been amply justified in the sphere of concrete achievement."

The inflated style is itself a kind of euphemism. A mass of Latin words falls upon the facts like soft snow, blurring the outlines and covering up all the details. The great enemy of clear language is insincerity. When there is a gap between one's real and one's declared aims, one turns as it were instinctively to long words and exhausted idioms, like a cuttlefish squirting out ink. In our age there is no such thing as "keeping out of politics." All issues are political issues, and politics itself is a mass of lies, evasions, folly, hatred and schizophrenia. When the general atmosphere is bad, language must suffer. I should expect to find—this is a guess which I have not sufficient knowledge to verify—that the German, Russian and Italian languages have all deteriorated in the last ten or fifteen years, as a result of dictatorship.

But if thought corrupts language, language can also corrupt thought. A bad usage can spread by tradition and imitation, even among people who should and do know better. The debased language that I have been discussing is in some ways very convenient. Phrases like *a not unjustifiable assumption, leaves much to be desired, would serve no good purpose, a consideration which we should do well to bear in mind,* are a continuous temptation, a packet of aspirins always at one's elbow. Look back through this essay, and for certain you will find that I have again and again committed the very faults I am protesting against. By this morning's post I have received a pamphlet dealing with conditions in Germany. The author tells me that he "felt impelled" to write it. I open it at random, and here is almost the first sentence that I see: "(The Allies) have an opportunity not only of achieving a radical transformation of Germany's social and political structure in such a way as to avoid a nationalistic reaction in Germany itself, but at the same time of laying the foundations of a cooperative and unified Europe." You see, he "feels impelled" to write—feels, presumably, that he has something new to say—and yet his words, like cavalry horses answering the bugle, group themselves automatically into the familiar dreary pattern. This invasion of one's mind by ready-made phrases (*lay the foundations, achieve a radical transformation*) can only be prevented if one is constantly on guard against them, and every such phrase anaesthetizes a portion of one's brain.

I said earlier that the decadence of our language is probably curable. Those who deny this would argue, if they produced an argument at all, that language merely reflects existing social conditions, and that we cannot influence its development by any direct tinkering with words and constructions. So far as the general tone or spirit of a language goes, this may be true, but it is not true in detail. Silly words and expressions have often disappeared, not through any evolutionary process but owing to the conscious action of a minority. Two recent examples were *explore every avenue* and *leave no stone unturned,* which were killed by the jeers of a few journalists. There is a long list of flyblown metaphors which could similarly be got rid of if enough people would interest themselves in the job; and it should also be possible to laugh the *not un-* formation out of existence,[3] to reduce the amount of Latin and Greek in the average sentence, to drive out foreign phrases and strayed scientific words, and, in general, to make pretentiousness unfashionable. But all these are minor points. The defense of the English language implies more than this, and perhaps it is best to start by saying what it does *not* imply.

To begin with it has nothing to do with archaism, with the salvaging of obsolete words and turns of speech, or with the setting up of a "standard English" which must never be departed from. On the contrary, it is especially concerned with the scrapping of every word or idiom which has outworn its usefulness. It has nothing to do with correct grammar and syntax, which are of no importance so long as one makes one's meaning clear, or with the avoidance of Americanisms, or with having what is called a "good prose style." On the other hand it is not concerned with fake simplicity and the attempt to make written English colloquial. Nor does it even imply in every case preferring the Saxon word to the Latin one, though it does imply using the fewest and shortest words that will cover one's meaning. What is above all needed is to let the meaning choose the word, and not the other way about. In prose, the worst thing one can do with words is to surrender to them. When you think of a

---

[3] One can cure oneself of the *not un-* formation by memorizing this sentence: *A not unblack dog was chasing a not unsmall rabbit across a not ungreen field.*

concrete object, you think wordlessly, and then, if you want to describe the thing you have been visualizing you probably hunt about till you find the exact words that seem to fit it. When you think of something abstract you are more inclined to use words from the start, and unless you make a conscious effort to prevent it, the existing dialect will come rushing in and do the job for you, at the expense of blurring or even changing your meaning. Probably it is better to put off using words as long as possible and get one's meaning as clear as one can through pictures or sensations. Afterwards one can choose—not simply *accept*—the phrases that will best cover the meaning, and then switch round and decide what impression one's words are likely to make on another person. This last effort of the mind cuts out all stale or mixed images, all prefabricated phrases, needless repetitions, and humbug and vagueness generally. But one can often be in doubt about the effect of a word or a phrase, and one needs rules that one can rely on when instinct fails. I think the following rules will cover most cases:

(i) *Never use a metaphor, simile or other figure of speech which you are used to seeing in print.*

(ii) *Never use a long word where a short one will do.*

(iii) *If it is possible to cut a word out, always cut it out.*

(iv) *Never use the passive where you can use the active.*

(v) *Never use a foreign phrase, a scientific word or a jargon word if you can think of an everyday English equivalent.*

(vi) *Break any of these rules sooner than say anything outright barbarous.*

These rules sound elementary, and so they are, but they demand a deep change of atttude in anyone who has grown used to writing in the style now fashionable. One could keep all of them and still write bad English, but one could not write the kind of stuff that I quoted in those five specimens at the beginning of this article.

I have not here been considering the literary use of language, but merely language as an instrument for expressing and not for concealing or preventing thought. Stuart Chase and others have come near to claiming that all abstract words are meaningless, and have used this as a pretext for advocating a kind of political quietism. Since you don't know what Fascism is, how can you struggle against Fascism? One need not swallow such absurdities as this, but one ought to recognize that the present political chaos is connected with the decay of language, and that one can probably bring about some improvement by starting at the verbal end. If you simplify your English, you are freed from the worst follies of orthodoxy. You cannot speak any of the necessary dialects, and when you make a stupid remark its stupidity will be obvious, even to yourself. Political language—and with variations this is true of all political parties, from Conservatives to Anarchists—is designed to make lies sound truthful and murder respectable, and to give an appearance of solidity to pure wind. One cannot change this all in a moment, but one can at least change one's own habits, and from time to time one can even, if one jeers loudly enough, send some worn-out and useless phrase—some *jack-boot, Achilles' heel, hotbed, melting pot, acid test, veritable inferno* or other lump of verbal refuse—into the dustbin where it belongs.

LOOKING AT ENGLISH IN USE

Randolph Quirk

We have seen something of what is involved in grammatical and lexical distinctions. Let us now look at the way distinctions of these kinds actually manifest themselves in the English we are liable to come upon any day within a single linguistic community, inspecting varieties of English with a somewhat different focus.

Rather more than a century ago, Thomas Wade started off on the road to becoming one of the outstanding Chinese scholars of his time. He sought out the best-qualified man he could find and said, 'Please teach me Chinese'. We may imagine his dismay at the reply: 'Which Chinese is it you want to learn, Sir? There is the Chinese of the ancient Classics, the Chinese of official documents, the Chinese used in writing letters, and there is the spoken Chinese, of which there are many dialects. Now which Chinese is it that you want to learn?'

Now, of course, Chinese is a notoriously extreme case, but as we have seen, the situation with English is certainly analogous. We are all aware of the distinctiveness of the regional dialects, but we less generally acknowledge the comparable distinctiveness—both in spoken and written English—of other kinds of 'dialect' which are comparably self-consistent and (with a different concept of speech 'community') comparably justified. The incomplete recognition of these makes us too liable to join in the intolerant and ill-informed tirades upon jargon—a wholly pejorative word

From The Uses of English *by Randolph Quirk. Used by permission of St. Martin's Press and Longmans, Green & Co., Ltd.*

often applied to a perfectly respectable 'trade dialect' which has its own rules and the users of which have their own rights. We become susceptible also to the great deal of nonsense which is written about incorrectness and impropriety of expression, insisting mistakenly that a given form is either 'correct' or 'incorrect' in all styles and circumstances.

We have seen that the word 'English'—like 'Chinese'—is an abstraction, conveniently summarising a wide range of different, partly self-contained forms of communication. Only the individual forms themselves have an 'actual existence' as English, but they all have enough in common to justify the application of the generic term 'English' to all of them. One may compare the word 'dog'. Everyone can tell the difference between a dog and a cat, but there is an immense range of animals which share the designation 'dog', and one cannot point to one dog that has all the features present in all dogs: there is no actual embodiment of 'dogginess'. Nor can we say (if the analogy may be pressed a little further) that one dog is 'doggier' than another: a feature that is 'correct' in one variety of dog is 'incorrect' in another.

So it is with English, and in Chapter 6[1] we attempted to show something of the total range of English, and singled out from that range some features and forms which we said could be called 'Standard English'. The object now is to look at the corresponding range that exists within educated usage itself and especially at the forms of English that characterise the various *uses* of Standard English. No attempt can be made, however, to discuss *all* the varieties even within this relatively narrow band which is loosely called 'Standard'. But it is worth emphasising that the few, very distinctive varieties exemplified in this chapter could easily have come from the lips and pens of people who, for ordinary purposes, would seem to be using as uniform a type of English as it is possible to find. The distinctive features revealed are no less real for that, and may be all the more noteworthy.

Let us consider first an example of religious English, written within the past few years:

1. Eternal God, Who dost call all men into unity with Thy Son, Jesus Christ our Lord, we pray Thee to pour Thy spirit upon the students of all nations, that they may consecrate themselves to Thy service; that being joined together by their common faith and obedience, they may come more perfectly to love and understand one another, that the world may know that Thou didst send Thy Son to be the Saviour and the Lord of all men; through the same Jesus Christ our Lord Who with Thee and the Holy Spirit liveth and reigneth one God world without

[1] Not reprinted here.

end. Amen. (Prayer published for the Universal Day of Prayer for Students, 15 February 1953.)

Even the opening two words embody a construction which is almost entirely restricted to religious usage—adjective plus noun in direct address. One may compare the epistolary formula, 'Dear (Sir)', and beyond that there is little except some colloquial expressions like 'old man'. We notice that in religious English the noun in direct address may be post-modified by a relative clause, a feature which is a common and living one in this kind of English but virtually unknown outside it.

Perhaps the most obvious characteristic is the use of the distinctive second person pronoun and the equally distinctive second and third person singular verb forms. What is more, the pronoun has separate subject and object forms, a feature absent from the usual second person pronoun: something more is involved than a straightforward one-for-one correspondence such as we find between *lives* and *liveth; you* corresponds to *thou* or *thee* according to rules which do not affect *you.* Such special pronoun and verb forms are all but absent from other varieties of Standard English, though some continue to crop up in poetry from time to time. And some, of course, continue to flourish in several regional dialects. Of them all perhaps the third person inflexion in *-eth* is the most restricted. Nearly two hundred years ago, the grammarian John Ash tells us that the termination is 'used in the *grave* and *formal* Style; but *s* . . . in the *free* and *familiar Style'.* From this time there has been a severe limiting of the functions grave enough to require the *-eth* forms and a corresponding extension of the occasions on which *-s* would not sound too flippant. Even today, however, the special pronoun and verb forms are not merely optional in religious usage; if we were to repeat the last part of the prayer, replacing *Thee* by *You,* and *liveth and reigneth* by *lives and reigns,* it would sound to most people intolerably impertinent and irreverent, perhaps even profane. It is a matter of common observation that forms which are thoroughly to be expected in one variety of English give us a sensation of shock when they are introduced into a variety in which they are not expected.

There are several other features that one might mention even in this short passage. There is the special use of *through* in 'through . . . Jesus Christ' which we nevertheless accept so readily in religious discourse. And there are lexical words which, if not actually confined to religious use (*saviour, consecrate, amen*), are used in other kinds of English chiefly when it is desirable to convey the echo or suggestion of devotion, piety, or high seriousness. But we must turn our attention to other varieties.

The English of laws and regulations is an easy butt, and passages like the following can be cited as almost beyond the reach of ridicule and derision:

> 2. In the Nuts (Unground) (Other than Groundnuts) Order, the expression nuts shall have reference to such nuts, other than groundnuts, as would, but for this Amending Order, not qualify as nuts (Unground) (Other than Groundnuts) by reason of their being nuts (Unground). (Quoted in the *Daily Telegraph,* 3 April 1956.)

Yet even this style of writing has its justification undiminished by the fact that some specimens of writing in this style may be bad or unnecessarily clumsy. Any of us with the smallest experience of drawing up regulations even for a small society or club must find it easy to sympathize with the lawyer.

Contrary to popular belief, there are few lawyers who contrive obscurity to make a mystery of their profession: they regret it, as much as we, that a contract is difficult to understand—and indeed impossible if it is heard instead of being studied visually. The sad fact is that regulations and deeds have to be drawn up with one's eye steadily on the potential cheat, not on the majority of us who merely want to know as simply as possible what our liabilities or rights are. To this extent, the style of legal English, too, then, is obligatory and not optional. As the late Lord Justice Birkett has said (*The Magic of Words,* English Association, 1955), 'the lawyer . . . must resolutely eschew the words that have colour, and content himself with the "hereinbefores" and "aforesaids" in order to achieve precision'. He does not actively wish to write obscurely, nor does he wish to omit the commas which would make his document so much easier to read. But he knows that commas are the easiest thing for a dishonest person to introduce and that dishonestly introduced commas are an easy way to make apparent changes in grammatical constructions, and so it is a protection to have none at all—thus making it obvious that any subsequently discovered must have been unauthorised alterations. It follows that the more he can weave the stipulations into unbroken chains of grammatical constructions, the less possibility again there is of deliberate misinterpretation of fraudulent manipulation. Here is an example of legal English:

> 3. Whereas the Insured described in the Schedule has by the proposal the date of which is specified in the Schedule which proposal and declaration the Insured has agreed shall be the basis of this Contract and be held as incorporated herein applied to The —— Assurance Company Limited (hereinafter called 'the Company') for insurance against the

contingencies hereinafter specified Now this Policy witnesseth that in consideration of the Insured paying to the Company for this Insurance the First Premium specified in the Schedule the Company hereby agrees (subject to the conditions contained herein or endorsed or otherwise expressed hereon which conditions shall so far as the nature of them respectively will permit be deemed to be conditions precedent to the right of the Insured to recover hereunder) that in the event of any of the said contingencies happening. . . . (Preamble to a current Insurance Policy.)

The suffixed prepositions (as in *hereunder*) are well in evidence, and we see a good deal of the 'continuous chain' type of grammatical expression that has also been mentioned. Both are in fact long-standing characteristics of legal expression. In the eighteenth century, Robert Lowth writes of the suffixed preposition as being a feature of the 'complicated periods' which 'are so curiously strung, or hook'd on, one to another, after the long-spun manner of the bar'. What Lowth calls the 'hook'd on' manner can be seen in the compound reference expressions like 'which conditions' and 'the said contingencies', both making the reference back more precise and unambiguous (if clumsier) than an ordinary relative clause in the first case or an article without 'said' in the second.

The fact that we still have these characteristics which Lowth noticed shows that legal language is very traditional. It is also, of course, formulaic. Thus *witnesseth* in this passage does not indicate a general use of *-eth* forms as in religious English (*agrees* also occurs in the passage); the archaic *witnesseth* stands in a set piece (additionally marked typographically in the original) dividing the preamble from the main undertaking. The way in which such a fixed formula can stand apart from ordinary linguistic structure reminds us of similar phenomena in (for example) proverbs.

The language of officialdom, which has some affinities with that of the Law, is worth a separate mention, though its features have been the object of much widely read criticism in the past thirty years, from the Fowlers to Sir Alan Herbert and Sir Ernest Gowers. One characteristic is the use of words and phrases that we condemn with the value-judgment 'pompous'. This generally means that words have been chosen which have as little popular echo as possible, since the composing official is afraid— and often with good reason—of being accused by superiors or the public of lacking a proper command of 'dignified', remote, impersonal English. The story is told of how Canning included the phrase 'He died poor' in the text of a monument to Pitt; an official was scandalised by this, feeling that it was grossly deficient in dignity, and he proposed instead of Canning's words, 'He expired in indigent circumstances.' Smile as we may, we must all have felt similar pressures and inhibitions at some time, even in drafting something simple to put up on a notice-board. Official English has become a little less obtrusive in recent years, and here is a typical example of it:

4. The symbol † against a subscriber's entry in the Directory denotes that the telephone number is withheld from publication at the subscriber's request and the Post Office is not authorised to supply it to enquirers. The names and addresses of such subscribers are, however, shown in the Directory in cases where frequent enquiries are received by the Post Office for the exchange number, with a view to saving members of the public the trouble of fruitless enquiry. (*London Telephone Directory*, 1955.)

Even here, we may note the phrases 'in cases where' (reminding us of Quiller-Couch's devastating criticism) and 'with a view to', not to mention the rather formidable 'authorised'. We notice also the impersonal style: the writer did not put 'We show the names and addresses', as he might have *said* if he had been explaining the system to an inquirer orally, but 'The names and addresses . . . are . . . shown'. Such a use of the passive (and it occurs a little earlier, too, in 'the . . . number is withheld') was attacked not long ago in a speech at Nottingham, which was reported in *The Guardian* beneath the headline, 'Too Much of the Passive Voice in Local Government' (4 September 1956). The speaker, Mr. Derek Senior, had said: 'Half the dilatoriness, the passing of the bucks, the shirking of responsibility, the lazymindedness, and the want of initiative . . . could be eradicated overnight by the simple expedient of forbidding the use of the passive voice in any official document.' This is no doubt a little optimistic, but we can see what is in Mr. Senior's mind.

There are similarities to both legal and official usage in the English of industry and commerce, but here we run deeply into the much-discussed, much-misunderstood question of 'jargon'. Let us take the following passage:

5. The programme has included the replacement of existing coke ovens, a new material handling terminal, a sinter plant, the redesign and enlargement of the Company's eight fixed open hearth steel melting furnaces, the installation of two Bessemer converters and a mixer and blower to raise the potential of the melting shop, the installation of a combined slabbing, blooming and continuous billet mill and construction of a new basic refractory brick works at Jarrow.

The five per cent. redeemable Debenture Stock 1975/85 was created by resolution of the Directors and will be constituted and secured by a trust deed charging the undertaking and all the property and assets of the Company present and future (including any uncalled capital) by way of a first floating charge. The stock will be redeemable by a cumulative sinking fund calculated to redeem by annual operation not less than half of the stock at par by 30th September, 1985. (Public Notice of the Consett Iron and Steel Company, December 1955.)

At 'melting shops' and 'floating charges' and 'sinking funds' many may throw up well-bred hands in horror, but though this be jargon, yet there is method in it. Indeed, since the word 'jargon' carries such overtones of disapproval, it would be best to reserve it for recurrent slipshod pomposities as distinct from technical expressions like 'sinter plant' which are admirably clear to those who understand these things, and which are therefore completely legitimate. One frequently hears writing like this condemned because it is incomprehensible, but criticism on this score is often grossly unjust: if we do not understand the *processes* of a given context of activity and situation, we cannot expect to understand the labels for those processes, however they are 'addressed', so to speak. Replacing the terms *sinter plant* or *sinking fund* by something comprehensible to all would involve replacing them with manuals of instruction in metallurgy and finance respectively!

We find the same problem with modern scientific usage, which is particularly fertile in producing expressions totally obscure to the general public:

6. Neuraminic acid in the form of its alkali-stable methoxy derivative was first isolated by Klenk from gangliosides and more recently from bovine sub-maxillary gland mucin and from a urine muco-protein, its composition being $C_{11}H_{21}NO_9$ or perhaps $C_{10}H_{19}NO_8$. This substance has no reducing power, but is ninhydrin-positive. Sialic acid and the methoxy derivative of neuraminic acid are characterised by the purple colour they give on heating with Ehrlich's *p*-dimethylaminobenzaldehyde reagent even without alkali pretreatment (direct Ehrlich reaction), by the violet colour they produce on treatment with Bial's orcinel reagent and by the considerable humin formation on heating with dilute mineral acid . . . Neuraminic acid may be regarded as an aldol type of condensation product of 2-amino-2-deoxy-hexose with pyruvic acid, the aldol type of linkage rendering recovery of the amino sugar by acid treatment impossible. (Letter in *Nature,* November 1955.)

But quite apart from the *lexical* problems confronting us in these industrial and scientific passages, there is a prominent *grammatical* feature that has been subjected to a good deal of criticism. Thus, in place of what we find in passage 5, 'eight fixed open hearth steel melting furnaces', many critics of this style would prefer to see something like 'eight furnaces, of a fixed type with open hearth, for the melting of steel'. Similarly in place of 'bovine submaxillary gland mucin' in passage 6 they would prefer a rephrasing to 'mucin from the sub-maxillary gland of cattle'. In terms of grammatical description, they would in other words prefer to see more 'postmodified nominal groups' and fewer of the heavily 'premodified' ones.

Premodification was roundly condemned by Dr. John Baker, of Oxford (himself a scientist), in the number of *Nature* from which passage 6 was taken. As a matter of taste, of course, it must remain an open question, though obviously protagonists of the style will rightly advance its brevity on the credit side. But Dr. Baker's objection seems to derive its vigour from his conviction that the habit of premodification is reaching Britain from the United States, where in turn it springs from the usage of the many German-born scientists now working in American laboratories. This seems rather dubious, since the premodification of nouns by nouns was a common feature of English before Germans studied science or America was discovered. Heavy modifications in this manner are very frequent in the most commonplace and least scientific English. We not only have 'refreshment room' and 'railway station' but also 'railway station refreshment room', which few would prefer to see broken down into 'room for refreshments at the station of that special kind of way which consists of rails'.

Of course, we should always do well to remember that the excessive use of any stylistic device, be it never so genuinely native and natural, can become a serious source of irritation. Some of the varieties of English used in journalism bear this out only too well. In the last resort, the determiners of any linguistic form are mainly habit and fashion, however much we may like to believe there is some useful purpose justifying it. Probably, therefore, it is to these two that outstanding peculiarities in journalistic writing owe their persistence rather than to the demands of brevity and other factors sometimes offered as excuses. One such peculiarity is a piling up of adjectives and relative clauses, even though the information so conveyed is frequently not properly relevant to the rest of the sentence. Consider the following:

7. . . . this dark, slimly built young chemistry student from New South Wales is England-bound next April. A Sydney colleague tells me that the modest, 17-year-old Craig—who celebrated his recent double century against the South Africans by week-ending at his local Youth Club camp —is considered a certainty for the England tour. Craig, who has been handling a bat since he was eight, celebrated his entry into first-class

cricket with a streamlined 91 against South Australia at the belligerent age of 16. His tally to date is 654 runs in 13 first-class innings—twice not out. Complementary to his cricket, Craig was planning to have started a pharmacy course at Sydney University next March. (*Evening Standard*, January 1953.)

Apparently, the Sydney colleague did not say simply that 'Craig is considered a certainty for the England tour' but that *'the modest 17-year-old* Craig is considered a certainty for the England tour', which surely very few people would in fact be heard saying. And in the middle, the writer has interposed (presumably from other sources) the lengthy relative clause about 'week-ending' at the camp, which neither helps to identify Craig nor concerns the certainty of his 'England tour'. Craig's age, of course, is fair material here, but often age and other 'personal angles' dominate a journalistic sentence with less justification. Take the following, for example:

8. Mr. John William Allaway, a 46-year-old plumber, his wife, Florence, aged 32, and their 15-year-old son, John, escaped unhurt in their nightclothes after fire broke out at their 200-year-old home, Rose Hill Cottage at Gallows Hill, King's Langley, Herts. (*Ibid.*)

Notice first the special journalistic function of the indefinite article—'a 46-year-old plumber': it conveys the information that Mr. Allaway has not been in the news before (otherwise he would be 'the well-known 46-year-old plumber' or at any rate *the* something). It is the more noteworthy, therefore, that in this single sentence about a man we have not heard of, we are given not only *his* age but also that of his house and of its every occupant.

Now, this heavy modification of nouns leads to another fairly widespread feature in journalese. In the *Daily Mail,* July 1958, we find: 'Her 35-year-old Etonian husband, grandson of a millionaire steelmaster, said . . .' Here is a rhythm which is atypical in English structure, the heavy qualification of the subject (normally the first noun) of a sentence; in general, the English balance is found by making such heavy modifications to a noun after the main verb (normally the object or complement). And so there develops a tendency to inversion, illustrated in the same column, same 'story', in the *Daily Mail;* a paragraph begins: "Said the new owner, 31-year-old Mrs. Sheena Simmons, wife of a retired auctioneer from Bourne End . . .' We may compare the following piece from the *Daily Express,* August 1958: 'Presiding at the victims' funeral service will be rugged Army chaplain Captain Robin Roe, ex-Ireland international Rugby player, who was one of the first on the scene of the disaster.'

The stylistic traits shown here are widely current in an extreme form in some American journalistic writing, particularly that associated with *Time*. They were amusingly pilloried as long ago as 1937 by the late Wolcott Gibbs in *A Bed of Neuroses;* his by no means unfair parody includes the following:

> Sad-eyed last month was nimble, middle-sized *Life*-President Clair Maxwell as he told newshawks of the sale of the 53-year-old gagmag to *Time*. . . . Behind this latest, most incomprehensible Timenterprise looms, as usual, ambitious, gimleteyed, Baby Tycoon Henry Robinson Luce. . . . Once to interviewer who said, 'I hope I'm not disturbing you,' snapped Luce, 'Well, you are.'

Here we see how writers in this style have reconciled a passion for piling adjectives on to the subject of a sentence with the English rhythmic pattern which requires heavily modified nouns to follow the verb; it has been done by reversing the normal English word-order with such results as 'Presiding . . . will be rugged Army chaplain Captain Robin Roe' and 'Sad-eyed last month was nimble, middle-sized *Life*-President Clair Maxwell'.

Not all writing in journalism is 'journalistic' in the sense that it necessarily embodies features found in the passages quoted here. That is to say, we define the features of this style only on positive grounds: they characterise journalistic writing in that they rarely occur outside it. A corresponding caveat is equally required when we come to consider 'literary' English; there are many varieties and degrees of 'literariness' and much good literature has been written which has few features that one can label 'literary'. But this does not mean that a category labelled 'literary' is unreal; when we say of a person that his conversation has a literary flavour, it means something; there are linguistic features which, although not having of necessity to be used in literary writing, are fairly rare in other kinds of usage. Let us consider the three following passages in this connexion:

> 9. It has given me pain to have to relate this incident. To suppress it indefinitely would be impossible. Besides, the Australian people have a right to know what happened and why. On the other hand, it must be remembered that, apart from the limitations of their rigid party system, the Australian Governments had little reason to feel confidence at this time in British direction of the war, and that the risks their troops had run when the Desert Flank was broken, and also in the Greek campaign, weighed heavily upon them. (W. S. Churchill, *The Alliance*, 1950.)

10. That a great many people in this country are but dimly aware of what the banishment of the artist has cost them is certainly true. The tidal wave of ugliness has swept away all but a few of the older, finer things which provided a salutary comparison.

Nor have many manufacturers perceived that the artist-craftsman of yesterday, who has been put out of business by their machines, might at least be replaced by the industrial designer of today, who could show them how to bring seemliness and beauty into the products of the machine. (Gordon Russell, in *The Observer*, February 1953.)

11. Although the power to communicate with others is no longer regarded as a characteristically human achievement, for which no other animal possesses the capacity, the habit of speaking in different languages is peculiar to Man. Thus there has arisen a situation which is biologically unique—the existence of a species in which some individuals are unable to understand the words and meanings of some other individuals. (T. Savory, *The Art of Translation*, 1957.)

If one had to say in three words how these passages differed from the varieties previously discussed, one might reasonably choose 'precision with elegance'. The writer seeks the *mot juste* from a fairly large vocabulary and embeds it in an elegant pattern of word-order and clause interrelationship. Thus in the second paragraph of the Russell passage, one recognises the precision of *perceived* (a word uncommon except in 'literary' usage) and the elegant network in which it appears; this opens with an inversion preceded by *nor* (again, a literary connective when used after positive statements) and proceeds to a pretty balance of 'yesterday' plus relative clause against 'today' plus relative clause.

Some other features in these passages which have a literary flavour may be mentioned briefly. As already stated, the typical and unremarkable English utterance has a light subject followed by the verb with the heavily modified parts then following; this pattern applies also to the disposition of subordinate clauses: they generally follow a part of the sentence which can be seen as in some way nuclear, thus conforming with the broad underlying pattern of having the main fabric of a structure take shape before the qualifications are added. The opening of the Savory passage illustrates how differently this matter can be treated in literary English: a concessive clause and a relative clause (one of an uncolloquial type) precede the nuclear part which even so begins with a 'heavy' subject. The second sentence of the Churchill passage and the first of the Russell one have as subjects an infinitive phrase and a noun clause respectively; in spoken English, both would probably have had 'it' as the subject ('It would be impossible . . .' and 'It is certainly true . . .'). Churchill's last sentence has a noun clause interrupted by a lengthy parenthetic phrase, and a parallel noun clause whose subject is followed by a relative clause, a temporal clause and a parenthetic phrase before the verb, reserved in the majestic Ciceronian manner, makes its appearance.

Although in the criticism of a piece of literary English one may sometimes have occasion to draw attention to the flavours of religious, journalistic, scientific, or even legal style which the author has introduced, it is more usual to find oneself weighing the style against that of *colloquial* usage: 'literary' chiefly operates in contrast with 'colloquial'. Let us therefore turn to the features which characterise conversational usage, and consider first of all the following passage:

> 12. I often pop an odd paper in here. Do look at this! A bell-ringer's outing to Skegness, before the war, in one of those charabancs with a hood and, I should think by the look of our hair, no mica side curtains that buttoned and split half your nails! Would you remember those, dear? This is the most likely spot in the house. I know I put the recipe in just such a hidey-hole. The bicarb goes in with the warm milk. Take a look at that! Got up by a crank uncle of mine. He had eccentric ideas on breathing. One long in, and two short out, I think he advocated, or am I thinking of Morse? (*Punch,* February 1953.)

At once one notices words which would not appear in a prayer or a law or in Mr. Savory's book on translation: 'pop', 'hidey-hole', 'bicarb'. And there is colloquial syntax too: an expanded form of the imperative with *do* ('Do look at this'), the indefinite *you* ('split half your nails'), the special use of *would* ('Would you remember those, dear?'). A noun clause introduced without *that* ('I know I put') is also usually colloquial; compare Churchill's 'it must be remembered *that*' and Russell's 'perceived *that*'. Two verb expressions may also be mentioned as commoner in colloquial than in other varieties of English. The first is the 'phrasal verb', as it is usually called, illustrated in *'Got up* by a crank uncle'; one may compare 'put up with' meaning 'tolerate' and 'take in' meaning 'deceive'. Secondly, there is the feature illustrated by 'Take a look at that'—in other words, the use of a copula-type verb plus noun in place of a fully 'lexical' verb; other common examples are 'have a swim' for *swim,* 'have a smoke', 'have a try', 'take a bath'. It may be recalled that one of the outstanding characteristics of the late C. K. Ogden's system of Basic English is the replacement of practically all our verbs by nouns preceded by one of a small number of 'operators': instead of 'a war to end war', Basic has 'a war to put an end to war'.

But the piece of spoken English quoted above was never spoken: it is a writer's imaginative attempt to capture the style of spoken English, and although it captures certain aspects of that style very well, one must not leave the impression that spoken English is typically and only this. The writer here is using literary conventions (punctuation marks, for instance) to convey one type of frivolous talk, and the conventions of writing cannot express such features as intonation, stress, tempo and rhythm which belong specifically to *speech*. Moreover, a great deal of spoken English is concerned with topics as serious as those which occupy the writers of 'literary' English. In the following passage, we have a transcript of a piece of serious conversation, recorded from life. The dashes indicate pauses; 'er' and 'um' give conventional expression to voiced pauses:

13. You see um the the um the chief lecturer there is is er um—he is the main lecturer though really he has one or two subordinates but he is the—he gives the lectures the main lectures—there are seminars as well and discussions following upon those but the main lectures are given by him—and he tries—to maintain—um a balance I mean he talks so far he's talked about I missed the last one um unfortunately but he's talked—er and given various sides he's given what he called the er the religious—um aspects of philosophy those who have—a religious point of view who believe in values you know er existing outside the human community—and then what he calls—the—the the secular point of view or the transsecular I think oh no secular point of view—opposed to the transsecular which embodies religious and er the other—er mystical er um approaches I suppose. (Part of a recent conversation, transcribed from a recording.)

If we are struck by the clumsiness of expression and the inelegant hesitations, we must remember that the conventional orthography used for the transcription has no means of showing those features like intonation which were mentioned above, and which are described in Supplement I. Because of the features which belong *only* to speech, the conversation itself did not sound unduly clumsy. It was in fact fairly representative of the talk we hear around us every day. It serves to emphasise the art which the novelist has to cultivate in order to make his dialogue seem natural *and yet* readable.

There are numerous varieties of English that have not been illustrated in this chapter. It is important to realise, after all, that conversation itself can take place on many different subjects and that these subjects will influence the selection of linguistic forms in speech somewhat as we have seen them doing in the written language. And there are some spoken varieties, even among educated people, that we rarely find represented in writing. Mothers and fathers (or at any rate aunts and grannies) are still liable to address a baby with some such verbiage as:

Will the baby-boodlum havums teeny-weeny drinkum-winkum now? Will he then! There now! Mummy wipum baby's mouffy.

Even this kind of 'specialised' language has its traditional characteristics. In his book on English grammar, the pioneer chemist, Joseph Priestley, noted in 1768 that in addressing very young children 'we sometimes use the third person singular instead of the second; as *will he* or *she* do it'.

It is hoped that enough of the varieties of English have been discussed to bring out the extent to which they have characteristic linguistic features. Whether or not we need to be proficient in *producing* all these varieties in our own usage, it is surely useful to be able to *recognise* them and to cultivate a sympathetic, urbane reaction to them. Each has a good deal of interest for the objective student of English and their degree of internal consistency should make us look with a critical eye on any handbook which would seem to suggest that there is a single set of Standard English forms which are 'right' for all occasions.

HOW SHALL I WORD IT?

Max Beerbohm

It would seem that I am one of those travellers for whom the railway bookstall does not cater. Whenever I start on a journey, I find that my choice lies between well-printed books which I have no wish to read, and well-written books which I could not read without permanent injury to my eyesight. The keeper of the bookstall, seeing me gaze vaguely along his shelves, suggests that I should take "Fen Country Fanny" or else "The Track of Blood" and have done with it. Not wishing to hurt his feelings, I refuse these works on the plea that I have read them. Whereon he, divining despite me that I am a superior person, says "Here is a nice little handy edition of More's 'Utopia' " or "Carlyle's 'French Revolution' " and again I make some excuse. What pleasure could I get from trying to cope with a masterpiece printed in diminutive grey-ish type on a semitransparent little grey-ish page? I relieve the bookstall of nothing but a newspaper or two.

The other day, however, my eye and fancy were caught by a book entitled "How Shall I Word It?" and sub-entitled "A Complete Letter Writer for Men and Women." I had never read one of these manuals, but had often heard that there was a great and constant "demand" for them. So I demanded this one. It is no great fun in itself. The writer is no fool. He has evidently a natural talent for writing letters. His style is,

From the book And Even Now *by Max Beerbohm. Copyright, 1921, by E. P. Dutton & Co., Inc. Renewal, 1949, by Max Beerbohm. Reprinted by permission of E. P. Dutton & Co., Inc., and William Heinemann Ltd., Publishers.*

for the most part, discreet and easy. If you were a young man writing "to Father of Girl he wishes to Marry" or "thanking Fiancée for Present" or "reproaching Fiancée for being a Flirt," or if you were a mother "asking Governess her Qualifications" or "replying to Undesirable Invitation for her Child," or indeed if you were in any other one of the crises which this book is designed to alleviate, you might copy out and post the specially-provided letter without making yourself ridiculous in the eyes of its receiver—unless, of course, he or she also possessed a copy of the book. But—well, can you conceive any one copying out and posting one of these letters, or even taking it as the basis for composition? You cannot. That shows how little you know of your fellow-creatures. Not you nor I can plumb the abyss at the bottom of which such humility is possible. Nevertheless, as we know by that great and constant "demand," there the abyss is, and there multitudes are at the bottom of it. Let's peer down . . . No, all is darkness. But faintly, if we listen hard, is borne up to us a sound of the scratching of innumerable pens—pens whose wielders are all trying, as the author of this handbook urges them, to "be original, fresh, and interesting" by dint of more or less strict adherence to sample.

Giddily you draw back from the edge of the abyss. Come!—here is a thought to steady you. The mysterious great masses of helpless folk for whom "How Shall I word It?" is written are sound at heart, delicate in feeling, anxious to please, most loth to wound. For it must be presumed that the author's style of letter-writing is informed as much by a desire to give his public what it needs, and will pay for, as by his own beautiful nature; and in the course of all the letters that he dictates you will find not one harsh word, not one ignoble thought or unkind insinuation. In all of them, though so many are for the use of persons placed in the most trying circumstances, and some of them are for persons writhing under a sense of intolerable injury, sweetness and light do ever reign. Even "yours truly, Jacob Langton," in his "letter to his Daughter's Mercenary Fiancé," mitigates the sternness of his tone by the remark that his "task is inexpressibly painful." And he, Mr. Langton, is the one writer who lets the post go out on his wrath. When Horace Masterton, of Thorpe Road, Putney, receives from Miss Jessica Weir, of Fir Villa, Blackheath, a letter "declaring her Change of Feelings," does he upbraid her? No; "it was honest and brave of you to write to me so straight-forwardly and at the back of my mind I know you have done what is best. . . . I give you back your freedom only at your desire. God bless you, dear." Not less admirable is the behaviour, in similar case, of Cecil Grant (14, Glover Street, Streatham). Suddenly, as a bolt from the blue, comes a letter from Miss Louie Hawke (Elm View, Deerhurst), breaking off her betrothal to him. Haggard, he sits down to his desk; his pen traverses the note-paper —calling down curses on Louie and on all her sex? No; "one cannot say good-bye for ever without deep regret to days that have been so full of happiness. I must thank you sincerely for all your great kindness to me. . . . With every sincere wish for your future happiness," he bestows complete freedom on Miss Hawke. And do not imagine that in the matter of self-control and sympathy, of power to understand all and pardon all, the men are lagged behind by the women. Miss Leila Johnson (The Manse, Carlyle) has observed in Leonard Wace (Dover Street, Saltburn) a certain coldness of demeanour; yet "I do not blame you; it is probably your nature"; and Leila in her sweet forbearance is typical of all the other pained women in these pages: she is but one of a crowd of heroines.

Face to face with all this perfection, the not perfect reader begins to crave some little outburst of wrath, of hatred or malice, from one of these imaginary ladies and gentlemen. He longs for—how shall he word it?—a glimpse of some bad motive, of some little lapse from dignity. Often, passing by a pillar-box, I have wished I could unlock it and carry away its contents, to be studied at my leisure. I have always thought such a haul would abound in things fascinating to a student of human nature. One night, not long ago, I took a waxen impression of the lock of the pillar-box nearest to my house, and had a key made. This implement I have as yet lacked either the courage or the opportunity to use. And now I think I shall throw it away . . . No, I shan't. I refuse, after all, to draw my inference that the bulk of the British public writes always in the manner of this handbook. Even if they all have beautiful natures they must sometimes be sent slightly astray by inferior impulses, just as you and I.

And, if ever they must, surely it were well they should know how to do it correctly and forcibly. I suggest to our author that he should sprinkle his next edition with a few less righteous examples, thereby both purging his book of its monotony and somewhat justifying its sub-title. Like most people who are in the habit of writing things to be printed, I have not the knack of writing really good letters. But let me crudely indicate the sort of thing that our manual needs. . . .

letter from poor man to obtain money from rich one

(The English law is particularly hard on what is called blackmail. It is therefore essential that the applicant should write nothing that might afterwards be twisted to incriminate him.—Ed.)

Dear Sir,
    Today, as I was turning out a drawer in my attic, I came across a letter which by a curious chance fell into my hands some years ago, and which, in the stress of grave pecuniary embarrassment, had escaped my memory. It is a

letter written by yourself to a lady, and the date shows it to have been written shortly after your marriage. It is of a confidential nature, and might, I fear, if it fell into the wrong hands, be cruelly misconstrued. I would wish you to have the satisfaction of destroying it in person. At first I thought of sending it on to you by post. But I know how happy you are in your domestic life; and probably your wife and you, in your perfect mutual trust, are in the habit of opening each other's letters. Therefore, to avoid risk, I would prefer to hand the document to you personally. I will not ask you to come to my attic, where I could not offer you such hospitality as is due to a man of your wealth and position. You will be so good as to meet me at 3.00 A.M. (sharp) tomorrow (Thursday) beside the tenth lamp-post to the left on the Surrey side of Waterloo Bridge; at which hour and place we shall not be disturbed.

> I am, dear Sir,
> Yours respectfully
> *James Gridge.*

letter from young man refusing to pay his tailor's bill

Mr. Eustace Davenant has received the half-service, half-insolent screed which Mr. Yardley has addressed to him. Let Mr. Yardley cease from crawling on his knees and shaking his fist. Neither this posture nor this gesture can wring one bent farthing from the pockets of Mr. Davenant, who was a minor at the time when that series of ill-made suits was supplied to him and will hereafter, as in the past, shout (without prejudice) from the housetops that of all tailors in London Mr. Yardley is at once the most grasping and the least competent.

letter to thank author for inscribed copy of book

Dear Mr. Emanuel Flower,

It was kind of you to think of sending me a copy of your new book. It would have been kinder still to think again and abandon that project. I am a man of gentle instincts, and do not like to tell you that "A Flight into Arcady" (of which I have skimmed a few pages, thus wasting two or three minutes of my not altogether worthless time) is trash. On the other hand, I am determined that you shall not be able to go around boasting to your friends, if you have any, that this work was not condemned, derided, and dismissed by your sincere well-wisher, *Wrexford Cripps.*

letter to member of parliament unseated at general election

Dear Mr. Pobsby-Burford,

Though I am myself an ardent Tory, I cannot but rejoice in the crushing defeat you have just suffered in West Odgetown. There are moments when political conviction is overborne by personal sentiment; and this is one of them. Your loss of the seat that you held is the more striking by reason of the splendid manner in which the northern and eastern divisions of Odgetown have been wrestled from the Liberal Party. The great bulk of the newspaper-reading public will be puzzled by your extinction in the midst of our party's triumph. But then, the great mass of the newspaper-reading public has not met you. I have. You will probably not remember me. You are the sort of man who would not remember anybody who might not be of some definite use to him. Such, at least, was one of the impressions you made on me when I met you last summer at a dinner given by our friends the Pelhams. Among the other things in you that struck me were the blatant pomposity of your manner, your appalling flow of cheap platitudes, and your hoggish lack of ideas. It is such men as you that lower the tone of public life. And I am sure that in writing to you thus I am but expressing what is felt, without distinction of party, by all who sat with you in the late Parliament.

The one person in whose behalf I regret your withdrawal into private life is your wife, whom I had the pleasure of taking in to the aforesaid dinner. It was evident to me that she was a woman whose spirit was well-nigh broken by her conjunction with you. Such remnants of cheerfulness as were in her I attributed to the Parliamentary duties which kept you out of her sight for so very many hours daily. I do not like to think of the fate to which the free and independent electors of West Odgetown have just condemned her. Only, remember this: chattel of yours though she is, and timid and humble, she despises you in her heart.

I am, dear Mr. Pobsby-Burford,

Yours very truly,

Harold Thistlake.

letter from young lady in answer to invitation

from old schoolmistress

My dear Miss Price,

How awfully sweet of you to ask me to stay with you for a few days but how *can* you think I may have forgotten you for of course I think of you so very often and of the three years I spent at your school because it is such a joy not to be there any longer and if one is at all down it bucks one up directly to remember that *thats* all over atanyrate and that one has enough food to nurrish one and not that awful monottany of life and not the petty fogging daily tirrany you went in for and I can imagin no greater thrill and luxury in a way than to come and see the whole dismal grind stil going on but without me being in it but this would be rather beastly of me wouldn't it so please dear Miss Price dont expect me and do excuse mistakes of English Composition and Spelling and etcetra in your affectionate old pupil,

Emily Therese Lynn-Royston,

ps, I often rite to people telling them where I was edducated and highly reckomending you.

letter in acknowledgment of wedding present

Dear Lady Amblesham,

Who gives quickly, says the old proverb, gives twice. For this reason I have purposely delayed writing to you, lest I should appear to thank you more than once for the small, cheap, hideous present you sent me on the occasion of my recent wedding. Were you a poor woman, that little bowl of ill-imitated Dresden china would convict you of tastelessness merely; were you a blind woman, of nothing but an odious parsimony. As you have normal eyesight and more than normal wealth, your gift to me proclaims you at once a Philistine and a miser (or rather did so proclaim you until, less than ten seconds after I had unpacked it from its wrappings of tissue paper, I took it to the open window and had the satisfaction of seeing it shattered to atoms on the pavement). But stay! I perceive a possible flaw in my argument. Perhaps you were guided in your choice by a definite wish to insult me. I am sure, on reflection, that this was so. I *shall not forget.*

Yours, etc.,

Cynthia Beaumarsh.

P.S. My husband asked me to tell you to warn Lord Amblesham to keep out of his way or to assume some disguise so complete that he will not be recognized by him and horsewhipped.

PPS. I am sending copies of this letter to the principal London and provincial newspapers.

letter from . . .

But enough! I never thought I should be so strong in this line. I had not forseen such copiousness and fatal fluency. Never again will I tap these deep dark reservoirs in a character that had always seemed to me, on the whole, so amiable.

special problems

METAPHOR AND OTHER FIGURES OF SPEECH

Herbert Read

We have seen that words used as epithets are words used to analyze a direct statement. We have in mind a complex image, and to express this image in its fullness we break it up into its constituent units:

> The hills stand snow-powdered, pale, bright.
>
> *Carlyle*

Metaphor is the opposite process: it is the synthesis of several units of observation into one commanding image; it is the expression of a complex idea, not by analysis, nor by abstract statement, but by a sudden perception of an objective relation. The complex idea is translated into a simple concrete equivalent.

The nature and importance of metaphors was clearly stated by Aristotle, in the *Poetics* (xxii. 16, 17):

> . . . much the most important point is to be able to use metaphors, for this is the one thing that cannot be learned from others; and it is also

From English Prose Style *by Herbert Read, copyright 1952 by Herbert Read. Reprinted by permission of Pantheon Books, a Division of Random House, Inc., and G. Bell & Sons, Ltd.*

a mark of genius, since a good metaphor implies an intuitive perception of the similarity in dissimilars.[1]

But in this passage Aristotle is writing of poetry. The ability to invent new metaphors is a sign of a poetic mind; and the main use of metaphors is always poetical. To say that a metaphor "is the result of the search for a precise epithet"[2] is misleading. The precision sought for is one of equivalence, not of analytical description. And as prose is essentially the art of analytical description, it would seem that metaphor is of no particular relevance to it; for poetry it is perhaps a more necessary mode of expression.

We may say quite generally that the use of metaphor tends to obscure the essential nature of prose, because it substitutes a poetic equivalence for a direct statement. For this reason many of our best writers have been chary of this mode of writing—as Swift. "The rogue never hazards a metaphor," said Johnson. "Never" is perhaps an exaggeration, but it is true that we may read Swift for many pages without encountering imagery of any kind, except such as was at that time embodied in common speech.

> On the fifth of November, which was the beginning of summer in those parts, the weather being very hazy, the seamen spied a rock, within half a cable's length of the ship; but the wind was so strong, that we were driven directly upon it, and immediately split. Six of the crew, of whom I was one, having let down the boat into the sea, made a shift to get clear of the ship and the rock. We rowed, by my computation, about three leagues, till we were able to work no longer, being already spent with labour while we were in the ship. We therefore trusted ourselves to the mercy of the waves, and in about half an hour the boat was overset by a sudden flurry from the north. What became of my companions in the boat, as well as of those who escaped on the rock, or were left in the vessel, I cannot tell; but conclude they were all lost. For my own part, I swam as fortune directed me, and was pushed forward by wind and tide. I often let my legs drop, and could feel no bottom: but when I was almost gone, and able to struggle no longer, I found myself within my depth; and by this time the storm was much abated. The declivity was so small, that I walked near a mile before I got to the shore, which I conjectured was about eight o'clock in the evening. I then

[1] "The art of producing good metaphors is a token of the faculty for recognizing the universal and the common element underlying externally dissimilar objects." Note to the translation of this passage of the *Poetics* by E. S. Bouchier (Oxford, 1907).

[2] J. Middleton Murry, *The Problem of Style*, p. 83. Fenollosa gives a perfect definition of metaphor: "the use of material images to suggest immaterial relations." *The Chinese Written Character*, ed. Ezra Pound, London, 1936.

advanced forward near half a mile, but could not discover any sign of houses or inhabitants; at least I was in so weak a condition that I did not observe them. I was extremely tired, and with that, and the heat of the weather, and about half a pint of brandy that I drank as I left the ship, I found myself much inclined to sleep. I lay down on the grass, which was very short and soft, where I slept sounder than ever I remember to have done in my life, and as I reckoned, about nine hours; for when I awaked it was just daylight. I attempted to rise, but was not able to stir: for as I happened to lie on my back, I found my arms and legs were strongly fastened on each side to the ground; and my hair, which was long and thick, tied down in the same manner. I likewise felt several slender ligatures across my body, from my armpits to my thighs. I could only look upwards, the sun began to grow hot, and the light offended my eyes. I heard a confused noise about me, but in the posture I lay, could see nothing except the sky. In a little time I felt something alive moving on my left leg, which advancing gently forward, over my breast, came almost up to my chin; when bending my eyes downward as much as I could, I perceived it to be a human creature not six inches high, with a bow and arrow in his hands, and a quiver at his back.

Swift, Gulliver's Travels, *pt. i. ch. i.*

In this passage there is not a single simile or metaphor; there is not even a direct comparison, such as we find later in the book. "They climbed high trees as nimbly as a squirrel, for they had strong extended claws before and behind, terminating in sharp points, and hooked." But a direct or simple *comparison,* where the objects compared are of a common nature, is not a figure of speech at all; to climb high trees comes naturally to both Yahoos and squirrels. But if we say of a man, or a horse, that he climbed high trees as nimbly as a squirrel, then we compare the particular qualities of one object to the general qualities of another, and this constitutes a *simile.* If we go a step further, and in a manner *identify* the man and the squirrel, as in "This man, the squirrel of his clan, climbed the high trees"—then we invent a metaphor.

Simile and Metaphor differ only in degree of stylistic refinement. The Simile, in which a comparison is made directly between two objects, belongs to an earlier stage of literary expression: it is the deliberate elaboration of a correspondence, often pursued for its own sake. But a Metaphor is the swift illumination of an equivalence. Two images, or an idea and an image, stand equal and opposite; clash together and respond significantly, surprising the reader with a sudden light.

This light may either illuminate or decorate the sentence in which it is found; and perhaps we may divide all metaphors into the *illuminative* and the *decorative.* By doing so we can make more distinct the limited relevance of metaphor to prose writing; for while both kinds are appropriate to poetry, only the illuminative metaphor will be found appropriate in pure prose style.

In narrative prose, such as the passage already quoted from Swift, there is no need for either illumination or decoration; metaphors would merely impede the action and are therefore properly discarded.

In exposition, whether of the descriptive kind or of the persuasive kind, . . . it is again difficult to see any justification for decorative metaphors. These are generally introduced either to display the poetic tendency of the writer's mind, and are therefore out of place; or to give an alternative expression to a thought which has already been expressed in direct language. In this case they are redundant.

But it often happens in exposition that abstract language is inadequate to express a meaning clearly, and then metaphor may be introduced to illuminate the thought. Paradoxically, it is in scientific prose that the illuminative metaphor is most effectively used. The history of language and of early poetry, as well as the general results of modern psychology, according to a well-known logician, confirm the view that "metaphors are not merely artificial devices for making discourse more vivid and poetical, but are also necessary for the apprehension and communication of new ideas." Metaphors "are often the way in which creative minds perceive things, so that the explicit recognition that we are dealing with an analogy rather than a real identity comes later as a result of further reflection and analysis."[3]

The language of scientific pioneers like Faraday, Darwin and Huxley abounds in illuminative metaphors. Here, for example, is a paragraph from the work of a modern physicist:

> I have said that all atoms are in motion, and that there is a constant struggle between some form of attractive force which would draw all the atoms together and this motion which would keep them independent. The existence of an attractive force which we here take into account as something very important does not at first seem to be reconcilable with the atomic structure we have just considered, because in this we supposed that the outer shells of electrons would prevent the atoms from coming too close to each other. It is a difficult point, because both views are entirely correct. It is, no doubt, our present ignorance of the nature of these forces that prevents us from arriving at a clear understanding. We have seen how it can happen that when two atoms approach each other at great speeds they go through one another, while at moderate speeds they bound off each other like two billiard balls. We have to go a step further, and see how, at very slow speeds of approach, they may actually stick together. We have all seen those swinging gates which,

[3] Morris R. Cohen: *A Preface to Logic* (Holt, Rinehart and Winston, Inc.).

when their swing is considerable, go to and fro without locking. When the swing has declined, however, the latch suddenly drops into its place, the gate is held and after a short rattle the motion is all over. We have to explain an effect something like that. When the two atoms meet, the repulsions of their electron shells usually cause them to recoil; but if the motion is small, and the atoms spend a longer time in each other's neighbourhood, there is time for something to happen in the internal arrangements of both atoms, like the drop of the latch-gate into its socket, and the atoms are held. It all depends on some structure of the atom which causes a want of uniformity over its surface, so that there is usually a repulsion; but the repulsion will be turned into attraction if the two atoms are allowed time to make the necessary arrangements, or even if at the outset they are presented to each other in the right way.

Sir William Bragg, Concerning the Nature of Things[4]

The following passage shows the use of merely decorative metaphors:

The Oxford Movement may be a spent wave, but, before it broke on the shore, it reared, as its successor is now rearing, a brave and beautiful crest of liturgical and devotional life, the force of which certainly shifted the Anglican sands, though it failed to uncover any rock-bottom underlying them. It is enough if now and then a lone swimmer be borne by the tide, now at its full, to be dashed, more or less ungently, upon the Rock of Peter, to cling there in safety, while the impotent wave recedes and is lost in the restless sea.

M. A. Chapman, in Blackfriars, *April, 1921*
(Quoted by Stephen J. Brown, The World
of Imagery, *p. 308.)*

By translating this passage into direct language the meaning could be preserved without any loss, and even clarified. Because of their vagueness, it is not always possible to be sure that exact equivalents have been found for the metaphors; but this only reveals the weakness of decorative metaphorical writing. The translation which follows may not be so emotive as the original, but it is more definite, and to be definite is the proper aim of expository writing:

The Oxford Movement may belong to the past, but before its end it produced, like its successor of to-day, a fine sense of liturgical devotional life, the force of which certainly had some effect on the looser elements of the Anglican Church, though it failed to reach any fundamental body of opinion. It is enough that the Movement, when at its

[4] Bell.

height, led a few desperate individuals to become converted to the Church of Rome, and there these remained in security of mind when the Movement, losing its force, became a merely historical phenomenon.

Hazlitt called such writers *hieroglyphical* writers. Here is his description of them (itself not free from the vices it castigates):

> . . . Such persons are in fact besotted with words, and their brains are turned with the glittering but empty and sterile phantoms of things. Personifications, capital letters, seas of sunbeams, visions of glory, shining inscriptions, the figures of a transparency, Britannia with her shield, or hope leaning on an anchor, make up their stock-in-trade. They may be considered as *hieroglyphical* writers. Images stand out in their minds isolated and important merely in themselves, without any ground-work of feeling—there is no context in their imaginations. Words affect them in the same way, by the mere sound, that is, by their possible, not by their actual application to the subject in hand. They are fascinated by first appearances, and have no sense of consequences. Nothing more is meant by them than meets the ear: they understand or feel nothing more than meets their eye. The web and texture of the universe, and of the heart of man, is a mystery to them: they have no faculty that strikes a chord in unison with it. They cannot get beyond the daubings of fancy, the varnish of sentiment. Objects are not linked to feelings, words to things, but images revolve in splendid mockery, words represent themselves in their strange rhapsodies. The categories of such a mind are pride and ignorance—pride in outside show, to which they sacrifice everything, and ignorance of the true worth and hidden structure both of words and things. With a sovereign contempt for what is familiar and natural, they are the slaves of vulgar affectation—of a routine of high-flown phrases. Scorning to imitate realities, they are unable to invent anything, to strike out one original idea. They are not copyists of nature, it is true; but they are the poorest of all plagiarists, the plagiarists of words. All is far-fetched, dear bought, artificial, oriental in subject and allusion; all is mechanical, conventional, vapid, formal, pedantic in style and execution. They startle and confound the understanding of the reader by the remoteness and obscurity of their illustrations; they soothe the ear by the monotony of the same everlasting round of circuitous metaphors. They are the *mock-school* in poetry and prose. They flounder about between fustian in expression and bathos in sentiment. They tantalise the fancy, but never reach the head nor touch the heart.
>
> *William Hazlitt,* Essay on Familiar Style

In the following passage an idea is stated and is then followed by a metaphor (it is hardly a simile) which has the effect of illuminating and fixing the meaning in our minds. Incidentally this passage shows an example of a metaphor followed out in all its implications, extending and branching out and at each stage bringing fresh light to illuminate the idea:[5]

> Heathenism, if we consider life at large, is the primal and universal religion. It has never been my good fortune to see wild beasts in the jungle, but I have sometimes watched a wild bull in the ring, and I can imagine no more striking, simple, and heroic example of animal faith; especially when the bull is what is technically called noble, that is, when he follows the lure again and again with eternal singleness of thought, eternal courage, and no suspicion of a hidden agency that is mocking him. What the red rag is to this brave creature, their passions, inclinations, and chance notions are to the heathen. What they will they will; and they would deem it weakness and disloyalty to ask whether it is worth willing or whether it is attainable. The bull, magnificently sniffing the air, surveys the arena with the cool contempt and disbelief of the idealist, as if he said: "You seem, you are a seeming; I do not quarrel with you, I do not fear you. I am real, you are nothing." Then suddenly, when his eye is caught by some bright cloak displayed before him, his whole soul changes. His will awakes, and he seems to say: "You are my destiny; I want you, I hate you, you shall be mine, you shall not stand in my path. I will gore you. I will disprove you. I will pass beyond you. I shall be, you shall not have been." Later, when sorely wounded and near his end, he grows blind to all these excitements. He smells the moist earth, and turns to the dungeon where an hour ago he was at peace. He remembers the herd, the pasture beyond, and he dreams, "I shall not die, for I love life. I shall be young again, young always, for I love youth. All this outcry is nought to me, this strange suffering is nought. I will go to the fields again, to graze, to roam, to love."
>
> So exactly, with not one least concession to the unsuspected reality, the heathen soul stands bravely before a painted world, covets some bauble, and defies death. Heathenism is the religion of will, the faith which life has in itself because it is life, and in its aims because it is pursuing them.
>
> *George Santayana*[6]

The passage from Swift (p. 180) has shown us narrative prose that is completely independent of the use of metaphor. The following passage from a work of great clarity and precision, will show the same independence in expository prose:

[5] A difficult feat, more often than not involving the author in runaway and mixed metaphors, and a general violence of statement. The greatest master of the branching metaphor is perhaps Henry James. Cf. the passage quoted in *The London Book of English Prose*, II, viii, 23.

[6] From *Egotism in German Philosophy* by George Santayana. Reprinted by permission of Charles Scribner's Sons. Copyright 1916.

Physical Science is that department of knowledge which relates to the order of nature, or, in other words, to the regular succession of events.

The name of physical science, however, is often applied in a more or less restricted manner to those branches of science in which the phenomena considered are of the simplest and most abstract kind, excluding the consideration of the more complex phenomena, such as those observed in beings.

The simplest case of all is that in which an event or phenomenon can be described as a change in the arrangement of certain bodies. Thus the motion of the moon may be described by stating the changes in her position relative to the earth in the order in which they follow one another.

In other cases we may know that some change of arrangement has taken place, but we may not be able to ascertain what that change is.

Thus when water freezes we know that the molecules or smallest parts of the substance must be arranged differently in ice and in water. We also know that this arrangement in ice must have a certain kind of symmetry, because the ice is in the form of symmetrical crystals, but we have as yet no precise knowledge of the actual arrangement of the molecules in ice. But whenever we can completely describe the change of arrangement we have a knowledge, perfect so far as it extends, of what has taken place, though we may still have to learn the necessary conditions under which a similar event will always take place.

Hence the first part of physical science relates to the relative position and motion of bodies.

J. Clerk Maxwell, Matter and Motion, *pp. 9 and 10.*[7]

The historical evolution of an art often runs from complexity to simplicity, and Jespersen has suggested that this is true also of the development of language. It would seem to be true not only of language itself but also of the arts of language. Early literature is characterized by the frequent use of *riddles* and *periphrases* ("kennings"). Riddles are primitive metaphors, roundabout descriptions or stories designed to convey their subject as a sudden and vivid revelation in the mind of the reader.[8]

My nose is downward; I go deep and dig into the ground; I move as the grey foe of the wood guides me, and my lord who goes stooping as guardian at my tail; he pushes me in the plain, bears and urges me, sows in my track. I hasten forth, brought from the grove, strongly bound, carried on the wagon, I have many wounds; on one side of me as I go there is green, and on the other my track is clear black. Driven through my back a cunning point hangs beneath; another on my head fixed and

[7] S. P. C. K.
[8] Cf. Aristotle, *Rhet.,* III, ii. 12.

prone falls at the side, so that I tear with my teeth, if he who is my lord serves me rightly from behind.

"Plough"—from Anglo-Saxon Poetry
(Everyman Library), p. 327.

Kennings are very characteristic of Anglo-Saxon literature; for examples: "world-candle" (sun), "word-hoard" (mind or speech), "battle-adders" (arrows), "the head jewels" (eyes). They differ from later metaphors in that they have a deceptive intention, and may, indeed, have their origin in some form of taboo. Primitive man associated the thing and its name in an intimate fashion, and when the thing was an object of veneration or fear, he would seek for some form of periphrasis so as to avoid a direct reference. A kenning is a simple periphrasis of this kind.

Metonymy is a special form of periphrasis; something associated with an idea is made to serve for the expression of that idea. "From the *cradle* to the *grave*," "Loyalty to the *throne*," "an officer of the *Crown*."

Synecdoche is still another type of concise periphrasis; a part of a thing is made to serve for the expression of the whole. "A fleet of fifty *sail*," "All *hands* on deck," "A force of a thousand *rifles*."

The use of all these forms of periphrasis is a matter of discretion; they are better avoided unless they are fresh enough to add to the vividness or significance of a passage; or unless they have become so current as to pass without equivocation for the master word.

Personification or *Actualization* is another figure of speech related to metaphor, and has its origins in primitive modes, such as the Anglo-Saxon riddle; but like metaphor, of which, indeed, it is a collapsed form (for one of the terms of comparison has been suppressed, or identified with the object to which it is compared), it is more appropriate to poetic expression. It consists in endowing inanimate things with animate (and generally human) action. A sustained process of personification or actualization may sometimes be used to give vitality to descriptive prose, but only with discretion.

It was a hot July afternoon, the world laid out open to the sun to admit its penetration. All nature seemed swollen to its fullest. The very air was half asleep, and the distant sounds carried so slowly that they died away before they could reach their destination; or perhaps the ear forgot to listen.

The house, too, had indulged itself, and had lost a little its melancholy air. The summer decked it with garlands, for still newly-green creepers crept up the walls and on to the roof, almost high enough to gain the chimney-pots. But the house held them like hats, carefully out of reach, and the creepers, snubbed, pried into the open windows. The smooth lawns lay tantalizingly about, just out of the way of the blunder-ing, clumsy house kept prisoner by the chain of gravel. The lawn, a green-clad monster, arched its back against the yew hedge, and put out emerald feelers all through the garden and turfed alley-ways.

Valentine Dobrée, Your Cuckoo Sings by Kind, *pp. 51–52.*[9]

The concision of personification, of metonymy and of synecdoche, was one way of escape from the complexity and unwieldiness of the periphrasis and the riddle. Comparison, simile and metaphor renounce the mere love of indirectness; they denote a growth in poetic sensibility, and in the use of metaphor we have, indeed, one of the main agents in the growth of intelligence. It has been a main agent, too, in the growth of language, most words and idioms being in the nature of dead metaphors. But whatever we may say of it, and however great and inclusive the function we assign to it, essentially it belongs to the sphere of poetry. But it is equally possible to say that science itself, in its formative stage, also belongs to the sphere of poetry.[10]

[9] Knopf.

[10] Cf. Fenollosa: "In diction and in grammatical form science is utterly op-posed to logic. Primitive men who created language agreed with science and not with logic. Logic has abused the language which they left to her mercy. Poetry agrees with science and not with logic."

SIMILE AND METAPHOR

F. L. Lucas

"As prose is essentially the art of analytical description,[1] it would seem that metaphor is of no particular relevance to it; for poetry it is perhaps a more necessary mode of expression. . . . But whatever we may say of it, and however great and inclusive the function we assign to it, essentially it belongs to the sphere of poetry. Poetry alone is creative.[1] The art of prose is not creative, but constructive or logical."[1]

Such is the austere view of Sir Herbert Read.[2] Aristotle, on the other hand, thought more highly of metaphor. After discussing the value of unusual and poetic words, he continues: "But far the greatest thing is a gift for metaphor. For this alone cannot be learnt from others and is a sign of inborn power." (*Poetics,* xxii.)

Sir Herbert, citing this passage, pleads that Aristotle is here writing only of poetry. But Aristotle—more wisely, I think—did not fix this gulf between poetry and prose; Socrates, indeed, had done so; but Aristotle's *Rhetoric* (III, 2) explicitly stresses the value of metaphor for *prose* oratory as well: "In conversation all of us use metaphors and ordinary,

Reprinted with permission of Crowell-Collier and Macmillan, Inc. from Style *by F. L. Lucas. Copyright 1955 by F. L. Lucas. Reprinted also with permission of Cassell and Company, Ltd. This essay is abridged as indicated. Footnotes renumbered.*

[1] Why?
[2] *English Prose Style* (1928), pp. 26, 34. In the second edition (1952) the last two sentences are omitted.

current words. Evidently by a proper combination of these one may attain a style that will remain clear, yet unobtrusively avoid the commonplace. . . . In prose there is all the *more* need to take pains with this because prose has fewer resources than verse."

Here, then, are two flatly opposite views on the value of metaphor in prose. Which of them we adopt, remains ultimately a matter of personal preference. Taste is relative. But you will soon see, if you read the enduring prose-works of the past, that most men, in many ages and nations, have felt with Aristotle. Childish of them, maybe, or meretricious; but, for myself, I will own at once that a style without metaphor and simile is to me like a day without sun, or a woodland without birds.

Living metaphor is a kind of two-headed Janus, looking two ways at once and making us see two things almost simultaneously.

> Ah would that from earth and Heaven all strife were for ever flung,
> And wrath, that makes even a wise man mad! Upon the tongue
> Its taste is sweeter than honey, that drips from the comb—but *then*
> Like a smother of blinding smoke it mounts in the hearts of men.

So cries Homer's Achilles in his remorse above Patroclus; and the likeness of wrath and honey is even more vividly concentrated in the metaphor than the likeness of blinding anger and blinding smoke in the simile. The simile sets two ideas side by side; in the metaphor they become superimposed. It would seem natural to think that simile, being simpler, is older. Indeed, it might be thought that this is why the prehistoric Homer, whose similes are so lovely, should be less remarkable for metaphor; whereas in Aeschylus and Pindar, some four or five centuries later, simile is overshadowed by a bold skill in metaphor such as poetry has never since surpassed.

But this explanation will hardly work. Of the not very numerous metaphors in Homer, many seem already old traditional formulae (such as "wingéd words," "paths of the fishes," and so on), not new inventions.[3] Similarly Old English and Scandinavian poetry, more primitive than *Iliad* or *Odyssey*, abounds in metaphorical kennings already stereotyped.

The truth seems that metaphor too is older than any literature—an immemorial human impulse perhaps as much utilitarian as literary. For there appears little ground for assigning poetic motives to the first man who called the hole in a needle its "eye," or the projections on a saw its "teeth." In fine, metaphor is an inveterate human tendency, as ancient

---

[3] See Milman Parry, "The Traditional Metaphor in Homer," *Classical Philology,* 1933; W. B. Stanford, *Greek Metaphor,* 1936.

perhaps as the days of the mammoth, yet vigorous still in the days of the helicopter.[4] Why then should it be banned from prose?

It is, indeed, astonishing how much ordinary language is built of dead metaphors; as a coral-reef is formed of the skeletons of dead madrepores and constantly increased by those of their living brethren. In the words of Professor Weekley,[5] "Every expression that we employ, apart from those that are connected with the most rudimentary objects and actions, is a metaphor, though the original meaning is dulled by constant use." Consider the words of that very sentence: an "expression" is something squeezed out; to "employ" something is to wind it in (*implicare*); to "connect" is to tie together (*conectere*); "rudimentary" comes from the root RAD, "root, sprout"; an "object" is something thrown in the way, an "action" something driven or conducted; "original" means "rising up," like a plant or spring or heavenly body; "constant" is "standing firm." "Metaphor" itself is a metaphor, meaning the "carrying across" of a term or expression from its normal usage to another.

Even in so humdrum a phrase as "well off" there is said to have lurked once the metaphor of a ship well away from the perils of a lee shore. Even a seemingly simple word like "zest" has gained its meaning metaphorically; from its literal sense of "orange or lemon peel" (Fr. *zeste*) it came to be used for "flavour, relish," and thence for "a feeling of relish." Even our most ideal terms are metaphors with material roots; an "idea" is merely a "shape"; "$\pi\nu\varepsilon\hat{\upsilon}\mu\alpha$," "anima," "spirit" meant once no more than "breath."

If languages are so largely built of dead metaphors, this is no doubt partly for reasons of obvious convenience; picture-thinking is as natural at a primitive stage as picture-writing; but it shows also, I think, how deeply innate is the human pleasure in simile and metaphor themselves, quite apart from their utility. "A good saying well spit out is a Christmas fire to my withered heart."

Why? Partly, I suppose, because imagery pleases the simpler side of us, as pictures please children. And again it is a relief and a reassurance to descend from the clouds of the abstract to the solid world of things tangible, visible, or audible. Concepts are enlivened and illumined by percepts. But it is only the dream-interpretation of modern psychology that has fully revealed what a persistent and fundamental part is played in our less conscious thinking by symbols—how much our dream-life is devoted to disguise and masquerade; so that, for example, a man who is afraid of being carried away by some passion will dream, without ever having heard of the chariot of the soul in Plato's *Phaedrus,* that he is

---

[4] *Lit. "screw-wing."*
[5] *The Romance of Words* (1912), p. 97.

endangered by some uncontrollable horse. The visions of our sleep are often a fancy-dress ball of symbolic figures.

> Is it Murder whets his blade?
>   No!—a woodman, axe in hand.
> (*That,* for sure, 's an honest trade.)
>   What, Priapus? There you stand?
> Veil you in our masquerade
>   As a churchtower old and grey,
>   Primly pointing Heaven's way.
> Aphrodite brazen there,
>   Bare in beauty?—quickly mask it!
> Though Pandemos otherwhere,
>   Seem you here a simple casket.
> Rhadamanthus, Minos, sleep!
> Blameless revels here we keep.

But whatever the reasons and origins, anyone who troubles to look will, I think, be surprised to find how often the power and pleasure of the most memorable passages of prose and verse spring mainly from a gift for metaphor. No doubt its use is often difficult, often dangerous. It is difficult because, after so many centuries, new metaphors are not so easy to find. And weary old metaphors, decrepit with long years of service, bring at each reappearance, not pleasure, but nausea. "The long arm of coincidence" has become palsied with overwork; the non-existent "snakes of Iceland" have long lost their bite; "the jam that sweetens the powder," telling enough once in Lucretius, no longer sweetens the reader's temper; "trump-cards" are dog-eared, "burning questions" leave us cold, and "the eleventh hour" no longer strikes.

There are also ways in which metaphor can prove dangerous. It does not do to adore *this* sort of image with one's eyes shut. The writer who informs us that "there is no life in standing water," or that "meaning is an arrow that reaches its mark when least encumbered with feathers," simply appears never to have seen a duckpond or shot an arrow. Or take the following sentences from Robert Byron's[6] *The Byzantine Achievement.*

"But not only are we poised on the footboard of the encyclopaedic civilisation now being launched; in addition, we are gathered to the brow of infinity by the initial achievement of the scientific revoluton."

(Of Constantinople.) "It was here at this thwarted kiss of two continents, that the trade between the richest extremities of Europe, Asia and Africa, was sucked and spewed at the lips of the Golden Horn."

---

[6] For Robert Byron, Gibbon was "a pseudo-historian." But at least Gibbon could write. Nor would he have spelt Cilicia "Silicia."

Ships with footboards? Humanity as a swarm of midges deposited on the noble forehead of infinity? Asia and Europe trying to kiss like Hero and Leander, in the intervals of vomiting? Horns with lips? Imagery is not for those who cannot use, and control, their imaginations.

The mixed metaphor comes simply from failure to visualize. There seems no harm, whatever some may suppose, in a rapid succession of metaphors. These need not trouble any mind of ordinary quickness. And by this means Shakespeare has produced some of his most tumultuously brilliant passages. The objection is only to any coupling of ideas that breeds monstrous hybrids. The orator who cries "we will burn our ships and . . . steer boldly out into the ocean of freedom," the journalist who urges the government to "iron out vicious circles of bottlenecks," are ludicrous merely because they have not *seen* what they are talking about, and therefore amuse, or irritate, readers who do.

Yet such lapses are surprisingly common. One can only conclude that many imaginations are strangely blind. Sir Herbert Grierson cites an extraordinary instance from Mark Pattison: "Even at this day a country squire or rector, on landing with his cub under his wing" (a sort of lion of St. Mark?) "at Oxford, finds himself at sea." Then there is that enthusiastic vision I once encountered in a book on the Oxford Group: "the University atmosphere is stabbed with praying giants." And here are two examples from Saintsbury:

> But brevity has the Scylla and Charybdis of obscurity and baldness ever waiting for it; and balance those of monotonous clock-beat and tedious parallelism. The ship is safe through all these in such things as the exquisite symmetry of the Absolution.[7]

(A truly strange voyage of vessels manned by Brevity and Balance through seas perilous with obscurity and baldness, clock-beats and parallels. Besides, Scylla and Charybdis were alternative dangers: whereas there is, unfortunately, nothing to prevent a writer from being *both* bald *and* obscure, *both* monotonous in rhythm *and* tedious in antithesis. On the contrary, such faults can easily be combined.)

Similarly Saintsbury writes of Ruskin:

> Whether he shows any influence from the older prose harmonists who had begun to write, as it were, like fairy parents over his cradle, I must leave to some industrious person to expiscate or rummage out; for the haystack of Ruskinian autobiography is not only mighty in bulk but scattered rather forbiddingly.

---

[7] *English Prose Rhythm*, p. 126.

(An equally odd vision of prose-musicians as fairy godparents scribbling, like a posse of reporters, above an infant's cradle; of angling; and of haystacks scattered before being built.)

When a man as clever as Saintsbury can produce such absurdities, all of us may well be on our guard. The trouble comes partly from employing hackneyed imagery like fairy godparents, or Scylla and Charybdis, which have done such long service that they might now be allowed a rest. Their very familiarity is apt to blur the image that a living metaphor should present; and the writer allows these half-dead metaphors to collide with other metaphors less dead.

It must, of course, be owned that very distinguished authors have written things as queer. There are plenty of examples in Shakespeare. There is that phrase of Milton's which, when pointed out by Rogers to Coleridge, is said to have given him a sleepless night:

> Sight so deform what heart of rock could long
> Dry-eyed behold?

There is Cromwell's—"God has kindled a seed in this nation." There is De Quincey's—"The very recognition of these or any of these by the jurisprudence of a nation is a mortal wound to the very keystone upon which the whole vast arch of morality reposes." But whoever may have written so, I still feel they would have done better not to. In any case they are hardly for imitation; especially in prose.

Really dead metaphors, like really dead nettles, cannot sting; but often the metaphors are only half dead; and these need careful handling. It may, of course, be argued that some mixed metaphors bother none but readers with too vivid imaginations. Yet I doubt if readers *can* have too vivid imaginations. At all events you will find, I think, that you lose esteem with many readers if they come to feel that you have a less vivid imagination than they have themselves. A main purpose of imagery is to make a style more concrete and definite; and it is interesting to note how much that imagery itself may gain by being made still more concrete and still more definite, as when Webster borrows images from Sidney or Montaigne.

> She was like them that could not sleepe, when they were softly layd.
> *Sidney,* Arcadia

> You are like some, cannot sleepe *in feather-beds,*
> But must have *blockes for their pillowes.*
> Duchess of Malfi

> See whether any cage can please a bird. Or whether a dogge grow
> not fiercer with tying.
> *Sidney,* Arcadia

Like *English Mastiffes,* that grow fierce with tying.
Duchess of Malfi

The opinion of wisedome is the plague of man.
Montaigne

Oh Sir, the opinion of wisedome is *a foule tettor,* that runs all over a mans body.
Duchess of Malfi

Never, it seems to me, was the theft better justified—the plagiarist here is far more praiseworthy than his victims; simply because in each case the picture becomes much more precisely visualized. "A dogge" is vague beside "English Mastiffes"; a "plague" is feeble compared to "a foule tettor." Here, as with other kinds of clarity, preferences may indeed differ according to taste and temperament; there are doubtless times when, here too, writing gains by half-lights, mists, and shadows; but I own that I love, particularly in prose, keen vision; sharp focus; and clearest air.

Imagery, however, is also exposed to other dangers. It can become too far-fetched. Aeschylus is magnificent when he speaks of

the jaw of Salmydessus,
Sour host to sailors, stepmother of ships:

but many of us smile when we come upon things so fantastic as "the thirsty dust, twin-sister unto mud." On this point, indeed, at least in prose, ancient taste tended to be far more cautious than ours. Thus Aristotle objects to the image of Alcidamas that "the Odyssey is a lovely mirror of human life"; "Longinus," to Plato's phrase in *The Laws* about allowing the walls of his ideal city to sleep beneath the earth (that is, to remain unbuilt). Yet it is not easy to see why these should be blamed; especially when Pericles is praised for calling hostile Aegina "the eyesore of Peiraeus," or for saying over the young Athenians fallen in the Samian War that "the spring had been taken out of the year." Some, however, will agree that many Elizabethan conceits and much bad Metaphysical poetry are based on comparisons too hyperbolical. Similarly with some oriental imagery (for "Metaphysical" poetry is far older than some of us realize).

Night black as pitch[8] she bids bright day[9] bestride;
Two sugar-plums[10] stars two-and-thirty[11] hide;
O'er the red rose[12] a musky scorpion[13] strays,
For which she keeps two antidotes[14] well-tried.

Abul-Quasim Al-Bakharzi, d. A.D., 1075

---

[8] Her hair.   [10] Her lips.   [12] Her cheek.   [14] Her lips.
[9] Her face.   [11] Her teeth.   [13] A lovelock.

And here is a strange modern specimen of metaphors both mixed and forced.

> To the Giorgione in the Cathedral at Castel Franco a man must come should the dry biscuit of the desert have stuck in his throat or should the subtlety of life have bent his sleep. Here is the certain rejoinder to the intricacy of bitterness, here the sane assumption that is not keyed to mark the loaded hiss that whistles a drugging breath through the undergrowth of a Catholic dispensation.[15]

Again, imagery may lapse into grossness and crudity, like Robert Byron's spewing Constantinople (above), or the already quoted French Revolutionary orator who cried to his adversary, "There is not a louse on your body but has a right to spit in your face." Or again imagery can become precious and affected as in *Euphues:* which also illustrates yet another danger—that metaphor and simile, instead of being used as a means to clearer meaning, may be abused as ends in themselves. When Sir Thomas Browne trots out his "Bivious Theorems and Janus-faced Doctrines" and his Negroes "in the black Jaundice"; when he bids us not look "for *Whales* in the Euxine Sea, or expect great matters where they are not to be found"; then it becomes clear that he is more concerned with his art than with his matter, with beauties and quaintnesses than with truth. In lesser men such things became a fashion frivolous and futile; and they were bound to provoke revolt in practical minds. Even at the beginning of the seventeenth century, "it was," Aubrey records, "a shrewd and severe animadversion of a Scotish lord, who, when King James asked him how he liked Bishop A's sermon, said that he was learned, but he did play with his Text, as a Jack-an-apes does who takes up a thing and tosses and playes with it, and then he takes up another, and playes a little with it. Here's a pretty thing, and there's a pretty thing."[16]

Again, Bishop Samuel Parker (1640–88) would have liked preachers prohibited by Act of Parliament from using "fulsome and lushious Metaphors." And Hobbes, no favourite of bishops, was at least in agreement here—"metaphors . . . are like *ignes fatui.*"[17]

It is, too, familiar enough how, as the seventeenth century drew towards its close, the men of the Royal Society reacted still more drastically against this "luxury and redundance of speech." But it is worth quoting a little more fully from the tirades of their historian, Sprat. "Who can behold, without Indignation, how many mists and uncertainties their

[15] Quoted in Sir Herbert Read, *English Prose Style* (1928 ed.), p. 31.
[16] *Aubrey's Brief Lives,* ed. O. L. Dick (1950), "Lancelot Andrewes," p. 7.
[17] Cf. Locke's view that, in writings which aim at truth, all figurative expressions are "perfect cheats."

specious *Tropes* and *Figures* have brought in our Knowledge? . . . Of all the Studies of men, nothing may be sooner obtain'd, than this vicious abundance of *Phrase,* this trick of *Metaphors,* this volubility of *Tongue* which makes so great a noise in the World. . . . And indeed, in most other parts of Learning, I look on it as a thing almost utterly desperate in its cure; and I think, it may be plac'd among those *general mischiefs;* such as the *dissention* of Christian Princes, the *want of practice* in Religion, and the like; which have been so long spoken against, that men are become insensible about them." Hence, he says, the Royal Society formed "a constant Resolution to reject all amplifications, digressions, and swellings of style: to return back to the primitive purity, and shortness, when men deliver'd so many *things* almost in an equal number of *words."*

Never, surely, was verbal imagery subjected to so tremendous an anathema. "The *dissention* of Christian Princes"—"the *want of practice* in Religion"—one may wonder if the iconoclastic Sprat was himself being very scientific, or (for a future bishop) very religious.[18] Naturally no serious scientist could be expected to have much patience with minds still fancifully medieval like Sir Thomas Browne, who is capable of beginning a chapter on lampreys: "Whether Lampries have nine eyes, we durst refer it unto *Polyphemus,* who had but one, to judge it. An error concerning eyes, occasioned by the error of eyes. . . ." But even the scientist who wishes to persuade the world may find metaphor and simile far from valueless. Montesquieu, I suppose, may claim to be called a political scientist. And not the least part of his greatness is that, as Sainte-Beuve has said (with an admirable metaphor), "Dans la pensée de Montesquieu, au moment où l'on s'y attend le moins, tout d'un coup la cime se dore."

*　　　*　　　*　　　*　　　*

And, to take one more scientific example among many, has not Einstein excellently said (though of course for a popular audience) that it is hard to split atoms because it is like shooting birds in the dark, in a country where there are few birds?

But our concern is not, after all, with science but with literature, and

---

[18] Nor was he even very consistent in avoiding simile and metaphor himself. He begins the first passage quoted above with a metaphor. Of alchemists seeking the Philosopher's Stone he says: "if an Experiment lye never so little out of their rode, it is free from their discovery: as I have heard of some violent creatures in Africk, which still going a violent pace straight on, and not being able to turn themselves, can never get any prey but what they meet just in their way." And again: "Now there is an universal *desire,* and *appetite* after *knowledge,* after the peaceable, the fruitful, the nourishing *knowledge:* and not after that of the antient Sects, which only yielded hard indigestible *arguments,* or sharp contentions instead of *food:* which when the minds of men requir'd *bread,* gave them only a *stone,* and for *fish* a *serpent."*

with ordinary writing (and speech). Here, great as are the dangers of imagery, its gifts can be greater still. Metaphor, above all, can give strength, clarity, and speed; it can add wit, humour, individuality, poetry. After all, the one unpardonable fault in an author—and perhaps the commonest—is tediousness. It is easy for a monologue in conversation to become a bore; easier still for a speech; easiest of all for a book. But against boredom there are no better antidotes than these qualities that vivid metaphor can often bring.

Consider, first, the gain in energy and clarity of impression. Hundreds of thousands have groaned in the bitterness of homeless banishment; but their lamentations have been stifled in the silence of the years, while we still remember that double metaphor in which Dante cried how bitterly salt was the bread of exile, and how steep for him its stairs.[19] Many an actor or dramatist must have suffered from the sense of prostituting his own soul to amuse an audience; but could any direct form of utterance have been as moving as Shakespeare's simile "my nature is subdu'd, To what it workes in, like the Dyers hand," or the metaphor of Hugo, telling how, as the curtain rose for the first night of *Hernani,* "Je voyais se lever la jupe de mon âme"?

Many an observer of human life has groaned at the fickle brevity of human grief. Abstractly, it could hardly be put with finer eloquence than Chateaubriand's—"Croyez-moi, mon fils, les douleurs ne sont point éternelles; il faut tôt ou tard qu'elles finissent, parce que le coeur de l'homme est fini; c'est une de nos grandes misères; nous ne sommes pas même capables d'être longtemps malheureux." But, for one who remembers this, there are a thousand who never forget the more concrete vision that Shakespeare has created with the homely aid of a dish and a pair of shoes.

> Thrift, thrift, *Horatio:* the Funerall Bakt-meats
> Did coldly furnish forth the Marriage Tables.

> A little Month, or ere those shooes were old,
> With which she followed my poore Fathers body
> Like *Niobe,* all teares.

Without metaphor could misogyny have found such barbed invectives against women as Pope's phrase about "the moving toyshop of their heart," or Balzac's savage "des poêles à dessus de marbre"? Metternich,

---

[19] *Tu proverai sì come sa di sale*
  lo pane altrui, e com' è duro calle.
  lo scendere e il salir per l'altrui scale.
          Paradiso, XVII.
  Thou shalt make trial what salt and bitter fare
  The bread of others; and how hard a path
  Still to toil up and down another's stair.

I think, was right: "In politics calm clarity is the only true eloquence; but, to be sure, this clarity can at times be best gained by an image."[20]

Next, speed. I know no better example of the power of metaphor to crowd the maximum of ideas into every minute than Ulysses' famous speech in *Troilus and Cressida*.

> Time hath (my Lord) a wallet at his backe,
> Wherein he puts almes for oblivion:
> A great-siz'd monster of ingratitudes:
> Those scraps are good deedes past,
> Which are devour'd as fast as they are made,
> Forgot as soone as done: perserverance, deere my Lord,
> Keepes honor bright, to have done, is to hang
> Quite out of fashion, like a rustie mail,
> In monumentall mockrie: take the instant way,
> For honour travels in a straight so narrow,
> Where one but goes abreast, keepe then the path:
> For Emulation hath a thousand Sonnes,
> That one by one pursue; if you give way,
> Or hedge aside from the direct forthright,
> Like to an entred Tyde, they all rush by,
> And leave you hindmost:
> Or like a gallant Horse falne in first ranke,
> Lye there for pavement to the abject rear,
> Ore-run and trampled on: then what they doe in present,
> Though lesse then yours in past, must ore-top yours.
> For Time is like a fashionable Hoste,
> That slightly shakes his parting Guest by th' hand;
> And with his armes out-stretcht, as he would flye,
> Graspes in the commer: the welcome ever smiles,
> And farewel goes out sighing: O let not vertue seeke
> Remuneration for the thing it was:
> For beautie, wit,
> High birth, vigor of bone, desert in service,
> Love, friendship, charity, are subjects all
> To envious and calumniating Time:
> One touch of nature makes the whole world kin:
> That all with one consent praise new-borne gaudes,
> Though they are made and moulded of things past,
> And give to dust, that is a little gilt,
> More laud then gilt oredusted.

"I use the metaphorical," said Meredith, "to avoid the long-winded." Often he did this effectively.

[20] Varnhagen von Ense, *Denkwürdigkeiten* (1843–59), **VIII**, p. 112.

Slave is the open mouth beneath the closed.

Time leers between above his twiddling thumbs.

When the renewed for ever of a kiss
Whirls life within the shower of loosened hair.

A kiss is but a kiss now! And no wave
Of a great flood that whirls me to the sea.
But as you will! We'll sit contentedly
And eat our pot of honey on the grave.

Strain we the arms for Memory's hours,
We are the seized Persephone.

Thousand eyeballs under hoods
   Have you by the hair.
Enter these enchanted woods
   You who dare.

Unfortunately, I feel, Meredith lacked a Greek sense of restraint; as might be expected from one who held the somewhat simple faith that "the core of style" is "fervidness," and would even rebuke young ladies because their nostrils were not lively, nervous, and dilated. Vitality became for him, at times, a sort of St. Vitus' dance; and in the coils of his twisted ideas he would writhe and mouth like a new Laocoön. Thus sharing Browning's cult for mere violence, he shared also Browning's slightly vulgar itch to astonish; so that Morley could describe him at home, on the approach of a new visitor, "forcing himself without provocation into a wrestle for violent effects"; and Stevenson lament the admixture with his finer qualities of "the high intellectual humbug." Hence a frequent abuse of metaphor in his later work, such as these lines from *The Empty Purse.*

He cancelled the ravaging Plague
   With the roll of his fat off the cliff.
Do thou with thy lean as the weapon of ink,
Though they call thee an angler who fishes the vague
   And catches the not too pink.
Attack one as murderous, knowing thy cause
Is the cause of community. Iterate,
Iterate, iterate, harp on the trite:
Our preacher to win is the supple in stiff:
Yet always in measure, with bearing polite.

Yet to Meredith there does belong the credit of seeing and stating the truth that metaphor need not be, as some suppose, an otiose and time-wasting ornament, like a maze in a country-house garden; but can provide at times a most trenchant short-cut.

As for the humour that imagery can give, I do not know who illustrates this better than dear Fuller. Naturally he got into trouble for it, then and since, with critical owls. Sometimes, indeed, it is not clear whether his humour is intended, or is just the quaintness of his wit—whether we are laughing with him or at him. But often there is no doubt; and, for me, passages like the following make him much more congenial than some Metaphysical minds before him, in the school of Donne, who display their quips with such peacock gravity, and seem too conceited about mere conceits.

Some serious books that dare flie abroad, are hooted at by a flock of Pamphlets.

There are some Birds (Sea-pies by name) who cannot rise except it be by flying against the winde, as some hope to achieve their advancement, by being contrary and paradoxical in judgement to all before them.

(Of tall men.) Ofttimes such who are built four stories high, are observed to have little in their cockloft.

(Of Sir Francis Drake.) In a word, should those that speak against him fast till they fetch their bread where he did his, they would have a good stomach to eat it.

Thus dyed Queen Elizabeth, whilest living, the first maid on earth, and when dead, the second in heaven.

They who count their calling a prison, shall at last make a prison their calling.

(Of a crippled saint.) God, who denied her legs, gave her wings.

Wherefore I presume my aunt Oxford will not be justly offended, if in this book I give my mother[21] the upper hand and first begin with her history. Thus desiring God to pour his blessing on both, that neither may want milk for their children, nor children for their milk, we proceed to the business.

(Of Cambridge Castle.) At this day the castle may seem to have run out of the gate-house, which only is standing and employed for a prison.

Take away Fuller's images, and you rob his humour of half its charm.

[21] Cambridge.

For wit in simile and metaphor, let us turn to Swift. His case is the more interesting in that he is sometimes supposed to have almost wholly disdained such imagery. But to say "the Rogue never hazards a figure"[22] is absurd. He put one (a half-dead metaphor, it is true) even on his tomb—"ubi saeva indignatio ulterius *cor lacerare* nequit." It would be special pleading to point out that *The Tale of a Tub* is a series of metaphors, or to recall the Big-endians and Little-endians, the high Heels and low, of *Gulliver*. But the comparative rarity of Swift's images is not more marked than their point, and often their deadliness, when they do occur. It was Swift that provided Matthew Arnold with a famous watchword in the allegory of the bee's "sweetness and light," as contrasted with the dirt and poison of the spider (though Swift himself, unhappily, too often chose to be more spider than bee). And when Swift proclaims "Surely man is a broomstick"; when he compares Dryden under Virgil's helmet to a mouse under a canopy of state; or poets preyed on by poets to fleas bit by lesser fleas; when he predicts "like that tree, I shall die at top"; when he groans that he *is* dying "in a rage, like a poisoned rat in a hole," could his rancour have found utterance half so telling without the images? And how bitter is the wit of these!

> Old men and comets have been reverenced for the same reason; their long beards, and pretences to foretell events.

> The reason why so few marriages are happy, is, because young ladies spend their time in making nets, not in making cages.

> (Of lovers.) They seem a perfect moral to the story of that philosopher, who, while his thoughts and eyes were fixed upon the constellations, found himself seduced by his lower parts into a ditch.

> If the quiet of the state can be bought by only flinging men a few ceremonies to devour, it is a purchase no wise man would refuse. Let the mastiffs amuse themselves about a sheepskin stuffed with hay, provided it will keep them from worrying the flock.

It remains true, however, that Swift is, in general, unusually sparing of simile and metaphor. (And the images he does use are mainly meant not to charm, but to wound.) That is partly why, to me, he is on the whole an unattractive writer—bleak, monotonous, and depressing, though impressive, like a Pennine moorland—not like the Highlands. But Johnson has

[22] Joseph Warton (*Pope's Works* (1797 ed.), IX, p. 84) asserts that Johnson said this to him. Johnson, as he himself admitted, could talk at times very "loosely"; but I feel some doubt whether he can really have uttered anything so inaccurate. (See G. B. Hill, *Johnson's Lives of the Poets* (1905), III, p. 51; and contrast p. 204 below.)

already said it. "That he has in his works no metaphor, as has been said, is not true, but his few metaphors seem to be received rather by necessity than choice."[23] "This easy and safe conveyance," Johnson continues, "it was Swift's desire to attain, and for having attained he deserves praise. For purposes merely didactic, when something is to be told that was not known before, it is the best mode; but against that inattention by which known truths are suffered to lie neglected, it makes no provision; it instructs, but does not persuade." This, I think, is just. That widening of sympathy which, for me, is so largely the true end of literature, in Swift's writing remains rare. He does not persuade.

It is idle to wish, as Swift trots like a lean grey wolf, with white fangs bared, across his desolate landscape, that he were more like a benevolent Saint Bernard; he would cease to be Swift. Being what he was, he made a striking addition to the infinite variety of the world; but one Swift seems to me quite enough. And his style is of interest as showing both what trenchancy the presence of imagery can give, and how much charm and colour its absence takes away.

We have so far seen how imagery can add strength and speed, wit and humour. But no less important is its power to stamp a work with the writer's particular individuality. This was clear long before psychologists began using the images of our dreams to reveal mental conflicts hidden even from ourselves. The light thrown on Shakespeare's mind by the imagery of his plays, and of one play as contrasted with another, has been abundantly—perhaps too abundantly—examined.[24] Writers, again, have used imagery to mark the personality of their characters. It is not least by his metaphors and similes that the tone of impatient impetuousness in Hotspur is brought to life.

> I had rather be a Kitten and cry mew.

> Oh, he's as tedious
> As a tyred Horse, a rayling Wife,
> Worse than a smoakie House. I had rather live
> With Cheese and Garlick in a Windmill farre,
> Than feede on Cates, and have him talke to me,
> In any Summer-House in Christendome.

23 This I do not feel.
24 See especially W. H. Clemen, *The Development of Shakespeare's Imagery,* 1951—an excellent study, though at times, I think, a little apt to grow too microscopic in the search for hidden significances; too forgetful that the stage is not the study. Not the least interesting thing in Shakespeare's images is their advance from being ornamental to become relevant, concentrated, suggestive. In his prentice work he often uses them merely to impress; but later to express what in no other way could have been expressed so poignantly. They had been mere jewellery: they become the life and feature of his characters.

> You sweare like a Comfit-makers Wife . . .
> Sweare me, *Kate,* like a Lady, as thou art,
> A good mouth-filling Oath: and leave "In sooth",
> And such protest of Pepper Ginger-bread,
> To Velvet-guards and Sunday-Citizens.

Or consider that pair of very different soldiers, Uncle Toby and his corporal. " 'Tis supposed, continued the Benedictine, that St. Maxima has lain in this tomb four hundred years, and two hundred before her canonization—'Tis but a slow rise, Brother Toby, quoth my father, in this selfsame army of Martyrs.[25]—A desperate slow one, an' please your Honour, said Trim, unless one could purchase. I should rather sell out entirely, said my uncle Toby.—I am pretty much of your opinion, Brother Toby, said my father.—Poor St. Maxima, said my uncle Toby low to himself."[26]

But a more solid instance may be found in Johnson of the way a man's images can make him still more himself. "His mind," says Boswell, "was so full of imagery, that he might have been perpetually a poet; yet it is remarkable, that, however rich his prose is in this respect, his poetical pieces, in general, have not much of that splendour, but are rather distinguished by strong sentiment and acute observation." Take away Johnson's figures, especially in his talk, and you will weaken a good deal that impression of snorting, militant energy which made Goldsmith say of him, in another metaphor, that if his pistol missed fire, he would knock you down with the butt; and Boswell, no less vividly, that he used no vain flourishes with his sword—"he was through your body in an instant." Typical, for example, are Johnson's troops of "dogs"—not only "Whig dogs," or "factious dogs," or (of Chesterfield) "I have hurt the dog too much already"; but also (before his own portrait) "Ah ha! Sam Johnson, I see thee! And an ugly dog thou art!"—"I had rather see the portrait of a dog I know than all the allegorical pictures they can shew me in the world"[27]—"If you call a dog Hervey, I shall love him"— "What, is it you, you dogs! I'll have a frisk with you."

Then there are the bulls he launched at Hume and at Rousseau.

> Truth, sir, is a cow which will yield such people no more milk, and so they are gone to milk the bull.

[25] Compare Sterne's own remark: "If ever the army of martyrs was to be augmented or a new one raised—I would have no hand in it, one way or t'other."

[26] Another example of this somewhat obvious form of humour is the nautical Ben of Congreve's *Love for Love.*

[27] A little curious when one recalls Johnson's rather excessive fondness for allegory in *The Rambler.*

If a bull could speak, he might as well exclaim: "Here am I with this cow and this grass; what being can enjoy greater felicity?"

And again, of Edwards's attack on Warburton: "Nay, he has given him some smart hits to be sure; but there is no proportion between the two men; they must not be named together. A fly, sir, may sting a stately horse and make him wince; but one is but an insect, and the other is a horse still." Omit the second sentence, and how much less Johnsonian the whole becomes!

So with Johnson's criticisms. Today they may at times seem false, or old-fashioned; but often, by their gift of metaphor, they still outlive the more meticulous judgements of lesser men. "He treads upon the brink of meaning"—"if their conceits were far-fetched, they were often worth the carriage"—"a quibble was to him the fatal Cleopatra for which he lost the world and was content to lose it"—"if blank verse be not tumid and gorgeous, it is crippled prose." When he dismissed Gray's Odes as "cucumbers," it was in the scornful heat of conversation; but the more considered judgment in the *Life of Gray*—"He has a kind of strutting dignity, and is tall by walking on tiptoe"—lives longer, I find, in the memory than whole chapters by lesser critics. Again what mockery of literary vanity can compare with Johnson on Richardson?—"that fellow Richardson, on the contrary, could not be contented to sail quietly down the stream of reputation, without longing to taste the froth from every stroke of the oar"—"that fellow died merely for want of change among his flatterers; he perished for want of more, like a man obliged to breathe the same air till it is exhausted." And finally when Johnson is himself confronting critics, how typically and genially gigantic is the figure with which he ends! (He is writing to Thomas Warton about the *Dictionary*.) "What reception I shall meet with upon the shore, I know not . . . whether I shall find upon the coast a Calypso that will court, or a Polyphemus that will eat me. But if a Polyphemus comes to me, have at his eye!"[28]

Lastly, the poetry of metaphor. There are owls who want prose to be wholly prosaic. Some kinds of it, yes. Like Locke's.[23] But, whereas poetry is better without any prose in it, prose can often embody a great deal of poetry. Prose in poetry is a blemish like ink on a swan; but prose without poetry becomes too often as drab and lifeless as a Sunday in London. By "poetry" in this sense I do not mean "fine writing," such as De Quincey or Ruskin were sometimes tempted to overdo; I mean a

[28] Johnson wrote "eyes"; but this plural must surely be a slip of his pen.
[29] Cf. Lock, *Of Education:* "If he have a poetic vein, it is to me the strangest thing in the world, that his father should desire or suffer it to be cherished or improved." At least, admirably honest!

feeling for the beauty, grace, or tragedy of life. It is thanks to this that some can find more essential poetry in Sir Thomas Browne than in Dryden; in Landor than in Byron; in some paragraphs of Yeats' prose than in twenty shelves of minor verse. And one of the things that reduce me to annual rage and despair in correcting examination papers is the spectacle of two or three hundred young men and women who have soaked in poetry for two or three years, yet seem, with rare exceptions, not to have absorbed one particle of it into their systems; so that even those who have acquired some knowledge yet think, too often, like pedants, and write like grocers.

*   *   *   *   *

In fine, Johnson, like Aristotle, seems to me right: "And, Sir, as to metaphorical expression, that is a great excellence in style, when it is used with propriety, for it gives you two ideas for one; conveys the meaning more luminously, and generally with a perception of delight."

To say, then, that "metaphor is of no particular relevance" to prose, seems to me stupefying. My confusion is that those who have no gift for metaphor and imagery are doubtless wise to keep clear of it; but that those who have it, whether in writing or in speech, will find few qualities that better repay cultivation.

ROUSING THE EMOTIONS

Bonamy Dobrée

Pure emotive prose, if one can imagine such a thing, would make the reader experience an emotion without direct relation to anything in life: it would work as music does—or at least as it does with semi-musical people, that is, with the majority of those who listen to music, among whom I number myself. Yet writing cannot be utterly unrelated to experience. Unless the words used carry with them some suggestion of moving events or things, they have very little effect, as anybody can tell who has listened to poetry in a language he does not know at all. There may be some degree of pleasure or emotion, but it is very slight. Therefore the purest examples of emotive prose one can find, turn out to be those which deal with ideas whose very vastness makes them diffuse as well as portentous:

> Of all the arts, Tragedy is the proudest, the most triumphant; for it builds its shining citadel in the very centre of the enemy's country, on the very summit of his highest mountain; from its impregnable watchtowers, his camp and arsenals, his columns and forts are all revealed; within its walls the free life continues, while the legions of Death and Pain and Despair, and all the servile captains of tyrant Fate, afford the burghers of that dauntless city new spectacles of beauty. Happy those sacred ramparts, thrice happy the dwellers on that all-seeing eminence.

From Modern Prose Style *by Bonamy Dobrée, 1934. Reprinted by permission of The Clarendon Press, Oxford.*

207

Honour to those brave warriors who, through countless ages of warfare, have preserved for us the priceless heritage of liberty, and have kept undefiled by sacrilegious invaders the home of the unsubdued.

But the beauty of tragedy does but make visible a quality which, in more or less obvious shapes, is present always and everywhere in life. In the spectacles of Death, in the endurance of intolerable pain, and in the irrevocableness of a vanished past, there is a sacredness, an over-powering awe, a feeling of the vastness, the depth, the inexhaustible mystery of existence, in which, as by some strange marriage of pain, the sufferer is bound to the world by bonds of sorrow. In these moments of insight, we lose all eagerness of temporary desire, all struggling and striving for petty ends, all care for the little things that, to a superficial view, make up the common life of day by day; we see, surrounding the narrow raft illumined by the flickering light of human comradeship, the dark ocean on whose rolling waves we toss for a brief hour; from the great night without, a chill blast breaks in upon our refuge; all the loneli-ness of humanity amid hostile forces is concentrated upon the individual soul, which must struggle alone, with what courage it can command, against the whole weight of a universe that cares nothing for its hopes and fears. Victory, in this struggle with the powers of darkness, is the true baptism into the glorious company of heroes, the true initiation into the overmastering beauty of human existence. From that awful encounter of the soul with the outer world, renunciation, wisdom and charity are born; and with their birth a new life begins. To take into the inmost shrine of the soul the irresistible forces whose puppets we seem to be— Death and change, the irrevocableness of the past, and the powerlessness of man before the blind hurry of the universe from vanity to vanity—to feel these things and know them is to conquer them.[1]

There is very little, if any, intellectual idea to be wrested from that passage: its main, one might say, its only effect is to arouse some emo-tion in the reader (perhaps a temporary suspension of the judgment is necessary), an emotion which need not be in the least like the one that impelled the writer. It does not direct the mind to anything in particular, unless you say that to suggest to the reader that tragedy is a comprehensive art form is to direct the mind particularly; for to induce musings on the universe is not to guide a mental process.

There are several interesting things to notice about that passage if we are to try to arrive at any general notions as to how emotive prose is written. The first, to choose at random, though it seems to be one of the most important, is the use of archaic words and expressions (for I need not stress the emotivity of the suggestions), "burghers," "dauntless," "brief

[1] From *Mysticism and Logic,* by Bertrand Russell. Reprinted by permission of George Allen & Unwin, Ltd.

hour," "thrice happy. . . ." There is, of course, all the romantic imagery of the shining citadel and the impregnable watchtowers; and there are the abstract words such as pain, death, and fate. Then there are the adjectives that add nothing to the actual meaning, because it is otherwise stated: "*brave* warriors," "*strange* marriage," words which are, however, valuable in the effect; for consider the difference in the context between writing "some strange marriage" and "a marriage." But possibly more important than all of these is the way the rhythms are sustained. Take the sentence "Honour to those brave warriors who, through countless ages of warfare, have preserved for us the priceless heritage of liberty, and have kept undefiled by sacrilegious invaders the home of the unsubdued." As keynote take the first clause, "Honour to those brave warriors who, through": for if Lord Russell had written "Honour to those brave warriors, who through . . ." the effect would be quite different, until at the very end you came on the very weakened effect of "the home of the unsubdued." It is, perhaps, humiliating to think that the placing of a comma may be much more important than any of your ideas. Then again there are the burdened phrases such as "the dark ocean on whose rolling waves we toss for a brief hour," and a reminiscence or two, an echo of other moving passages, "from vanity to vanity." Also we can note the words "does but." This is common in emotive prose; it serves as a kind of warning bell to tell us that it is our emotions that are going to be attacked. It does indeed have a curious effect. Suppose Lord Russell had written the beginning of his second paragraph: "But the beauty of tragedy makes visible a quality, which in . . ." instead of "But the beauty of tragedy does but make visible a quality which, in . . .": we might then feel more certain that the author of *Mysticism and Logic* really was identical with the writer of *The Analysis of Mind*.

For it is extremely curious how a man's style will change according to what he is doing with it: to note this is once more to present us with the problem of how much it is subject-matter and how much it is personality that decides how a man shall write. [Read the following passage by Professor Trevelyan:]

The morning hours slipped by, and still with impassive countenance he watched the men he treasured fall under the cannon shots. Messenger after messenger galloped off to hasten Eugene, struggling through marsh and woodland far away. But till his colleague was ready to attack, the Duke would not give the word. What were his thoughts as he lunched among his staff in the open field, perhaps for the last time? He well knew it was the day that either made or undid him quite: his fortunes could not survive defeat. And with his own ambitions, the liberties of England and of Europe had come to the last hazard, to be decided, not in any famous city or crowded meeting-place of men, but here in a naked plain of reaped stubble, between villages and farms of names unknown—that tallest spire was called Blindheim, the guides said—places where un-lettered peasants had for ages tilled the soil and for ages more would till it, caring nothing what the great world in its madness had come there to do that day—save only that their poor houses and barns would assuredly be burned. Yet in this uncouth, rustic spot, the texture of Eighteenth Century civilization and thought was to take its colour for good or ill. Hasten, Eugene! Flesh and blood can no longer stand still under this carnage of a cannonade, and the very gods are impatient to see the invisible event. Here at last comes his messenger galloping from the north. He is ready: and we are more than ready. It is past noon, but August days are long. Cutts, the Salamander, is to lead the British and Dutch against Blindheim. And everywhere, along four miles of the Nebel's course, the regiments and squadrons shake themselves and move down towards the marshy edges of the brook.[2]

There again we at once notice the use of archaic expressions: "undid him quite," "to the last hazard," "tilled the soil," "assuredly," "rustic spot." But apart from that there is not much likeness between the two passages quoted in this chapter. Professor Trevelyan does not manage to sustain his rhythms, and the long sentence in the middle of the passage is broken by the spire of Blindheim. Of course, the purpose of the two passages is different. Professor Trevelyan is trying to move his readers not by purely literary means so much as by sitting him next to Marl-borough, and trying to make him share his hopes and his fears. "Hasten, Eugene!" (the archaic word again) does not, in me at least, provide the emotional jolt evidently hoped for, and I must confess that the invisible gods leave me unexcited. What this would seem to suggest is that prose to be emotive must be written with long, sustained rhythms, and abstract words heavily weighted with association. I do not mean that the sentences need be long, for you can maintain rhythm across sentences, as is done in one of the finest emotive passages known to me, in De Quincey's *Levana and Our Lady of Sorrow:*

The second sister is called *Mater Suspiriorum*—Our Lady of Sighs. She never scales the clouds, nor walks abroad upon the winds. She wears no diadem. And her eyes, if they were ever seen, would be neither sweet nor subtle; no man could read their story, they would be found filled with perishing dreams, and with wrecks of forgotten delirium. But she raises not her eyes; her head, on which sits a dilapidated turban, droops for ever, for ever fastens on the dust. She weeps not. She groans not. But

[2] From G. M. Trevelyan, *England Under Queen Anne:* vol. i, *Blenheim.* Re-printed with permission of Longmans, Green & Co., Ltd. Copyright 1930.

she sighs inaudibly at intervals. Her sister, Madonna, is oftentimes stormy and frantic, raging in the highest against heaven, and demanding back her darlings. But Our Lady of Sighs never clamours, never defies, dreams not of rebellious aspirations. She is humble to abjectness. Hers is the meekness that belongs to the hopeless. Murmur she may, but it is in her sleep. Whisper she may, but it is to herself in the twilight. Mutter she does at times, but it is in solitary places that are desolate as she is desolate, in ruined cities, and when the sun has gone down to his rest.

These two latter passages at least give one some concrete imagery, and the words still have meaning. We are not left with questions in our minds such as when, . . . with Lord Russell, we want to know how you can endure pain that is intolerable. That is, in the earlier passage words have ceased to have any precise meaning, and are only suggestive.

In a sense, naturally, all prose is emotive, but I hope there is no confusion here about the kind of prose we are at the moment discussing: it is prose which aims directly at the emotions of the reader, not at his mind. One would naturally expect to find this prose most commonly among novelists, but it is rather curious that to-day the passages which strike me as being addressed to the feelings rather than to the mind are to be found in England mainly among the scientists, philosophers, historians, and critics. It is easier to find the sort of prose we are talking about here among American novelists than among English ones; for reasons I must leave to sociologists. I will begin with a short example:

On the sea the helmsman suffered the downpour, and on the high pastures the shepherd turned and drew his cloak closer about him. In the hills the long-dried stream-beds began to fill again and the noise of water falling from level to level, warring with the stones in the way, filled the gorges. But behind the thick beds of clouds the moon soared radiantly bright, shining upon Italy and its smoking mountains. And in the East the stars shone tranquilly down upon the land that was soon to be called Holy and that even then was preparing its precious burden.[3]

The archaic "suffered" prepares us, and again the effect is produced largely by the extent of the view, which by its size is necessarily vague, first a vision of Italy, and then a historical glimpse of Christianity, the note of remoteness once more being struck at the very end with a familiar echo in "precious burden." But we need not be taken quite so far away from actuality:

[3] From *The Woman of Andros,* by Thornton Wilder, Longmans, 1930.

The Mother Superior and Magdalena and Bernard attended the sick man. There was little to do but to watch and pray, so peaceful and painless was his repose. Sometimes it was sleep, they knew from his relaxed features; then his face would assume personality, consciousness, even though his eyes did not open.

Toward the close of day, in the short twilight after the candles were lighted, the old bishop seemed to become restless, moved a little, and began to murmur; it was in the French tongue, but Bernard, though he caught some words, could make nothing of them. He knelt beside the bed: "What is it, Father? I am here."

He continued to murmur, to move his hands a little, and Magdalena thought he was trying to ask for something or to tell them something. But in reality the Bishop was not there at all: he was standing in a tip-tilted green field among his native mountains, and he was trying to give consolation to a young man who was being torn in two before his eyes by the desire to go and the necessity to stay. He was trying to forge a new Will in that devout and exhausted priest; and the time was short, for the *diligence* for Paris was already rumbling down the mountain gorge.

When the Cathedral bell tolled just after dark, the Mexican population of Stanta Fé fell upon their knees, and all American Catholics as well. Many others who did not kneel prayed in their hearts. Eusabio and the Tesuque boys went quietly away to tell their people; and the next morning the old Archbishop lay before the high altar in the church he had built.[4]

That is almost free of archaisms: there is just a faint flavour given by the phrase "the close of day," and perhaps by "in the French tongue," instead of "in French." But otherwise the method is as different as possible from that of the passages already quoted. It is that of extreme simplicity and direct statement. The voice is kept deliberately dry. You are made to feel that nothing that the voice can do, nothing that words crammed with association might suggest, could increase the poignancy, the sorrow, the acceptance, of the fact. It goes without saying that the theme itself is moving, for however common death may be, it can never be commonplace. Yet the method breaks down unless you feel that the event described really is so stupendous that it needs no more than the bare telling of it to produce the effect (as in Biblical stories, especially in the New Testament): and it breaks down here because the death of this particular archbishop cannot be important enough to you to carry a very great emotion with it. So Miss Cather slips your mind back to an earlier crucial moment of the dying man's life: she is giving you a complete view—like Mr. Wilder's map of Italy—as Lytton Strachey did in his (regrettably)

---

[4] From *Death Comes to the Archbishop,* by Willa Cather, Heinemann, 1927.

often-quoted Death of Queen Victoria. In the main, however, simplicity of statement is relied on, but the words are very carefully chosen, with an ear for alliteration—"so peaceful and painless was his repose," and the sentences are very carefully balanced to give an effect of quietness. The monosyllables make for slow prose. A certain effect of sonority suggested here and there in the earlier paragraphs is rigorously kept out of the last.

Writers, novelists especially, would find it too limiting to confine emotive passages merely to vast, distant, or quiet things, and we find that in describing emotion authors often try to make you feel what their characters felt. They are describing something immediate, vivid, part of life at the moment, at the moment for you just as much as at the moment for their characters. Here any trace of the archaic would be disastrous:

> From the throats of the ragged black men, as they trotted up and down the landing-stage, strange haunting notes. Words were caught up, tossed about, held in the throat. Word-lovers, sound-lovers—the blacks seemed to hold a tone in some warm place, under their red tongues perhaps. Their thick lips were walls under which the tone hid. Unconscious love of inanimate things lost to the whites—skies, the river, a moving boat—black mysticism—never expressed except in song or in the movements of bodies. The bodies of black workers belonged to each other as the sky belonged to the river. Far off now, down river, where the sky was splashed with red, it touched the face of the river. The tones from the throats of black workers touched each other, caressed each other. On the deck of the boat a red-faced mate stood swearing as though at the sky and the river.
>
> The words coming from the throats of the black workers could not be understood by the boy, but were strong and lovely. Afterwards when he thought of that moment Bruce always remembered the singing voices of the negro deck-hands as colors. Streaming reds, browns, golden yellows coming out of black throats. He grew strangely excited inside himself, and his mother, sitting beside him, was also excited. "Ah, my baby! Ah, my baby!" Sounds caught and held in black throats. Notes split into quarter-notes. The word, as meaning, of no importance. Perhaps words were always unimportant. There were strange words about a "banjo dog." What was a "banjo dog"? "Ah, my banjo dog! Oh, oh! Oh! oh! Ah, my banjo dog!"
>
> Brown bodies trotting, black bodies trotting. The bodies of all the men running up and down the landing-stage were one body. One could not be distinguished from another. They were lost in each other.[5]

That is without echoes from other things, and while being as free of archaisms as the piece quoted from De Quincey (allowing for the passage

[5] *From Dark Laughter,* by Sherwood Anderson, Jarrolds, 1926.

of a hundred years or so), it does not take you into either a strange visionary realm, or an abstract one. At the same time it gets its poetic effects: and realizing that emotive prose is primarily poetic, we may remember Mr. Eliot's belief that more prose is bad because it is like bad poetry, than poetry is bad because it is like bad prose. Good emotive prose is very rare, and it seems likely that Mr. Eliot has hit upon the reason why it is so. However, let us look at the poetic effects here. They are almost entirely caused by repetitions. Look how often the word "river" is repeated at the end of the first paragraph, or how often the word "body" is repeated in the last. The words, separately, are not moving ones; they have no profound associations. Colour is a most important element in this passage: black, red, brown; a touch of white; then the stream of reds, browns, golden yellows, and black again at the end. It is clear, I think, that Mr. Anderson's intention in writing this passage was to give you some emotion; but what the precise emotion was to be, even what it was to be about, is not so clear. In the previous passages, except for Lord Russell's and De Quincey's we know both these things: the absence of that knowledge makes for more purely emotive writing.

We still feel here, that although the subject is immediate and modern, some vast issue lies behind the words: we are intended to get a glimpse of a world more primitive (and thus, it is suggested, superior, more intuitive, more in tune with the infinite) than the one white men live in. The piece which follows narrows the issue down to an intellectual attitude:

> This talk of sincerity, I confess, fatigues me. If the fellow was sincere, then so was P. T. Barnum. The word is disgraced and degraded by such uses. He was, in fact, a charlatan, a mountebank, a zany without shame or dignity. His career brought him into contact with the first men of his time; he preferred the company of rustic ignoramuses. It was hard to believe, watching him at Dayton, that he had traveled, that he had been received in civilized societies, that he had been a high officer of state. He seemed only a poor clod like those around him, deluded by a childish theology, full of an almost pathological hatred of all learning, all human dignity, all beauty, all fine and noble things. He was a peasant come home to the barnyard. Imagine a gentleman, and you have imagined everything that he was not. What animated him from end to end of his grotesque career was simply ambition—the ambition of a common man, to get his hand upon the collar of his superiors, or, failing that, to get his thumb into their eyes. He was born with a roaring voice, and it had the trick of inflaming half-wits. His whole career was devoted to raising those half-wits against their betters, that he himself might shine. His last battle will be grossly misunderstood if it is thought of as a mere exercise in fanaticism—that is, if Bryan the Fundamentalist Pope is mistaken for one of the bucolic fundamentalists. There was much more in

it than that, as every one knows who saw him on the field. What moved him, at bottom, was simply hatred of the city men who had laughed at him so long, and brought him at last to so tatterdemalion an estate. He lusted for revenge upon them. He yearned to lead the anthropoid rabble against them, to punish them for their execution upon him, by attacking the very vitals of their civilization. He went far beyond the bounds of any merely religious frenzy, however inordinate. When he began denouncing the notion that man is a mammal even some of the hinds at Dayton were agape. And when, brought upon Darrow's cruel hook, he writhed and tossed in a very fury of malignancy, bawling against the boldest elements of sense and decency like a man frantic—when he came to that tragic climax of his striving there were snickers among the hinds as well as hosannas.

Upon that hook, in truth, Bryan committed suicide, as a legend as well as in the body. He staggered from the rustic court ready to die, and he staggered from it ready to be forgotten, save as a character in a third-rate farce, witless and in poor taste. It was plain to everyone who knew him, when he came to Dayton, that his great days were behind him— that for all the fury of his hatred, he was now definitely an old man, and headed at last for silence. There was a vague, unpleasant manginess about his appearance; he somehow seemed dirty, though a close glance showed him as carefully shaven as an actor, and clad in immaculate linen. All the hair was gone from the dome of his head, and it had begun to fall out, too, behind his ears, in the obscene manner of the late Samuel Gompers. The resonance had departed from his voice; what was once a bugle blast had become reedy and quavering. Who knows that, like Demosthenes, he had a lisp? In the old days, under the magic of his eloquence, no one noticed it. But when he spoke at Dayton it was always audible. . . .

That is, so far. The Fundamentalists, once apparently sweeping all before them, now face minorities prepared for battle even in the South —here and there with some assurance of success. But it is too early, it seems to me, to send the firemen home; the fire is still burning on many a far-flung hill, and it may begin to roar again at any moment. The evil that men do lives after them. Bryan, in his malice, started something that it will not be easy to stop. In ten thousand country towns his old heelers, the evangelical pastors, are propagating his gospel, and everywhere the yokels are ready for it. . . .[6]

That, to the curious, is an extremely interesting passage. It is, if you like, journalism, but if all journalism was of that quality we should not hear so many complaints about it. What is so odd about it is, that although it

[6] Reprinted with permission of Alfred A. Knopf, Inc. from *Prejudices, Fifth Series* by H. L. Mencken. Copyright, 1926 by Alfred A. Knopf, Inc. Renewed, 1954 by H. L. Mencken.

seems a piece of straight hard hitting, it is not emotive as invective is emotive, but in some quite different way. There is, of course, a slight feeling of pity for the decayed Bryan, but only very slight, because of the biting picture we are given of his "grotesque" career. There are one or two emotive turns of speech, such as "headed at last for silence," "so tatterdemalion an estate" (instead of "such a tatterdemalion state"), "many a far-flung hill," and the repetition of "he staggered"; but I do not think the effect is in the main traceable to them. What makes it so puzzling to find out the way the effect is produced is that we are not quite certain what the effect is. It is not pity, it is not scorn, nor derision, nor anger, nor fear, certainly not a vague brooding. One wonders if it may not be accidental, or I should say that I wonder whether it is not peculiar to myself. As I read the last sentence an echo came into my mind of, of all things, Browne's *Garden of Cyrus:* "The huntsmen are up in America, and they are already past their first sleep in Persia." There is something of the same movement. And if we look again at Mr. Mencken's prose, we see that it has a continuous rhythm which quickens the pulse: the vigor behind it imparts a kind of excitement which has nothing to do with the subject-matter. What then is really happening to you is that you are being made warmly sympathetic, not towards Bryan, or any anti-Fundamentalist cause, but towards Mr. Mencken. There is a continual change of speed, with a kind of lilt which gives the main pace, that of "anthropoid rabble against them," "clad in immaculate linen," "minorities prepared for battle." There may follow a pause, a drop in the voice; in fact we realize that what is working upon us is a sort of oratory. I do not defend it as classic prose, yet I submit that of its kind it is worth studying.

Given that emotive prose is a sort of poetry, one would expect that poets would write it best, and that the place where it might most legitimately be found would be the drama. It is certainly to be met with at its highest level in Shakespeare. Unfortunately the drama to-day has become divorced from poetry; we no longer go to the theatre to hear the words, with the result that these are usually lamentably thin, though Mr. Shaw has at least superb phrasing it is a delight to listen to. Occasionally, however, a poet does take to the theatre—usually to be repulsed—and then we sometimes get speeches worth paying attention to. Here, Samuel, old and disappointed, is praying:

> . . . I eat bread, but my soul faints, and wine will not heal my bones. Nothing is good for me but God. Like waters He moves through the world, like a fish I swim in the flood of God Himself. Answer me, Mover of the waters, speak to me as waves speak without mouths. Saul has fallen off, as a ripe fig falls and bursts. He, anointed, he moved in the

flood of power, he was God's, he was not his own. Now he is cast up like a fish among the dry stones, he beats himself against the sun-licked pebbles. He jumped out from the deeps of the Lord, the sea of God has seen him depart. He will die within the smell of his own violence. Lord, Lord, Ocean and Mover of Oceans, lick him into the flood of Thyself. Wilt Thou not reach for him with the arm of a long wave, and catch him back into the deeps of living God? Is he lost from the sway of the tide for ever and for ever? When the rain wets him, will it wet him Godless, and will the wind blow on him without God in it? Lord, wilt Thou not reach for him, he is Thine anointed? Bitter are the waters of old age, and tears fall inward on the heart. Saul is the son whom I anointed, and Saul has crawled away from God, he creeps up the rocks in vanity, the stink of him will rise up like a dead crab. Lord, is it verily so with Saul, is he gone out from Thee for ever, like a creeping thing crawled in vanity from the element of elements? I am old, and my tears run inward, they deaden my heart because of Saul. For Saul has crawled away from the Fountain of Days, and the Ancient of Days will know him no more. I heard the voice of the Lord like waters washing through the night, saying: *Saul has fallen away and is no more in the way of the power of God.* Yea, what is love, that I should love him! He is fallen away, and stinketh like a dead crab, and my love stinks with him. I must wash myself because of Saul, and strip myself of him again, and go down into the deeps of God. Speak, Lord, and I will obey. Tell me, and I will do it. I sink like a stone in the sea, and nothing of my own is left me. I am gone away from myself, I disappear in the deeps of God. And the oracle of the Lord stirs me, as the fountains of the deep. Lo! I am not mine own. The flood has covered me and the waters of the beginning sound in the shell of my heart. And I will find another King for Israel, I shall know him by the whispers of my heart. Lo, I will fill the horn with oil again, with oil from the body of Him, and I will go into the hills of Judah. I will find out one, in whom the power sleeps. And I will pour potency over his head and anoint him with God's fecundity, and place him beyond forgetting. I will go into the hills of Judah, where the sheep feed among the rocks, and find a man fresh in the morning of God. And he shall be King. On the morrow I will gather myself and go, silently, carrying the kingship away from Saul, because the virtue is gone out of him. And Saul will kill me with a spear, in one stroke, for rage he will kill me, if I tell him. But I shall not tell him. I shall say: I must away to the land of Judah, it is the time to sacrifice in the place of Bethlehem, the appointed time is at hand.—So I shall go away from Saul for ever, and never shall I see his face again. I shall hide myself away from his face, lest he hurt himself, slaying me. I shall go in the morning with sure feet, but the shell of my heart will be weary. For I am the Lord's and servant of the Lord, and I go in obedience, even with the alacrity of willingness. But alas, that I should have loved Saul, and had pride in him! I am old.[7]

[7] From *David*, by D. H. Lawrence, Secker, 1926. Reprinted by permission of Laurence Pollinger Limited and the estate of the late Mrs. Frieda Lawrence.

The difficulty there is to assess the effect of the archaistic style, because in this place it is perfectly fitting, and does not give any impression of quaintness. It can probably be discounted. What we get instead is the emotive effect of Biblical English, which, from the enormous weight of its associations, impresses the atheist as much as it does the believer. Over and above this, Lawrence has used every art of the poet; a decided pattern of rhythm, varied according to need; poetic imagery—"Wilt Thou not reach for him with the arm of a long wave," or "the stink of him will rise up like a dead crab;" a good deal of repetition or refrain. The vividness of these things increases as the prayer goes on: the imagery gets more rapturous—"a man fresh in the morning of God"—and the phrase chosen for refrain is more striking, while together with these things the rhythm becomes more insistent, so that you cannot be unaware of the variations in it; "The flood has covered me and the waters of the beginning sound in the shell of my heart," followed later by "I shall go in the morning with sure feet, but the shell of my heart will be weary." The whole passage is almost free verse, though it very rarely falls into actual verse rhythms. What makes this passage particularly striking is that Lawrence has combined the poignancy of something actually moving, the old disillusioned prophet stretching out to God for help, with all the vague apprehensions of eternity and infinity which are Lord Russell's whole stock-in-trade; yet he never lets these get out of hand, but focuses them almost at once by a physical image. Saul, for instance, moved in the flood of power; that is a vast abstract idea: then immediately he is cast up like a fish among the dry stones. This continual shifting of the level of vision, so to speak, is very disturbing; and it is in this way that Lawrence brings into play so many more of your intellectual and emotional faculties than any other of the authors I have quoted do. That, of course, is what makes his passage real poetic prose, not sham poetry written in prose form. There are plenty of other things one could point out as making this extract still more moving: for instance, all of us, however young we may be, are to some extent open to the suggestion of "Bitter are the waters of old age, and tears fall inward on the heart," of which we are reminded when Samuel says "I am old, and my tears run inward"; and again when the idea comes at the end, but still more shortened and so more compressed, with the final, utterly final, "I am old." There is another observation I would like to make. I said in reference to Miss Cather's prose, and earlier, that monosyllables make for slowness; they make for it, but do not necessarily impose it. . . . Lawrence does not let monosyllables interfere with [the passage] or delay it: "I sink like a stone in the sea, and nothing of my own is left me." Where he does not use the polysyllable (which usually has a small proportion of stressed syllables, e.g.: "in vanity from the element of elements") he uses his small words to make feet, one might say, of triple measure: "I sínk like a stóne in the séa," and so on, not, after Miss Cather's manner, making shall we say iambic feet: "a yóung mán who was being tórn in twó befóre his eýes." The more one looks at Lawrence's passage, the more one is struck with its consummate artistry.

When I said that emotive prose might most "legitimately" be found in the drama, I did not wish to suggest that it is not successfully used in other forms of writing, only that it tends to arouse our suspicions when we find it in critical, philosophic, scientific, or historical work. For as a rule, when we analyse these passages, we find, not necessarily that they mean very little, but that they mean one thing while pretending to convey another. Sometimes, however, the art critic can use no way but that of arousing the emotions to make you understand what he is talking about. Is it any good trying to describe low-relief carving by telling you what the subjects are, giving you the measurements (if you could), and so on? The only possible way, though it may be full of dangers, is to try to describe it emotionally, as Mr. Adrian Stokes does in dealing with the sculpture of Agostino di Duccio in the Tempio Malatestiano:[8]

> . . . On an island of jungle land surrounded by the dolphin-populated flux, the elephant and the lion have walked down to join the inspired flood and to vouchsafe the secret places of the wood. Mountains jump up in mid-ocean, scattering the sea. Now Diana re-enters her pagan grave and submits to being resurrected as the sods are upturned by the process she has set in motion. Her place in the sky is taken by the Crab who has stolen up out of the Adriatic over Rimini. Due to the ineluctable union of water and air, under the aegis of Diana, natural forces are suspended, in the flood of moonlight trees may root in the sea, dolphins sport the land, and ships brush their rigging against the fortress, moonlight twanging at the spars. Now Diana has mounted her chariot, and as she climbs the sky to displace the Crab, fish slip off the board, their metallic bodies strike the moonlight. For all is molten silver, and up from the earth comes a bucolic Mercury, his sodden garments limp and worn by the grave to single threads. Immediately he assumes his position, one foot on land, one in water, and to give the effect of continuity, as if no interruption had occurred, he has gathered the cock of vigilance to him, also several spirits of the dead; and now he ties on his winged sandals and fixes a cloud to his knee as if he had this moment (forgetting the spirits of the dead) rushed down from Olympus. The influence at work sets the lute he carries a-whirring, and two serpents hasten to join his caduceus.
>
> Diana is at her height. Sea and sea-life mount the shore still higher without harm to the land because of the infusion of air and moonlight in the heavy water. The mysteries of ocean and of earth, taut now

[8] From *Stones of Rimini,* by Adrian Stokes, Faber and Faber, 1934.

and exemplified to the last atom, at peace, together they are forging the new element which shall the better sustain the offspring of dust and water, the living form, their offspring of a now-remembered marriage before the feud. Entranced human forms flash up, their sex alone indistinct as with the alert and hypnotised Mercury, as with Jupiter. Here are the Twins, hand in hand: their young bodies glisten beneath the filmy draperies that guard their breasts like administering clouds that hasten to tend the moon, to hide her tired eyes some night when her laborious tears of cold silver shall not fall into gravity; and thus she cannot set influence to work as now she does. Indeed, Diana is at her height, and in an excess of hypnotic power she summons the yet remaining lords of the universe. Saturn comes in haste, his beard unkempt, a Phrygian night-cap upon his head. But Mars has never unhammered his armour since the ancient times, his chariot is ready, and it needed but one word from him to set the wolf baying at his horses' feet. They hasten to enrich the element that sustains the human form to its greatest glory. The mountains rise and drop in the even, chorded light, a god in ecstasy on every peak as, breaking the leaf of tuneful silver, Venus comes reborn out of the further sea into the new element, her chariot drawn this time by two white swans. Trees stand upon the tallest waves that move in procession behind her. Doves descend to give her greeting and to inspect the open shell, her birthplace, that she flourishes. As she touches land she disappears. Infusion is complete. Nothing remains to the outer senses, all is music now, imperceptible to the ear, loud in the blood.

It is easy enough to say "That is 'literature'; it has nothing to do with sculpture." Yet you will note that unlike most "literature" of this kind, it does not attempt to interpret the artist, to arrive at his metaphysics: it limits itself to imaginative description, which, to judge from the illustrations in the book, does not seem at all too fanciful. Mr. Stokes is not trying to convey his emotion to you, so much as directing your attention to the things from which you may derive emotion.[9] What kind of emotion it is, he leaves to you. This makes us feel more easy, for we resent prose which has a palpable design upon us, especially critical prose. We prefer to be left to ourselves so far as our feelings are concerned.

At the same time it is emotive prose, and Mr. Stokes does not attempt to hide his emotion from us. Like all the examples we have taken, this sort of prose deals with something vast and eternal, but in this instance, only at second hand: what it deals with primarily is the sculpture, hard rock you can touch and see. And Mr. Stokes is so much in control of his emotion that he never lets you forget this: he does not let you drift

[9] "All emotion depends on real solid vision or sound. It is physical." "But in *rhetoric* and really exceptional prose, we get words divorced from any real vision." T. E. Hulme.

off into cosmic musings. Nevertheless this passage has characteristics in common with others of the sort we are discussing. There is repetition: "Diana is at her height . . ." There are words which, if not archaic (there is no hint of this throughout the passage) are curiously used: the elephant and the lion *vouchsafe* the secret places of the wood: the dolphins *sport* the land. These are examples of modern syntactical compression. But again, as always, it is the voice, the rhythm, which is mainly responsible for the effect: the sustained clauses, the regular marked stresses: "Indeed, Diana is at her height, and in an excess of hypnotic power she summons the yet remaining lords of the universe." The emotive word is occasionally used: "entranced," "ecstasy," "ineluctable" (also somewhat strangely applied): it is, however, a delicate piece of work, and the effective additions made to the main rhythmic structure are never harsh or obvious.

In this chapter I have dealt with only one kind of emotive prose: there are others, such as invective, or the comic, both meant primarily to arouse your feelings, though invective may to some extent be expository, and the comic may be descriptive of action, of persons, or of things. Invective is very rare to-day, perhaps because people are kinder, perhaps because they are indifferent; possibly also, being less robust than our ancestors, we do not take invective in good part, but go and see a lawyer about our prospects of winning a libel action. Also writers of personal invective would not wish to have their scathing words reprinted when their indignation has died down. I can, however, point to Professor A. E. Housman's Preface to *Manilius* as an admirable example of invective prose aimed at (and hitting) bad editors of the classics. The comic is a little outside the range of this book; it does, it is true, depend to some extent on the tone of voice in which it is uttered—take, for instance, Mr. Max Beerbohm's *Zuleika Dobson:* but on the whole it depends more upon the images and ideas presented, on the words put into the mouths of comic characters, than on the writer's style. Think of Mr. W. W. Jacobs, or Mr. P. G. Wodehouse. . . . I feel it would be better to leave the reader to make his own researches into these styles, if he wishes to, to compare for instance the opposite comic styles of overstatement and understatement. . . .

THE GRACES OF PROSE

Robert Graves and Alan Hodge

There is a Debateable Land between the region governed by our numbered principles,[1] those concerned with the secure conveyance of information, and the region governed by our lettered principles, those concerned with its graceful conveyance. For example, most cases of the
use of obscure references, discussed under Principle F, also come under
Principle 3, which concerns general unintelligibility of expression; and
most cases of the circumlocution discussed under Principle G also come
under Principle 20, which concerns irrelevancies. That does not trouble
us. We have separated the two classes of principles because a failure to
conform with the lettered ones is an offence against sensibility, rather
than sense; whereas with the numbered ones the offence is against sense,
rather than sensibility.

principle a

METAPHORS SHOULD NOT BE MATED IN SUCH A WAY AS TO CON-
FUSE OR DISTRACT THE READER.

Metaphors are used more often in English than in most modern
European languages, and far more often than in Latin or Greek. A metaphor is a condensed simile. Here are two similes:

Reprinted with permission of the publisher from The Reader Over Your Shoulder
*by Robert Graves and Alan Hodge. Copyright 1943 by Crowell-Collier and
Macmillan, Inc.*

[1] A reference to an earlier chapter of *The Reader Over Your Shoulder*. [Ed.
Note.]

Marriage is like a lottery—with a great many blanks and very few prizes.

Our struggle against sin resembles a cricket-match. Just as the batsman strides out to the wicket, armed with pads, gloves and bat, and manfully stands up to demon bowling, with an adversary behind him always ready to stump him or catch him out . . . and when the sun sets, and stumps are drawn, he modestly carries his bat back to the pavilion, amid plaudits. So likewise the Christian . . . And when, finally, safe in the celestial pavilion, he lays aside the bat of the spirit, unbuckles the pads of faith, removes the gloves of doctrine and casts down the cap of sanctity upon the scoring-table,—lo, inside, is the name of The Maker!

Examples of metaphors derived from these two similes are:

Poor Edwin has indeed drawn a blank in the matrimonial lottery.

St. Paul, that great sportsman, faced the bowling manfully in the struggle against Paganism.

When two unconnected similes are reduced to metaphors, and these are combined in the same sentence, the effect on the reader is to blur both of the mental pictures which the metaphors call up:

Edwin's matrimonial record deserves our praise rather than our pity: he drew two blanks but on each occasion faced the bowling manfully.

The mismating of metaphors is justified only in facetious contexts. For example, Mr. R. A. Butler, M.P. remarked in a Commons debate:

The Hon. Member for East Wolverhampton is to be congratulated on producing a very tasty rehash of several questions which have been fully ventilated in this House up to date.

Here, the unpleasant implications of the word "ventilated" were sure of a laugh. The columnist "Atticus" often makes genial use of the mismated metaphor. For example:

Colonel Moore-Brabazon's predecessor, Sir John Reith, continues on his Gulliver's travels, and is now on his way to that distant land, the House of Lords, from whose bourne no traveller returns.

But there is no facetiousness in this remark by Mr. Arthur Greenwood, M.P. (1939):

> While we strive for peace, we are leaving no stone unturned to meet the situation should the fateful blow fall.

In what conceivable circumstances could anyone turn up a stone to ward off a fateful blow? Mr. Greenwood meant:

> We who strive for peace are seeking every means of warding off the fateful blow.

The Archbishop of Canterbury in a pamphlet (1940):

> But just as truly pioneers of that far-off age are those who accept the common obligations of men and strive to live in the spirit of Christ as they discharge them.

One may be the pioneer of a new route to some far-off land; one may be the herald or harbinger of a new age; one may be the prophet of a far-off age. But "a pioneer of a far-off age" is a difficult conception.

From a letter to the Press by Eden Phillpotts:

> Exorcize forever the vision of Germany as a bleeding martyr who calls upon civilization to cut the cancer from her bosom; since Germany is herself the cancer. . . .
> She penetrates web and woof, destroying the fabric of human society, pouring her venom through every existing channel of international relations, creating nests and pockets in the healthy tissue of her neighbours, fouling and destroying the forests of human kind that her own fungus breed alone shall inherit the earth and the fulness thereof . . .

A ready test of the legitimacy of a metaphor is whether it can be illustrated even in a fantastic caricature or diagram. Mr. Phillpotts fails to pass the test here: it would puzzle the most ingenious and morbid-minded painter alive, even Salvador Dali, to show a seeming cancer which is really a fungus in the world's bosom, pouring venom through channels in the universal cloth fabric, at the same time creating nests and pockets in the healthy tissues of her neighbour fungus-cancers (?), and destroying forests of mankind.

There are many nearly dead metaphors in English; but they are apt to revive when two or three are included in the same sentence.

From a newspaper article:

> The I.F.S. had held out the olive branch, but nothing of a concrete nature had come out of it.

principle b

METAPHORS SHOULD NOT BE PILED ON TOP OF ONE ANOTHER.

Constant change of metaphor is very tiring to the reader: the visualizing of metaphors requires a different sort of mental effort from that required for visualizing facts.

Here is an account from the American magazine, *Time,* of President Roosevelt's electoral campaign in 1940:

> No ivory tower held Candidate Roosevelt. He knew well that a candidacy should reach its crest on Election Day and not one moment before. But the Gallup Poll, giving him a terrific majority, left no option now but to go ahead and kill off Candidate Willkie, for any slip from that lead might still be fatal in a year as full of loose electricity as 1940. He decided to go ahead full steam.

It would be have better to write this report in a simple sustained metaphor —for example, that of a boxer who has planned to win a match on points, intending not to go all out until the last round, but getting an unexpected chance to knock out his opponent in an early one. In the *Time* version the change from the electricity to the steam metaphor is particularly confusing.

"Atticus" sometimes overdoes his trick of mismating metaphors. An occasional mismating may be good fun, but an orgy disgusts.

> After a series of punishing defeats the Premier's son, Mr. Randolph Churchill, has won a bloodless victory and will now join the gallant six hundred at Westminster. No doubt he will have mellowed since the days when as a young politician he not only rode ahead of the hounds but in front of the fox.

H. G. Wells is being solemn, not facetious, in this sentence from a newspaper article:

> And the raw material, that hairy ape, is so made over that it is only in some moment of crazy lust, panic, rage or bestial vitality that we realize he is still the core, the blood injection at the root of us all.

Mr. Wells tends to take a scientific view of language—that words are tools, and those with the strongest pictorial associations have the keenest cutting edge: if he wishes to express himself trenchantly why should he not use "hairy ape," "the core," "blood injection," "at the root of us all"? Because it is dangerous to play with edged tools.

Readers would understand and accept Mr. Well's meaning far better if he had written:

> And the passionate material of which we all are made has been so carefully processed in the factory of our social habits that it is only an occasional crazy moment of lust, rage, or panic that suddenly recalls our bestial origin.

principle c

METAPHORS SHOULD NOT BE USED IN SUCH CLOSE ASSOCIATION WITH UNMETAPHORICAL LANGUAGE AS TO PRODUCE ABSURDITY OR CONFUSION.

The principle is best illustrated by this short sentence from a melodramatic chapter in Graham Greene's novel *It's a Battlefield:*

> Kay Rimmer sat with her head in her hands and her eyes on the floor.

And her teeth on the mantelpiece? A slip like this will break the spell of a novel for any intelligent reader.

In the following quotation from J. N. W. Sullivan's *The Bases of Modern Science* (1928), the fantastic metaphor in the first sentence is disconcertingly given an appearance of reality in the second and third sentences:

> The principle requires us to believe that, *to an observer mounted on such an electron,* a ray of light would pass the electron with the speed of 186,000 miles per second, whether the electron was moving in the direction of the ray or whether it was moving in the opposite direction. We have said "to an observer," but we do not intend to imply thereby

that any merely psychological effect is involved. We may replace the observer by scientific apparatus making the necessary measurements automatically. What is essential is that the apparatus should be mounted on the electron.

From the Minutes of a Municipal Council:

> The sub-committee have reported that though every avenue has been explored, no street in the central district bounded by Station Road on the North and High Street on the South could be used as a permanent parking-place for cars without incommoding tradesmen and/or impeding traffic.

There were no avenues in the central district—only narrow streets lined with shops.

principle d

CHARACTERISTICALLY POETICAL EXPRESSIONS SHOULD NOT BE USED IN PROSE

Except, of course, in quotations. When Daphne du Maurier writes in a pamphlet:

> All that remained of the gallantry, the courage, the brotherhood and sacrifice, of four years in Flanders, were the graves of the fallen and the blown and scarlet poppies.

The reader is entitled to make such burlesque variants on "the blown and scarlet poppies" as "the infant and chestnut foals," "the adolescent and Red Indian."

Our phrase "poetical expressions" includes such conceits as these from a novel by Dr. A. J. Cronin:

> The force of the hurricane almost bowled him off his feet. The station was deserted. The young poplars planted in line at its entrance bent like bows, whistling and shivering at every blast. Overhead the stars were polished to a high glitter.

Prose decency demands rather: "Overhead, the stars glittered with such brilliance that he fancied them burnished by the force of the wind."

These are conceits in the French style. French is a less poetic language than English, since fewer liberties can be taken with it and possible meanings are therefore restricted. If, obeying the traditional rules of French, one attempts to write great poetry, the result, judged by English poetic standards, is at best merely magnificent verse. This is what André Gide meant when, asked who was the greatest French poet, he answered "Victor Hugo —*hélas!*" Modern poets who are born French have despairingly cultivated an anarchic "disorientation of the senses," following the example of Rimbaud, a true poet. Such characteristically French movements as impressionism, symbolism, and surrealism all began from disorientation. Impressionism is a hit-or-miss way of describing the general appearance of things without consideration of details; symbolism is a way of describing things with conscious disregard of how one intellectually knows them to be, for the purpose of emphasizing their emotional significance; surrealism is the realistic expression of disturbingly anticonventional fancies.

Many feelings and scenes are extremely difficult to describe accurately in prose. Here, for example, is a description of a "damnable room" by Rebecca West, in her novel *Harriet Hume,* as it looked when one Arnold Condorex switched out all the lamps but an alabaster urn on the chimney-piece:

> The fluted pilasters, their grooves black with shadow, looked like claw-nails drawn down the walls, and the gold convoluted capitals might have been the claws that traced them. The painted lunettes on the panels and ceiling were black oily smears from which shone only the whiter details of a universe lackadaisically falsified, swan necks bent by angelic meekness to re-entrant curves, profiles so tense with nobility that the breath must rush forth from the nostrils like the shriek of a police whistle, forearms like fins with languishment.

This reads queerly, but then the room was damnably queer; and when one examines the words in detail there is not one to which one could justly take exception, except "like claw-nails drawn" for "as though claw-nails had been drawn": it is as intelligibly expressed as so difficult a scene could be. But in the same novel occurs another passage:

> Tenderly he reflected that her little head, which was almost egg-like in its oval blandness was as full as an egg is of meat with the desire to please. But for that his shrewdness rebuked him. There must be much else besides. She had mastered the shining black leviathan that just behind her proclaimed Bechstein its parent. Like him she had crawled up the dark tunnel which leads from obscurity to the light, and had performed the feat more expeditiously.

This does not seem written in the same sensitive style as the other passage. Some sort of "ism" pervades it. The reader feels that Rebecca West is trying to put something over on him, some sort of verbal hypnotism. When he examines the words in detail they do not answer for themselves in a commonsense way. Blandness cannot be oval. "But for that" is ambiguous. "Shrewdness" cannot rebuke; though a "shrewder self" can. Bechstein was not a shining black leviathan who spawned other black leviathans and crawled up dark tunnels rather less expeditiously than Harriet.

Here is an example of impressionism from W. E. Woodward's biography *George Washington:*

> Writers, historians, philosophers and men of that tribe have more inner life than they really need. On the other hand, there are many people who could take on a larger amount of inner life without being harmed at all.
>
> McMaster thought that Washington's inner life had never been understood and probably never would be.
>
> From him we get the impression of a great figure, sitting in dusky isolation, like a heroic statue in an empty plain. To reach it we must travel a road that has been worn so deep by McMaster, and Irving, and Sparks, and Wilson, and Lodge—and innumerable others—that we cannot see over its sides. It is cluttered with the prayer tablets of the pilgrims who have preceded us; and we are out of breath from climbing over the hurdles of reverence and fancy. We approach on tiptoe; we utter the sibilant whispers of awe.
>
> No wonder Washington's character appears elusive. Anybody's would under the circumstances. . . .
>
> The background of elusiveness has been painted in the picture by biographers who have looked into Washington's soul for the quivering inner life which they themselves possessed. When they did not find it there they lost their bearing and ran round in circles.
>
> Washington's mind was the *business mind.*

This is a plausible argument and a sensible conclusion; but it would carry far more weight with the ordinary reader if written more soberly. It is not merely that the metaphors are mismated—one does not expect to find hurdles across a well-worn road, or a three-dimensional statue melting into a two-dimensional background; nor merely that the contrast between the crudely facetious "take on a large amount of inner life" and the rhetorical "sitting in dusky isolation, like a heroic statue in an empty plain" is shocking. The worst is that the reader feels himself written *at,* not written *for*—especially in the de Quinceyesque: "We approach on tiptoe; we utter the sibilant whispers of awe."

Here is an impressionistic passage from a short-story by H. A. Manhood:

> They kissed, and happiness was a singing colour in the stillness. They lay down, and their passion was an exquisite winging of time and beyond reason, a glimpse of harmony at its uttermost source, a moment of immortal growth. And, having raced to rapture and savoured all creation, they came laughing back like guests to sleep where sleep was known, lying close in a gracious half-state that made the final waking less like bruising, gave them time to secure memory for ever. . . .
>
> They never lost the first ecstasy. The richness and marvel of their oneness increased to a deep, sustained over-beat within them, a radiance which seemed larger even than death.

These are wild words. How can a winging be a glimpse? How can a source be uttermost? How can harmony have even an original source? What is immortal growth? How can a glimpse be a growth? What is the meaning of even so apparently simple a phrase as "like guests to sleep where sleep was known"?—is the first "sleep" a verb or a noun? "Half-smile," "half-apple," or "half-century," yes!—but what is a half-state?—does he mean "intermediate state"?—if so between what extremes? How can an overbeat be a radiance, and how can a radiance seem larger than death?

principle e

EXCEPT WHERE THE WRITER IS BEING DELIBERATELY FACETIOUS, ALL PHRASES IN A SENTENCE, OR SENTENCES IN A PARAGRAPH, SHOULD BELONG TO THE SAME VOCABULARY OR LEVEL OF LANGUAGE.

Scholars and clergymen are seldom able to keep their language all of a piece.

The following is from a newspaper sermon:

> It is one of the mysteries of that inner life of man (one so replete with mysteries hard to accept or solve) that some of us are clearly, as it were, freeborn citizens of grace, whilst others—alas! many others—can only at great price buy this freedom. Of this there can be no doubt. The Gospel appointed for to-day reports to us, in the words of our Lord

Himself, a story at once simple and mystifying, about day-labourers in an Eastern vineyard. Some of them had worked a full day, whilst others had only "clocked in," so to speak, when it was nearly time to go. Yet each received from the employer the same flat rate of remuneration— a Roman penny. Our Lord said that was all right, which must be enough for us.

It begins with ecclasiastical-scholarly language "whilst others—alas! many others—can only at great price buy this freedom"; gradually presses through the apologetically modern, "others had only 'clocked in', so to speak, when it was nearly time to go," and the commercial, "each received from the employer the same flat rate of renumeration"; descends to the downright vulgar, "Our Lord said that was all right . . ."

Scholars are at their worst in translations, especially when trying to give antique work a modern flavour: over-attention to the Classics has blinded them to the moods of their own language. From Dr. Rouse's translation of Seneca's *Apocolocyntosis:*

Citius mihi verum, ne tibi alogias excutiam.
Out with the truth and look sharp, or I'll knock your quips and quiddities
    out of you.

Contentus erit his interim convictoribus.
These boon-companions will satisfy him for the nonce.

Vosque in primis qui concusso
Magna parastis lucra fritillo.
And you, above all, who get rich quick
By the rattle of dice and the three-card trick.

This is to dart about confusingly between the seventeenth and twentieth centuries.

The same uncertainty of language-level is found in Michael Heseltine's translation of Petronius's *Satyricon.* Here there is an attempt at brisk modernity:

"*Oro te,*" *inquit Echion centonarius,* "*melius loquere.*"
"Oh, don't be so gloomy," said Echion, the old-clothes dealer.

But there are sad lapses into the antique:

In pinacothecam perveni vario genere tabularum mirabilem. Nam et Zeuxidos manus vidi nondum vetustatis injuria victas.

Mr. Heseltine's translation is:

> I came into a gallery hung with a wonderful collection of various pictures. I saw the works of Zeuxis not yet overcome by the defacement of time.

This, to match the other quotation, should have read:

> I visited the gallery. The exhibition of paintings there was most representative and contained some fine old-masters, among which I even found a few Zeuxises that had kept their original tones surprising well.

principle f

NO REFERENCE SHOULD BE UNNECESSARILY OBSCURE.

If everyone had to write for the stupidest reader, as a regiment on the march accommodates itself to the pace of the slowest soldier, literature would be as tedious as a tenpenny nail,[1] and since the precise degree of literary and historical education with which one's public can be credited varies greatly with its estimated size, this principle is a difficult one to observe.

The Parliamentary Correspondent of a daily paper who writes: "The "ouse couldn't but do it' as Bunce remarked on a similar occasion" is expecting too much of even his educated readers. A few of them will have read Trollope's *Phineas Finn,* but of those not all will remember the minor character Bunce and hardly one of those who do will be able to recall the "similar occasion."

From a detective novel by Dorothy Sayers:

> "I feel," said the lawyer, carefully stirring his coffee, "that . . . Mr. Arbuthnot is right in saying it may involve you in some—er— unpleasant publicity. Er—I . . . cannot feel that our religion demands that we should make ourselves conspicuous—in such very painful circumstances."
>
> Mr. Parker reminded himself of a dictum of Lord Melbourne.
>
> "Well, after all," said Mrs. Marchbanks, "as Helen so rightly says, does it matter? . . ."

---

[1] We use this to exemplify the sort of incidental expression that one should avoid. A "tenpenny nail" is an old-fashioned school reading-book, but (except in Scotland) the phrase has been a hundred years out of fashion.

The particular dictum of Lord Melbourne appropriate to this context cannot be unerringly singled out by any of Miss Sayers's readers, who number hundreds of thousands, nor even guessed at by more than a dozen or so Melbourne experts—none of whom is necessarily a reader of Miss Sayers's novels. That Mr. Parker, a police inspector, could recall a dictum of Lord Melbourne's is not an indication, either, that he was an educated person: he might have come across it in a "Great Thoughts" calendar or in a popular newspaper.

Malcolm Muggeridge writes in his history, *The Thirties:*

> In the restless determination to extract ever more material satisfaction from life to compensate for other satisfactions which were lacking, ever heavier drafts were drawn on the future. Expense of shame in a waste of passion. . . .

This crooked reference to the 129th sonnet of Shakespeare's which begins:

> Th' expence of spirit in a waste of shame
> Is lust in action . . .

seems to us indefensible. The line is first inverted, then misquoted, and in its new form does not explain itself as prose.

principle g

ALL IDEAS SHOULD BE EXPRESSED CONCISELY, BUT WITHOUT DISCOURTEOUS ABRUPTNESS

Circumlocution is one of the few bad habits in writing that have gradually gone out of fashion since the daily newspapers first set an example of snappy reporting of events. Yet there is still plenty of verbosity left over from the leisured days before the First World War when it was often considered a sign not of pomposity but of ingenuity to make five words, without irrelevance or repetition, do the work of one. Pontifical critics, who wish to fill up a column easily, politicians and retired Headmasters who wish to be regarded as men of letters, and officials who wish to be portentous for reasons of policy are, in general, the most verbose writers of to-day.

Victorian readers did not much mind having their time wasted; a few survivors still feel that they are not getting their money's worth unless, say, an article on modern novels in the leading literary weekly begins in the leisurely expansive style of the following (1940):

> Nothing is vainer at the present time, of course, than prediction. But one broad conclusion seems reasonably safe. If, as is most likely, we come out after the war into rather a different sort of world, we shall almost certainly be getting a rather different sort of novel.
>
> English fiction of the past two years throws little light on precisely what differences may be expected. So far, that is, the war has not stimulated any noticeable "new tendencies" in the novel; there is nothing to indicate the birth of either new ideals or new methods. But at the same time there is evidence, admittedly slight and possibly unreliable except in rough outline, of a deepening selectiveness among old ideals and methods. For what it is worth this evidence may supplement certain general deductions from the course of events since the outbreak of war that concern much else besides literature.

This amounts to no more than:

> Though the style of English novels is likely to change after the war is over, it is not safe to prophesy just how it will change. Fiction published during this war has shown signs, not of new ideals and methods, but only of what I, perhaps mistakenly, judge to be a more conscientious choice of old ones. I will relate this judgement to certain general deductions from events of the last two years.

From the Minutes of a Debating Society:

> It was proposed by Mr. J. H. Dix and unanimously carried: that whereas discussions in this Society are not liable to end in the breaking of furniture or fixtures, so long as they are checked when they become too noisy; and whereas discussions unwisely conducted endanger the peacefulness of this Society; and whereas discussions that go on under the chairmanship of Mr. E. B. Silvoe sometimes end in the breaking of furniture or fixtures; and whereas discussions in this usually peaceful Society are, if wisely conducted, always checked when they become too noisy—Mr. E. B. Silvoe be not again appointed to take the chair at a meeting of this Society.

This can be reduced simply to:

> It was proposed by Mr. J. H. Dix and unanimously carried: that whereas, when Mr. E. B. Silvoe is appointed chairman, the discussions

of this usually peaceful Society are not always checked before furniture or fixtures are broken, he be not again appointed.

Verbosity, as in the last example, is often due to over-conscientiousness; in the following instance, from a Head Warden's circular, it is due to embarrassment at having to point out something obvious:

> With the coming of the longer periods of darkness the possibility of enemy action is increasing and it is necessary that all steps should be taken by the civilian population to minimize the dangers attendant on the falling of bombs, by organizing themselves into stirrup-pump parties, and so face up to the war.

This would have been put more simply as:

> As the nights draw out, civilians must face the increased danger of enemy bombing, by forming stirrup-pump parties.

This, from Professor A. N. Whitehead's *Science and the Modern World* (1925), is probably written in an embarrassment similarly caused.

> The inevitableness of destiny can only be illustrated in terms of human life by incidents which in fact involve unhappiness.

Since destiny is by definition inevitable, this reduces to:

> Human destiny can be exemplified only with unhappy instances.

principle h

THE DESCRIPTIVE TITLE OF A PERSON OR THING SHOULD NOT BE VARIED MERELY FOR THE SAKE OF ELEGANCE.

Elegant variation of names and titles is a common French trick, derived from Latin verse. A Latin poet, writing about the God Bacchus, for example, or the God Jupiter, would have thought meanly of himself if he could not present the God under ten or twelve aliases, each recording a part of his legendary history and attributes. The French novelist Balzac, similarly, used as many as six different descriptive identifications of the same person at the beginning of successive sentences. Mr. Philip

Guedalla emulates Balzac. Here is a passage from his *Mr. Churchill: a Portrait:*

> . . . he prepared a discourse, learned it off, and established himself in his father's seat. His predecessor in debate was a Welsh Radical, a few years older than himself, who had been ten years in the House already, and, courageous in his criticism of the war, emulated Winston Churchill's escape from Pretoria in a Dutch pastor's hat by escaping from a hostile audience at Birmingham Town Hall in a policeman's helmet.
>
> The black-haired orator resumed his seat, and Mr. Churchill followed Mr. Lloyd George. It was an unimpressive little speech . . . Though he managed to be loyal to the Government, the new member's tone about the Boers was a shade unusual. . . .
>
> The ordeal was over; and when someone introduced him to Lloyd George, the fervent Welshman told him that he was "standing against the light." The Tory novice answered that his new friend seemed to "take a singularly detached view of the British Empire."

Anyone who read this passage hurriedly would imagine that at least four or five people, not two, were involved in this historic meeting.

An official leaflet, E D L 66, circulated by the Ministry of Labour to women who registered under the "Registration for Employment Order, 1941," contains this paragraph:

> Women are wanted for the work of supplying the Forces with aeroplanes, guns, shells, and all the munitions and equipment that they need. Large numbers are also required in the Women's Auxiliary Services —the W.R.N.S., the A.T.S., the W.A.A.F., . . . The Nursing Services also require a great many additional recruits. More women are wanted by the Women's Land Army and N.A.A.F.I. There are also many other essential industries and services which must be maintained.

This constant change of formula is unnecessary, confusing and invidious. The paragraph would have read more persuasively as follows:

> Large numbers of women are needed in industry, especially in the factories that supply the Forces with aeroplanes, guns, tanks, ammunition and equipment. Large numbers are needed also in the W.R.N.S., the A.T.S., the W.A.A.F., in the Women's Land Army, in the N.A.A.F.I., in the Nursing Associations—these and many other vital services must be maintained.

From an historical article on the American War of Independence:

> When news of the disaster came, Cornwallis sought to retrieve it by cutting off Morgan, but that general had dropped back with such celerity that the force sent out was too late, the troops being detained by torrents of rain which made the creeks almost impassable.

"That general," "that gentleman," "that worthy" are never either neat or necessary substitutes for "he." The author should have written something of this sort:

> When news of the disaster came, Cornwallis sought to retrieve his position by cutting General Morgan's line of retreat. But Morgan moved quickly and the force that Cornwallis sent out arrived too late [at the Dan River], having been detained by torrential rain which made the intervening creeks almost impassable.

Expressions such as "the former, the latter," "the first, the second," should be used as seldom as possible: they are invitations to the reader's eye to travel back—and it should be encouraged always to read straight on at an even pace.

An Air Ministry announcement was phrased:

> One of our fighters attacked and destroyed three enemy bombers in as many minutes.

This is a device for avoiding the repetition of "three." But why trouble to avoid it? Why ask the reader to work out an equation sum—which is not even amusingly complex?

An American magazine takes this device a stage further into absurdity:

> For the second time in as many months the panic was on.

principle i

SENTENCES SHOULD NOT BE SO LONG THAT THE READER LOSES HIS WAY IN THEM.

A sentence may be as long as the writer pleases, provided that he confines it to a single connected range of ideas, and by careful punctuation prevents the reader from finding it either tedious or confusing. Modern journalists work on the principle that sentences should be as snappy as possible; they seldom, therefore, use colons or semi-colons. Historians and biographers have learned to be snappy too. Here is H. C. Armstrong writing about Mustapha Kemal Ataturk in his *Grey Wolf:*

> Enver was always inspired by great ideas, by far-flung schemes. The big idea absorbed him. He cared nothing for details, facts or figures.
>
> Mustafa Kemal was cautious. He was suspicious of brilliancy. Big, vague ideas did not rouse him. His objectives were limited, and undertaken only after long and careful consideration and calculation. He wanted exact facts and figures. He had no sympathy with and no ability at handling Arabs or any foreigners. He was a Turk, and proud of being a Turk. . . .

A biographer of the old school would have fittted these ten sentences into a single one, connected by a semi-colon at the place where Mr. Armstrong has begun a new paragraph.

Sentences by eighteenth-century authors sometimes continue for a page or more, yet are not allowed to get out of hand. Here, however, are a couple of modern instances where even a seven-line sentence is too long. From an article by D. R. Gent, the sporting-journalist:

> I spent many hours dipping into Rugby books of all kinds, and two especially suggested lots of subjects that, I think, will interest my readers these days, when we can face up to the strenuous times we are living in, even more bravely when we can refresh ourselves occasionally with memories of great days behind us, and especially days on the Rugby field or watching glorious matches.

This would have read better if he had broken it up into three sentences, in some such way as this:

> I spent many hours dipping into a variety of books about Rugby, and two especially interested me. I think that they would have interested my readers too, for they concerned great events in the history of the game. In these strenuous times we can face up to our trials and responsibilities more bravely if we occasionally refresh ourselves with memories of the glorious matches which we have witnessed or in which we have been fortunate enough to take part ourselves.

This is from an article by Ernest Newman, the music critic:

Berlioz's faults as a composer are obvious, but not more so than those of many other composers who, however, had the good luck to have their misses counted as hits by umpires whose sense of values had been perverted by too long a toleration of bad art so long as it was bad in the orthodox way, whereas Berlioz's directest hits were often debited to him as misses.

This is too long a sentence only because it is mismanaged. Commas are not enough to separate so many complex ideas into poorly related parts of a single argument. We suggest this alternative version:

Berlioz's faults are obvious to us modern listeners, as are those of many other composers who in their time fared far better with the critics than he did: their misses were often counted as hits, his most direct hits as misses—merely because musical standards had been perverted by a long toleration of work which, though bad, was not eccentrically so.

This is from an article by Arthur Krock in a New York newspaper (1941):

It is Morava-Varda that is the military stake for which Hitler is playing in his game of high-tension diplomacy with the Yugoslavs. Should he be confined to the Struma because of unwillingness or inability to add to his enemies the Yugoslavs massed against a Salonica front which would be the result if the people and their government fulfil the expectation noted above, Hitler's designs would be obstructed.

The second sentence is too long only because too many ideas have been tied to one another in a bundle. They should have been separated in this sort of way:

If the people and government of Yugoslavia, fulfilling my expectation of them noted above, decide to forbid Hitler the use of the Morava-Varda valleys, and if he is unwilling or unable to add them to his enemies, he will be unable to approach Salonica except by the Struma valley and his designs will thereby be obstructed.

principle j

NO UNNECESSARY STRAIN SHOULD BE PUT ON THE READER'S MEMORY.

Some writers think in far longer stretches than others: they start an essay or article with some unobtrusive point and, after introducing a whole new body of argument, slowly circle round and pick the point up again two or three pages later as if it had only just been made. They should remember that most people, though they may be expected to retain the general sense of any paragraph until the end of the chapter, will forget a particular phrase in it (unless heavily accentuated) after three sentences and a word (unless very remarkable) as soon as they have finished the sentence.

Here are examples, from two leaders by J. A. Spender, of excessive strain put on the reader's memory:

> There could, for example, be no better contribution to "Federal Union" than the pooling of resources for mutual defence recently achieved by the United States, Britain and Canada. Here, for the first time, is shown the way to break down the obstacle of "sovereignty" which worked so disastrously before the war to isolate and divide the smaller nations and leave them at the mercy of the Dictators. Lord Lothian, who has long been a student of this subject, brings back this sheaf with him on his visit to London.

The phrase "this subject" in the third sentence presumably refers to "Federal Union"; and "this sheaf" to "the pooling of resources for mutual defence." But because of the intervening sentence few readers will have been able to identify these references without a quick look-back to the first sentence.

> Our habit of taking the whole world into our confidence about our casualties and the damage done by German raiders to our buildings and property is, I am sure, well justified. A free and self-respecting people needs to be assured that nothing is being concealed from it, and that there will not some day be a sudden shock of discovery when concealment is no longer possible. Yet contrasted with the grim silence of the dictators about what is happening in their countries, it produces a one-sided psychological effect which needs to be corrected by some effort of imagination.

Here, the "it" of the third sentence has separated from the subject to which it refers by a longish sentence. Few readers will have been immediately able to identify the "it" with "our habit of taking the whole world into our confidence about our casualties and the damage done by German raiders to our buildings and property."

The Archbishop of Canterbury writes in a pamphlet (1940):

Especially we must remember that it is very hard to extract justice from strife. The passions evoked by war blind the vision and distort the judgement. We dare not hope to make our victory result in pure justice. We can, indeed, make it result in something far nearer justice than a Nazi domination; that alone would justify our fighting. But we must not ignore the perils inseparable from our enterprise; and we must steadfastly determine that we will resist, so far as by God's help we can, these corrupting influences, so that if He gives us victory we may be found faithful to the principles for which we have striven.

Here, similarly, the "corrupting influences" in the last sentence are not easily identified with "the passions evoked by war" mentioned three sentences previously: most readers will be able to think back only as far as "a Nazi domination."

principle k

THE SAME WORD SHOULD NOT BE SO OFTEN USED IN THE SAME SENTENCE OR PARAGRAPH THAT IT BECOMES TEDIOUS.

For emphasis it is legitimate to go on using the same word or phrase time after time:

The crow has been peculiarly my bird ever since I can remember. Indeed, my earliest recollection of childhood is a crow perched on my nursery window-sill. On my third birthday a crow came to my party and helped himself to my birthday cake. On my first journey to school I was accompanied by a crow. A crow perched on a tree outside the room where I sat for my first successful examination. A crow was the cause of my meeting my first wife; a crow attended our wedding; a crow nested on the chimney of my first freehold house. Finally, a crow gave the alarm when I was drowning in the Regent's Canal in June 1886. It has always been a crow, not lark, robin, blackbird, raven, owl nor lapwing— no other bird but a crow!

Or:

Fethi had this tradition from the sage Abdul ibn Rashid, who had it from the sage Daoud ibn Zaki, who had it from his father who was a judge in Homs, who had it from his brother Ali the Copyist, who had it from Mahomed the guardian of the Mosque of Tarjid, who had it from his predecessor of the same name, who had it from [etc. etc.] who had it from Ali, the muezzin of Al Ragga, who had it from his father

Akbar, the saddle-maker, who had it from the lips of the blessed Prophet Himself!

But here are instances where the continued use of the same word becomes tedious. From a "lay sermon":

> I admire the man who is man enough to go up to a man whom he sees bullying a child or a weaker man and tell him, as man to man, that he must lay off.

This should read:

> I admire the man who is courageous enough to go up to someone whom he sees bullying a child or a man weaker than himself, and tell him plainly that he must lay off.

The word "of" is often a difficulty. From a report on broadcasting by the Committee of Convocation (1931):

> There has been . . . an honest dread on the part of many of the popularization of a form of godliness that lacked its power, of the substitution of an emotional appeal at the fireside for the organized fellowship. . . .

This should have read:

> Many have honestly dreaded the popularization of a form of godliness that lacked its power, the substitution of an emotional appeal at the fireside for organized fellowship. . . .

The word "in" is often a difficulty. From an agricultural report in a newspaper:

> In fact, in countless villages in England in this war and in a variety of ways, there has been a most astonishing adaptation of local products to war needs.

This should have read:

In countless English villages during this war, and in a variety of ways, there has been, indeed, etc. etc.

principle I

WORDS WHICH RHYME OR FORM A JINGLE SHOULD NOT BE AL-LOWED TO COME TOO CLOSE TOGETHER.

Though modern prose is intended to be read silently and two or three times faster than at the ordinary speaking rate, some people read with their mental ear not quite closed. Obstrusive accidental rhymes or jingles are therefore avoided by careful prose writers, as possibly distracting their readers' attention.

The terminations "otion" and "ation" are often a difficulty:

The need of registration or re-registration at this station of all workers on probation is to be the subject of examination by the Administration.

There is usually a way out—here, for example:

The Administration will examine the need of registering or reregistering at this station all probationary workers.

The termination "ing" is often a difficulty. This is from a Gossip column (1940):

I have heard something interesting which, anticipating the approaching ending of the Peiping Puppet Government, illustrates popular feeling in Northern China to-day.

The way out here was:

I have heard an interesting piece of news which illustrates popular feeling in Northern China to-day and anticipates the early collapse of the Puppet Government at Peiping.

This is from *English Villages,* by Edmund Blunden:

> Our great game is cricket; our summer is incomplete without its encounters . . . and however the actual process of play may seem to the uninitiated visitor, the centre scene . . . with pigeons flying over and cuckoos calling across, and now and then the church clock measuring out the hour with deep and slow notes, cannot but be notable.

To avoid the jingle with "notes," "notable" should have been "memorable."

Terminal "y" is often a difficulty. From an article by Hilaire Belloc on air-superiority:

> We have established, and are increasing, our superiority in quality, while time makes steadily for ultimately establishing superiority in quantity as well.

The way out was:

> We have established and are increasing our qualitative superiority, and are making steady progress towards the ultimate establishment of quantitative superiority as well.

The persistent recurrence of the same vowel-sound is often very ugly. For example, this sentence from an article on the Baconian Theory:

> But my main contention is that, though great claims may be made for the name of Bacon, "Shakespeare's plays" remain unchangeably the same.

Many of these "a" sounds can be removed:

> But my chief contention is that, however strongly it may be urged that Bacon was the author of "Shakespeare's plays," this cannot result in the slightest textual alteration in them.

Another example, from an article by Herbert Read:

> Art as we know it now will have disappeared in the flames like so much plush. . . .

Or like so much crushed, mushy, touchwood.

principle m

ALLITERATION SHOULD BE SPARINGLY USED.

The use of alliteration need not be altogether discarded. Indeed, when one writes with feeling in English there is a natural tendency for words to well up in a strongly alliterative way; and this should be checked only when the emphasis seems too heavy for the context. The foregoing sentence, for example, has got one "w" too many in the middle of it: on reading it over we should naturally have changed "well up" to "start up," had we not seen that it illustrated our point.

In the following passage from a newspaper article, Mr. J. B. Priestley might well have cut out five of the eight "w"s and two of the four rhymes in *-ore*.

The world before the war produced the war, and we want no more such worlds. But we want . . .

He could have written:

There must be no more worlds like that which produced this war. Instead, there must be . . .

The B.B.C. news-bulletin editors might well have trimmed off a few *p's* from the following item (1940):

A feature of to-day's news has been important public pronounce-ments on peace by the Pope and President Roosevelt.

They could have written:

Important declarations on peace are a feature of to-day's news: they have been made by the Pope and by President Roosevelt.

principle n

THE SAME WORD SHOULD NOT BE USED IN DIFFERENT SENSES IN THE SAME PASSAGE, UNLESS ATTENTION IS CALLED TO THE DIF-FERENCE.

If one searches in the kitchen-cupboard for a missing egg-cup and does not find it, though it is there, the chances are that it is doing duty as a mustard-pot—the eye refuses to recognize it as an egg-cup. Similarly, if the same word is used in different senses in a passage, the reader's eye will often fail to recognize the second word—it cannot grasp, as it were, that an egg-cup can also be a mustard-pot.

Here are examples. From a pamphlet by Dr. Hugh Dalton, M.P.:

> I have already said that Britain holds the key to this key-problem of Franco-German relations.

The word "key" is here used in two different senses. A key-problem is a metaphor derived from the key-stone of an arch; the key to a problem is a metaphor derived from unlocking a chest.

From a newspaper leader (1941):

> Roumania must remember that though she has now chosen to take what she believes to be the safest course, namely, to *range* herself with Germany, the *range* of our heavy bombers based on Greek aerodromes constitutes a serious threat to her oil fields.

From a newspaper report:

> The mob of frightened little children reached the fire-alarm but were unable to reach it.

The probable meaning is:

> The frightened little children ran in a mob to the fire-alarm, but none was tall enough to reach the knob.

From the organ of the International Brigade Association:

> A few letters written in July have reached this country from German and Polish International Brigaders, interned at the concentration camp of Le Vernet. Two hundred prisoners still remain there. All efforts should be concentrated to save them.

The odium in the word "concentration camp" should have made the writer avoid using "concentrated" in a good sense.

principle o

THE RHETORICAL DEVICE OF PRETENDING TO HESITATE IN A
CHOICE BETWEEN TWO WORDS OR PHRASES IS INAPPROPRIATE TO
MODERN PROSE.

Many orators have built their reputations on passages such as
this:

> Mr. Hacksaw—oh, I beg his pardon, our friend served two whole
> days in the State militia, so I suppose I ought to call him *Captain
> Hacksaw*—well, this gallant Captain was born in Clay County getting
> on for thirty years ago, I reckon. His father was a dishonest, possessed
> Baptist minister—forgive the slip of the tongue, I should have said "an
> honest, dispossessed Baptist minister"—from a wretched living near
> Taunton, Conn. Well, this Rev. Jackstraw—I should say Chopstraw—oh,
> the devil take it, Hacksaw—was a sheep-stealer, or if that sounds too
> blackguardly, let us say he was a man who used to rob his fellow-ministers
> of their flocks and rush them down to the stream to be *dipped*. . . .

Prose writers, however, are assumed to be able to correct their first inaccurate remarks before publication; so that their play with second thoughts
is not amusing, but indicates mere indecision between two ideas.

From an article by Brigadier-General Morgan, K.C.:

> When the great explosion of 1914 occurred, the doctrine was there
> ready to the hands of the German armies to justify, or rather to excuse,
> every outrage they committed.

From an article by Negley Farson:

> This might all be fruitless were it not that, in his self-overhaul, the
> Englishman has begun to question some of his traditions, or (let us call
> them correctly) his obsessions.

From a woman's column in a weekly paper:

> Typewriting, from the very beginning, has been a woman's means
> of earning a livelihood—or, more correctly, a girl's perhaps because
> women, taking them all round, are nimbler with their fingers than men.

From Sir Walter Citrine's *My Finnish Diary:*

> Below us were masses of trees fringing tracts of snow, which quite possibly were small lakes, or to put it more correctly, perhaps, creeks.

(Or shall we say "fjords"?)

In each of these cases, if second thoughts were best, the writer should have expunged the first.

principle p

EVEN WHEN THE NATURAL ORDER OF ITS WORDS IS MODIFIED FOR THE SAKE OF EMPHASIS, A SENTENCE MUST NOT READ UNNATU-RALLY.

The three following examples of inversion suggest too-literal translations from a foreign language:

From a note by "Atticus," the columnist:

> Colonel Bishop became a truly remarkable shot and the higher his score of victims amounted the more his china-blue eyes grew humourously pensive.

(Here "amounted" is probably a slip for "mounted.")
From an article by Ivor Brown:

> News comes of the death of a clown absolute . . . one of a dynasty adored . . . The clown absolute is quite a different person from the actor-droll.

(Yes, quite a person different.)
From an unsigned book-review:

> That till he had installed himself at Ferney never, surely, in his whole life had he been so much of his fate the master, this was the burden, or under-song, of all Voltaire's later writings. . . .

From an American news magazine:

Unhappily, the Rome radio admitted: "There is a possibility of our having to yield some further points."

The effect in this last sentence is ambiguity. The writer did not mean that he was made unhappy by the admission, but that the Rome radio was unhappy.

LUCIDITY, SIMPLICITY, EUPHONY

W. Somerset Maugham

I have never had much patience with the writers who claim from the reader an effort to understand their meaning. You have only to go to the great philosophers to see that it is possible to express with lucidity the most subtle reflections. You may find it difficult to understand the thought of Hume, and if you have no philosophical training its implications will doubtless escape you; but no one with any education at all can fail to understand exactly what the meaning of each sentence is. Few people have written English with more grace than Berkeley. There are two sorts of obscurity that you find in writers. One is due to negligence and the other to wilfulness. People often write obscurely because they have never taken the trouble to learn to write clearly. This sort of obscurity you find too often in modern philosophers, in men of science, and even in literary critics. Here it is indeed strange. You would have thought that men who passed their lives in the study of the great masters of literature would be sufficiently sensitive to the beauty of language to write if not beautifully at least with perspicuity. Yet you will find in their works sentence after sentence that you must read twice to discover the sense. Often you can only guess at it, for the writers have evidently not said what they intended.

Another cause of obscurity is that the writer himself not quite sure

From The Summing Up *by W. Somerset Maugham. Copyright 1938 by W. Somerset Maugham. Reprinted by permission of Doubleday & Company, Inc., W. Heinemann, Ltd., and the author.*

of his meaning. He has a vague impression of what he wants to say, but has not, either from lack of mental power or from laziness, exactly formulated it in his mind and it is natural enough that he should not find a precise expression for a confused idea. This is due largely to the fact that many writers think, not before, but as they write. The pen originates the thought. The disadvantage of this, and indeed it is a danger against which the author must be always on his guard, is that there is a sort of magic in the written word. The idea acquires substance by taking on a visible nature, and then stands in the way of its own clarification. But this sort of obscurity merges very easily into the wilful. Some writers who do not think clearly are inclined to suppose that their thoughts have a significance greater than at first sight appears. It is flattering to believe that they are too profound to be expressed so clearly that all who run may read, and very naturally it does not occur to such writers that the fault is with their own minds which have not the faculty of precise reflection. Here again the magic of the written word obtains. It is very easy to persuade oneself that a phrase that one does not quite understand may mean a great deal more than one realizes. From this there is only a little way to go to fall into the habit of setting down one's impressions in all their original vagueness. Fools can always be found to discover a hidden sense in them. There is another form of wilful obscurity that masquerades as aristocratic exclusiveness. The author wraps his meaning in mystery so that the vulgar shall not participate in it. His soul is a secret garden into which the elect may penetrate only after overcoming a number of perilous obstacles. But this kind of obscurity is not only pretentious; it is shortsighted. For time plays it an odd trick. If the sense is meagre time reduces it to a meaningless verbiage that no one thinks of reading. This is the fate that had befallen the lucubrations of those French writers who were seduced by the example of Guillaume Apollinaire. But occasionally it throws a sharp cold light on what had seemed profound and thus discloses the fact that these contortions of language disguised very commonplace notions. There are few of Mallarmé's poems now that are not clear; one cannot fail to notice that his thought singularly lacked originality. Some of his phrases were beautiful; the materials of his verse were the poetic platitudes of his day.

Simplicity is not such an obvious merit as lucidity. I have aimed at it because I have no gift for richness. Within limits I admire richness in others, though I find it difficult to digest in quantity. I can read one page of Ruskin with delight, but twenty only with weariness. The rolling period, the stately epithet, the noun rich in poetic associations, the subordinate clauses that give the sentence weight and magnificence, the grandeur like that of wave following wave in the open sea; there is no doubt that in all this there is something inspiring. Words thus strung together fall on the ear like music. The appeal is sensuous rather than intellectual, and the beauty of the sounds leads you easily to conclude that you need not bother about the meaning. But words are tyrannical things, they exist for their meanings, and if you will not pay attention to these, you cannot pay attention at all. Your mind wanders. This kind of writing demands a subject that will suit it. It is surely out of place to write in the grand style of inconsiderable things. No one wrote in this manner with greater success than Sir Thomas Browne, but even he did not always escape this pitfall. In the last chapter of *Hydriotaphia* the matter, which is the destiny of man, wonderfully fits the baroque splendour of the language, and here the Norwich doctor produced a piece of prose that has never been surpassed in our literature; but when he describes the finding of his urns in the same splendid manner the effect (at least to my taste) is less happy. When a modern writer is grandiloquent to tell you whether or no a little trollop shall hop into bed with a commonplace young man you are right to be disgusted.

But if richness needs gifts with which everyone is not endowed, simplicity by no means comes by nature. To achieve it needs rigid discipline. So far as I know ours is the only language in which it has been found necessary to give a name to the piece of prose which is described as the purple patch; it would not have been necessary to do so unless it were characteristic. English prose is elaborate rather than simple. It was not always so. Nothing could be more racy, straightforward and alive than the prose of Shakespeare; but it must be remembered that this was dialogue written to be spoken. We do not know how he would have written if like Corneille he had composed prefaces to his plays. It may be that they would have been as euphuistic as the letters of Queen Elizabeth. But earlier prose, the prose of Sir Thomas More, for instance, is neither ponderous, flowery nor oratorical. It smacks of the English soil. To my mind King James's Bible has been a very harmful influence on English prose. I am not so stupid as to deny its great beauty. It is majestical. But the Bible is an oriental book. Its alien imagery has nothing to do with us. Those hyperboles, those luscious metaphors, are foreign to our genius. I cannot but think that not the least of the misfortunes that Secession from Rome brought upon the spiritual life of our country is that this work for so long a period became the daily, and with many the only, reading of our people. Those rhythms, that powerful vocabulary, that grandiloquence, became part and parcel of the national sensibility. The plain, honest English Speech was overwhelmed with ornament. Blunt Englishmen twisted their tongues to speak like Hebrew prophets. There was evidently something in the English temper to which this was congenial, perhaps a native lack of precision in thought, perhaps a naive delight in fine words for their own sake, an innate eccentricity and love of embroidery, I do not know; but the fact remains that ever since, English prose has had to struggle against the tendency to luxuriance. When from time to time the spirit of the language has reasserted itself, as it did with Dryden and the writers of Queen Anne, it was only to be submerged once more by the pomposities of Gibbon and Dr. Johnson. When English prose recovered simplicity with Hazlitt, the Shelley of the letters and Charles Lamb at his best, it lost it again with De Quincey, Carlyle, Meredith and Walter Pater. It is obvious that the grand style is more striking than the plain. Indeed many people think that a style that does not attract notice is not style. They will admire Walter Pater's, but will read an essay by Matthew Arnold without giving a moment's attention to the elegance, distinction and sobriety with which he set down what he had to say.

The dictum that the style is the man is well known. It is one of those aphorisms that say too much to mean a great deal. Where is the man in Goethe, in his birdlike lyrics or in his clumsy prose? And Hazlitt? But I suppose that if a man has a confused mind he will write in a confused way, if his temper is capricious his prose will be fantastical, and if he has a quick, darting intelligence that is reminded by the matter in hand of a hundred things he will, unless he has great self-control, load his pages with metaphor and simile. There is a great difference between the magniloquence of the Jacobean writers who were intoxicated with the new wealth that had lately been brought into the language, and the turgidity of Gibbon and Dr. Johnson, who were the victims of bad theories. I can read every word that Dr. Johnson wrote with delight, for he had good sense, charm and wit. No one could have written better if he had not wilfully set himself to write in the grand style. He knew good English when he saw it. No critic has praised Dryden's prose more aptly. He said of him that he appeared to have no art other than that of expressing with clearness what he thought with vigour. And one of his Lives he finished with the words: "Whoever wishes to attain an English style, familiar but not coarse, and elegant but not ostentatious, must give his days and nights to the volumes of Addison." But when he himself sat down to write it was with a very different aim. He mistook the orotund for the dignified. He had not the good breeding to see that simplicity and naturalness are the truest marks of distinction.

For to write good prose is an affair of good manners. It is, unlike verse, a civil art. Poetry is baroque. Baroque is tragic, massive and mystical. It is elemental. It demands depth and insight. I cannot but feel that the prose writers of the baroque period, the authors of King James's Bible, Sir Thomas Browne, Glanville, were poets who had lost their way. Prose is a rococo art. It needs taste rather than power, decorum rather than inspiration and vigour rather than grandeur. Form for the poet is the bit and the bridle without which (unless you are an acrobat) you cannot ride your horse; but for the writer of prose it is the chassis without which your car does not exist. It is not an accident that the best prose was written when rococo, with its elegance and moderation, at its birth attained its greatest excellence. For rococo was evolved when baroque had become declamatory and the world, tired of the stupendous, asked for restraint. It was the natural expression of persons who valued a civilized life. Humour, tolerance and horse sense made the great tragic issues that had preoccupied the first half of the seventeenth century seem excessive. The world was a more comfortable place to live in and perhaps for the first time in centuries the cultivated classes could sit back and enjoy their leisure. It has been said that good prose should resemble the conversation of a well-bred man. Conversation is only possible when men's minds are free from pressing anxieties. Their lives must be reasonably secure and they must have no grave concern about their souls. They must attach importance to the refinements of civilization. They must value courtesy, they must pay attention to their persons (and have we not also been told that good prose should be like the clothes of a well-dressed man, appropriate but unobtrusive?), they must fear to bore, they must be neither flippant nor solemn, but always apt; and they must look upon "enthusiasm" with a critical glance. This is a soil very suitable for prose. It is not to be wondered at that it gave a fitting opportunity for the appearance of the best writer of prose that our modern world has seen, Voltaire. The writers of English, perhaps owing to the poetic nature of the language, have seldom reached the excellence that seems to have come so naturally to him. It is in so far as they have approached the ease, sobriety and precision of the great French masters that they are admirable.

Whether you ascribe importance to euphony, the last of the three characteristics that I mentioned, must depend on the sensitiveness of your ear. A great many readers, and many admirable writers, are devoid of this quality. Poets as we know have always made a great use of alliteration. They are persuaded that the repetition of a sound gives an effect of beauty. I do not think it does so in prose. It seems to me that in prose alliteration should be used only for a special reason; when used by accident it falls on the ear very disagreeably. But its accidental use is so common that one can only suppose that the sound of it is not universally offensive. Many writers without distress will put two rhyming words together, join a monstrous long adjective to a monstrous long noun, or between the end of one word and the beginning of another have a conjunction of consonants that almost breaks your jaw. These are trivial and obvious instances. I mention them only to prove that if careful writers can do such things it is only because they have no ear. Words have weight, sound and appearance; it is only by considering these that you can write a sentence that is good to look at and good to listen to.

I have read many books on English prose, but have found it hard to profit by them; for the most part they are vague, unduly theoretical, and often scolding. But you cannot say this of Fowler's Dictionary of Modern English Usage. It is a valuable work. I do not think anyone writes so well that he cannot learn much from it. It is lively reading. Fowler liked simplicity, straightforwardness and common sense. He had no patience with pretentiousness. He had a sound feeling that idiom was the backbone of logic and was willing enough to give usage right of way through the exact demesnes of grammar. English grammar is very difficult and few writers have avoided making mistakes in it. So heedful a writer as Henry James, for instance, on occasion wrote so ungrammatically that a schoolmaster, finding such errors in a schoolboy's essay, would be justly indignant. It is necessary to know grammar, and it is better to write grammatically than not, but it is well to remember that grammar is common speech formulated. Usage is the only test. I would prefer a phrase that was easy and unaffected to a phrase that was grammatical. One of the differences between French and English is that in French you can be grammatical with complete naturalness, but in English not invariably. It is a difficulty in writing English that the sound of the living voice dominates the look of the printed word. I have given the matter of style a great deal of thought and have taken great pains. I have written few pages that I feel I could not improve and far too many that I have left with dissatisfaction because, try as I would, I could do no better. I cannot say of myself what Johnson said of Pope: "He never passed a fault unamended by indifference, nor quitted it by despair." I do not write as I want to; I write as I can.

But Fowler had no ear. He did not see that simplicity may sometimes make concessions to euphony. I do not think a far-fetched, an archaic or even an affected word is out of place when it sounds better than the blunt, obvious one or when it gives a sentence a better balance. But, I hasten to add, though I think you may without misgiving make this concession to pleasant sound, I think you should make none to what may obscure your meaning. Anything is better than not to write clearly. There is nothing to be said against lucidity, and against simplicity only the possibility of dryness. This is a risk that is well worth taking when you reflect how much better it is to be bald than to wear a curly wig. But there is in euphony a danger that must be considered. It is very likely to be monotonous. When George Moore began to write, his style was poor; it gave you the impression that he wrote on wrapping paper with a blunt pencil. But he developed gradually a very musical English. He learned to write sentences that fall away on the ear with a misty languor and it delighted him so much that he could never have enough of it. He did not escape monotony. It is like the sound of water lapping a shingly beach, so soothing that you presently cease to be sensible of it. It is so mellifluous that you hanker for some harshness, for an abrupt dissonance, that will interrupt the silky concord. I do not know how one can guard against this. I suppose the best chance is to have a more lively faculty of boredom than one's readers so that one is wearied before they are. One must always be on the watch for mannerisms and when certain cadences come too easily to the pen ask oneself whether they have not become mechanical. It is very hard to discover the exact point where the idiom one has formed to express oneself has lost its tang. As Dr. Johnson said: "He that has once studiously formed a style, rarely writes afterwards with complete ease." Admirably as I think Matthew Arnold's style was suited to his particular purposes, I must admit that his mannerisms are often irritating. His style was an instrument that he had forged once for all; it was not like the human hand capable of performing a variety of actions.

If you could write lucidly, simply, euphoniously and yet with liveliness you would write perfectly: you would write like Voltaire. And yet we know how fatal the pursuit of liveliness may be: it may result in the tiresome acrobatics of Meredith. Macaulay and Carlyle were in their different ways arresting; but at the heavy cost of naturalness. Their flashy effects distract the mind. They destroy their persuasiveness; you would not believe a man was very intent on ploughing a furrow if he carried a hoop with him and jumped through it at every step. A good style should show no sign of effort. What is written should seem a happy accident. I think no one in France now writes more admirably than Colette, and such is the ease of her expression that you cannot bring yourself to believe that she takes any trouble over it. I am told that there are pianists who have a natural technique so that they can play in a manner that most executants can achieve only as the result of unremitting toil, and I am willing to believe that there are writers who are equally fortunate. Among them I was much inclined to place Colette. I asked her. I was exceedingly surprised to hear that she wrote everything over and over again. She told me that she would often spend a whole morning working upon a single page. But it does not matter how one gets the effect of ease. For my part, if I get it at all, it is only by strenuous effort. Nature seldom provides me with the word, the turn of phrase, that is appropriate without being far-fetched or commonplace.

I have read that Anatole France tried to use only the constructions and the vocabulary of the writers of the seventeenth century whom he so greatly admired. I do not know if it is true. If so, it may explain why there is some lack of vitality in his beautiful and simple French. But simplicity is false when you do not say a thing that you should say because you cannot say it in a certain way. One should write in the manner of one's period. The language is alive and constantly changing; to try to write like the authors of a distant past can only give rise to artificiality. I should not hesitate to use the common phrases of the day, knowing that their vogue was ephemeral, or slang, though aware that in ten years it might be incomprehensible, if they gave vividness and actuality. If the style has a classical form it can support the discreet use of a phraseology that has only a local and temporary aptness. I would sooner a writer were vulgar than mincing; for life is vulgar, and it is life he seeks.

I think that we English authors have much to learn from our fellow authors in America. For American writing has escaped the tyranny of King James's Bible and American writers have been less affected by the old masters whose mode of writing is part of our culture. They have formed their style, unconsciously perhaps, more directly from the living speech that surrounds them; and at its best it has a directness, a vitality and a drive that give our more urbane manner an air of languor. It has been an advantage to American writers, many of whom at one time or another have been reporters, that their journalism has been written in a more trenchant, nervous, graphic English than ours. For we read the newspaper now as our ancestors read the Bible. Not without profit either; for the newspaper, especially when it is of the popular sort, offers us a part of experience that we writers cannot afford to miss. It is raw material straight from the knacker's yard, and we are stupid if we turn up our noses because it smells of blood and sweat. We cannot, however willingly we would, escape the influence of this workaday prose. But the journalism of a period has very much the same style; it might all have been written by the same hand; it is impersonal. It is well to counteract its effect by reading of another kind. One can do this only by keeping constantly in touch with the writing of an age not too remote from one's own. So can one have a standard by which to test one's own style and an ideal which in one's modern way one can aim at. For my part the two writers I have found most useful to study for this purpose are Hazlitt and Cardinal Newman. I would try to imitate neither. Hazlitt can be unduly rhetorical; and sometimes his decoration is as fussy as Victorian Gothic. Newman can be a trifle flowery. But at their best both are admirable. Time has little touched their style; it is almost contemporary. Hazlitt is vivid, bracing and energetic; he has strength and liveliness. You feel the man in his phrases, not the mean, querulous, disagreeable man that he appeared to the world that knew him, but the man within of his own ideal vision. (And the man within us is as true in reality as the man, pitiful and halting, of our outward seeming.) Newman had an exquisite grace, music, playful sometimes and sometimes grave, a woodland beauty of phrase, dignity and mellowness. Both wrote with extreme lucidity. Neither is quite as simple as the purest taste demands. Here I think Matthew Arnold excels them. Both had a wonderful balance of phrase and both knew how to write sentences pleasing to the eye. Both had an ear of extreme sensitiveness.

If anyone could combine their merits in the manner of writing of the present day he would write as well as it is possible for anyone to write.

ONLY TOO CLEAR

C. E. Montague

I

You will hear people say that this or that is only too clear. It is only too clear that Thompson—whom they do not like—has taken to drink, or that Brown—with whom they disagree—has not a leg to stand on. In these cases the "only too clear" may be taken to mean that the speaker only wishes that it *were* quite clear that the facts are as he states them. The words serve the same useful office as phrases like "It is beyond dispute that," or "All thinking men are agreed that" so-and-so is this or that. Every question-beggar has them in his tool bag. As soon as you hear them you know that some statement is coming which is not likely to go down without a good deal of ramming.

People say less often that some written thing is only too clear—that an essay is disagreeably lucid, or that limpidity has gone mad in some-body's novel or poem. Were we not taught at school to admire clearness as the queen of literary virtues? And "saying a plain thing in a plain way," "not beating about the bush," "simply hitting the nail on the head"— a dozen such phrases seem to show that in this matter the great world stands for once on the side of the schoolmasters.

They seem, besides, to imply that the act of writing is always a kind of rendering unto Caesar, or some other clear-minded and masterful per-

From A Writer's Notes on His Trade *by C. E. Montague. Copyright 1930. Reprinted by permission of Chatto & Windus, Ltd. This essay is abridged as indicated.*

son, of something predetermined, measurable and unmistakable, like a quarter's tribute, or a tailor's bill, something that has to be faced as it stands and got rid of, neither a penny more nor a penny less.

II

A few of us would like to pipe up, in a modest way, against this indiscriminate cult of clearness. We suspect that we are sometimes over-dosed with lucidity in leading articles and sermons, in novels and verse. There is that light-drenched controversial way of writing which seems to be always forcing us up against some glaring, tight-drawn dilemma: X, we are told plainly, must equal either A or B; if it equals A, then some-thing, which establishes the writer's point, must inevitably happen to C and D; if it equals B, then some situation equally favourable to the desired conclusion must arise between E and F. We jib, we few plain people. In the rude world that we know, things are not like that: A never quite equals B, nor C either; any real C and D, or E and F, have enough pig-headed individual ways of their own to upset any calculation that they will give a certain exact response to a certain supposed stimulus from A or B or X. Moral stresses, somehow, are not transmitted with that fine precision; causation leaks, or it gets pushed out of its course just a little.

The syllogism itself grows suspect, rigged out though it be with the whole plant of logical clearness, major and minor premise and everything ostentatiously luminous about it, and nothing, it seems, to keep it from leading up to some conclusion that any honest mind will reject at sight, as the very madness of partisanship. And "crystallisation," that sovereign dodge—the compression and recompression and yet further compression of some crafty freak of argument or of detraction; the gist of the thing grows, at each stage of the progress, terser, more pungent, more crystal clear, more cunningly unqualified by any deference to the truth. No, the sun's lucidity used to seem straight enough, once. Then came Einstein and showed what bad twist even those rectitudinous rays may contract. Such incidents make a man cautious.

You must, at some time or other, have groaned dumbly under a flood of clearness from a pulpit. First the giving out of a text, clear as noon, perhaps the words, "A city set on a hill." Then the illumination of this heavenly lamp by setting out, all round it, pound after pound of tal-low candles. From word to word of the text the hapless divine straggles onward, match-box in hand. " 'A city,' mark you. Not two cities! Not twin cities like Assisi and Perugia, each set on its Umbrian hill. Not one of those potent leagues of cities which shine in the storied page of history like constellations in the natural firmament! And yet a *city!* No mere village! No hamlet perched on a knoll, as the traveller to-day may see them in the Apennines," and so on and on till the martyred Christian below has to ask, in his heart, "Shall I never hit back?" as Juvenal did when his author friend recited the epic once more.

To relieve the lack of pence, which so often vexes first-rate men, a friend of my youth, a waterman on the Thames, used to dive into the river from Richmond Bridge, for gain. As he passed the tin can round the expectant crowd, before the performance, he used to explain: "I dives, gentleman, I dives. I don't jump. I don't fall. I don't flop. I don't leap. I don't waller. I dives." If "style is clearness," as it has been called, and if there be nothing more to be said, my friend was a stylist to rank with many shining lights of churches and chapels.

III

Clearness at any price is supposably the aim of some writers of fiction and of that slender handmaiden of fiction, the "sketch." You know the insipid veracity with which Crabbe used to report some of the most trite doings of Nature and of man?

> Something had happened wrong about a bill
> Which was not drawn with true mercantile skill.
> So, to amend it, I was told to go
> And seek the firm of Clutterbuck & Co.

The spirt of Crabbe is not dead. You can feel it breathing faintly in a kind of modern prose that is cut up into little systems of infantine paragraphs. They all begin with "And." The whole work looks, at a sufficient distance, like a poem by Whitman or Rabindranath Tagore. It is turned out with an air of pride in the bleached and vacuous purity of its simplicity. The idea seems to be that if you can achieve a certain pitch of literal and copious fidelity in the description of a bald fact—any fact— that larks sing and nettles sting and so on—quite frigidly contemplated, you will at least have wedged one foot inside the doorway of the antechamber of Art, so that no one can kick you right out of the Palace.

The themes of these chaste exercises are often of a studied thinness. You may find that the author is disclaiming, almost anxiously, the idea of tarnishing the minute mirror of his sensibilities with any breath of thought. "Nothing in my brain I bring"—he seems to hymn with a pious and complacent humility his freedom from intellectual baggage.

We simple readers begin to fancy we have been too easily taken in by the virtuous demeanour with which these simplicists make themselves perfectly clear about trifles, and throw floods of light upon the nakedness of their several small patches of land. We are too reverent and good-natured. We feel that the writing person is trying, at any rate, to become as a little child; and, of course, everyone ought to do that; so perhaps there is more chance of finding ourselves on the side of the angels if we do not pelt or boot him. If that is the line we take, any genuinely little child could lead us into a wiser one. For if you put four dots on one i and hope that a little child will think well of this abundance of lucidity in writing, your hope will come to naught. He will call you "a silly."

Worse, he may be affronted. Perhaps it might, to his mind, have been more civil to take it for granted that he knows about dots. So may we readers, however humble our intellectual standing, take a little reasonable umbrage at the assumption of writers that we cannot see a church by daylight. They are discourteous to us. "I do not rhyme," says the polite Sir Walter Scott,

> to that dull elf[1]
> Who cannot image to himself

this, that and the other thing that happens. But that is just what these too lucid folk do. They use us as dull elves or blind horses to whom no mere wink, nor nod either, means much.

Even in his most explicit moments a courteous writer will stop short of rubbing into our minds the last item of all that he means. He will, in a moderate sense of the term, have his non-lucid intervals. At times he will make us wrestle a little with him, in the dark, before he yields his full meaning, as God made the patriarch wrestle with the angel, to the patriarch's ultimate advantage. Or perhaps he will lead you right up to the verge of a full comprehension of what he is at; he will edge you into the right corner and put the pie within reach of your hand, and then he will withdraw gently and leave you to put in your thumb and pull out a plum and think what a bright boy or girl you are. As keenly as a good talker he will feel the value of ellipse, within the bounds of reason; he will know how much more blessed it is for a reader to guess right than to be told; know, too, that in a picture the high lights depend, for their value, on the low. Were it not so, we might find our best light reading in Acts of Parliament, because their whole aim in life is to be clear; the same bright, even light beats shadowlessly down upon every square inch of their level expanses of verbiage. Yet most of us find them plain stuff in the worse sense as well as the better.

[1] I cannot guess why Scott should have imputed dullness to elves. I had always thought of elves as quick-witted. Still, you can see what he means, in the main.

IV

On scores even graver, if any there be, than that of incivility you may demur to an overdoing of clearness. A writer might have all the good manners that were ever housed in Versailles and yet make a show of clearness to which he has no lawful title. Until you know a thing right to the bottom, you should not speak as if you did; meanwhile, your description ought to be edged with something akin to that dim borderland in which your half-knowledge gradually loses itself; wisps of its mists should be visible in your report.

From age to age the value currently put upon clearness in writing varies rather freely. The times when it has stood highest were also times when our chances of getting to know, pretty soon, whatever there is to be known were over-rated, as we see now. A typical fruit of such a period, vigorous, positive, bold, sure of the sufficiency of whatever data it had, impatient of doubts, reservations or awe, was our received political economy of the middle nineteenth century. In it a thin, fallacious lucidity seemed to make everything clear, but did it by failing to see that there was anything to be cleared up where the worst difficulties lay.

The psychology accepted fifty years ago had the same illusory sharpness of outline, the same false finality. It took as the unit of mental life the idea, the single, separable idea, isolating each idea as a detached, clearly describable thing by which, in turn with other ideas, the mind could be wholly occupied. The books of psychology then in vogue might make you think of your consciousness as if it were a railway signal lamp, at one moment wholly red and nothing but red, at the next wholly green and nothing but green. Now, during the last forty years, as you know, psychology has looked more closely at the mental life and has found it a good deal less simple. The result has been an entirely new way of envisaging that life.

The unit of mental life, as modern psychologists see it, is not the insulated idea but the whole wave, or field, as it is variously called, of consciousness at any given instant. From moment to moment the mind, like an eye, puts itself forth on successive fields of consciousness, each field melting or modulating into the next in chronological order, like the successive photographs forming a cinematographic film. Each of these fields of consciousness has its centre of interest, on which there is at least a relative concentration of the mind. Of the contents of the surrounding portions of the field the mind grows less and less intensely conscious as their distances from the centre of interest increase; they fade away in widening circles of diminishing interest towards the margin of the field, and there, without any definite frontier line, they merge in the outer dimness.

What the modern psychologists mean is illustrated by what happens when you look at a landscape as a painter does, with your eye fixed on some central point in it—say, a tree in the foreground. That tree itself you realise fairly fully—the kind that it is, and its youth or age, and the shape of its trunk and the colour of its leaves—you know lots about it. If you keep your eye still fixed on that centre and ask yourself what you know about the trees a little to its right and left, you find you know something about them, but much less. You may feel sure that they *are* trees, and perhaps that one of them is shaped like a spike and another more like a cauliflower, and you are conscious of a mass of darker colour in one than in another. But that will be all, or about all. If you still keep your eyes fixed and interrogate your sensations as to the trees still further to the left and right, you will find there are still fewer definite things that you can say about them. They are merely causes of a vague consciousness of masses of darkness, perhaps, against a lighter sky. You are aware of them; the landscape would not be the same landscape to you if they were not there, but you are not aware of them even with the semi-distinctness with which you were aware of the trees in the middle zone, still less with the intense and articulate distinctness with which you are aware of the centre of interest.

So, in every moment of consciousness, every phase of feeling or thought, your mind is applied to some centre that it finds or makes for its attention in a field of consciousness which sinks into dimness and shadowy vagueness as it recedes from that centre towards an indeterminate border, lying you cannot exactly tell where.

The size of the field of consciousness varies a good deal, as between one person and another; and also as between one and another state of the same person. A man of genius—whether poet, scientific thinker or business organiser—may be supposed to have, at his best, a much greater width of field than most of us: he can see, in their right relation to each other, things so far apart that most of us do not find them both present on our field of consciousness at any one moment. A person ill, depressed or fatigued has his field of consciousness dwarfed for the time: a toothache may contract the field to a speck; almost nothing may exist for you except a tiny detail of your body. Some stirring experience, the drastic stimulus given by some masterpiece in an art or by some personal emotion, may swiftly dilate your field of consciousness, so that you feel invisible things drifting into sight and hearing, and unhoped-for achievements of comprehension and insight coming as magically within your power, like Lear's flash of recognition of what it means to be destitute—"O! I have ta'en too little care of this!" That is the natural utterance of a person whose field of consciousness has been suddenly dilated, bringing within its borders an unthought-of call upon sympathy.

So, to a writer happily engaged on his work and excited by it, there

may come a curious extension of his ordinary faculties; he will find portions of knowledge floating back into his brain, available for use, which
he had supposed to be thrown away long ago on the rubbish-heap outside the back door of his mind; relevant passages will quote themselves
to his mind from books that he scarcely remembers to have ever read; and
he suddenly sees germane connections where in his ordinary state of mind
he would see nothing. The field of consciousness has expanded again.
People of strong social instinct often derive the same experience from
animated conversation; the exercise of their own vivacity stirs latent
powers of apprehension in them; the area upon which they are able to
draw for those piquant incongruities, which are the chief material of wit,
is for the moment widened; the field of comic consciousness is enlarged.

In matters of conduct, again, you may find rapid enlargement of an
ordinary field of consciousness leading to actions, heroic or criminal,
which those who have done them can only ascribe, when the field has
contracted again, to unaccountable impulse. From the uncharted region
of the outer consciousness one of these impulses strikes in and impinges
on us, as the cyclones come up incalculably from the Southern Atlantic
and impinge on South-West Britain. A kindred effect, or a simulacrum of
these effects, is producible in some measure by alcohol and other drugs;
no doubt their tragic hold on mankind is mainly due to their power of
giving at least the illusion of temporary release from narrow, cold and
cramping fields of consciousness.

In all these cases it is not that anything wholly unknown, wholly
outside the range of the mind, has been brought within its reach. It is
rather as if some outer zone of an estate which you already own were
brought back into use after lying derelict. At the centre of the consciousness of each of us there is, as it were, the highly cultivated garden plot
of our habitual thoughts, feelings, observations and memories; they are
more or less arranged and registered; they can be readily summoned.
Outside and surrounding this central disc of worked soil there extends an
unmapped outer estate of dormant personal or ancestral memories, of
residual impulses, of inchoate powers and dexterities, and of forgotten or
unrealised knowledge. Each mind lives, like a prehistoric inhabitant of
Britain, in a small clearing among thick forest; only, the forest is part of
the mind itself, and the mind lives surrounded by all that dark part of its
own contents and powers which at ordinary times remains potential only.

V

To reclaim for us some portions of that forest is the business of
imaginative literature. It offers us inlets by which to penetrate into the
surrounding twilight. At the climax of a great tragedy you feel sure, at

any rate, that some sort of veil has been lifting; you are, for the moment, in a finer and more understanding state of yourself. A similar sense of release and of opened eyes can be generated by comedy, even low comedy; you may feel that, as Mr. Masefield says, the roystering scene in *Twelfth Night* "rouses the heart with the thought that life is too wonderful to end." You have the same sense of a glorious incursion, of having penetrated securely into an outer darkness, of having got beyond the region where the writs of ordinary thought run. The normal luminousness of the centre of the field of consciousness has for the moment flooded out all round over its dim borderland, lighting up what was previously the complete darkness outside, so that more and more new things swim into your ken as more stars do when you are coming up a shaft to the surface of the earth at night; and not only more things outside you, but more powers in yourself, more capacities for comprehension, co-ordination and sympathy.

Where Wordsworth's imagination has travelled far and has wrought hard to express itself, as in the *Intimations of Immortality,* he seems to have first experienced so unusual an enlargement of the ordinary field of consciousness that on the murky verge of the field certain mystic shapes —dim, but still shapes—have begun to take form for his mind, and this at a radius from the centre so great that for most of us it is a region of mere obscurity, yielding us nothing but some vague promptings and cravings and regrets. And then Wordsworth has contrived, in a remarkable measure, to express this visionary revelation of his own in a way that renders mystic reverie in the reader more coherent and articulate than it could otherwise have been. But in doing this he has not achieved, nor attempted to achieve, the clearness of an advertisement.

8
>   . . . those obstinate questionings
>   Of sense and outward things,
>   Fallings from us, vanishings;
>   Blank misgivings of a Creature
> Moving about in worlds not realised,
> High instincts before which our mortal Nature
> Did tremble like a guilty Thing surprised:

Well, that is wonderful, but it is not clear as an election poster is clear. It is almost as far from being clear as are the four Michelangelo statues in the Church of San Lorenzo at Florence, of which Pater says that "they concentrate and express, less by way of definite conceptions than by the touches, the promptings of a piece of music, all those vague fancies, misgivings, presentiments, which shift and mix and are defined and fade again, whenever the thoughts try to fix themselves with sincerity on the conditions and surroundings of the disembodied spirit." And again, Pater says that this memorial sculpture of Michelangelo's expresses "dumb enquiry over the relapse after death into the formlessness which preceded life, the change, the revolt from that change, then the correcting, hallowing, consoling rush of pity; at last, far off, thin and vague . . . the new body—a passing light, a mere intangible, external effect, over those too rigid, or too formless faces; a dream that lingers a moment, retreating in the dawn, incomplete, aimless, helpless; a thing with faint hearing, faint memory, faint power of touch; a breath, a flame in the doorway, a feather in the wind."

That is a good deal to express, in four white marble figures, or in twenty lines of print. We need hardly expect so many elusive things to be expressed with the explicit lucidity of handbooks of popular science. Yet there is evidently some demand, even in such contexts, for a shallow positivism of clearness, a kind of insistence upon the trivially and superficially clear, a note of distrust and dislike of anything which calls for salutary efforts of comprehension or makes a demand upon us to disengage ourselves from common, indolent, incurious states of mind.

VI

Ours is a free country; anyone may take his mental ease if he likes. Only, if you are going to stand out for clearness at any price, then you are going to shut yourself out from a good many things. For a good many things cannot be put quite clearly except by being put falsely. If everything in every shadowy corner of a Rembrandt interior were painted so that you could tell just what it was, what would become of the picture, its beauty and truth? Where would be the song that ends *Twelfth Night* if its inconsequence were gone and its unreason put to rights? It gaily defies any meagre and captious rationalism that it may meet in a reader's mind; it flaunts in his face a divine new clearness of its own, a clearness that passes understanding; with unsurpassable distinctness it calls up precisely that mood that its author desires, however incoherent the terms of the summons may seem.

Such incoherence or obscurity can scarcely be a blunder or an accident. All of us feel, while we delight in the song, that it must have a kind of submerged logic; we have faith in its fundamental coherence and rightness, although we cannot see them and cannot exactly say why we have faith. And this feelings of ours is accountable. We may suppose that Shakespeare wrote with his field of consciousness so enlarged as to bring within his view many connections between things apparently remote— at any rate not visibly connected within any common field of consciousness. Thus an utterance of his, framed in that rare state of his mind, may well seem disconnected to ours, and yet the connections that it assumes or implies may not be far out of our reach; though not at our command, an understanding of them may at all times be floating somewhere on the twilight border of our field of consciousness. And when we are fired by the beauty of the song, it may well be that this subconscious recognition almost breaks through into clearness; the underlying logic of the lines all but rises to the surface.

From feeling that kind of faith in the greatest of imaginative writers it is not a long step to the feeling that every imaginative writer should have some such calls to make upon faith, and should not shrink from making them. Between that which we consciously know and that which we know in no sense at all, there extend the waters of our subconscious or incomplete and imperfectly available knowledge. In those waters he is a pilot licensed to ply; and we must leave him free, like a pilot, to do things which we cannot always quite follow, though we rely on him to bring us through. In fact we might doubt his command of his craft and mystery if his doings were never even a little beyond us. If a writer is really lifted above himself; if as he writes he is veritably making forays far beyond our ordinary field of consciousness, even beyond his own as it is at most times, it is not merely pardonable that his written report of these raids should ask us for some little effort of comprehension; if it were all a plain tale you might even suspect that he had not gone very far.

*   *   *   *   *2

VIII

Such writers may carry a wilful unclearness too far. If so, they differ only by a few degrees from the greatest of imaginative artists. In some of these the enigmatic suggestion is conveyed under the most cunning semblance of absolute clearness.

> The boat rocks at the pier o'Leith;
> Fu' loud the wind blaws frae the ferry;

The whole of Burns's song has an air of straight dealing; a child can understand the first intentions of all the words, but these seeming simplicities are craftily charged, by the subtlety of their choice and arrangement, with secondary purposes, ulterior intimations; they evoke ideas, or prompt you to group your thoughts, in ways which the words, in their primary senses, will not account for. In the much-quoted lines,

2 Section VII has been deleted here.

> Brightness falls from the air,
> Queens have died young and fair,
> Dust hath closed Helen's eye,

all that is said, on the surface, is an old truism; you might excusably say that Nashe was putting a commonplace baldly. Yet you don't. For you feel that the show of shallow clearness is illusive, behind their obvious meanings the words have been given an energy that can raise in you certain emotions as unmistakable as elephants, although also as undefinable. Among the youthful stuff, clever and bookish, that makes up most of *Love's Labour's Lost,* you strike here and there on lines rich in that virtue, such as Armado's note about Hector:

> The sweet war-man is dead and rotten; sweet chucks, beat not the bones of the buried; when he breathed, he was a man.

Coming in the middle of so much writing which strives hard to be full of meaning, beauty, and wit, and to get the last ounce of its meaning well out, such passages shine the more brightly, because they come of a more cunning art that knows how to charge with high evocative power phrases which on the face of them may be platitudinous to a degree approaching drivel. Here, of course, we tread close to one of the thorniest of critical thickets. All the prickly topic of symbolism, with its malign power to set the wise by the ears, is very near. Mine be it to steer clear of the question whether this special quality of poetry, this keeping open of its communications with the subconscious part of our mental life, is mainly a Celtic contribution to literature or is a survival from the primeval poetry and legend of many races. And also clear of the question whether, in this effort to unpack the luggage of the mind, the imagination is trying to get past the malignity and obstructiveness of a delusive world of sense and of intellect—a hostile host of "things" and of reasoned thoughts— or whether things and thoughts are themselves portions of Reality, and not even the blackest sheep among her flocks. All that I want to touch here is the contrast between the traditional pregnancy of all great art— you find it even in the rather hard, dry poetry of Pope—and a kind of writing in which, almost as a matter of principle, nothing is left unsaid and no more is meant than meets the ear. You read this super-lucid stuff; you do your best to believe that the writer must have got hold of something more than he directly says; you hope he may be like the Sphinx, who used often to seem to be asking her clients an easy one when she really gave them something much tougher to tackle. But no; the pellucid rubbish has no camouflaged fullness of meaning; it is all like hard, literal painting on tin; the trees have no dryads; and the Sphinx is just a foolish old lady without any secret to keep or to tell.

IX

How much one has to leave out! Here is nothing said, nor room left to say it, about the cardinal difference between the expression of obscurity and obscurity of expression. Of course it is no virtue to say relatively simple things with a relatively high degree of indistinctness. Indeed it must be half the work of education to cure this malady in its grosser forms. You find it in schoolboys' essays, where it comes of helplessness, and in the work of some minor poets who want to be crepuscular and to bring on Celtic or other twilights, but do not know how. It is for criticism to distinguish this obscurity of the confused or astigmatic mind, or of affectation, or of a small or ill-used vocabulary, from that other element of enigma which may remain when the greatest powers of expression have been most strenuously used. Perhaps one might say, roughly, that it is the difference between a muddled statement of something already known, and an indication—necessarily indeterminate and ambiguous—of some unexplored possibility of further knowledge. Since Einstein made his great finds we have all seen how far from clear the most faithful statements of an unfamiliar fact of nature may be. They have to partake of the dim profundity of their theme. But some of the accounts that appeared in the press were perfectly clear because they were perfectly bad and left out whatever it needed some skill to convey. Just like that is the contrast between excess of clearness in imaginative art and its just renunciation.

Another shoal that deserves to be better buoyed out than can now be done here is the difficulty of teaching the young the proper limits of clearness. In most of the workaday uses of the spoken or written word we suffer much more from want of clearness than from excess of it; so it might seem like reversing the engines of education to warn a boy or girl that one may be too clear. Anyhow it is not done; and now that we have had nearly fifty years of popular half-education, we naturally have an enormous number of people whose education has not reached the point at which any critical attitude towards this virtue of clearness is practicable or, perhaps, safe. Hence a strong economic pressure, which cannot be ignored, upon popular writers in the direction of extreme clearness or at least the appearance of it. A common result is a kind of writing rather like a watch with a highly luminous face, but no hands. Or it is like a tree with no roots—nothing more about it than what first takes the eye, whereas the best of imaginative writing has its leaves in the light and its roots in the darkness, and does not deny its own nature nor the continuity of the known with the unknown.

A NOTE ON STYLE AND THE LIMITS OF LANGUAGE

Walker Gibson

Questions about style can most usefully be approached if we think of a style as the expression of a personality. I do not mean at all that our words necessarily reveal what we are "really like." I do mean that every writer and talker, more or less consciously, chooses a role which he thinks appropriate to express for a given time and situation. The personality I am expressing in this written sentence is not the same as the one I orally express to my three-year-old who at this moment is bent on climbing onto my typewriter. For each of these two situations, I choose a different "voice," a different mask, in order to accomplish what I want accomplished. There is no point in asking here which of these voices is closer to the Real Me. What may be worth asking is this: what kind of voices, in written prose, may be said to respond most sensitively and efficiently to the sort of contemporary world that this book[1] has been describing?

First, let's be logical about it. Given the kind of dilemma with respect to knowledge and language that this book defines, what sort of style might we *expect* in our own time? What sort of speaking voice adopted by the writer, what mask, would be appropriate in a world where, as we have seen, the very nature of nature may be inexpressible? If we live in a pluralistic and fluxlike universe, what manner of word-man should we become in order to talk about it? Well, we might at least expect a man who knows his limits, who admits the inevitably subjective character of his wisdom. We might expect a man who knows that he has no right in

From The Limits of Language *by Walker Gibson,* © *1962 by Walker Gibson. Reprinted by permission of Hill and Wang, Inc.*

[1] In this essay, references to "this book" refer, of course, to Mr. Gibson's book.

a final sense to consider himself any wiser than the next fellow, including the one he is talking to. The appropriate tone, therefore, might be informal, a little tense and self-conscious perhaps, but genial as between equals. With our modern relativistic ideas about the impossibility of determining any "standard dialect" for expressing Truth in all its forms, we might expect the cautious writer to employ many dialects, to shift from formal to colloquial diction, to avoid the slightest hint of authoritarianism. The rhythm of his words will be an irregular, conversational rhythm— not the symmetrical periods of formal Victorian prose. Short sentences alternating erratically with longer sentences. Occasional sentence fragments. In sum we might expect a style rather like *this!*[2]

This style, indeed, is easily recognizable and can be discovered all around us in modern prose. Thirty years ago in a book called *Modern Prose Style,* Bonamy Dobrée described it much as we have done here. "Most of us have ceased to believed, except provisionally, in truths," he wrote, "and we feel that what is important is not so much truth as the way our minds move toward truth." The consequence is a kind of self-searching need for frankness and humility on the part of the writer. "The modern prose-writer, in returning to the rhythms of everyday speech, is trying to be more honest with himself than if he used, as is too wreckingly easy, the forms and terms already published as the expression of other people's minds." Finally, in a touching sentence, "In our present confusion our only hope is to be scrupulously honest with ourselves." That was written in 1933: since then the confusion has multiplied spectacularly, while our hopes of ever being "scrupulously honest" about anything look pretty dim. Still, the relation Dobrée made, between an intellectual difficulty and a style, is essentially the relation we are making here.

The trouble with it—and a reminder of the awful complexity of our subject—is that sometimes this proposition simply doesn't work. Some contemporary writers, sensitively aware of the limits of language, indeed conceding them explicitly, nevertheless write in a *style* that sounds like the wisdom of Moses, or like Winston Churchill. Far from echoing the rhythms of ordinary speech, they pontificate or chant in authoritarian rhythms the assertion that one cannot be authoritarian. We have a fine example of this paradox in the paragraph by Oppenheimer that I have

---

[2] A few of the writer's obvious attempts to echo a conversational tone in that paragraph can be quickly summarized. Contractions (let's). Colloquialisms (well . . . , the next fellow). Some very short sentences. Capitalization in an effort to place an ironical turn on a Big Fat Abstraction (Truth)—an effort that is of course much easier to accomplish with the actual voice. Italics (*except,* like *this!*), again in mimicry of the way one speaks in conversation. And so on. The purpose of such devices, to compensate for the loss of oral intonation, is strictly speaking impossible to achieve. If only you were here I could *say* all this to you!

so much admired,[3] Oppenheimer uses a vocabulary, sentence structure, tone, and rhythm all highly structured and formalized; there is no unbending there. The theme of his discourse—that style is "the deference that action pays to uncertainty"—seems at odds with the *personality* we hear uttering this theme. That personality, because of the way the words are chosen and arranged, appears curiously self-confident, even dictatorial, with echoes perhaps of Johnsonian prose, or Macaulay's elegant sentences. Thus the first sentence is built around a handsome triplet of alliterative abstractions ("the implicit, the imponderable, and the unknown"); the second sentence is built out of another triplet of nicely balanced clauses. The extraordinary final sentence approaches incantation in its parallel repetitions of structure. The "voice" we hear, remote indeed from ordinary conversation, seems to *know* even as it asserts its own humility. Different readers will explain all this in different ways: some will argue that the traditional manner lends sincerity and persuasiveness to the message, while others will be set off by what they consider a real discrepancy between matter and manner. We recall that the passage was taken from an address delivered at a formal occasion. I have heard Mr. Oppenheimer's platform manner described as "arrogant"; our stylistic observations might well account in part for such an impression. In any case it is clear that no easy formula—Dobrée's or any one else's—is going to account for all the vagaries of modern prose.

Other writers in this collection will illustrate Dobrée's thesis with less embarrassment—that is, will show clear evidence of a "conversational" voice. Thus [Herbert J.] Muller:

> Emerson remarked that it is a good thing, now and then, to take a look at the landscape from between one's legs. Although this stunt might seem pointless when things are already topsy-turvy, it can be the more helpful then. One may say that what this chaotic world needs first of all

[3] The paragraph, from J. Robert Oppenheimer's "The Open Mind," reads as follows:

> The problem of doing justice to the implicit, the imponderable, and the unknown is of course not unique to politics. It is always with us in science, it is with us in the most trivial of personal affairs, and it is one of the great problems of writing and of all forms of art. The means by which it is solved is sometimes called style. It is style which complements affirmation with limitation and with humility; it is style which makes it possible to act effectively, but not absolutely; it is style which, in the domain of foreign policy, enables us to find a harmony between the pursuit of ends essential to us and the regard for the views, the sensibilities, the aspirations of those to whom the problem may appear in another light; it is style which is the deference that action pays to uncertainty; it is above all style through which power defers to reason.

is *dis*sociation; by breaking up factitious alliances and oppositions, one may get at the deep uniformities. Or. . .

The simplicity of the diction in that first sentence, and the absurdity of the described action, support a familiar relation of equality between the speaking voice and the reader. There is no talking down; we all know who Emerson is. (Not "That great American Transcendentalist, Ralph Waldo Emerson. . . .") "Now and then," "stunt," "topsy-turvy" contribute the colloquial touch. The slightly awkward "then" at the end of the second sentence suggests that in this particular communication formal grace would be inappropriate. But with the third sentence the writer boldly shifts his tone as his diction becomes more polysyllabic and his sentence structure more complex. "Enough of geniality," he seems to say, "you must now follow me into a serious tangle." With this abruptness, Muller is perhaps "breaking up factitious alliances" *in his style,* so that his own prose both expresses and dramatizes the point he is making.

The trick, if that is what it is, of mingling formal and colloquial vocabulary can convey a kind of ironical thrust by the writer at his own pretensions. Thus he can have it both ways—make his great assertion and kid himself for his own gall. It is a device much employed in circles that are verbally sophisticated, including academic circles. Consider an extreme example, from a professor of law at Chicago, here discussing a flexible approach to problems of judicial interpretation:

> But it leads to *good* rules of law and in the main toward flexible ones, so that most cases of a given type can come to be handled not only well but easily, and so that the odd case can normally come in also for a smidgeon of relief. The whole setup leads above all—a recognition of imperfection in language and in officer—to *on-going and unceasing judicial review of prior judicial decision* on the side of rule, too, and technique. That, plus freedom and duty to do justice *with* the rules but *within* both them and their whole temper, that is the freedom, the leeway for own-contribution, the scope for the person, which the system offers.[4]

Here style and message work with a degree of co-operation: a call for unceasing flexibility in the operations of judicial review is expressed in an idiom that is itself almost wildly flexible. The speaker in this passage betrays the strains of an impassioned conversationalist, with his heavy reliance on italics and his interrupted sentence structures. We are button-

[4] From Karl N. Llewellyn, *The Common Law Tradition: Deciding Appeals,* Little, Brown, 1960.

holed. This is a technical discussion, and most of the vocabulary has to be fairly heavy, but we have "smidgeon" and "whole setup" to cut across the formality. We have even a jazzy bit of alliteration and rhyme—"rule, tool, and technique." The "recognition of imperfection in language," therefore, which is explicitly granted by the text, is implicitly conveyed as well by the unorthodox scramblings of language. Nobody has to like this style (many are simply irritated), but at least one can see what is going on, and why.

Or consider another extreme example, from a professor of English at Wisconsin, here discussing problems of usage:

> Bad, fair, good, better, best. Only the best is Correct. No busy man can be Correct. But his wife can. That's what women are for. That's why we have women to teach English and type our letters and go to church for us and discover for us that the English say "Aren't I?" while we sinfully hunt golf-balls in the rough on Sunday and, when our partner finds two of them, ask "Which is me?" (Webster: *colloq.*—Professor K of Harvard: I speak colloq myself, and sometimes I write it.) . . . Only a few of us today are aware of the other scales of English usage. It is our business to consciously know about their social utility.[5]

These sentences from a treatise on language admirably demonstrate that self-consciously unbuttoned informality which the subject nowadays seems to demand. To some, again, it will appear offensively "cute," idiosyncratic. Short sentences, some without predicates, surround one almost endless rambling sentence. The ironical capital in Correct (cf. Truth *supra*). Indifference to the rule that pronouns should have specific antecedents ("That's what women are for. That's why . . ."). Muddled number in using personal pronouns (we hunt golf-balls, our partner [sing.] finds, [we] ask "Which is me?"). Deliberately split infinitive in the last sentence quoted, at a point in the utterance when a conventionally formal tone has begun to enter. We may anticipate, I am sure, a time when writers will endeavor to carefully split their infinitives, at whatever cost in awkwardness, just as writers of a former generation endeavored so elaborately to avoid the "error." All this should prove to at least be amusing.

To many readers, the style displayed by a Professor Llewellyn or a Professor Joos will seem undisciplined, vulgar, and chaotic. A sign of academic deterioration. A result of wild "permissiveness" in education and in society generally. But such readers will be missing the point. There is nothing indiscriminately permissive in this style, but the writers do accept and reject different kinds of language from those accepted and

[5] From Martin Joos, *The Five Clocks*. Copyright 1961 by Martin Joos.

rejected by traditional stylists. They express different personalities. Without insisting on the merits of these particular passages, which are certainly debatable, it ought nevertheless to be clear that you do not write in this way simply by saying anything that occurs to you. The process of selection can be, indeed, *more* discriminating because the available supply of language and experience is larger. As this is being written, in the autumn of 1961, a mild flurry about such extensions of language is going on in the press, relating to the publication of a new edition of *Webster's New International Dictionary.* *The New York Times* has editorialized as follows:

> A passel of double-domes at the G. & C. Merriam Company joint in Springfield, Mass., have been confabbing and yakking for twenty-seven years—which is not intended to infer that they have not been doing plenty work—and now they have finalized Webster's Third New International Dictionary, Unabridged, a new edition of that swell and esteemed word book.
>
> Those who regard the foregoing paragraph as acceptable English prose will find that the new Webster's is just the dictionary for them. The words in that paragraph all are listed in the new work with no suggestion that they are anything but standard.
>
> Webster's has, it is apparent, surrendered to the permissive school that has been busily extending its beachhead on English instruction in the schools. This development is disastrous. . . .

The *Times* goes on to acknowledge "the lexical explosion that has showered us with so many words in recent years," and to congratulate the Dictionary for including 100,000 new words or new definitions. "These are improvements, but they cannot outweigh the fundamental fault." Webster's has always been a "peerless authority on American English," and therefore its editors have "to some degree a public responsibility." "A new start is needed."

There is, I think, something wrong about all this. If you are acknowledging a "lexical explosion," a language changing with accelerating rapidity, then it seems rather difficult to insist at the same time on a "peerless authority." The editors of the Dictionary may have fulfilled their public responsibility by taking the only wise course—by including as many new words and definitions as they could without making "authoritative" judgments about "standard," "colloquial," and "slang." This is not to say that the modern writer ignores such distinctions; on the contrary he is sensitively aware of them as never before. But he knows, and the dictionary editors know, that no such label is good for long in a culture as volatile as this one. Yesterday's slang is today's standard, and the writer who remains resonant to these shifts has at his disposal a huge and varicolored vocabulary for his art.

The reason we call that opening paragraph in the *Times* editorial "unacceptable English" is not that it contains slang. The reason is that it contains too many kinds of slang at once, without any awareness of their differences. You do not say "passel of double-domes" unless you have some good reason for juxtaposing terms from utterly distinct language worlds. "Passel" is presumably of western-frontier origin and now has a kind of weary whimsy about it, while "double-domes" is recent, cheaply anti-intellectual, with a history something like "egghead" but without the popular acceptance of "egghead." It is conceivable that these words could be included in one sentence, but it would take more skill than the *Times* man has employed. Of course the appearance of clumsiness was just what served his purpose.

Meanwhile the writer who looks backward to "authority," who takes a static view of Standard Language, is likely to sound like the "straight" paragraphs of that editorial. The voice there is closer to a chiding or dictatorial professor than were the voices of the actual professors quoted. And when such a writer uses "modern" terms, he uses them in ways that are long overused before he gets to them—ways like "extending its beachhead on English instruction" or "lexical explosion that has showered us with so many words." It is this sort of thing that is the true vulgarity in our time.

Nevertheless our society remains generous with half-conscious concessions to the imperfections of its language. It may be, for example, that the language of the beatniks, especially their oral conventions, could be looked at in the light of such concessions. Consider just one curious symptom of jive-talk (now dated)—the suffix-plus-prefix *like*. "We came to this big town like and all the streets were like crazy, man." This attempt at rendering beat dialect is doubtless inaccurate but it should serve to make the point. That point is that the beats have (deliberately?) modified or qualified their nouns and adjectives by suggesting that they are not quite accurate, not quite the way things are. "This big town like"—it is a one-ended metaphor. Like what? We have a tenor but no vehicle, or is it a vehicle without a tenor? I have been told that many beats are determinedly antiverbal, preferring to listen to jazz while lying on beaches in Zenlike silence. It fits. The skepticism about the validity of words that "like" implies is a peculiarly twentieth-century skepticism, it seems to me, though there may be analogies with other ages such as the seventeenth century, when scientific developments encouraged similar self-scrutinies and self-doubts. In any event the beats, in their crude and sloppy way of course, have surrounded much of their language with a metaphorical blur by using (among other things) the simple device of "like." They suggest, with this blur, their conviction of the impossibility of anybody else's doing any better with words. Only squares believe you can speak "precisely."

The complexities of experience do occasionally get faced one way or another—if not with the beats' pose of inarticulateness, then with some other pose that will serve to avoid the charge of *really knowing*. Modern novelists adopt a "point of view" which is often no point of view at all, but several points of view from which to indicate various inadequate interpretations of various fictitious characters. It is a technique that will show how two novels as apparently unlike as *The Waves* and Faulkner's *As I Lay Dying* belong after all to the same age. There is no narrator, no one of whom the reader might conceivably say, "There! That's the author talking." The technique is not new; there is *The Ring and the Book,* to mention one example. But the difference is that when you read *The Ring and the Book,* you feel how firmly and finally Browning is on Pompilia's "side," in spite of his wonderful multiplicity throughout that great poem. Whereas in many modern novels you scarcely know who is on anybody's side—you must simply flow in the flux. Sometimes it is so lifelike you can hardly stand it.

And of course that road—the road of chaos chaotically expressing chaos—is a dead end of imitative form where we end with a grunt, or maybe a whimper. The very point is that language will never *say* our experience "as is," and recognizing this truth, we have immense freedom of possibility to make, create, form what we can out of words or out of anything else. The most elaborate of villanelles is not much further removed from Real Life than the latest Allen Ginsburg poem, or a slice of Mr. Bloom's day. So write a villanelle if that will meet your need. But whatever it is, there remains this simple blasphemy to be avoided, and that is the blasphemy of ignoring the limits, of assuming that one's words do indeed tell the reader what is going on. There is an important sense in which nobody knows what he is talking about.

I hope I do not except myself and everything uttered here.

3 ANALYSES OF STYLE

general or period styles

THE MANDARIN AND VERNACULAR STYLES

Cyril Connolly

- ■ The Mandarin Dialect

Before continuing with our diagnosis it becomes necessary to have a definition of style. It is a word that is beginning to sound horrible, a quality which no good writer should possess. Stephen Spender can even brashly say of Henry James:

> As always with great æstheticians there is a certain vulgarity in his work, and this vulgarity found its expression in violence. It is vulgarity of a kind that we never find in the work of coarser writers like Fielding, Smollett and Lawrence, but which we always are conscious of in writers like Flaubert, or Jane Austen, or Wilde.

The dictionary defines style as the "collective characteristics of the writing or diction or artistic expression or way of presenting things or decorative methods proper to a person or school or period or subject, manner of exhibiting these characteristics." This suggests a confusion since the word means both the collective characteristics and the manner of exhibiting them, and perhaps this confusion may account for the distaste in which the topic is held. For a surprising number of people to-day would agree in principle with Spender, or would argue that the best writers have

Reprinted with permission of Crowell-Collier and Macmillan Inc. from Enemies of Promise *by Cyril Connolly. Copyright 1938.*

no style. Style to them seems something artificial, a kind of ranting or of preening. "The best writing, like the best-dressed man," as Samuel Butler said, is sober, subdued and inconspicuous.

In point of fact there is no such thing as writing without style. Style is not a manner of writing, it is a relationship; the relation in art between form and content. Every writer has a certain capacity for thinking and feeling and this capacity is never quite the same as any other's. It is a capacity which can be appreciated and for its measurement there exist certain terms. We talk of a writer's integrity, of his parts or his powers, meaning the mental force at his disposal. But in drawing from these resources the writer is guided by another consideration; that of his subject. Milton's prose style, for example, is utterly unlike his verse. Not because one is prose and the other poetry; it reveals a quite different set of qualities. The Milton of *Paradise Lost* is an aloof and dignified pontiff who makes no attempt to enter into a relationship with the reader, whose language exhibits a classical lack of detail, whose blank verse is restrained, and whose sublime sentences, often ending in the middle of a line, suggest the voice of a man who talks to himself trailing off into silence. The Milton of the pamphlets is out to persuade the reader and confute his enemy, the style is forceful, repetitive and prolix; he bludgeons away at his opponent until he is quite certain that there is no life left in him, the magnificent language is remarkable for detailed exuberance and masculine vitality. The same distinction can be made between the prose and verse style of Marvell. The style of these writers varies with their subject and with the form chosen. One might say that the style of a writer is conditioned by his conception of the reader, and that it varies according to whether he is writing for himself, or for his friends, his teachers or his God, for an educated upper class, a wanting-to-be-educated lower class or a hostile jury. This trait is less noticeable in writers who live in a settled age, as they soon establish a relationship with a reader whom they can depend on and he, usually a man of the same age, tastes, education and income, remains beside them all their life. Style then is the relation between what a writer wants to say—his subject, and himself—or the powers which he has: between the form of his subject and the content of his parts.

Style is manifest in language. The vocabulary of a writer is his currency but it is a paper currency and its value depends on the reserves of mind and heart which back it. The perfect use of language is that in which every word carries the meaning that it is intended to, no less and no more. In this verbal exchange Fleet Street is a kind of bucket shop which unloads words on the public for less than they are worth and in consequence the more honest literary bankers, who try to use their words to mean what they say, who are always "good for" the expressions they employ, find their currency constantly depreciating. There was a time when this was not so, a moment in the history of language when words expressed what they meant and when it was impossible to write badly. This time I think was at the end of the seventeenth and the beginning of the eighteenth centuries, when the metaphysical conceits of the one were going out and before the classical tyranny of the other was established. To write badly at that time would involve a perversion of language, to write naturally was a certain way of writing well. Dryden, Rochester, Congreve, Swift, Gay, Defoe, belong to this period and some of its freshness is still found in the *Lives of the Poets* and in the letters of Gray and Walpole. It is a period which is ended by the work of two great Alterers, Addison and Pope.

Addison was responsible for many of the evils from which English prose has since suffered. He made prose artful, and whimsical, he made it sonorous when sonority was not needed, affected when it did not require affectation; he enjoined the essay on us so that countless small boys are at this moment busy setting down their views on Travel, the Great Man, Courage, Gardening, Capital Punishment, to wind up with a quotation from Bacon. For though essay-writing was an occasional activity of Bacon, Walton and Evelyn, Addison turned it into an industry. He was the first to write for the entertainment of the middle classes, the new great power in the reign of Anne. He wrote as a gentleman (Sir Roger is the perfect getleman), he emphasized his gentle irony, his gentle melancholy, his gentle inanity. He was the apologist for the New Bourgeoisie who writes playfully and apologetically about nothing, casting a smoke screen over its activities to make it seem harmless, genial and sensitive in its non-acquisitive moments; he anticipated Lamb and Emerson, Stevenson, *Punch* and the professional humorists, the delicious middlers, the fourth leaders, the memoirs of cabinet ministers, the orations of business magnates, and of chiefs of police. He was the first Man of Letters. Addison had the misuse of an extensive vocabulary and so was able to invalidate a great number of words and expressions; the quality of his mind was inferior to the language which he used to express it.

I am one, you must know, who am looked upon as a Humanist in Gardening. I have several Acres about my House, which I call my Garden, and which a skilful Gardener would not know what to call. It is a confusion of Kitchen and Parterre, Orchard and Flower Garden, which lie so mixt and interwoven with one another, that if a Foreigner who had seen nothing of our Country should be conveyed into my Garden at his first landing, he would look upon it as a natural Wilderness, and one of the uncultivated Parts of our Country. My flowers grow up in several Parts of the Garden in the Greatest Luxuriancy and Profusion. I am so far from being fond of any particular one, by reason of its

Rarity, that if I meet with any one in a Field which please me, I give it a place in my Garden. . . . I have always thought a Kitchen-garden a more pleasant sight than the finest Orangerie, or artificial Green-house [etc.].

Notice the presentation of the author (whose mind is also a *jardin anglais*): he is eccentric, unpractical, untidy, but glories in it and implies superiority over the foreigner; he prefers home-grown vegetables to exotic fruits and in short flatters the Little Man and also the city Soames Forsytes of his day. The court jester with his cap and bells is now succeeded by the upper middle-class with his "awkward-squad" incompetence, his armchair, carpet slippers, and gardening gloves.[1]

I shall christen this style the Mandarin, since it is beloved by literary pundits, by those who would make the written word as unlike as possible to the spoken one. It is the style of all those writers whose tendency is to make their language convey more than they mean or more than they feel, it is the style of most artists and all humbugs and one which is always menaced by a puritan opposition. To know which faction we should belong to at a given moment is to know how to write with best effect and it is to assist those who are not committed by their temperament to one party alone, the grand or the bald, the decorative or the functional, the baroque or the streamlined that the following is written.

Here are two more examples by Lamb and Keats of its misuse.

(I) My attachments are all local, purely local. I have no passion (or have had none since I was in love, and then it was the spurious engendering of poetry and books) to groves and vallies. The rooms where I was born, the furniture which has followed me about (like a faithful dog, only exceeding him in knowledge) wherever I have moved—old chairs, old tables, streets, squares, where I have sunned myself, my old school—these are my mistresses.

(II) I had an idea that a man might pass a very pleasant life in this manner. Let him on a certain day read a certain page of full Poesy or distilled Prose, and let him wander with it, and muse upon it, and reflect from it, and bring home to it, and prophesy upon it, and dream upon it. until it becomes stale—but when will it do so? Never! When Man has arrived at a certain ripeness in intellect any one grand and spiritual passage serves him as a starting-post towards all the two and thirty Palaces. How happy is such a voyage of conception, what delicious

---

[1] "For these reasons there are not more useful Members in a Commonwealth than Merchants. They knit Mankind together in a mutual Intercourse of good Offices, distribute the gifts of Nature, find Work for the Poor, add Wealth to the Rich, and Magnificence to the great." Compare Addison's attitude to the Merchants with Congreve's, for whom a decade earlier they were comic cuckolds.

diligent indolence! A doze upon a sofa does not hinder it, and a nap upon Clover engenders ethereal finger-pointing. The prattle of a child gives it wings . . . [etc., etc.].

Notice how untrue these sentiments are. Lamb's old school is not a mistress, nor is an old bookcase. The bookcase has to be packed up and put on a van when it moves; to compare it to a faithful dog is to suggest that Lamb is beloved even by his furniture. The delicious middlers probably believe it, for Essayists must be lovable, it is part of their rôle.

"Until it becomes stale—but when will it do so? Never!" Now, Keats is lying. "I am often hard put to it not to think that never fares a Man so far afield as when he is anchored to his own Armchair!" One could turn this stuff out almost fast enough to keep up with the anthologies. "The Man," "your Man," always occurs in these essayists. (Addison: "There is nothing in the World that pleases a Man in love so much as your Nightingale.")

Here are two recent examples (also from the *Oxford Book of English Prose*). The authors are Compton Mackenzie and Rupert Brooke.

(I) Some four and twenty miles from Curtain Wells on the Great West Road is a tangle of briers among whose blossoms an old damask rose is sometimes visible. If the curious traveller should pause and examine this fragrant wilderness, he will plainly perceive the remains of an ancient garden, and if he be of an imaginative character of mind will readily recall the legend of the Sleeping Beauty in her mouldering palace; for some enchantment still enthralls the spot, so that he who bravely dares the thorns is well rewarded with pensive dreams, and, as he lingers a while gathering the flowers or watching their petals flutter to the green shadows beneath, will haply see elusive Beauty hurry past. *The Basket of Roses* was the fairest dearest inn down all that billowy London Road . . .

Heigh ho! Georgian prose! Notice the words, especially the adverbs, which do not aid but weaken the description, serving only to preserve the architecture of the sentence. They are Addison's legacy. A catalogue of flowers follows. I will begin at flower thirty-five.

There was Venus' Looking-glass and Flower of Bristol, and Apple of Love and Blue Helmets and Herb Paris and Campion and Love in a Mist and Ladies' Laces and Sweet Sultans or Turkey Cornflowers, Gillyflower Carnations (Ruffling Rob of Westminster amongst them) with Dittany and Sops in Wine and Floramer, Widow Wail and Bergamot, True Thyme and Gilded Thyme, Good Night at Noon and Flower de

Luce, Golden Mouse–Ear, Prince's Feathers, Pinks and deep red Damask Roses.

It was a very wonderful garden indeed.

(II) He was immensely surprised to perceive that the actual earth of England held for him a quality which he found in A——— and in a friend's honour, and scarcely anywhere else, a quality which, if he'd ever been sentimental enough to use the word, he'd have called "holiness." His astonishment grew as the full flood of "England" swept him on from thought to thought. He felt the triumphant helplessness of a lover. Grey, uneven, little fields, and small, ancient hedges rushed before him, wild flowers, elms, and beeches. Gentleness, sedate houses of red brick, proudly unassuming, a countryside of rambling hills and friendly copses. He seemed to be raised high, looking down on a landscape compounded of the western view from the Cotswolds, and the Weald, and the high land in Wilshire, and the Midlands seen from the hills above Princes Risborough. And all this to the accompaniment of tunes heard long ago, an intolerable number of them being hymns.

"England has declared war," he says to himself, "what had Rupert Brooke better feel about it?" His equipment is not equal to the strain and his language betrays the fact by what might be described as the "Worthington touch." "If he'd ever been sentimental he'd have called it 'holiness,'" i.e. he calls it holiness. "Triumphant helplessness of a lover" has no meaning. It is a try-on. "Little, small, grey, uneven, ancient, sedate, red, rambling, friendly, unassuming"—true escapist Georgian adjectives. They might all be applied to the womb.

Pope as an Alterer is a very different case. He is one of the great poets of all time and the injury he did to English verse consisted in setting it a standard to which it could not live up. He drove lyricism out except from isolated artists like Burns and Blake and left his successors the task of continuing in a form which he had already perfected, and for which they had neither the invention nor the ear.

A waving glow the blooming beds display
Blushing in bright diversities of day

After this plenty poetry had become by the time of the Romantics barren and pompous, once again the content of the poetical mind was unequal to the form. The first Romantics, Wordsworth, Southey and Coleridge, therefore, set themselves to write simply, to entice poetry away from the notion of the Grand Style and the Proper Subject; their language was monosyllabic, plebeian, their subjects personal or everyday. They wore their own hair.

■ The Challenge to the Mandarins

The quality of mind of a writer may be improved the more he feels or thinks or, without effort, the more he reads and as he grows surer of this quality so is he the better able to make experiments in technique or towards a simplification of it, even to its apparent abandonment and the expression of strong emotion or deep thought in ordinary language. The great speeches in *Lear* and *Samson Agonistes* do not seem revolutionary to us because we do not recognize them as superb and daring manipulations of the obvious. Any poet of talent could write: "The multitudinous seas incarnadine" or "Bid Amaranthus all his beauty shed," but only a master could get away with "I pray you undo this button," or Lear's quintuple "Never."

Style is a relation between form and content. Where the content is less than the form, where the author pretends to emotion which he does not feel, the language will seem flamboyant. The more ignorant a writer feels, the more artificial becomes his style. A writer who thinks himself cleverer than his readers writes simply (often too simply), while one who fears they may be cleverer than he will make use of mystification: an author arrives at a good style when his language performs what is required of it without shyness.

The Mandarin style at its best yields the richest and most complex expression of the English language. It is the diction of Donne, Browne, Addison, Johnson, Gibbon, de Quincey, Landor, Carlyle and Ruskin as opposed to that of Bunyan, Dryden, Locke, Defoe, Cowper, Cobbett, Hazlitt, Southey and Newman. It is characterised by long sentences with many dependent clauses, by the use of the subjunctive and conditional, by exclamations and interjections, quotations, allusions, metaphors, long images, Latin terminology, subtlety and conceits. Its cardinal assumption is that neither the writer nor the reader is in a hurry, that both are in possession of a classical education and a private income. It is Ciceronian English.

The last great exponents of the Mandarin style were Walter Pater and Henry James, who, although they wrote sentences which were able to express the subtlest inflexions of sensibility and meaning, at the worst grew prisoners of their style, committed to a tyranny of euphonious nothings. Such writers, the devotees of the long sentence, end by having to force everything into its framework, because habit has made it impossible for them to express themselves in any other way. They are like those birds that weave intricate nests in which they are as content to hatch out a pebble as an egg. But the case of Henry James is sadder still, for his best writing, that found in his later books, charged with all the wisdom and feeling of his long life, went unappreciated. As he reminded Gosse, he remained "insurmountably unsaleable," and of his collected edition of 1908 he could say, like Ozymandias, "Look on my *works* ye mortals and despair."

The reason for this failure of James to reach an audience lay in the change that had come over the reading public, a change to which he could not adapt himself. The early books of James appeared as three-volume novels which sold at thirty-one and sixpence. They reached a small leisured collection of people for whom reading a book—usually aloud—was one of the few diversions of our northern winters. The longer a book could be made to last the better, and it was the duty of the author to spin it out. But books grew cheaper, and reading them ceased to be a luxury; the reading public multiplied and demanded less exacting entertainment; the struggle between literature and journalism began. Literature is the art of writing something that will be read twice; journalism what will be grasped at once, and they require separate techniques. There can be no delayed impact in journalism, no subtlety, no embellishment, no assumption of a luxury reader and since the pace of journalism waxed faster than that of literature, literature found itself in a predicament. It could react against journalism and become an esoteric art depending on the sympathy of a few or learn from journalism and compete with it. Poetry, which could not learn from journalism, ran away an 1 so we find, from the nineties to the last war, desolate stretches with no poets able to make a living and few receiving any attention from the public. The stage is held by journalist-poets like Kipling and Masefield, while Hopkins, Yeats, Bridges, de la Mare, Munro and a few others blossom in neglect.

Prose, with the exception of Conrad, who tried to pep up the grand style, began to imitate journalism and the result was the "modern movement"; a reformist but not a revolutionary attack on the Mandarin style which was to supply us with the idiom of our age. Shaw, Butler and Wells attacked it from the journalistic side—George Moore, Gissing and Somerset Maugham, admirers of French realism, of the Goncourts, Zola, Maupassant, from the aesthetic.

Only Wilde belonged to the other camp, and the style he created was his own variation of the introspective essayist:

On that little hil' by the city of Florence, where the lovers of Giorgione are lying, it is always the solstice of noon, of noon made so languorous by summer suns that hardly can the slim naked girl dip into the marble tank the round bubble of clear glass, and the long fingers of the lute-players rest idly upon the chords. It is twilight also for the dancing nymphs whom Corot set free among the silver poplars of France. In eternal twilight they move, those frail diaphanous figures, whose tremulous white feet seem not to touch the dew-drenched grass they tread on.

Notice the amount of "romantic" words, now well-known hacks, "solstice, languorous, eternal, frail, diaphanous, tremulous," which help to date the passage, while Shaw, who was the same age, was then writing:

This is the true joy in life, the being used for a purpose recognised by yourself as a mighty one; the being thoroughly worn out before you are thrown on the scrap-heap; the being a force of Nature instead of a feverish selfish little clod of ailments and grievances complaining that the world will not devote itself to making you happy. And also the only real tragedy in life is the being used by personally minded men for purposes which you recognise to be base. All the rest is at worst mere misfortune or mortality; this alone is misery, slavery, hell on earth; and the revolt against it is the only force that offers a man's work to the poor artist, whom our personally minded rich people would so willingly employ as pander, buffoon, beauty monger, sentimentaliser, and the like.

This sentence with its boisterous sentiments and creaking gerunds might have been written to-day. It is not a question of subject. The beauty of the Giorgione picture is just as alive as a sense of social injustice. Giorgione is not Sir Alma Taddema. But while the first passage is dead, constructed out of false sentiment and faulty linguistic material, the second is in the idiom of our time. For the idiom of our time is journalistic and the secret of journalism is to write the way people talk. The best journalism is the conversation of a great talker. It need not consist of what people say but it should include nothing which cannot be said. The Shaw passage could be talked; the Wilde passage would hardly stand recitation.

Moore also was not to remain a realist for long—but Moore, after his *Esther Waters* period, carried on his warfare against the Mandarin style from another position. In his *Ave, Salve, Vale* books he describes the Irish rebellion against the official literary language.

Alas, the efforts of the uneducated to teach the educated would be made in vain; for the English language is perishing and it is natural that it should perish with the race; race and grammatical sense go together. The English have striven and done a great deal in the world; the English are a tired race and their weariness betrays itself in the language, and the most decadent of all are the educated classes.

He perceived, however, the increasing unreality of Anglo-Irish, of Yeats and Synge filling their notebooks with scraps of tinker's dialogue which could be used only in plays, and in plays only about tinkers, and instead he moulded for himself a simplified prose in which he could describe pictures, books, people, places, and complex sensations—yet always maintain an unassuming unsophisticated equality with the reader.

> The artist should keep himself free from all creed, from all dogma, from all opinion. As he accepts the opinions of other he loses his talent, all his feelings and ideas must be his own.

> I never knew a writer yet who took the smallest pains with his style and was at the same time readable. Plato's having had seventy shies at one sentence is quite enough to explain to me why I dislike him.

> Men like Newman and R. L. Stevenson seem to have taken pains to acquire what they called a style as a preliminary measure—as something that they had to form before their writings could be of any value. I should like to put it on record that I never took the smallest pains with my style, have never thought about it, and do not know or want to know whether it is a style at all, or whether it is not, as I believe and hope, just common, simple straightforwardness. I cannot conceive how any man can take thought for his style without loss to himself and his readers.

Here in the colloquial English of 1897 is Samuel Butler attacking the Mandarin style. The musing introspective attitude of Pater and of Wilde's essays is replaced by one more social and argumentative.[2] This *arguing style* (as opposed to the soliloquy) is typical of the new relationship with the reader which is to sweep over the twentieth century and dominate journalism and advertising. It may be described as *you*-writing from the fact that there is a constant tendency to harangue the reader in the second person. It is a buttonholing approach. The Addison manner, on the other hand, has degenerated into whimsical *we*-writing. "We have the best goods. We like quality. We're funny that way," is one sort of advertising. "You realise the inconveniences of inadequate plumbing. Then why not of inadequate underclothing?" is the other.

Meanwhile, Wells, also, was not inactive (though it was not till 1915 that he attacked Henry James in *Boon,* a bogus autobiography). Henry James, in two magnificent letters (Vol. II, pp. 503–8, of his letters) answers Wells's criticism.

---

[2] "Mr. Walter Pater's style is, to me, like the face of some old woman who has been to Madam Rachel and had herself enamelled. The bloom is nothing but powder and paint and the odour is cherry blossom. Mr. Matthew Arnold's odour is as the faint sickliness of hawthorn."—Butler.

Wells wrote:

> To you literature, like painting, is an end, to us literature is a means, it has a use. Your view was, I felt, altogether too prominent in the world of criticism and I assailed it in lines of harsh antagonism. I had rather be called a journalist than an artist, that is the essence of it, and there was no antagonist possible than yourself.

James replied that his view can hardly be so prominent or it would be reflected in the circulation of his books.

> But I have no view of life and literature, I maintain, other than that our form of the latter [the novel] in especial is admirable exactly by its range and variety, its plasticity and liberality, its fairly living on the sincere and shifting experience of the individual practitioner . . . Of course for myself I live, live intensely and am fed by life, and my value, whatever it be, is in my own kind of expression of that . . . Meanwhile I absolutely dissent from the claim that there are any differences whatever in the amenability to art of forms of literature aesthetically determined, and hold your distinction between a form that is [like] painting and a form that is [like] architecture for wholly null and void. There is no sense in which architecture is æsthetically "for use" that doesn't leave any other art whatever exactly as much so; and so far from that of literature being irrelevant to the literary report upon life, and to its being made as interesting as possible, I regard it as relevant in a degree that leaves everything else behind. It is art that *makes* life, makes interest, makes importance, for our consideration and application of these things, and I know of no substitute whatever for the force and beauty of its process. If I were Boon I should say that any pretence of such a substitute is helpless and hopeless humbug; but I wouldn't be Boon for the world, and am only yours faithfully, Henry James.

The justification for Wells' attack must lie in the defence it provoked, for these two majestic letters from the dying giant form a creed which he might not otherwise have left us. One is reminded of a small boy teasing an elephant which gets up with a noble bewilderment, gives him one look, and shambles away.

We are not concerned here with the people who prefer to be journalists rather than artists, but with those who have tried to make journalism into an art, and already it is possible to define the opponents of the Mandarin style, all those who tried to break it up into something simpler and terser, destroying its ornamentation, attacking its rhythms and giving us instead the idiom of to-day. Thus Moore's new language is somewhat lyrical, for his standards are æsthetic. Norman Douglas is intellectual, with a strong imaginative side. Maugham is also imaginative, though playwriting interferes with his literary development, but Butler, Shaw, Wells, Bennett, write as plainly as they can. If Henry James could have given up all hope of being read, had abandoned novels and written but a few magnificent pages about ideas that stirred him, he might have been happier and had greater influence. But he was obsessed with the novel to the neglect even of his long short stories; he still considered the novel the supreme art form, as it had been for Turgenev, Balzac and Flaubert. So he continued to write novels which came into competition with the journalistic novels of Wells and Bennett or the speeded-up Jamesian of Conrad, rather than take refuge in the strongholds of the leisurely style—memoirs, autobiography, books of criticism, or else venture out into the experimental forms of the short story. The younger writers whom he patronised—Rupert Brooke, Compton Mackenzie and Hugh Walpole[3]—were more remarkable for talent, personal charm and conventionality than for the "beginning late and long choosing" of genius, the crabwise approach to perfection.

[3] It is interesting to speculate on the effect Henry James might have had on, say, E. M. Forster, Virginia Woolf and Lytton Strachey had he bestowed on them the loving criticism which he lavished on his more personable disciples.

ON STYLE

Rudolf Flesch

Mr. Malderton was a man whose whole scope of ideas was limited to Lloyd's, the Exchange, the India House, and the Bank. A few successful speculations had raised him from a situation of obscurity and comparative poverty, to a state of affluence. As frequently happens in such cases, the ideas of himself and his family became elevated to an extraordinary pitch as their means increased; they affected fashion, taste, and many other fooleries, in imitation of their betters, and had a very decided and becoming horror of anything which could, by possibility, be considered *low*. He was hospitable from ostentation, illiberal from ignorance, and prejudiced from conceit. Egotism and the love of display induced him to keep an excellent table: convenience, and a love of the good things of this life, ensured him plenty of guests. He liked to have clever men, or what he considered such, at his table, because it was a great thing to talk about; but he never could endure what he called "sharp fellows." Probably, he cherished this feeling out of compliment to his two sons, who gave their respected parent no uneasiness in that particular. The family were ambitious of forming acquaintances and connexions in some sphere of society superior to that in which they themselves moved; and one of the necessary consequences of this desire, added to their utter ignorance of the world beyond their own small circle, was that any one who could lay claim to an acquaintance with people of rank and title, had a sure passport to the table at Oak Lodge, Camberwell.

"On Style" by Rudolf Flesch, from The Writer's Book, *edited by Helen Hull. Copyright 1950 by Authors League of America, Inc. Reprinted by permission of Harper & Row, Publishers.*

This is Dickens. Not one of his famous passages, to be sure, but representative, recognizable Dickens. There can be little doubt that it is good writing—and that it has style.

It would be tempting to analyze such a passage and find out just how and where it bears the personal stamp of the author. But I want to do something else. I want to start with the fact—for it *is* a fact—that the style of this passage is unmistakably out of date. If written today, it could not be called good writing.

Let's look at the words and sentences. Dickens writes "from a situation of obscurity" where a good professional writer today would simply say "from obscurity"; he writes "by possibility" for what today would simply be "possibly"; he uses long, periodic sentences; and he uses words like "affluence" and "their respected parents" that are hardly permissible even in humorous usage today.

What is the reason for these differences between the Victorian style and ours? Obviously, since writing is done for the sake of readers, the difference lies with the reading public. Compared with the millions of potential readers today, Dickens, though immensely popular, wrote for a limited audience. His readers took their time over his novels and, in fact, read them aloud. They enjoyed his leisurely method of telling and his polysyllabic twinkle. He could safely write about Mr. Malderton's being "hospitable from ostentation, illiberal from ignorance, and prejudiced from conceit," because he knew his readers would not begrudge him the effort needed in understanding these phrases.

The writer today writes for a vastly larger audience. On both sides of the Atlantic, many millions more have acquired the habit of reading. These added millions are a different kind of people. They don't have the literary background of Victorian ladies and gentlemen; they don't have their leisure and patience; they are unwilling to put more effort into reading than they would into watching a movie or listening to the radio. A reader of today, reading "hospitable from ostentation, illiberal from ignorance, and prejudiced from conceit" with his customary newspaper-reading speed, would stop, turn back, and reread—or, more probably, he would just read on and let the matter go.

So the Victorian style just isn't adequate today. But what style is? Let's look at a paragraph written in 1948 that performs roughly the same function as Dickens' description of Mr. Malderton's home and family:

> The Caffreys are substantial people in Wakefield. Mrs. Caffrey is the daughter of Grafton Kenyon, whose grandfather, William G. Kenyon, founded Kenyon's Department Store in 1856. It is the only department store in Wakefield. Caffrey works in the family store. He is thirty-five

and fair-haired, and looks like a photogenic football player. When he was at Providence College, from which he graduated in 1936, he did play some football. The Caffreys, who have two children—a seven-year-old daughter named Carol and a four-year-old son named Kenyon—live in a pleasant twelve-room house of two and a half stories. It is painted white and has a well-kept lawn on three sides.

This happens to be from John McNulty's "Jackpot" story in *The New Yorker*. But it is irrelevant who wrote it. The passage certainly isn't recognizable McNulty; it isn't even recognizable *New Yorker*. In fact, the most significant thing about it is that it has no personal style at all. It could have been written by anyone among thousands of today's writers who have learned how to do a good reporting job. Its style is *the* accepted, mid-Twentieth-Century, "anonymous" style.

This style is not inferior to the personal styles developed by the great writers of the past. On the contrary: it is superior. It is superior because it can be learned, because it is more economical, and because it does its job by sticking to observable facts. Dickens uses a good many abstractions to tell his reader about Mr. Malderton's status in society. McNulty simply says that the Caffreys' house is painted white and has a well-kept lawn on three sides. On balance, I think, McNulty tells us more.

Comparison of the two passages shows the characteristics of what I called today's "anonymous" style. McNulty's fourteen-word sentences are about one-third shorter than Dickens'; he uses no complex words where simple words will do; and he strictly avoids expression of his own thoughts and sentiments. This is the crisp reportorial style hammered out by Hemingway and his followers, by *The New Yorker,* and by *Time.* It is admittedly journalistic writing—factual, simple, and idiomatic.

This journalistic writing is so respectable today that authors like Steinbeck or Thurber don't hesitate to occasionally sandwich a reporting job between their other literary work. They take pride in doing these menial literary tasks, and pride in writing the style that goes with them. Actually, what happened to writing is not too different from what happened to scientific invention and research. Fifty years ago our inventions came from individual geniuses like Edison; today most great inventions are made by anonymous researchers, following a fixed procedure.

To be sure, for the beginner the choice does not lie between his own personal style and the generally used reporter style. Usually, his problem is simply that of getting rid of bad writing and getting the hang of good writing. Ordinary people don't write like Dickens or Conrad or Henry James. What they write is more apt to resemble the following random sample from yesterday's paper:

Although the music dramas of Wagner remain among the mainstays of the Metropolitan Opera Association's repertoire and concerts of the excerpts from them are rarer nowadays than was the case not so many years ago there is still much pleasure to be derived from such a concert when it is devised as intelligently as the one planned for the Philadelphia Orchestra in Carnegie Hall last night by Eugene Ormandy, but conducted by his associate, Alexander Hilsberg, because Mr. Ormandy was suffering from a virus infection.

This is ridiculously bad writing. In fact, it probably wasn't written at all, but hurriedly dictated. And yet, it is a fair sample of the kind of prose that surrounds us on all sides.

Anyone who wants to call himself a writer must first graduate from this kind of thing to being able to write "It is painted white and has a well-kept lawn on three sides." But after he has done that, should he proceed from there to fashion his own personal style?

Some people say he should. The English critic Cyril Connolly, for instance, recently quoted the following passage from Virginia Woolf:

Considering how common illness is, how tremendous the spiritual change that it brings, how astonishing, when the lights of health go down, the undiscovered countries that are then disclosed, what wastes and deserts of the soul a slight attack of influenza brings to view, what precipices and lawns sprinkled with bright flowers a little rise of temperature reveals, what ancient and obdurate oaks are uprooted in us by the act of sickness, how we go down into the pit of death and feel the waters of annihilation close above our heads and wake thinking to find ourselves in the presence of the angels and the harpers when we have a tooth out and come to the surface in the dentist's armchair and confuse his "Rinse the mouth—rinse the mouth" with the greeting of the Deity stooping from the floor of Heaven to welcome us—when we think of this, as we are so frequently forced to think of it, it becomes strange indeed that illness has not taken its place with love and battle and jealousy among the prime themes of literature. Novels, one would have thought, would have been devoted to influenza; epic poems to typhoid; odes to penumonia; lyrics to toothache. But no.

Mr. Connolly rightly admires the "long, effortless, masterly first sentence, eighteen book-page lines without a full stop." And he adds nostalgically: "Where will we find sentences like that one today?"

I admit that I cannot bring myself to feel the same kind of nostalgia. Long sentences are still being written today by some of our leading writers, but more often than not they seem rather like a kind of morbid growth. Opening William Faulkner's recent novel *Intruder in the Dust,* I read:

> It was just noon that Sunday morning when the sheriff reached the jail with Lucas Beauchamp though the whole town (the whole county too for that matter) had known since the night before that Lucas had killed a white man.
>
> He was there, waiting. . . .

It took me a second or two to realize that the word "he" referred neither to the white man nor to Lucas Beachamp nor even to the sheriff, but to the boy from whose point of view the novel is written. After identifying the "he," I naturally looked for the boy's name. But Faulkner does not care for satisfying a reader's natural curiosity. The boy's name, Charles Mallison Jr., appears for the first time, quite incidentally and inconspicuously, in the following sentence on page 68:

> Because he had already passed that long ago when that something —whatever it was—had held him here five minutes ago looking back across the vast, the almost insuperable chasm between him and the old Negro murderer and saw, heard Lucas saying something to him not because he was himself, Charles Mallison junior, nor because he had eaten the plate of greens and warmed himself at the fire, but because he alone of all the white people Lucas would have a chance to speak to between now and the moment when he might be dragged out of the cell and down the steps at the end of a rope, would hear the mute unhoping urgency of the eyes.

Intruder in the Dust is a powerful novel and Faulkner, of course, has the right to fashion his own style for his own artistic purposes. In a way, this is an admirable achievement. But maybe the social function of the artist goes beyond that. Maybe he has a moral obligation to make his work accessible to all who could be enriched by it. If so, then Faulkner, and most other writers who use an intensely personal style, have gone too far in their literary artistry. By foregoing the humble, reportorial, "style-less" style, they have betrayed the great audience ready for the fruits of their imagination.

THE ENGLISH BIBLE;
AND THE GRAND STYLE

J. Middleton Murry

. . . If we regard writing as the establishment of a relation between the author and his audience, it is clear that the amount of compulsive virtue he has to put into his language will depend upon the extent to which the feelings and thoughts he wishes to communicate are familiar or strange to his reader. Where his emotion is particular, his thought and feeling inseparably associated with circumstances that are unique, where his whole system of convictions is individual and in a sense even incommensurable, there he has practically to compel us to think and feel as he wills. He has to put something before us to which we must react in a certain way or not at all, and just in so far as those reactions are remote from our habitual method of thinking or feeling, his task will be more difficult, and his style will need to be more concrete. Not that this will be an alien effort to him. Writers have enough common humanity to ensure that they themselves will feel the necessity of employing their most impassioned exactness to express thoughts and feelings that are remote from the common experience. If they do not feel this necessity, then they are either mystics or madmen, and we have only to regret that the norm of the common experience is sometimes pitched so low, that when a man *has* made the effort he is still reckoned as mad. Two truly gifted minor poets—Christopher Smart and John Clare—were put into asylums, so far as I discover, mainly because of their genius.

From The Problem of Style *by J. Middleton Murry. Copyright 1922. Reprinted by permission of Oxford University Press. This essay is abridged as indicated.*

298

But there are certain realms of experience in which the level of emotional susceptibility of the audience is much higher than in others. There is, for instance, the realm of religion. Any deeply religious man is habituated to thoughts and feelings of a kind utterly remote from those which are the accompaniment of his practical life. A man who really believes in a just and omnipotent, a merciful and omniscient God has for his familiar companion a conception and an emotion which are truly tremendous. No suggestion of the poet or the prose-writer can possibly surpass them in force or vehemence. When an old Hebrew prophet wrote: "And the Lord said," he had done everything. The phrase is overwhelming. Nothing in *Paradise Lost* can compare with it.

> When the most High
> Eternal Father from his secret cloud,
> Amidst in thunder uttered thus his voice[1]

is almost trivial by its side. "And they heard the voice of the Lord God walking in the garden in the cool of the day." Two thousand years of Christian civilization bend our minds to these words; we cannot resist them. Nor can we refuse to them the title of great style. All that we have, as critics of literature, to remember, is that style of this kind is possible only when the appeal is to a habit of feeling and thought peculiar to religion. Possibly that very phrase "And the Lord said" might seem even ridiculous to one brought up in one of the transcendental religions of the East, just as some of the most poignant verses of the New Testament are said to be grotesque to an educated Mahommedan.

For this reason, I think, we have to be on our guard against the familiar suggestion that the English Bible is as a whole the highest achievement in English prose style. Not that I think this wholly untrue, but the manner in which the verdict is often pronounced seems to me dangerous. The Bible is a very heterogeneous book. Throughout, the Authorized Version has the high qualities of simplicity and firmness in phrasing. But there is all the difference in the world between the underlying style of Genesis and Job and Matthew. The style of Genesis is possible only to a strict and almost fanatical monotheism; its tremendous simplicity overwhelms us, and I suppose it overwhelms a Jew even more. The style of Job, on the other hand, is that of high and universal poetry. The God of Job is not left to our religious imagination; he expresses himself in language so creative and compulsive that—to use the phrase of Voltaire—if he did not exist, it would be necessary to invent him. And then, for a third distinct kind, we have the style of the Gospels of the

---

[1] *Paradise Lost,* x. 31.

New Testament. In the 27th chapter of Matthew there are two masterly effects—I hardly know whether to call them effects of style. They were contained in two quite simple statements: "Then all the disciples left Him, and fled"; and the words about Peter, after his third denial, "And he went out and wept bitterly." These approach to the condition of "And the Lord said" in Genesis, in the sense that the emotional suggestion is not in the words themselves; but they differ from those simple evocations of an awful conception of God; the reserves of emotion which Matthew's simple statements liberate in us have been accumulated during the reading of the narrative. The personality and the circumstances of Christ have been given to us: no words, no art could intensify the effect of the sudden, utterly unexpected statement: "Then all the disciples left Him, and fled." The situation given, the force of the words is elemental. So, too, nothing more needs to be told us of Peter than that "he went out and wept bitterly." We know what he felt; to attempt to describe or define it would only be to take away from that which we know. And all through the Gospel narratives there are these phrases charged with a similar emotional significance. "My God, my God, why hast thou forsaken me?" is surely the most terrible cry the world has ever heard. Put it back into the Hebrew, the only words of Hebrew most of us know, "Eli, Eli, lama sabacthani"—its force is hardly less. We know what it means.

And then, again, in yet another kind you have that sentence . . . of which Walter Pater said: "There's a mystery in it—a something supernatural."

> Come unto me all ye that labour and are heavy laden, and I will give you rest. Take my yoke upon you, and learn of me; for I am meek and lowly in heart: and ye shall find rest unto your souls. For my yoke is easy and my burden is light.

There the language itself has a surpassing beauty. The movement and sound of the first sentence is exquisite, I have no doubt a thousand times more beautiful than the Greek, which I have forgotten if I ever knew it. But still,—would it be so very different in its effect in the Greek? I doubt it. In whatever language that sentence was spoken to you, your depths would be stirred. Our common humanity reaches out after the comfort of the words; all that there is of weariness and disappointment, of suffering and doubt, in all men stretches out for some small share in this love that might have changed the world. Apply your coldest test to it, and it remains great style; and when a man appears who can use it again, perhaps the face of the earth will be changed, for assuredly there is a mystery in the love which finds expression in it.

But there is not much fear that we shall have to take such emotions as these into our modern calculations, nor is there much likelihood of a modern writer's being able to rely upon the religious conceptions and feelings of his audience, nor much probability that those conceptions and feelings will be predominant in himself. In so far as the predisposition to certain kinds of emotional experience plays a part in the style of the English Bible, we may leave it out of our reckoning.

The emotional predisposition of contemporary society is of another and altogether inferior kind; so far from being tempted to rely upon it, the conscientious writer finds himself continually fighting against any tendency to appeal to it. The modern mind is bemused by a cloud of unsubstantial abstractions—democracy, liberty, revolution, honour,—none of the people who use these words seem to have the faintest notion what they mean, or any desire that they should mean anything. And these obvious examples are not really the most characteristic; the flabbiness of modern thinking is not really comparable to the sloppiness of modern feeling. I can only pick out a couple of sentences from a perfectly reputable and fairly well-known modern novelist, whose book happened to be at hand. The love-making scene in which the words occur might be rather nauseating if it were not so perfectly ridiculous. The gentleman has addressed the lady as "You royal creature" twice, and once as "You unutterable queen." To which last she has replied, "Oh no! I'm a tiny child." Now comes my quotation:

> He laid his cheek against her. "I am your baby and your father. Your baby taken home again and reborn. Your father to tend you always."

I admit that is a singularly unpleasant example of modern sentimentality; but it is only in extreme manifestations that one can recognize a tendency of sentiment. I do not know whether the author actually believed in the verisimilitude of that conversation, but in any case he was appealing to the empty emotionalism that is current to-day. No condition of society is more dangerous to the writer; it is as though he found himself playing on a piano whose every key sounded the same note. In the exasperated endeavour to get some differentiation of response out of it he is tempted to exaggerate, to pound with a hammer upon those senseless keys. Compulsion of that kind—and it is the characteristic vice of modern writing—is utterly different from the compulsion that the writer has to employ. Every age has its peculiar form of rhetoric, of course, but I doubt whether there has been any age in which the temptation was so insistent and insidious as it is to-day.

Rhetoric is the opposite of the process which I have called crystallization. Instead of condensing your emotion upon the cause, which becomes the symbol; instead of defining and making concrete your thought, by the aid of your sensuous perception; you give way to a mere verbal exaggeration of your feeling or your thought. Instead of trying to make your expression more precise and true, you falsify it for the sake of a vague impressiveness. The result is that you forfeit all power of discrimination; instead of taking your emotion down to a solid and particular basis, which differentiates it permanently, you raise it up to an infinite power. You try to replace quality by quantity, and forget that all quantities raised to an infinite power are the same. By pounding on the keys with a hammer you merely break the strings.

To return to our discussion of the style of the English Bible. Putting aside the purity of the vocabulary, which was (I should imagine) deliberately made simpler and purer than the ordinary prose of the time, there is at least as much difference between the underlying styles of the book as there is between Shakespeare and Bunyan and a chap-book. There is high poetry; there is dramatic narrative in its simplest and crudest form; there is religious legend deriving its emotional intensity from a passionate monotheism shared by the audience. And it seems better to distinguish between these than to assimilate them, even at the risk of an apparent irreverence. It is obvious that the emotional susceptibility of the reader will vary with the degree of his belief. One who accepts the cosmogony of Genesis will be more profoundly moved by it than one who believes in evolution and the nebular hypothesis; one who believes in the divinity of Jesus will be more profoundly affected by the gospel narratives than one who does not. And yet I am not quite sure; I think that, on the whole, I prefer to say that the believer will be more deeply affected by each separate page of the Gospel narrative, while the man who approaches it as literature will be more deeply affected by certain pages. "My God, my God, why hast thou forsaken me?" is far less disturbing to the Christian than to the agnostic.

This brief and inadequate discussion of the style of the Bible at least suggests that a useful cross-section of literature could be obtained by regarding it as determined by the emotional and intellectual predispositions which the audience brings to it. I do not think that this method of approach would carry one so far as the attempt to envisage it from the side of production; but the auxiliary anatomy of style would be useful. I mean that we might begin by regarding as the norm of literary style those simple and overwhelming dramatic effects of which "He went out and wept bitterly" is so notable an example. Their force is supplied by the previous narrative; we have formed in our mind a picture of the circumstances; we know from his own words the nature of the man who has been denied. If we were to adopt, as one critic has done, the distinction between "kinetic" and "potential" language, we might say that the half-dozen words describing Peter are merely "potential."

"And the Lord said" is an example of potential speech where the charge comes wholly from the mind of the audience. "Come unto me all ye that labour" is partly kinetic—the actual beauty of the words has a positive effect—partly potential: the longing to which the appeal is made is universal in mankind. And it might be possible to analyse style by endeavouring to separate the kinetic from the potential elements, though, seeing that these elements are inextricably intertwined, I cannot see that it would be possible to do more than indicate the predominance of one element or another. I suppose that the sentence, "But the iniquity of oblivion blindly scattereth her poppy," is almost wholly kinetic; that is to say, it completely creates its own emotion. You need no context, and you bring no emotion to it. It is, in the words of M. Bergson, a creative and not merely a liberating cause. But, however far we may carry analysis of this kind, it will not help us much. For the general award, we can only say that, other things being equal, that style in which the kinetic elements preponderate is to be preferred; but since those other things include the comprehensiveness of the author's attitude to the universe, and his power of explicating that attitude in an appropriate plot or muthos, to judge style primarily by an analysis of language is almost on a level with judging a man by his clothes.

And this is the principal danger in allowing the dogma of the infallibility of the style of the English Bible to go unchallenged. By doing so we allow our attention to be concentrated on the accidents and not the essentials of style. It is difficult to object when we are told—as we very frequently are told—that there are two super-eminent works of literature in English—the Bible and Shakespeare; but I always feel uneasy when I hear it. I suspect that the man who says so does not appreciate Shakespeare as he ought; and that he is not being quite honest about the Bible. The reason why it is difficult to object is that there is a sense in which it is true that the style of the Bible is splendid. The vocabulary on which the translators drew is singularly pure; purer than Shakespeare's vocabulary, by far. But the strength of a vocabulary does not really lie in its purity—and purity is in itself a very arbitrary conception when applied to language—but in its adaptability as an instrument. Think what you could do with Shakespeare's vocabulary as compared with what you could do with the vocabulary of the Bible: no comparison is possible. I can conceive no modern emotion or thought—except perhaps some of the more Hegelian metaphysics—that could not be adequately and superabundantly expressed

in Shapespeare's vocabulary: there are very few that would not be muti-
lated out of all recognition if they had to pass through the language of the
Bible.

And, when we consider style in the larger sense, it seems to me
scarcely an exaggeration to say that the style of one half of the English
Bible is atrocious. A great part of the historical books of the Old Testament, the gospels in the New, are examples of all that writing should not
be; and nothing the translators might have done would have altered this.
On the other hand, though the translation of Job that we have is a superb
piece of poetry, I am convinced that it is finer in the Hebrew original.
All this may, I fear, be thought heresy, perhaps even a painful heresy;
but I should not have gone out of my way to utter it, if I did not feel
that the superstitious reverence for the style of the Authorized Version
really stands in the way of a frank approach to the problem of style.
I shall put my conviction most clearly if I say that the following proposition must be accepted in any consideration of style: *"The Life of Jesus* by
Ernest Renan is, as a whole, infinitely superior in point of style to the
narrative of the Authorized Version of the Gospels." The proposition is
really axiomatic. It is clear, from a mere consideration of the facts of
authorship, that to speak of the style of the Gospels is to say "the thing
that is not." There are four styles, if there is a style at all. And the same
varnish of propriety with which the good taste of the English translators
has covered them all cannot change their substance. If we examine this
we discover only two elements that can possibly lay claim to be considered
creative literature; the actual words of Christ reported, such as "Come
unto Me . . ." and "My God, my God . . ." and the dramatic effects,
such as, "Then all the disciples forsook him and fled." The first do not
belong to the Gospels, but to their author, and the second are really not
effects of style at all. It is not the authors of the Gospels who have given
us the imaginative realization of the character of Jesus on which these
dramatic effects depend. Take away the words of Jesus which they reproduce and nothing of that character remains. The written evidence of an
honest police-constable would give us as much. The most elementary conditions of the presence of style are lacking.

Style is organic—not the clothes a man wears, but the flesh, bone,
and blood of his body. Therefore it is really impossible to consider styles
apart from the whole system of perceptions and feelings and thoughts
that animate them. There is a downright viciousness of language which
is produced by a lazy or inflated thought, or an insensitiveness to the true
meanings of words, which may be called "bad style," so long as we
remember that correctness of language is at best merely a negative condition of good style, or better of a positive style. In Leigh Hunt's unduly

neglected poem *The Story of Rimini* there are a good many appalling lines, and there is in particular one couplet:

> The two divinest things this world has got,
> A lovely woman in a rural spot.

The concentrated abuse of language in those two rhyme words could not easily be paralleled. But the absence of such vulgarisms—against which, as Coleridge said a familiarity with the language of the Authorized Version is one of the best safeguards—is not in the least a guarantee of positive style. The most confusing of the many equivocations concealed in the word "style" is that by which good taste in language is allowed to masquerade as a creative principle. Good taste in language will not carry a writer anywhere. Massinger's taste in language was very fine indeed, but I do not hesitate to say that his style was generally bad. His way of feeling and thinking was not his own; his perceptions were blunted and clumsy. Webster, on the other hand, had not at all a good taste in language—at times it was shocking—but his way of thinking and feeling was individual, and he managed to project it into an expression that was by fits and starts tortuous and blindingly clear: he had style.

Purity of language, therefore, is a most unreliable clue to style. But this does not mean that it is always impossible to infer the whole from the part. There are some writers—of whom Shakespeare is the great exemplar—whose wealth of sensuous perception is such that in any piece of the texture of their writing you are bound to come upon some conclusive evidence of a distinct and individual mode of feeling. There will be a revealing image, or an epithet used with a new precision—some token of that process of crystallization which is the typical method of positive style—and these evidences, which may be found in all times and places, are reliable. But they are not always present throughout the texture of a positive style: you may infer from their presence, but you may not infer from their absence. With many great writers the main act of crystallization is done once for all when they have formed their plot, or their argument. All that one can say of them, negatively, is that they do not belong to the great revivifiers of language; their style is not the less real for that. . . .

If we accept the organic character of style, it becomes rather difficult to extract much valuable meaning from the familiar term, "the grand style." If the epithet is conceived as applying to the vocabulary, the distinction is not very important: if it applies to the system of emotions and thoughts that a great writer must have, it is not at all easy to see why Milton's is grander, say, than Mr. Thomas Hardy's. All great writers, or none, have the grand style. That is only another way of saying that the distinction does not convey very much to us. If we try to use the term "grand style" in Matthew Arnold's sense, and restrict it to poetry which contains "criticism of life," we find ourselves, as I tried to show, compelled to understand the phrase "criticism of life" in a very arbitrary sense. It is only by accident that the criticism of life which is contained in all great works of literature finds expression in general statements about life. Pope's *Essay on Man,* on the other hand, is full of them.

Probably there are a good many conflicting ideas tied together in a loose bundle by the words "the grand style"; sometimes, the emphasis is on the character of the vocabulary—and in that case, if Milton's poetry is in the grand style, Dr. Johnson's prose is also; sometimes, on the nature of the plot or muthos—if superhuman or majestic figures are involved; sometimes, on the expression of general ideas about life. Each of these elements is, in itself, accidental to a true anatomy of style. But there is a certain logical connexion between the first two: if the characters of the plot are superhuman and majestic, it seems more or less necessary that their manner of speech should differ from that of ordinary dramatic poetry by being more dignified, though it is worth while to remember that two of the most triumphant evocations of superhuman beings—of Mephistopheles in *Faust,* and of the Devil in *The Brothers Karamazov*—do not rely upon any particular dignity of speech. Dostoevsky's Devil, you will remember, looked like a decayed gentleman in a shabby frockcoat, and spoke like one. He was certainly not the less impressive for that.

If we approach the grand style from this angle, it appears as a means to dramatic propriety: the poet heightens the speech of his superhuman characters in order that they may appear truly superhuman. In *Hyperion* Keats goes one step farther; he does not profess to reproduce the speech of Thea, as Milton reproduces that of the Deity, but merely to give a human approximation to it:

> Some words she spake
> In solemn tenour and deep organ tone:
> Some mourning words, which in our feeble tongue
> Would come in these like accents; O how frail
> To that large utterance of the early Gods!

The grand style is, I believe, a technical poetic device for a particular end, and is not really an equivalent of the peculiar usage of classical poetry, which draws upon a different vocabulary from that of prose. The vocabulary of English poetry does not differ widely from that of English prose. The poets keep a good many words alive that have passed out of common speech, and there are a few definitely poetic words—though for the most part they are better avoided—and, I believe, a few unpoetic words. (I remember that when I first began to write verses, a poet of some renown warned me that "legs" could not be mentioned in poetry. I have never been able to decide whether it was a relic of the Victorian social convention, or some profound aesthetic conviction on his part.)

I do not think that in the golden age of English literature the Elizabethans made any particular distinction between the vocabularies of prose and poetry, though my scholarship is not enough to permit me to be dogmatic in the matter. The difference between the two languages was, as I have said, mainly one of tempo. Of course, there was the rant of *Tamburlaine,* that peculiar Elizabethan rhetoric which was natural to Marlowe, and which the rest of them could turn on when they liked. But that was a rhetoric of exaggeration: if you wished to suggest that some one in misery might as well kill herself, this is how you said it:

> When thy poor heart beats with outrageous beating
> Thou canst not strike it thus to make it still.
> Wound it with sighing, girl, kill it with groans;
> Or get some little knife between thy teeth,
> And just against thy heart make thou a hole;
> That all the tears that thy poor eyes let fall
> May run into that sink, and, soaking in,
> Drown the lamenting fool in sea-salt tears.[2]

But Elizabethan rhetoric has nothing to do with "the grand style." That is the deliberate invention of Milton, first for the special purposes of his celestial argument, and secondly because he was drawn by his deep classical sympathies towards the notion of a peculiar poetic vocabulary, and perhaps also because he felt the necessity of reacting against the influence of Shakespeare. It is much simpler, and I think more useful, to regard the grand style in English as the style of Milton. It is a true and a great style; the perfect medium of expression for a mode of thought and feeling that are absolutely individual. It is as different from the style of Dante—with which it is sometimes compared—as it is from the style of Donne; in other words, absolutely different.

One great attempt was made to imitate the Miltonic style, by Keats. By instinct he knew that it was foolish to attempt to write Miltonics; he had to feel and think Miltonics; and the surpassing interest of *Hyperion* is that it shows that he could, in a way, think and feel Miltonics better than Milton. But they were not natural to him; he could not maintain

[2] *Titus Andronicus,* III. ii. 13.

himself; he raised the pitch of his own thought to a level on which it could not operate any more. The reasons why he abandoned the poem were, I believe, two: one was the reason he gave, that the artifice of Miltonic rhythms and inversions went against the grain, the other that he had worked his superhuman argument into a position from which it was impossible to continue. He declared that he wished to devote himself "to another verse alone." There is, in the collected fragments of his work, a little passage in blank verse—there are good reasons for believing it to be the last poetry he wrote—which gives us an inkling of what the other verse might have been:

> This living hand, now warm and capable
> Of earnest grasping, would, if it were cold
> And in the icy silence of the tomb,
> So haunt thy days and chill thy dreaming nights
> That thou wouldst wish thine own heart dry of blood
> So in my veins red life might stream again
> And thou be conscience-calmed—see here it is—
> I hold it towards you.

It has nothing of "the grand style": but it has something of great style; it is simple, sensuous, and passionate.

I believe that "the grand style" is largely a bogey. There are styles, but no style; there are great styles and there are little ones: there are also non-styles. And, alas, no one can have a great style or a little one for the asking, nor even by taking pains. The best he can do is negative: but the smallest writer can do something to ensure that his individuality is not lost, by trying to make sure that he feels what he thinks he feels;—that he thinks what he thinks he thinks, that his words mean what he thinks they mean. Whether his individuality is worth anything is another matter; but mostly individualities are valuable, because they are rare. Nothing will teach a man to feel distinctly: but probably the best way for him to discover whether he does is to leave himself out of the reckoning. To be impersonal is the best way of achieving personality, and it gives him far less chance of deceiving himself. "A second promise of genius," wrote Coleridge, "is the choice of subjects very remote from the private interests and circumstances of the writer himself. At least I have found that where the subject is taken immediately from the author's personal experiences, the excellence of a particular piece of literature is but an equivocal mark, and often a fallacious pledge of genuine literary power."

particular styles

T. H. HUXLEY AS A LITERARY MAN

Aldous Huxley

. . . For the purposes of literary analysis, Huxley's writings may be divided into three classes: first, the purely descriptive; secondly, the philosophical and sociological; and thirdly, the controversial and (to use once more a repellant, but irreplaceable, word) the emotive. To the first of these classes belong the technical scientific papers; to the second, the studies of Hume and Berkeley and a number of essays on metaphysical, ethical and educational subjects; and to the third, certain of the essays on Christian and Hebrew tradition and the essays containing critcisms of other people's ideas or a defence of his own. It is hardly necessary to say that, in reality, the three classes overlap. The descriptive papers contain philosophical matter in the form of generalizations and scientific hypotheses. The philosophical and sociological essays have their controversial and their emotionally moving passages; and as most of the controversies are on philosophical subjects, the controversial essays are to a considerable extent purely philosophical. Still, imperfect as it is, the classification is none the less useful. The writings of the first two classes are strictly scientific writings; that is to say, they are meant to communicate facts and ideas, not passions. They are of the same kind as the passage from the *Encyclopaedia* quoted at an earlier stage in this lecture. The writings of the third class belong to the same genus as my quotation from Milton. They are intended to communi-

From The Olive Tree *by Aldous Huxley. Copyright 1937 by Aldous Huxley; renewed 1956 by Laura A. Huxley. Reprinted by permission of Harper & Row, Publishers.*

cate feelings as well as information—and biological feeling as well as pure aesthetic feelings. I propose now to deal with these three classes of Huxley's writings in order.

To describe with precision even the simplest object is extremely difficult. Just how difficult only those who have attempted the task professionally can realize. Let me ask you to imagine yourselves suddenly called upon to explain to some Martian visitor the exact form, function and mode of operation of, say, a corkscrew. The thing seems simple enough; and yet I suspect that, after a few minutes of stammering hesitations, most of us would find ourselves reduced to making spiral gestures with a forefinger and going through a pantomime of bottle-opening. The difficulties of describing in a clear and intelligible way such an incomparably more elaborate piece of machinery as a living organism, for example, are proportionately greater.

Not only is exact description difficult; it is also, of all kinds of writing, that which has in it the least potentialities of beauty. The object to be described stares the author uncompromisingly in the face. His business is to render its likeness in words, point by point, in such a way that someone who had never seen it would be able to reconstruct it from his description, as from a blue print. He must therefore call every spade consistently and exclusively a spade—never anything else. But the higher forms of literature depend for many of their most delicate effects on spades being called on occasion by other names. Non-scientific writers are free to use a variety of synonyms to express the same idea in subtly different ways; are free to employ words with variously coloured overtones of association; are free to express themselves, in terms now of one metaphor, now of another. Not so the maker of verbal blue prints. The only beauties he can hope, or, indeed, has any right to create are beauties of orderly composition and, in detail, of verbal clarity. Huxley's scientific papers prove him to have had a remarkable talent for this austere and ungrateful kind of writing. His descriptions of the most complicated organic structures are astonishingly lucid. We are reminded, as we read, that their author was an accomplished draughtsman. "I should make it absolutely necessary," he writes in one of his essays on education, "for everybody to learn to draw. . . . You will find it," he goes on, "an implement of learning of extreme value. It gives you the means of training the young in attention and accuracy, which are two things in which all mankind are more deficient than in any other mental quality whatever. The whole of my life has been spent in trying to give my proper attention to things and to be accurate, and I have not succeeded as well as I could wish; and other people, I am afraid, are not much more fortunate." No artist, I suppose, has ever succeeded as well as he could wish; but many have succeeded as well as other, less talented people could wish. In its own kind, such a book as Huxley's *Treatise on the Crayfish* is a model of excellence. Quotation cannot do justice to the composition of the book as a whole, and the unavoidable use of technical terms makes the citing even of short extracts unsuitable on such an occasion as the present. The following passage may serve, however, to give some idea of the lucidity of Huxley's descriptive style:

> In the dorsal wall of the heart two small oval apertures are visible, provided with valvular lips, which open inwards, or towards the internal cavity of the heart. There is a similar aperture in each of the two lateral faces of the heart, and two others in its interior face, making six in all. These apertures readily admit fluid into the heart, but oppose its exit. On the other hand, at the origins of the arteries there are small valvular folds directed in such a manner as to permit the exit of fluid from the heart, while they prevent its entrance.

This is nakedly plain and unadorned; but it does what it was intended to do—it gives the reader a satisfyingly accurate picture of what is being described. Some modern popularizers of science have sought to "humanize" their writing. The following is an example of the late Dr. Dorsey's humanized—his all-too-humanized—scientific style:

> If we find that the thing we trust to pick the mother of our children is simply a double-barrelled pump, knowledge of our heart or the liquid refreshment it pumps to our brains will not grow more nerve cells, but it should make us less nervous and more respectful of the pump and the refreshment it delivers; when it stops, the brain starves to death.

Obscure almost to meaninglessness, vulgar, vague—this is the humanization of science with a vengeance! Deplorably but, I suppose, naturally enough, this kind of popular science is thoroughly popular in the other, the box-office sense of the term. Tennyson's generalization, that we needs must love the highest when we see it, has but the slenderest justification in observable fact.

So much for the writings of the first class. Those of the second are more interesting, both to the general reader and to the literary critic. Philosophical writings have much higher potentialities of beauty than purely descriptive writings. The descriptive writer is confined within the narrow prison of the material objects whose likeness he is trying to render. The philosopher is the inhabitant of a much more spacious, because a purely mental, universe. There is, if I may so express myself, more room in the theory of knowledge than in a crayfish's heart. No doubt, if we could feel as certain about epistemology as we do about the shape and function of crustacean viscera, the philosopher's universe would be as narrow as the descriptive naturalist's. But we do not feel as certain. Ignorance has many advantages. Man's uncertainties in regard to all the major issues of life allow the philosopher much enviable freedom—freedom, among other things, to employ all kinds of artistic devices, from the use of which the descriptive naturalist is quite debarred.

The passages from Huxley's philosophical writings which I now propose to quote and analyze have been chosen mainly, of course, because they exhibit characteristic excellences of style, but partly, also, for the sake of their content. Huxley's philosophical doctrines are outside my province, and I shall not discuss them. What I have done, however, is to choose as my literary examples passages which illustrate his views on a number of important questions. They show how cautious and profound a thinker he was—how very far from being that arrogant and cocksure materialist at whom, as at a convenient Aunt Sally, certain contemporary publicists are wont to fling their dialectical brickbats.

Huxley's use of purely rhythmical effects was always masterly, and my first three examples are intended to illustrate his practice in this branch of literary art. Here is a paragraph on scientific hypotheses:

> All science starts with hypotheses—in other words, with assumptions that are unproved, while they may be, and often are, erroneous, but which are better than nothing to the searcher after order in the maze of phenomena. And the historical progress of every science depends on the criticism of hypotheses—on the gradual stripping off, that is, of their untrue or superfluous parts—until there remains only that exact verbal expression of as much as we know of the facts, and no more, which constitutes a perfect scientific theory.

The substance of this paragraph happens to be intrinsically correct. But we are the more willing to believe its truth because of the way in which that truth is expressed. Huxley's utterance has something peculiarly judicious and persuasive about it. The secret is to be found in his rhythm. If we analyze the crucial first sentence, we shall find that it consists of three more or less equal long phrases, followed by three more or less equal short ones. Thus:

All science starts with hypotheses—
in other words, with assumptions that are unproved,
while they may be, and often are, erroneous;
but which are better than nothing
to the searcher after order
in the maze of phenomena.

The long opening phrases state all that can be said against hypotheses—
state it with a firm and heavy emphasis. Then, suddenly, in the second
half of the sentence, the movement quickens, and the brisk and lively
rhythm of the three last phrases brings home the value of hypotheses with
an appeal to the aesthetic sensibilities as well as to the intellect.

My second example is from a passage dealing with "those who
oppose the doctrine of necessity":

> They rest [writes Huxley] on the absurd presumption that the
> proposition "I can do as I like" is contradictory to the doctrine of neces-
> sity. The answer is: nobody doubts that, at any rate within certain
> limits, you can do as you like. But what determines your likings and
> dislikings? Did you make your own constitution? Is it your contrivance
> that one thing is pleasant and another is painful? And even if it were,
> why did you prefer to make it after the one fashion rather than the
> other? The passionate assertion of the consciousness of their freedom,
> which is the favourite refuge of the opponents of the doctrine of necessity,
> is mere futility for nobody denies it. What they really have to do, if they
> would upset the necessarian argument, is to prove that they are free to
> associate any emotion whatever with any idea whatever; to like pain as
> much as pleasure, vice as much as virtue; in short, to prove that, what-
> ever may be the fixity of order of the universe of things, that of thought
> is given over to chance.

Again, this is a very sound argument; but its penetrative force and
immediate persuasiveness are unquestionably increased by the manner of
its expression. The anti-necessarian case is attacked in a series of short,
sharp phrases, each carrying a simple question demanding a simple and,
for the arguer's opponents, a most damaging answer:

But what determines your likings and dislikings?
Did you make your own constitution?
Is it your contrivance that one thing is pleasant and another is painful?

The phrases lengthen as the argument deals with subtler points of
detail; then, in the last sentence, where Huxley convicts his opponents of
upholding an absurdity, they contract to the emphatically alliterative
brevity of

to like pain as much as pleasure,
vice as much as virtue.

After which the absurdity of the anti-necessarian case is generalized; there
is a long preparatory phrase, followed by a brief, simple and, we are made
to feel, definitive conclusion:

to prove that, whatever may be the fixity of order of the universe of
things,
that of thought is given over to chance.

The persuasive effectiveness of these last phrases is enhanced by the
use of alliteration. "Things" and "thought" are key words. Their alliterative resemblance serves to emphasize the unjustifiable distinction which the
anti-necessarians draw between the two worlds. And the insistent recurrence in both phrases of the v-sound of *prove, whatever, universe* and of
given and *over* enhances the same effect.

> In whichever way we look at the matter, morality is based on feel-
> ing, not on reason; though reason alone is competent to trace out the
> effects of our actions and thereby dictate conduct. Justice is founded on
> the love of one's neighbour; and goodness is a kind of beauty. The moral
> law, like the laws of physical nature, rests in the long run upon instinc-
> tive intuitions, and is neither more nor less "innate" and "necessary"
> than they are. Some people cannot by any means be got to understand
> the first book of Euclid; but the truths of mathematics are no less
> necessary and binding on the great mass of mankind. Some there are
> who cannot feel the difference between the "Sonata Appassionate" and
> "Cherry Ripe," or between a gravestone-cutter's cherub and the Apollo
> Belvedere; but the canons of art are none the less acknowledged. While
> some there may be who, devoid of sympathy, are incapable of a sense
> of duty; but neither does their existence affect the foundations of mo-
> rality. Such pathological deviations from true manhood are merely the
> halt, the lame and the blind of the world of consciousness; and the
> anatomist of the mind leaves them aside, as the anatomist of the body
> would ignore abnormal specimens.
> And as there are Pascals and Mozarts, Newtons and Raphaels, in
> whom the innate faculty for science or art needs but a touch to spring
> into full vigour, and through whom the human race obtains new possi-
> bilities of knowledge and new conceptions of beauty; so there have been
> men of moral genius, to whom we owe ideals of duty and visions of
> moral perfection, which ordinary mankind could never have attained;
> though, happily for them, they can feel the beauty of a vision which lay
> beyond the reach of their dull imaginations, and count life well spent
> in shaping some faint image of it in the actual world.

As a piece of reflective writing, this is quite admirable; and it will
be worth while, I think, to take some trouble to analyze out the technical
devices which make it so effective. The secret of the peculiar beauty of
this grave and noble passage is to be found, I believe, in the author's use
of what, for lack of a better term, I will call "caesura-sentences." Hebrew

literature provides the classical type of the caesura-sentence. Open any of the poetical books of the Bible at random, and you will find all the examples you want. "His soul shall dwell at ease; and his seed shall inherit the earth." Or, "Then shall the dust return to the earth as it was; and the spirit shall return unto God who gave it." The whole system of Hebrew poetry was based on the division of each sentence by a caesura into two distinct, but related clauses. Anglo-Saxon verse was written on a somewhat similar principle. The caesura-sentence is common in the work of some of the greatest English prose-writers. One of them, Sir Thomas Browne, used it constantly. Here, for example, is a characteristic passage from the *Urn Burial:* "Darkness and light divide the course of time, and oblivion shares with memory a great part even of our living beings. We slightly remember our felicities, and the smartest strokes of affliction leave but short smart upon us. Sense endureth no extremities, and sorrows destroy us or themselves." It was Browne, I think, who first demonstrated the peculiar suitability of the caesura-sentence for the expression of grave meditations on the nature of things, for the utterance of profound and rather melancholy aphorisms. The clauses into which he divides his sentence are generally short. Sometimes the two clauses are more or less evenly balanced. Sometimes a longer clause is succeeded by a shorter, and the effect is one of finality, of the last word having been spoken. Sometimes the shorter comes first, and the long clause after the caesura seems to open up wide prospects of contemplation and speculative argument.

I could give other examples of the use of caesura-sentences by writers as far apart as Dr. Johnson and De Quincey. But time presses; and besides, these examples would be superfluous. For, as it so happens, Huxley's use of the caesura-sentence is very similar to Browne's. He employs it, in the great majority of cases, when he wants to express himself in meditative aphorisms about the nature of life in general. Thus: "Ignorance is visited as sharply as wilful disobedience—incapacity meets with the same punishment as crime." Again, "Pain and sorrow knock at our doors more loudly than pleasure and happiness; and the prints of their heavy footsteps are less easily effaced." Here is another example, where the clauses are much shorter: "There is but one right, and the possibilities of wrong are infinite." Here yet one more, in which, as the statement made is more complicated, the clauses have to be longer than usual: "It is one of the last lessons one learns from experience, but not the least important, that a heavy tax is levied upon all forms of success; and that failure is one of the commonest disguises assumed by blessings."

In the long passage quoted just now much of that effect of noble and meditative gravity is obtained by the judicious use of caesura-sentences. The tone is set by a sentence that might almost have been penned by Sir Thomas Browne himself: "Justice is founded on the love of one's neighbour; and goodness is a kind of beauty." All the rest of the first paragraph is built up of fundamentally similar caesura-sentences, some almost as brief and simple as the foregoing, some long and complicated, but preserving through their length and complication the peculiar quality (as of a sad and deeply reflective soliloquy, an argument of the mind with its inmost self), the musically pensive essence of the Brownean formula.

Before leaving the subject of Huxley's philosophical writings, I must say something about his use of images and his choice of words. Since accuracy and veracity were the qualities at which he consistently aimed, Huxley was sparing in the use of images. Ideas can be very vividly expressed in terms of metaphor and simile; but, since analogies are rarely complete, this vividness is too often achieved at the cost of precision. Seldom, and only with the greatest caution, does Huxley attempt anything like a full-blown simile. The most striking one I can remember is that in which he compares living beings to the whirlpool below Niagara:

> However changeful is the contour of its crest, this wave has been visible, approximately in the same place, and with the same general form, for centuries past. Seen from a mile off, it would seem to be a stationary hillock of water. Viewed closely, it is a typical expression of the conflicting impulses generated by a swift rush of material particles. Now, with all our appliances, we cannot get within a good many miles, so to speak, of the crayfish. If we could, we should see that it was nothing but the constant form of a similar turmoil of material molecules, which are constantly flowing into the animal on one side, and streaming out on the other.

Only where analogies were as close as this one between the living body and the vortex would Huxley venture to make use of similes. He was never prepared to enliven the manner of his books at the expense of their matter.

Huxley's vocabulary is probably the weakest point in all his literary equipment. True, it was perfectly adequate to the clear and forceful statement of his ideas. But the sensitive reader cannot help feeling that the choice of words might, without any impairment of scientific efficiency, have been more exquisite. For example, we miss in his writings that studied alternation of words of Greek and Latin with words of Teutonic origin— an alternation so rich, when skilfully handled, as by Milton, in powerful and startling literary effects. To illustrate the defects in Huxley's vocabulary would be a lengthy and laborious process, which I cannot undertake in the time at my disposal. It must be enough to say that, good as his choice of words generally is, it might unquestionably have been better.

Let us turn now to the third division of Huxley's writings, the controversial and emotive. As a controversialist, Huxley was severe, but always courteous. We must not expect to find in his polemical writings those thunderous comminations, that jeering and abuse which make Milton's prose such lively reading. Still, he could be sarcastic enough when he wanted, and his wit was pointed and barbed by the elegance with which he expressed himself. Here is a passage from a brief biography of Descartes, which shows what was the nature of his talents in this direction:

> Trained by the best educators of the seventeenth century, the Jesuits; naturally endowed with a dialectic grasp and subtlety which even they could hardly improve; and with a passion for getting at the truth which even they could hardly impair, Descartes possessed in addition a rare mastery of literary expression.

One could quote many similar passages. From the neat antithesis to the odd and laughter-provoking word—Huxley used every device for the expression of sarcasm and irony.

In the passages in which his aim was to convey, along with ideas, a certain quality of passion, Huxley resorted very often to literary allusion —particularly to biblical allusion. Here is a characteristic example:

> The politician tells us, "You must educate the masses because they are going to be masters." The clergy join in the cry for education, for they affirm that the people are drifting away from church and chapel into the broadest infidelity. The manufacturers and the capitalists swell the chorus lustily. They declare that ignorance makes bad workmen; that England will soon be unable to turn out cotton goods, or steam engines, cheaper than other people; and then, Ichabod! Ichabod! the glory will be departed from us. And a few voices are lifted up in favour of the doctrine that the masses should be educated because they are men and women with unlimited capacities of being, doing and suffering, and that it is as true now as ever it was, that the people perish for lack of knowledge.

Here the two, or rather the three, biblical references produce a variety of powerful emotional effects—produce them, let us note in passing, only upon those who know their Bible. Those who do not know their Bible will fail to appreciate the chief beauties of this passage almost as completely as those who do not know their Functions of Complex Variables must fail to appreciate the beauties of Niels Abel's mathematical literature. Every writer assumes in his readers a knowledge of the work of certain other writers. His assumptions, I may add, are frequently quite unjustified.

Let us now consider the emotional effects which Huxley aimed at producing and which, upon those who know the sacred writings as well as he, he did and still does produce. Ichabod, it will be remembered, was so named, "because the glory is departed from Israel, for the ark of God is taken." To mention Ichabod in this context is to imply a richly sarcastic disquisition on the nature of the capitalists' god. The tone changes, in the last sentence, from ironical to earnest and pathetic; and those final words, "the people perish for lack of knowledge," put us in mind of two noble biblical passages: one from the book of the prophet Hosea, who affirms that "the Lord hath a controversy with the inhabitants of the land" and that "the people are destroyed for lack of knowledge"; the other from the book of Proverbs, to the effect that "where there is no vision, the people perish." The double reference produces the effect Huxley desired. The true reason for universal education could not be stated more concisely or more movingly.

Occasionally, Huxley's biblical references take the form, not of direct citation, but of the use of little tags of obsolescent language borrowed from the Authorized Version. After a long passage of lucid and essentially modern exposition, he will sometimes announce the oncoming of his peroration by a phrase or two of sixteenth-century prayer-book or Bible English. Our modern taste has veered away from this practice; but among writers of the early and middle nineteenth century it was very common. Lamb and his contemporaries were constantly dropping into Wardour Street Elizabethan; Carlyle's writings are a warehouse of every kind of fancy-dress language; Herman Melville made a habit of breaking out, whenever he was excited, into bogus Shakespeare; the very love-letters of the Brownings are peppered with learned archaisms. Indeed, one of the major defects of nineteenth-century literature, at any rate in our eyes, was its inordinate literariness, its habit of verbal dressing up and playing stylistic charades. That Huxley should have made brief and occasional use of the literary devices so freely exploited by his contemporaries is not surprising. Fortunately, his passion for veracity prevented him from overdoing the literariness.

I have constantly spoken, in the course of these analyses, of "literary devices." The phrase is a rather unfortunate one; for it is liable to call up in the hearer's mind a picture of someone laboriously practising a mixture of card-sharping and cookery. The words make us visualize the man of letters turning over the pages of some literary Mrs. Beeton in quest of the best recipe for an epigram or a dirge; or else as a trickster preparing for his game with the reader by carefully marking the cards. But in point of fact the man of letters does most of his work not by calculation, not by the application of formulas, but by aesthetic intuition. He has something to say, and he sets it down in the words which he finds most satisfying aesthetically. After the event comes the critic, who discovers that he was using a certain kind of literary device, which can be classified in its proper chapter of the cookery-book. The process is largely irreversible. Lacking talent, you cannot, out of the cookery-book, concoct a good work of art. The best you can hope to do is to produce an imitation, which may, for a short time, deceive the unwary into thinking it the genuine article.

Huxley's was unquestionably the genuine article. In this necessarily perfunctory discussion of a few characteristic examples of his writing, I have tried to show why he was a great man of letters, and how he produced those artistic effects, which cause us to make this critical judgment. . . .

THE FUNCTION OF STYLE:
ERNEST HEMINGWAY

Wright Morris

Before I go on with this short history, let me make a general observation—the test of a first-rate intelligence is the ability to hold two opposed ideas in the mind at the same time, and still retain the ability to function. One should, for example, be able to see that things are hopeless and yet be determined to make them otherwise.

F. Scott Fitzgerald, The Crack-up

"All modern literature," Hemingway stated in *The Green Hills of Africa,* "comes from one book by Mark Twain called *Huckleberry Finn.*" In such a comment there is an uncanny amount of truth, but it is a characteristically revealing, oversimplified observation. What the master is saying is, "I began with Huckleberry Finn." It was perhaps inspired in order to settle the dust on that tiresome quarrel with Gertrude Stein—who claimed that she gave birth to Ernest—but, as he indicates, it was Twain who got in the first, and the *last* lick.

In the essentials, Ernest Hemingway, born in Illinois, is a latter-day Huckleberry Finn. His "Big Two-Hearted River" is a latter-day retreat into the wilderness. The differences are precisely those that time would have made, what time would have done to both Huck and the territory ahead. He would have learned, at a very early age, that there was no such animal. His life would have begun with disenchantment rather than en-

From The Territory Ahead, *1961, by Wright Morris. Reprinted by permission of the author.*

chantment: he would be the first of that new breed of young men who knew too much, who knew more than their fathers would admit to knowing.

The boy who witnessed the death in the Michigan woods came out of the woods a man no longer subject to change. He had had it. But it took time to learn *what* he had had. The nature of this disenchantment is described with classic finality in the stories and sketches of *In Our Time*. The man who emerged lived and wrote by the values forged in his fiction. Both the writer and his work, that is, resisted change. A process of "seasoning," rather than development, links the disillusion of *In Our Time* with the resolution of *The Old Man and the Sea*. The facts are the same. You can't win. In the long run, life will beat you. First the big fish eat the little ones, then the little fish eat the big ones. But a brave and simple man can win a bit of the laurel, nevertheless. In never giving up, win or lose, he enjoys a final triumph over death itself.

With this wisdom, dramatized in a tale that is a lucid model of his craft, few modern men will care to argue. It seems true to life, and we know it is true to Hemingway. It is what he has been saying, and how he has been living, since he stepped, just forty years ago, to the edge of the wilderness and did not like at all what he saw. To that shock of recognition he has been consistent. In his life and his art he has been his own man. His craft has cast a spell that both inspires and takes a yearly toll. In attempting to come to terms with this man—or, as I choose to believe, this *style*—we are essentially concerned with coming to terms with his age, with the fact that he is largely responsible for it. His style —like the clear water that flows at the heart of all of his fiction—sounds the note of enchantment to the very disenchantment it anticipates. The reader grasps, immediately, that this man is not so tough as he looks. Quite the contrary, he looks and sounds so tough because his heart is so soft. Behind the armor of his prose, the shell of his exile, lurks our old friend Huck Finn, American dreamer, the clean-cut boy who just wishes Aunt Sally would leave him alone, who wants nothing more, nor less, than a clearing of his own in the wilderness. The dream itself he left unchanged, he merely moved to a smaller river, but he brought to it a style that revealed the dream to itself. There was no need to cry "O lost, lost—lost!" in the voice of Tom Wolfe, since the style had absorbed the state of disenchantment: the style was it. It was not merely the man, nor a handful of crafty exiles, but the age itself, the old moon of enchantment with the new moon of disenchantment in its arms.

When the young man Hemingway came to the edge of the clearing, when he saw what man had left in the place of nature, he found it something more than an unpleasant shock. He found it unacceptable. In that early judgment he has never wavered. It is expressed with finality in his exile. In this feeling, and in his exile, he is not alone, but being an artist he has been able to give his judgment a singular permanence. As the style of Faulkner grew out of his rage—out of the impotence of his rage —the style of Hemingway grew out of the depth and nuance of his disenchantment. Only a man who had believed, with a child's purity of faith, in some haunting dream of life, in its vistas of promise, is capable of forging his disillusion into a work of art. It is love of life that Hemingway's judgment of life reveals. Between the lines of his prose, between the passage and the reader, there is often that far sound of running water, a pine-scented breeze that blows from a cleaner and finer world. It is this air that makes the sight of so many corpses bearable. Invariably it is there—a higher order than the one we see before us in operation— as if the legend of the past were stamped, like a signature, on his brow. We have never had a more resolute moralist. A dream of the good life haunts the scene of all the bad life he so memorably observes, and when under his spell it is the dream of the good life that we possess. For such an artist, should there be anything but praise? Could there be anything conceivably impotent about such a style? It is when we come to brood on his consistency—on the man who does not change, or seem aware of it —that we see that the author, as well as the reader, has been under a spell, the same spell—the spell of a style. The consistency lies in what the style will permit him to think, to feel, and to say.

Every writer who is sufficiently self-aware to know what he is doing, and how he does it, sooner or later is confronted with the *dictates* of style. If he *has* a style, it is the style that dictates what he says. *What* he says, of course, is *how* he says it, and when we say that the style is the man we have testified to this property. The writer who develops, as a man and a writer, cannot be self-contained in a style, however memorable and charming, that has served its purpose. The style must change, or the writer must adapt himself to it. This is notably true of the writers whose style is the most highly personalized, and distinctive: the most distinctive stylist of this order in our time is Hemingway. He *is* a style. He has never departed from it. Tentative departures—in *For Whom the Bell Tolls,* for example—have appeared as flaws in the marble, rather than as symptoms of development. It is the nature of Hemingway's style to prohibit development. When he remains within it, he sounds *like himself.* When he attempts to escape, we do not know what he sounds like. Neither does he. It is a lesson he has taken to heart. *The Old Man and the Sea* is a two-way fable, that of an old man who has mastered a fish, and that of an aging writer who bows to the mastery of his style. Within these stylistic commitments he sounds all right. He does *not* sound, however, like he did more than thirty years earlier, when this style, and these commitments, were being forged. *The Old Man and the Sea* is an act of will; within the terms of this will it is a moving achievement, but as an act of the imagination it is dead. The style, not the creative mind, dictates the range and nature of the experience, selects the cast, and determines what is permissible. Here again the Spanish language—the simplifying agent—is used to reduce the complexities, in the manner of that memorable night of love and conversation in the sleeping bag. This technique, on occasion, leads to revelation, but as a rule it is merely reduction. The apparent simplicity lies in the style, rather than in the nature of the material, but Hemingway takes pains to build up a consistently simple scene. Man, fish, and Joe DiMaggio are attuned to the demands of the simple epic; complexities, human complexities, are reduced to a minimum. Complicated types enter Hemingway's world only to lose their complications. Man must appear simple, subject to simple corruptions, so that NATURE, writ large, will appear complex. The restoration of Nature—the Nature undefiled of the "Big Two-Hearted River"—would seem to be the passion behind Hemingway's reduction of man. It is why his disillusion, limited to man, is still grained with hope. Man is a mess, but Nature will prevail. It is the sea that triumphs, the sea and the sky against which man's puny drama is enacted, but they are not used, as in Hardy, to dwarf man to insignificance; rather, they remind him, in the complex way Hemingway will not permit his characters, of the paradise lost that might still be regained, that green breast of the world Huck Finn preserved in the territory ahead.

This scale of values—Man finitely simple, and Nature infinitely complex—is the Hemingway palette and the key to the scale of his style. He is never reduced to tampering with personalities. A Cézanne-like simplicity of scene is built up with the touches of a master, and the great effects are achieved with a sublime economy. At these moments style and substance are of one piece, each growing from the other, and one cannot imagine that life could exist except as described. We think only of what is there, and not, as in the less successful moments, of all of the elements of experience that are not.

The Hemingway economy, his sublime economy, is one thing when dictated by the imagination, but another when merely by the mechanical blue pencil of his style. These two slices of life, superficially, will look the same. Both will have the authority of his craft. There is no litmus test that the reader can apply to distinguish between the prose, the economy of the prose, of *The Sun Also Rises* and *Across the River and into the Trees*. Both books are written. But only one has been creatively imagined. In the absence of the shaping imagination Hemingway can always rely on his *craft,* and he is one of the great craftsmen of the age. The proof of this, ironically enough, is less in the books that were intensely imagined than in the books that were primarily an act of will. Here it is craft, and craft alone, that sustains both the reader and the writer, and it is what we mean, what we feel to be true, in observing that the author has fallen under his own spell. Indeed he has. And the spell is almost enough. The response of a new generation to *The Old Man and the Sea* was evidence of how much an artist might achieve through pure technique.

This technique, this celebrated style, was born full-fledged—whatever the line of descent—and in nearly forty years it has undergone no visible change. Neither has the life it portrays, since the style and the slice of life are the same. In the interests of this style things remain as they are, they do not change. It is a lens of the finest precision; it records, accurately, the author's field of vision, but the price of the performance is that the field must remain the same. Time—in the sense of development—must stand still. The timeless quality of the Hemingway snapshot is truly timeless—growth and change have been removed. The illusion of things as they are is raised to a point that has seldom been equaled; a frieze-like sense of permanence enshrines the Big Two-Hearted River and its worldwide tributaries. This woodland stream, symbolic of all that is undefiled in both man and nature, rises at the source of Hemingway's young manhood and flows through his life and his work to the sea. Clear water, clear fast-moving water, links the exile, on a weekend in Spain, with the Big Two-Hearted River back in Michigan. From different streams the fisherman pulls the same trout. Good fish and running water serve him as the means of coming to terms with life.

As Thoreau went to Walden for the *facts,* Hemingway went to the Michigan woods and the bullfight. In the grain of both men was a passionate desire for reality—be it life or death. Both men feared only one thing: being cheated of life. The *big* cheat, for both men, was the world of Aunt Sally, and only in the woods could one see life cleanly, in the wilderness of nature, or, for Hemingway, in the *nature* of war. But one began in the wilderness.

> He sat on the logs, smoking, drying in the sun, the sun warm on his back, the river shallow ahead entering the woods, curving into the woods, shallows, light glittering, big water-smooth rocks, cedars along the bank and white birches, the logs warm in the sun, smooth to sit on, without bark, gray to the touch; slowly the feeling of disappointment left him. It went away slowly, the feeling of disappointment that came sharply after the thrill that made his shoulders ache. It was all right now.

Any man who has ever tried to write will feel in this passage the line-taut passion of a man who would die rather than cheat you with a cliché. It is *this* that is moving—rather than what he tells us. We feel, in this prose, the man's passion for the truth. We hang on every word, as he intends, secure in the feeling that the word will support us. There is no thin ice in this style. We have our hands on experience. We are in possession of the facts.

On the Big Two-Hearted River the artist cut his teeth, but it is not till his exile that he clamps down with them. He waits, appropriately, till his exiles do a little fishing. It is in Spain, that the trout in the Big Two-Hearted River get their bite.

> While I had him on, several trout had jumped at the falls. As soon as I baited up and dropped in again I hooked another and brought him in the same way. In a little while I had six. They were all about the same size. I laid them out, side by side, all their heads pointing the same way, and looked at them. They were beautifully colored and firm and hard from the cold water. It was a hot day, so I slit them all and shucked out the insides, gills and all, and tossed them over across the river. I took the trout ashore, washed them in the cold, smoothy heavy water above the dam, and then picked some ferns and packed them all in the bag, three trout on a layer of ferns, then another layer of ferns, then three more trout, and then covered them with ferns. They looked nice in the ferns, and now the bag was bulky, and I put it in the shade of the tree.

This is like a summing up and a prophecy. After the sad goings on of the lost generation, we have plunged, in this stream, back to clean reality, beautifully colored and firm and hard, like the trout. That is nature. That is the nature of life. Bulls are sometimes good, sometimes bad, but only man is vile. In returning to nature it is possible for man to cleanse himself.

It is in keeping with this style that man should undergo a progressive brutalization, and nature a progressive refinement and serenity; that man, who should speak for himself, fails to do so, and that nature, who cannot, should become articulate. The river that flows through *The Sun Also Rises,* reflecting what is lost in the lost generation, is a clearer and more incorrruptible stream than the one that flows through *In Our Time.* The Spanish stream has been tested. The trout are firm immortal trout. They lie before our eyes, all their heads pointing in the same direction, like the timeless fish in one of the paintings of Braque. Technique has snatched them from the river of life and made them into art.

The flowering of Hemingway's conception of life—and let us make no mistake, it is a conception—achieves its fullest expression in *Death in the Afternoon.* Although death is its subject, it is a book that teems with life. But all of this life, with the exception of the eating and the drinking, is life downgraded, reduced in scale to the elementary plane. The effect, however, is monumental—like the figures in the drawings of Goya. Deprived of all refinements, they loom with the starkness of some demonic force. It is nature that speaks, not the man himself. We are in a scene virtually crammed with young men who are nothing if not "eggheads"—but when this fact appears in their thinking it is laughed out of court. In the opening paragraph, that remarkable dictum that so well describes the healthy bird of prey is given the power and the sanction of Hemingway's style.

> So far, about morals, I know only that what is moral is what you feel good after and what is immoral is what you feel bad after and judged by these moral standards, which I do not defend, the bullfight is very moral to me because I feel very fine while it is going on and have a feeling of life and death and mortality and immortality and after it is over I feel very sad but fine.

We need not concern ourselves with this as philosophy. It is a remarkably accurate statement—with its built-in escape clause—of a profoundly primitive state of being, less human than subhuman, a voice of *laissez faire* from the well of the past that would have frightened Neanderthal man. It is the first cry of that man who did not *want* to be a man. He wanted his simple uncomplicated feelings, his simple uncomplicated gratifications, and he did not want them troubled, at the time or later, by a lot of probing into *what* they were. He liked to eat, since after eating he felt good. He liked to make love—but not when it started getting complicated. He didn't mean to go so far as to say this was a good thing, since he liked it, but he did mean to say that at least he knew what he liked.

Now this statement grows, in my opinion, from the style more than it does from the man. It is the style that dictated the turn of the thought, and the style that gives it the ring of truth. Anything, in our time, *anything* that cuts through the morass of talk and complications—that cuts through and gives light—understandably appeals to us. This sort of plain talk from the shoulder, when the shoulder is a good one, wins our attention. The frank admission and the manly qualification have been sorely abused since Hemingway set the fashion, but it is a fashion that is singularly American. In this voice, if not in these accents, speaks the spirit of Thoreau, Whitman, and Mark Twain. The American grain calls for plain talk, for the unvarnished truth. Better to err a little in the cause of bluntness than soften the mind with congenial drivel. Better a challenging half-truth than a discredited cliché.

The moralist in Hemingway, kept off stage in his fiction, comes to the footlights in *Death in the Afternoon* to shock the Old Lady with his "immoral" observations on life. What we have here is Huck Finn, grown a little older but not grown *up,* getting in a final lick, a last sassy word, on the subject of Aunt Sally. The style, here, serves him less well: it is the weapon of a bully rather than of an artist, wielded in the manner of his pronouncements on women, big-game hunting, and the press. However telling these pronouncements often are, they are chips from the rocks along the Big Two-Hearted River, and evidence that the man within the artist has not changed. He is still, like his master Mark Twain, a boy at heart. While we pause to read what he has to say he is already off for the territory ahead before the world, or Aunt Sally, tries to civilize him. He can't stand it.

NOTES ON THE EXTINCTION
OF STYLE

Richard Chase

Anyone who admires literature must at some time have been moved by Edward Gibbon's account of the genesis of his great book—how, watching the Christian friars among the ruins of Rome, he had a vision of the revolutions of history, of the transient achievements of men and institutions, of the splendor and pity of the human spectacle.

Surely every successful book must begin with some sort of personal vision, indeed a conversion, more or less like Gibbon's. What shall we expect of a book[1] whose genesis is described as follows:

> At mid-point, the twentieth century may properly establish its own criteria of literary judgment; indeed, the values as well as the facts of modern civilization must be examined if man is to escape self-destruction. We must know and understand better the recorders of our experience. Scholars can no longer be content to write for scholars; they must make their knowledge meaningful and applicable to humanity.

We shall hardly hope to see a fiery vision issue out of this pious, flat, and anonymous language. The vision which bequeaths style and makes

---

Reprinted by permission of The Sewanee Review, *copyright 1950. Published by* The University of the South, *and by permission of the author's widow.*

---

[1] *Literary History of the United States.* Edited by Robert E. Spiller, Willard Thorp, Thomas H. Johnson, and Henry Seidel Canby. (The Macmillan Company, 1948, 3 volumes.) [Volume III, a bibliography by Mr. Johnson, is indispensable to students of American literature.]

the book is in these times mostly confined to novelists and poets. The venturesome mind that once sought to comprehend history has now grown timid and speaks the featureless language of corporate benevolence. *Literary History of the United States* is one of those estimable productions, such as TVA, which are heralded across the land by a general breakdown of grammar and metaphor. In the advertising brochure, an eminent San Francisco reviewer praises the four editors, three associates, and forty-eight contributors to *LHUS* for displaying a "general unanimity in the over-all perspective among all hands" (surely he meant "on the part of all hands"). An eminent professor at Johns Hopkins says that *LHUS* "marks a milestone" (meaning "*is* a milestone"). A Yale tautologist says that it is "inclusive in scope and judicious in its acumen." And a Texan master of truism says that "only once in a generation can such an epochal work as this be produced."

These absurdities would not be worthy of note except for the fact that those who testify to the product of the editors are only somewhat less able to find proper words to describe the book than are the editors themselves. The problem of style in such an undertaking is finally *the* problem. The mixed metaphor on the surface bespeaks an underlying confusion of purpose. The bit of mindless jargon implies more momentous intellectual abdications. The slick "literary" paradox proclaims the writer's readiness to slip with equal facility into some horrific affirmation of the greatness of Carl Sandburg or the coming glorious internationalism of American literature. The style is the book. Here there is no style and no book—or several styles and several books.

That *LHUS* is not a great book *LHUS* itself admits. In his chapter on "How Writers Lived" (in the twentieth century), Malcolm Cowley was unaccountably allowed to write the following subversive words:

> Yet there was also a greater timidity among writers, of the sort that develops in any bureaucratic situation; and there was a tendency to forget that, though a great book expresses a whole culture and hence has millions of collaborators, including persons long since dead, in another sense it must finally be written by one man alone in his room with his conscience and a stock of blank paper.

That is the truth. This man alone in his room, this Gibbon or Taine or even this Parrington, is the man we ought to hold out for. The editors of *LHUS* reply that "the United States . . . has produced too much literature for any one man to read or digest." But how do they know? Doubtless a single writer would not be perfectly exhaustive or equitable, but neither is *LHUS* (which, for example, allots less than two pages to the work of Scott Fitzgerald—but more than two each to S. N. Behrman and Clifford

Odets). As for digestion, our single writer might not even eat Mrs. Helen Reimensynder Martin, the author of *Tillie: A Menonnite Maid*. And since some writers, good and bad, are bound to be slighted in *any* history, is it not better to slight them with some illuminating turn of language such as a single writer in control of his style can manage than by some soggy, half-hearted attempt at summation which has probably already been done better in some other book?

The editors are, to be sure, very conscious of style. And by a system of "group conferences" they have tried to achieve a degree of uniformity, to "iron out," as they must have said, obvious discrepancies of statement, and to provide a semblance of continuity by adding a paragraph or two of transition at the end or beginning of the chapters submitted by their contributors. This is what the editors call "relating" the contributions "to one another within a frame." The "frame" of the single writer is formed by the inclusions of his point of view and of his style. The "frame" referred to by the editors of *LHUS* may perhaps be defined as "an aspect of an integrated approach channeled at the level of dynamic group collaboration." However it may have happened, there are at least three different styles in *LHUS*.

The first of these is a slickly glamorous style which leaps nimbly from summing up Emily Dickinson as "a breathless, perceptive poet" to such prophetic announcements as "we must recognize that the future of art can only be international." The slick style is affected by contributors both in and out of the academy. Its locus is perhaps the intersection of Maxwell Geismar, Professor Stanley T. Williams, Henry Seidel Canby, and Professor Howard Mumford Jones. Its tone is middlebrow *bravura:*

> Emily Dickinson, with a terrible, beautiful intensity, expressed the most aspiring experience of the Puritan soul, sharp-reined in her by a new realism, and released in distilled, gnomic verse; her extraordinary seizure in art of the apexes of despair and ecstasy may well endure.

Captain John Smith is described as "a hard-boiled character" (in an introductory chapter which patronizes colonial America for being religious, aristocratic, and pre-capitalist). In the chapter called "The Discovery of Bohemia" we have alliterations:

> The Philistines were reduced by Gelett Burgess to Bromides, by Sinclair Lewis to Babbitts, and by Mencken to the *Booboisie*. The seacoast of Bohemia became the comic opera kingdom of James Branch Cabell's novels, and romantic bookishness was pushed to its illogical conclusion in his *Beyond Life* (1919).

Of Thomas Wolfe, Mr. Geismar writes:

> If he was ignorant and superstitious as the hill folks were, and stumbled into many gargantuan pitfalls—some those of his own making too— he had the persistence and cunning as well as the long legs of the hill people, and he walked with the mountain walk.

If he was as ignorant as the hill folks, then let us get on with someone who wasn't and a fig for his legs. Mr. Geismar also writes that "for sheer technical virtuosity Elinor Wylie was to be matched in prose by Katherine Anne Porter, and T. S. Eliot by William Faulkner." The fact that Mr. Geismar can imagine such painfully meticulous writers as Miss Porter (who washeth not her feet in soda water) and Mr. Eliot to be sheer technical virtuosi hints at the limitations of his idea of what literature is. It seems to be mere speciousness of style that leads Mr. Geismar to meaningless assertions.

A second style, appearing in *LHUS* less frequently than the glamorous style, is the jargon of bureaucrats, economists, and graduates of Teachers College. The same writer who speaks of Emily Dickinson's apexes of despair says that "the factor of conscious plan in the poetry of Emily Dickinson is almost negligible." An interesting confusion of styles occurs in the chapter on Emerson:

> The resulting unity of approach to living is the key to Emerson's hold on his own and later generations. Henry Adams called it "naif," and others have put it away with childish things.

The following sentence seems to have been written by the editors as a group (unless perchance they called in a major general to do the job) in an attempt to usher the reader with the proper *élan* into the midst of Emerson, Thoreau, Hawthorne, Melville, and Whitman:

> In other words, European philosophical theory, acting as a primary catalyst for forces already deeply indigenous to the American mind, had effected and accelerated a reorientation of literature which was tantamount to raising it to a new plane.

The glamorous hyper-metaphoric style of *LHUS* and its jargonistic style are the extremities between which there operates a third style—the featureless combination of both, which is the undistinguished manner of most of the book. It *is* a competent manner. But its competence includes not only the ability to convey useful information but also the ability to evade most of the hard problems posed by that still mysterious phenomenon, American literature. Most people who write about American literature are afraid of it.

The effort of the editors of *LHUS* to achieve continuity cannot help being frequently factitious. The Hawthorne chapter begins with a portentous "Meanwhile." But the "while" in the reader's mind is the present day, wherein (it is said at the end of the preceding chapter) he will do well to cherish Thoreau's sympathy for nature "as the lava flow of our material civilization licks up the natural beauty of earth." Harry Levin's chapter on Ambrose Bierce, Lafcadio Hearn, and James G. Huneker is said to present (apparently) a "further phase" of Henry James's response "to the predicament of a society which did not yet know that it had to be redeemed"— which sounds like the notes an obtuse student might take on the preceding chapter. At the end of Mr. Geismar's chapter we are launched in flight by these words:

> These underlying cultural pressures still determined the shape of American life on the brink of another postwar era—and the shape of its literature—and whether the new age would burst in splendor or in terror.

Yet in what follows nothing bursts. Another way of making transitions and giving a single tone to the whole is to send the reader from one chapter to another in such a happy glow that he would feel like a cad to ask for logic. The chapter on "Folklore" ends on this entirely unjustifiable note of optimism:

> Phonograph, radio, and sound movie now expand indefinitely the range of oral transmission. At the same time, with universally accessible print intelligible to a literate people, they diminish the need for memory [!]. Folklore may instantly become literature, and literature may speedily travel the road to folklore. Their interaction . . . will be beneficial for both.

The next chapter ends by affirming that American humor "has been democratic; it has made us one," apparently forgetting the lonely muse of Lincoln, Melville, and Mark Twain.

The editors of *LHUS* tend to regard the writers of the past, and especially the great ones, as consciously contributing to a group project sanctioned by the values of a culture which is liberal in politics and conservative-middlebrow in taste. Nevertheless the influence of avant-garde criticism is apparent. The few great writers of the nineteenth century are firmly in the saddle. The avant-garde has won its battle on this point, and with a vengeance. *LHUS* allots one chapter of twenty pages to "The New England Triumvirate: Longfellow, Holmes, and Lowell," fewer pages than are accorded severally to Melville, Henry Adams, and Henry James. "Defenders of ideality," as *LHUS* calls Stoddard, Taylor, Boker, Aldrich, and Stedman, are given the small notice they are now thought to deserve.

The book shows, however, the familiar cultural lag between conservative practice and the new truths proclaimed by the avant-garde. For it is clear that on the whole the editors think more highly of the Longfellows, Holmeses, and Stedmans of today than of the Melvilles, Hawthornes, and Whitmans. The chapter on "Humor," by Harold W. Thompson "with passages by Henry Seidel Canby," praises Dorothy Parker for "mordant wit," says that James Thurber is capable of "deadly satire," and tells us that the wartime editorials of E. B. White are "deeply incisive" and have "powerful emotional undercurrents."

Our literature is neither so great nor so coherent as *LHUS* would have us believe. The book sees our writers as aiming consciously and by duty bound to produce a "world literature," after having overcome the shock of the new American experience and declared their independence of European culture. *LHUS* invites us to see our broken past as a generally blithesome adolescence leading up to a happy one-world of tomorrow.

This is of course the kind of historical-moral vision produced by committees and bureaus—they can produce no other. A single literary historian, even an incorrigible optimist, would not be so bland, so vaguely and happily apocalyptic. Pre-eminent literary historians, even pre-eminent anthologists, do not come cheaply or every day. But it would be good for our culture to wait until one does and to deserve him when he appears. V. L. Parrington committed many literary crimes, but better a Parrington than a group conference.

For the time being, *Literary History of the United States* remains a monument to the era of culture which began in this country thirty years ago—the era of Roosevelt, the WPA, the UN, the era, among writers, of social realism and group activity. It was too generally assumed in this era that style in literature and conduct could take care of itself or would automatically issue out of the concerted action of well-meaning men who saw eye to eye on more important questions. It is this assumption which has produced *LHUS;* and the finished product reminds us once again that a humane, personal style in literature, in conduct, and in culture cannot be done without. The enormous labors, the good intentions, the modest successes of the editors should not be allowed to obscure the fact that the invasion of literature by methods more suitable to rural electrification or advertising campaigns is deplorable. Who are the custodians of language and culture if not our literary historians?

APPENDIX

SAMPLE PASSAGES FOR
ANALYSIS
AND DISCUSSION

IT'S ALL OVER BETWEEN US, ROSE MARIE. For years, you and your barrel-chested boyfriend have made us look relentless. Canadian Mounties in hot pursuit over the trackless wastes, and all that nonsense? Rose Marie, we are *finis*. Oh we do have Mounties. Even some trackless wastes. But what we really have a lot of are hot pursuits! Sophisticated supper clubs with big-name entertainers. Intimate "boîtes," bars and cocktail lounges. Exotic restaurants of every description. And discotheque-wise, you may be delighted to learn that it is now as easy to slip a disc in Montréal, Toronto or Vancouver as it is in good old New York City. Each Canadian city is a little different in personality. Vancouver nightclubs tend to soar to roof-garden altitudes, the better to admire the Rocky Mountains. Montréal digs wine cellars . . . although Montréal does offer a sky-scraping bar-restaurant known as Altitude 737, featured attractions being a 90-mile view and a 5-ounce martini. In that order. Drop up to Canada some evening soon, and see it like it is. With no apologies to Rudolph Friml.

Travel advertisement in the New Yorker

POLLY BERGEN TALKS TURTLE. "I have an ugly friend who's done wonders for my skin. A turtle. And if you have dry skin, *don't wait as long as I did to find out about her.*

"Maybe you already know what today's smoggy climate, indoor heat, outdoor living, and rush-rush pace can do to your skin. Age it. Dry it out early. I know, too. For years I'd wake up every morning with a face crackling-dry.

"Then I found Oil of the Turtle. First thing that ever worked for me— and lasted. Why? Although it's a rich and potent natural lubricant, it is lapped up quickly and easily by your skin. No grease. No parched feeling later!

"I formulated Oil of the Turtle in a pink foam moisturizer first. Then, because dry skin never quits, I put that same wonderful help into a basic series of dry skin treatments. All designed for my kind of busy life. All quick, simple, effective, and fun.

"The point is, you don't need a lot of rigamarole to get ahead of dry skin. You just need an ugly friend. Try mine."

Advertisement for Skin Cream

. . . I thought of white men arriving for the first time in an African village, strangers there, as I am a stranger here, and tried to imagine the astounded populace touching their hair and marveling at the color of their skin. But there is a great difference between being the first white man to be seen by Africans and being the first black man to be seen by whites. The white man takes the astonishment as tribute, for he arrives to conquer and to convert the natives, whose inferiority in relation to himself is not even to be questioned; whereas I, without a thought of conquest, find myself among a people whose culture controls me, has even, in a sense, created me, people who have cost me more in anguish and rage than they will ever know, who yet do not even know of my existence. The astonishment with which I might have greeted them, should they have stumbled into my African village a few hundred years ago, might have rejoiced their hearts. But the astonishment with which they greet me today can only poison mine.

James Baldwin, "Stranger in the Village"

Well, then, it comes to this. There are two kinds of men, those who live for appearances and comfort and those who live in a world of raw realities slugging their way to the graveyard proud, and sinking their teeth in life like it was Kansas City sirloin medium rare. The members of the group who go for Sunday afternoon drives with the kids and bowl on Thursdays can't for the life of them understand *how* the others ever busted loose. They know *why* well enough, but of course they won't even admit that much, the most of them. They talk as though they're perfectly satisfied with the squirrel-cage routine of life at the office and the Elks and, by God, pretty soon they *are* satisfied. Meanwhile cousin Slim, who "was always kinda harum-scarum," or brother Bill, who "was pretty erratic as a kid," is slogging the seven seas in rusty old tramp steamers, laying pipe line across the Persian sands, building bridges, booming oil in Manitoba, or, close to home, railroading or steamboating or pulling the transports across the plains, and sucking in a hundred dollars' worth of fresh air a minute. I guess it boils down to those who thrive on taking chances and those who turn pale at the thought. You'll never get past those city limits, boys, unless you just up and go.

Richard Bissell, River in My Blood

New music: new listening. Not an attempt to understand something that is being said, for, if something were being said, the sounds would be given the shapes of words. Just an attention to the activity of sounds.

Those involved with the composition of experimental music find ways and means to remove themselves from the activities of the sounds they make. Some employ chance operations, derived from sources as ancient as the Chinese *Book of Changes,* or as modern as the tables of random numbers used also by physicists in research. Or, analogous to the Rorschach tests of psychology, the interpretation of imperfections in the paper upon which one is writing may provide a music free from one's memory and imagination. Geometrical means employing spatial superimpositions at variance with the ultimate performance in time may be used. The total field of possibilities may be roughly divided and the actual sounds within these divisions may be indicated as to number but left to the performer or to the splicer to choose. In this latter case, the composer resembles the maker of a camera who allows someone else to take the picture.

John Cage, "Experimental Music"

"Going up that river was like traveling back to the earliest beginnings of the world, when vegetation rioted on the earth and the big trees were kings. An empty stream, a great silence, an impenetrable forest. The air was warm, thick, heavy, sluggish. There was no joy in the brilliance of sunshine. The long stretches of the waterway ran on, deserted, into the gloom of overshadowed distances. On silvery sandbanks hippos and alligators sunned themselves side by side. The broadening waters flowed through a mob of wooded islands; you lost your way on that river as you would in a desert, and butted all day long against shoals, trying to find the channel, till you thought yourself bewitched and cut off for ever from everything you had known once—somewhere—far away—in another existence perhaps. There were moments when one's past came back to one, as it will sometimes when you have not a moment to spare to yourself; but it came in the shape of an unrestful and noisy dream, remembered with wonder amongst the overwhelming realities of this strange world of plants, and water, and silence. And this stillness of life did not in the least resemble a peace. It was the stillness of an implacable force brooding over an inscrutable intention. It looked at you with a vengeful aspect. I got used to it afterwards; I did not see it any more; I had no time. I had to keep guessing at the channel; I had to discern, mostly by inspiration, the signs of hidden banks; I watched for sunken stones. . . ."

Joseph Conrad, Heart of Darkness

At the sight of a flight of marble-or-something steps framed by boundlessly flowering plants we verily tremble:is(impossibly)the candle worth the game? And just as if to answer said unsaidness,down something-or-marble vista visionary with vegetation waddles 1 prodigiously pompous,quite supernaturally unlovely,infratrollop with far(far)too golden locks;gotup rather than arrayed in ultraerstwhile vividly various whathaveyous;assertingly(if not pugnaciously)puffing a gigantic cigarette;vaguely but unmistakably clutching,to this more hulking than that mammiform appendage,a brutally battered skeleton of immense milkcan. ("And they talk of Swinburne's women" myself comfortingly quoted, floating meanwhile brisky upward and inward). A notimposing counter. Behind it,a ½bald notimposing clerk wailing DAs into a notimposing telephone. Above,around,unbelievable emanation of ex-;incredible apotheosis of isn't. Thither,hauntingly hither,glide a few uncouth ghosts. Near, lounge crepuscularly 2 comehithering poules(alive?) At my left elbow,anyone (with the air of having been someone and who is now merely patient and helpless)and for whom the ½bald is telephoning or pretending to telephone or probably both. In vain—patiently he abandons the instrument to its fate:regards my neighbour helplessly,boosting eyebrowless eyebrows; the regarded helplessly comrade patiently shrugs,copiously meanders. "Have you any rooms?" I said.

E. E. Cummings, Eimi

Can mass culture be "improved"? Buy us some prime time and find out, came the answer this summer from New York's TV artists. Lock out the sponsors and the admen and the network veeps and the talent monopolists, fire the chubby-chested ingenues and the socking cops—we'll guarantee improvements. We'll do more than that, in fact, once conditions are right. We'll make a revolution, we'll Take Off, we'll do all that high culture ever hoped to do, we'll *clobber* the airwaves with beauty and truth: if only you'll give us the chance. . . .

The occasion of this plea and pledge was an inquiry conducted at a courthouse in lower Manhattan by the Federal Communications Commission's Office of Network Study. The declared purpose of the inquiry was to complete a description of the working conditions of people engaged in creating "programs for network television exhibition"; the officer of interrogation was a handsome, large-voiced, knowledgeable government lawyer named Ashbrook P. Bryant. Present to answer questions were more than a score of famous playwrights, producers and performers. Present to listen and profit were the FCC's Chief Hearing Examiner and the head of its Broadcast Bureau; two TV camera crews; dozens of reporters and photographers; radio technicians from WNYC (a New York radio station that broadcast the hearings); minor executives from NBC, CBS and ABC sent by their superiors to make quickie telephone reports on proceedings; and, among other private citizens, a clutch of aluminum-haired, purple-lipped teenagers whose straw sacks were filled with Chiclets and giggles, and whose Star-haunted eyes glistened (at the entrances of heroes) with sweet secret passion and shame.

Benjamin Demott, Hells and Benefits

Veblen,

a greyfaced shambling man lolling resentful at his desk with his cheek on his hand, in a low sarcastic mumble of intricate phrases subtly paying out the logical inescapable rope of matteroffact for a society to hang itself by,

dissecting out the century with a scalpel so keen, so comical, so exact that the professors and students ninetenths of the time didn't know it was there, and the magnates and the respected windbags and the applauded loud-speakers never knew it was there.

Veblen

asked too many questions, suffered from a constitutional inability to say yes.

Socrates asked questions, drank down the bitter drink one night when the first cock crowed,

but Veblen

drank it in little sips through a long life in the stuffiness of classrooms, the dust of libraries, the staleness of cheap flats such as a poor instructor can afford. He fought the boyg all right, pedantry, routine, timeservers at office desks, trustees, collegepresidents, the plump flunkies of the ruling business-men, all the good jobs kept for yesmen, never enough money, every broadening hope thwarted. Veblen drank the bitter drink all right.

John dos Passos, U.S.A.

His preference for Fitzgerald and Moy's Adams Street place was another yard off the same cloth. This was really a gorgeous saloon from a Chicago standpoint. Like Rector's, it was also ornamented with a blaze of incandescent lights, held in handsome chandeliers. The floors were of brightly coloured tiles, the walls a composition of rich, dark, polished wood, which reflected the light, and coloured stucco-work, which gave the place a very sumptuous appearance. The long bar was a blaze of lights, polished wood-work, coloured and cut glassware, and many fancy bottles. It was a truly swell saloon, with rich screens, fancy wines, and a line of bar goods unsurpassed in the country.

At Rector's, Drouet had met Mr. G. W. Hurstwood, manager of Fitz-gerald and Moy's. He had been pointed out as a very successful and well-known man about town. Hurstwood looked the part, for, besides being slightly under forty, he had a good, stout constitution, an active manner, and a solid, substantial air, which was composed in part of his fine clothes, his clean linen, his jewels, and, above all, his own sense of his importance. Drouet immediately conceived a notion of him as being some one worth knowing, and was glad not only to meet him, but to visit the Adams Street bar thereafter whenever he wanted a drink or a cigar.

Theodore Dreiser, Sister Carrie

Yet if the only form of tradition, of handing down, consisted in following the ways of the immediate generation before us in a blind or timid adherence to its successes, "tradition" should positively be discouraged. We have seen many such simple currents soon lost in the sand; and novelty is better than repetition. Tradition is a matter of much wider significance. It cannot be inherited, and if you want it you must obtain it by great labour. It involves, in the first place, the historical sense, which we may call nearly indispensable to any one who would continue to be a poet beyond his twenty-fifth year; and the historical sense involves a perception, not only of the pastness of the past, but of its presence; the historical sense compels a man to write not merely with his own generation in his bones, but with a feeling that the whole of the literature of Europe from Homer and within it the whole of the literature of his own country has a simultaneous existence and composes a simultaneous order. This historical sense, which is a sense of the timeless as well as of the temporal and of the timeless and of the temporal together, is what makes a writer traditional. And it is at the same time what makes a writer most acutely conscious of his place in time, of his own contemporaneity.

T. S. Eliot, "Tradition and the Individual Talent"

. . . For that moment his state of mind was homicidal. He saw in this second flagrant abrogation of the ancient biblical edict (on which he had established existence, integrity, all) that man must sweat or have not, the same embattled moral point which he had fought singly and collectively with his five children for more than twenty years and in which battle, by being victorious, he had lost. He was a man past middle age, who with nothing to start with but sound health and a certain grim and puritanical affinity for abstinence and endurance, had made a fair farm out of the barren scrap of hill land which he had bought at less than a dollar an acre and married and raised a family on it and fed and clothed them all and even educated them after a fashion, taught them at least hard work, so that as soon as they became big enough to resist him, boys and girls too, they left home (one was a professional nurse, one a ward-heeler to a minor county politician, one a city barber, one a prostitute; the oldest had simply vanished completely) so that there now remained the small neat farm which likewise had been worked to the point of mute and unflagging mutual hatred and resistance but which could not leave him and so far had not been able to eject him but which possibly knew that it could and would outlast him, and his wife who possibly had the same, perhaps not hope for resisting, but maybe staff and prop for bearing and enduring.

William Faulkner, The Hamlet

. . . I believe in aristocracy though—if that's the right word, and if a democrat may use it. Not an aristocracy of power, based upon rank and influence, but an aristocracy of the sensitive, the considerate, and the plucky. Its members are to be found in all nations and classes, and all through the ages, and there is a secret understanding between them when they meet. They represent the true human tradition, the one permanent victory of our queer race over cruelty and chaos. Thousands of them perish in obscurity; a few are great names. They are sensitive for others as well as for themselves, they are considerate without being fussy, their pluck is not swankiness but the power to endure, and they can take a joke. I give no examples—it is risky to do that—but the reader may as well consider whether this is the type of person he would like to meet and to be, and whether (going further with me) he would prefer that the type should *not* be an ascetic one. . . . On they go—

an invincible army, yet not a victorious one. The aristocrats, the elect, the chosen, the best people—all the words that describe them are false, and all attempts to organize them fail. Again and again authority, seeing their value, has tried to net them and to utilize them as the Egypian priesthood or the Christian Church or the Chinese civil service or the Group Movement, or some other worthy stunt. But they slip through the net and are gone; when the door is shut they are no longer in the room; their temple, as one of them remarked, is the holiness of the heart's imagination, and their kingdom, though they never possess it, is the wide open world.

E. M. Forster, "What I Believe"

The highroad into the village of Weydon-Priors was again carpeted with dust. The trees had put on as of yore their aspect of dingy green, and where the Henchard family of three had once walked along, two persons not unconnected with that family walked now.

The scene in its broad aspect had so much of its previous character, even to the voices and rattle from the neighbouring village down, that it might for that matter have been the afternoon following the previously recorded episode. Change was only to be observed in details; but here it was obvious that a long procession of years had passed by. One of the two who walked the road was she who had figured as the young wife of Henchard on the previous occasion; now her face had lost much of its rotundity; her skin had undergone a textural change; and though her hair had not lost colour it was considerably thinner than heretofore. She was dressed in the mourning clothes of a widow. Her companion, also in black, appeared as a well-formed young woman about eighteen, completely possessed of that ephemeral precious essence youth, which is itself beauty, irrespective of complexion or contour.

Thomas Hardy, The Mayor of Casterbridge

Sometimes in the dark we heard the troops marching under the window and guns going past pulled by motor-tractors. There was much traffic at night and many mules on the roads with boxes of ammunition on each side of their pack-saddles and gray motor-trucks that carried men, and other trucks with loads covered with canvas that moved slower in the traffic. There were big guns too that passed in the day drawn by tractors, the long barrels of the guns covered with green branches and green leafy branches and vines laid over the tractors. To the north we could look across a valley and see a forest of chestnut trees and behind it another mountain on this side of the river. There was fighting for that mountain too, but it was not successful, and in the fall when the rains came the leaves all fell from the chestnut trees and the branches were bare and the trunks black with rain. The vineyards were thin and bare-branched too and all the country wet and brown and dead with the autumn. There were mists over the river and clouds on the mountain and the trucks splashed mud on the road and the troops were muddy and wet in their capes; their rifles were wet and under their capes the two leather cartridge-boxes on the front of the belts, gray leather boxes heavy with the packs of clips of thin, long 6.5 mm. cartridges, bulged forward under the capes so that the men, passing on the road, marched as though they were six months gone with child.

Ernest Hemingway, A Farewell to Arms

Between 1800 and 1900 the doctrine of Pie in the Sky gave place, in a majority of Western minds, to the doctrine of Pie on the Earth. The motivating and compensatory Future came to be regarded, not as a state of disembodied happiness, to be enjoyed by me and my friends after death, but as a condition of terrestrial well-being for my children or (if that seemed a bit too optimistic) my grandchildren, or maybe my great-grandchildren. The believers in Pie in the Sky consoled themselves for all their present miseries by the thought of posthumous bliss, and whenever they felt inclined to make other people more miserable than themselves (which was most of the time), they justified their crusades and persecutions by proclaiming, in St. Augustine's delicious phrase, that they were practicing a "benignant asperity," which would ensure the eternal welfare of souls through the destruction or torture of mere bodies in the inferior dimensions of space and time. In our days, the revolutionary believers in Pie on the Earth console themselves for *their* miseries by thinking of the wonderful time people will be having a hundred years from now, and then go on to justify wholesale liquidations and enslavements by pointing to the nobler, humaner world which these atrocities will somehow or other call into existence.

Aldous Huxley, Collected Essays

Merton Densher, who passed the best hours of each night at the office of his newspaper, had at times, during the day, to make up for it, a sense, or at least an appearance, of leisure, in accordance with which he was not infrequently to be met, in different parts of the town, at moments when men of business are hidden from the public eye. More than once, during the present winter's end, he had deviated, toward three o'clock, or toward four, into Kensington Gardens, where he might for a while, on each occasion, have been observed to demean himself as a person with nothing to do. He made his way indeed, for the most part, with a certain directness, over to the north side; but once that ground was reached his behaviour was noticeably wanting in point. He moved seemingly at random from alley to alley; he stopped for no reason and remained idly agaze; he sat down in a chair and then changed to a bench; after which he walked about again, only again to repeat both the vagueness and vivacity. Distinctly, he was a man either with nothing at all to do or with ever so much to think about; and it was not to be denied that the impression he might often thus easily make had the effect of causing the burden of proof, in certain directions, to rest on him. It was a little the fault of his aspect, his personal marks, which made it almost impossible to name his profession.

Henry James, The Wings of The Dove

In long lassoes from the Cock lake the water flowed full, covering green-goldenly lagoons of sand, rising, flowing. My ashplant will float away. I shall wait. No, they will pass on, passing chafing against the low rocks, swirling, passing. Better get this job over quick. Listen: a fourworded wavespeech: seesoo, hrss, rsseeiss ooos. Vehement breath of waters amid seasnakes, rearing horses, rocks. In cups of rocks it slops: flop, slop, slap: bounded in barrels. And, spent, its speech ceases. It flows purling, widely flowing, floating foampool, flower unfurling.

Under the upswelling tide he saw the writhing weeds lift languidly and sway reluctant arms, hising up their petticoats, in whispering water swaying and upturning coy silver fronds. Day by day: night by night: lifted, flooded and let fall. Lord, they are weary: and, whispered to, they sigh. Saint Ambrose heard it, sigh of leaves and waves, waiting, awaiting the fullness of their times, *diebus ac noctibus iniurias patiens ingemiscit.* To no end gathered: vainly then released, forth flowing, wending back: loom of the moon. Weary too in sight of lovers, lascivious men, a naked woman shining in her courts, she draws a toil of waters.

Five fathoms out there. Full fathom five thy father lies. At once he said. Found drowned. High water at Dublin bar. Driving before it a loose drift of rubble, fanshoals of fishes, silly shells. A corpse rising saltwhite from the undertow, bobbing landward, a pace a pace a porpoise. There he is. Hook it quick. Sunk though he be beneath the watery floor. We have him. Easy now.

James Joyce, Ulysses

In Oakland I had a beer among the bums of a saloon with a wagon wheel in front of it, and I was on the road again. I walked clear across Oakland to get to the Fresno road. Two rides took me to Bakersfield, four hundred miles south. The first was the mad one, with a burly blond kid in a souped-up rod. "See that toe?" he said as he gunned the heap to eighty and passed everybody on the road. "Look at it." It was swathed in bandages. "I just had it amputated this morning. The bastards wanted me to stay in the hospital. I packed my bag and left. What's a toe?" Yes, indeed, I said to myself, look out now, and I hung on. You never saw a driving fool like that. He made Tracy in no time. Tracy is a railroad town; brakemen eat surly meals in diners by the tracks. Trains howl away across the valley. The sun goes down long and red. All the magic names of the valley unrolled—Manteca, Madera, all the rest. Soon it got dusk, a grapy dusk, a purple dusk over tangerine groves and long melon fields; the sun the color of pressed grapes, slashed with burgundy red, the fields the color of love and Spanish mysteries. I stuck my head out the window and took deep breaths of the fragrant air. It was the most beautiful of all moments. The madman was a brakeman with the Southern Pacific and he lived in Fresno; his father was also a brakeman. He lost his toe in the Oakland yards, switching, I didn't quite understand how. He drove me into buzzing Fresno and let me off by the south side of town. . . .

Jack Kerouac, On the Road

Because we see one thing in another—life in the candle flame, death in sleep, time in the flowing stream, space in a bowl or in the sky that we see as an inverted bowl—the vast multiplicity of experiences compose one world for us. Our symbolic seeing is what gives that world its fundamental unity, much deeper than the unity of its causal connectedness—the gnomonic "likeness in difference" that unifies a nest of tables, rather than the simple concatenation of links that unifies a chain. Most of the things we encounter have no obvious causal connections: the roar of a passing plane, and the voice from the radio advertising toothpaste, the thermometer at freezing, the dog scratching himself under the table. It is an article of scientific faith (and a primary one) that all events are causally connected, however complex the web of their connections may be. We really see causal connections only in a few chains of events . . . so far as our direct observation is concerned, most things "just happen" at the moment when they do, and could have been otherwise. We believe them to have causes, but their causes have to be learned, or taken on faith.

Susanne Langer, "The Growing Center of Knowledge"

Well that is about all to tell you about the trip only they was one amuseing incidence that come off yesterday which I will tell you. Well they was a dame got on the train at Toledo Monday and had the birth opp. mine but I did not see nothing of her that night as I was out smokeing till late and she hit the hay early but yesterday A.M. she come in the dinner and sit at the same table with me and tried to make me and it was so raw that the dinge waiter seen it and give me the wink and of course I paid no tension and I waited till she got through so as they would be no danger of her folling me out but she stopped on the way out to get a tooth pick and when I come out she was out on the platform with it so I tried to brush right by but she spoke up and asked me what time it was and I told her and she said she guessed her watch was slow so I said maybe it just seemed slow on acct. of the company it was in.

I don't know if she got what I was driveing at or not but any way she give up trying to make me and got off at Albany. She was a good looker but I have no time for gals that tries to make strangers on a train.

Ring Lardner, "Some Like Them Cold"

As a matter of fact, our great-grandfathers, who never went anywhere, in actuality had more experience of the world than we have, who have seen everything. When they listened to a lecture with lantern-slides, they really held their breath before the unknown, as they sat in the village school-room. We, bowling along in a rickshaw in Ceylon, say to ourselves: "It's very much what you'd expect." We really know it all.

We are mistaken. The know-it-all state of mind is just the result of being outside the mucous-paper wrapping of civilization. Underneath is everything we don't know and are afraid of knowing.

I realized this with shattering force when I went to New Mexico.

New Mexico, one of the United States, part of the U.S.A. New Mexico, the picturesque reservation and playground of the eastern states, very romantic, old Spanish, Red Indian, desert mesas, pueblos, cowboys, penitentes, all that film-stuff. Very nice, the great South-West, put on a sombrero and knot a red kerchief round your neck, to go out in the great free spaces!

That is New Mexico wrapped in the absolutely hygienic and shiny mucous-paper of our trite civilization. That is the New Mexico known to most of the Americans who know it at all. But break through the shiny sterilized wrapping, and actually *touch* the country, and you will never be the same again.

D. H. Lawrence, Phoenix

But nobody can ever know what it was like to live in a community that left no written record of itself. Archaeologists and anthropologists hypothesize, but they can see only through their own eyes; they can do no more than present personal contrasts and comparisons. Different men also find different truths in the same document—but the document survives, to enlighten later arrivals. "Civilization" is a term which has picked up connotations of all sorts, but as a practical matter literacy is in itself a sufficient and a necessary definition of civilization. "In the beginning," as St. John once put it, "was the Word."

Literacy is also, as the leaders of the newly liberated nations in Africa and Asia have discovered, the indispensable foundation of political democracy. The illiterate man is a slave to his immediate environment and to what he is told. He can never hope to escape Francis Bacon's idols of the tribe, the marketplace, the den and the theater, all of which conduce to error. The man who reads may be a slave, too, but avenues of escape are available to him. So much has been written recently about the perils of propaganda and mass communications that many people—including teachers—are in danger of forgetting that reading and reading alone can make a man free in civilized society. Reading extends the possibilities of independent choice from the tight circle of individual experience to the great globe of the accomplishments of the species.

Martin Mayer, The Schools

Let us spell out the worst about this notorious mass-man and his mass-culture. He has a meager idea of the abundant life, confusing quantity with quality, size with greatness, comfort with culture, gadgetry with genius. He has as little appreciation of pure science as of the fine arts, and as little capacity for the discipline that both require; although he may stand in awe of them his real veneration goes to the engineers and inventors, the manufacturers of True Romances and Tin Pan Alley airs. He is frequently illiberal, suspicious of "radical" ideas, scornful of "visionary" ideals, hostile to "aliens"; in America he has developed a remarkable vocabulary of contempt that manages to embrace most of mankind—the nigger, the mick, the chink, the wop, the kike, et cetera. He is the chief foe of the individualism he boasts of, a patron of standard brands in tastes and opinions as in material possessions, with a morbid fear of being thought queer or different from the Joneses; individuality to him is "personality," which may be acquired in six easy lessons or his money back, is then turned on to win friends and influence people, and is confirmed by the possession of "personalized" objects, which are distinguished only by having his initials on them. In short, he appears to be a spoiled child, fundamentally ungrateful to the scientists, political philosophers, social reformers, and religious idealists who have given him his unprecedented opportunities. He is therefore the natural prey of advertisers, politicians, millionaire publishers, and would-be dictators.

Herbert J. Muller, The Uses of The Past

It is important to remember that, if a very much subtler view of the properties of an electron in an atomic system is necessary to describe the wealth of experience we have had with such systems, it all rests on accepting without revision the traditional accounts of the behavior of large-scale objects. The measurements that we have talked about in such highly abstract form do in fact come down in the end to looking at the position of a pointer, or the reading of time on a watch, or measuring out where on a photographic plate or a phosphorescent screen a flash of light or a patch of darkness occurs. They all rest on reducing the experience with atomic systems to experiment and observation made manifest, unambiguous, and objective in the behavior of large objects, where the precautions and incertitudes of the atomic domain no longer directly apply. So it is that ever-increasing refinements and critical revisions in the way we talk about remote or small or inaccessible parts of the physical world have no direct relevance to the familiar physical world of common experience.

J. Robert Oppenheimer, "Uncommon Sense"

The man of understanding can no more sit quiet and resigned while his country lets its literature decay, and lets good writing meet with contempt, than a good doctor could sit quiet and contented while some ignorant child was infecting itself with tuberculosis under the impression that it was merely eating jam tarts.

It is very difficult to make people understand the *impersonal* indignation that a decay of writing can cause men who understand what it implies, and the end whereto it leads. It is almost impossible to express any degree of such indignation without being called "embittered," or something of that sort.

Nevertheless the "statesman cannot govern, the scientist cannot participate his discoveries, man cannot agree on wise action without language," and all their deeds and conditions are affected by the defects or virtues of idiom.

A people that grows accustomed to sloppy writing is a people in process of losing grip on its empire and on itself. And this looseness and blowsiness is not anything as simple and scandalous as abrupt and disordered syntax.

It concerns the relation of expression to meaning. Abrupt and disordered syntax can be at times very honest, and an elaborately constructed sentence can be at times merely an elaborate camouflage.

Ezra Pound, ABC of Reading

Poe the maker betrayed the plastic world. By degrees he surrendered his effort to mold and shape matter into meaning. His mind arched over percept into concept, arched over the multiplicity of particulars into a kind of abstract truth that establishes relationships at the expense of particularity. It had to be so. Self had to be saved. The world could not be made to stand still, so the world became the enemy.

To depart, yet live. The question, then, is how the "exciting knowledge," the "never-to-be-imparted secret, whose attainment is destruction," can be gained without loss of identity. The explicit answer is that it can't, but that we have something even more satisfying: the self as God. Between the unanswerable question and the unquestioning answer we have the rhythm of the work of Poe; at one extreme, an infolding: the terror of annihilation, the embrace of self and a monomaniacal concern with the preservation of identity, the probing and dissecting of inner reality; at the other extreme, an unfolding: the quest for a personal unified field theory, the searching of the universe for introvertible evidence that no soul is greater than his own, the clipping and pasting of a cosmic reality.

From an Essay in PMLA, 1962

But while the trivial pleasures of culture have their place as a relief from the trivial worries of practical life, the more important merits of contemplation are in relation to the greater evils of life, death and pain and cruelty, and the blind march of nations into unnecessary disaster. . . . What is needed is not this or that specific piece of information, but such knowledge as inspires a conception of the ends of human life as a whole: art and history, acquaintance with the lives of heroic individuals, and some understanding of the strangely accidental and ephemeral position of man in the cosmos—all this touched with an emotion of pride in what is distinctively human, the power to see and to know, to feel magnanimously and to think with understanding. It is from large perceptions combined with impersonal emotion that wisdom most readily springs.

Life, at all times full of pain, is more painful in our time than in the two centuries that preceded it. The attempt to escape from pain drives men to triviality, to self-deception, to the invention of vast collective myths. But these momentary alleviations do but increase the sources of suffering in the long run. Both private and public misfortune can only be mastered by a process in which will and intelligence interact: the part of will is to refuse to shirk the evil or accept an unreal solution, while the part of intelligence is to understand it, to find a cure if it is curable, and, if not, to make it bearable by seeing it in its relations, accepting it as unavoidable, and remembering what lies outside it in other regions, other ages, and the abysses of interstellar space.

Bertrand Russell, "Useless Knowledge"

If you really want to hear about it, the first thing you'll probably want to know is where I was born, and what my lousy childhood was like, and how my parents were occupied and all before they had me, and all that David Copperfield kind of crap, but I don't feel like going into it, if you want to know the truth. In the first place, that stuff bores me, and in the second place, my parents would have about two hemorrhages apiece if I told anything pretty personal about them. They're quite touchy about anything like that, especially my father. They're *nice* and all—I'm not saying that—but they're also touchy as hell. Besides, I'm not going to tell you my whole goddam autobiography or anything. I'll just tell you about this madman stuff that happened to me around last Christmas just before I got pretty run-down and had to come out here and take it easy. I mean that's all I told D.B. about, and he's my *brother* and all. He's in Hollywood. That isn't too far from this crumby place, and he comes over and visits me practically every week end. He's going to drive me home when I go home next month maybe. He just got a jaguar. One of those little English jobs that can do around two hundred miles an hour. It cost him damn near four thousand bucks. He's got a lot of dough, now. He didn't *use* to. He used to be just a regular writer, when he was home. . . . Now he's out in Hollywood, D.B., being a prostitute. If there's one thing I hate, it's the movies. Don't even mention them to me.

J. D. Salinger, The Catcher in the Rye

[Josiah] Royce sometimes felt that he might have turned his hand to other things than philosophy. He once wrote a novel, and its want of success was a silent disappointment to him. Perhaps he might have been a great musician. Complexity, repetitions, vagueness, endlessness are hardly virtues in writing or thinking, but in music they might have swelled and swelled into a real sublimity, all the more that he was patient, had a voluminous meandering memory, and loved technical devices. But rather than a musician—for he was no artist—he resembled some great-hearted mediaeval peasant visited by mystical promptings, whom the monks should have adopted and allowed to browse among their theological folios; a Duns Scotus earnest and studious to a fault, not having the lightness of soul to despise those elaborate sophistries, yet minded to ferret out their secret for himself and walk by his inward light. His was a Gothic and scholastic spirit, intent on devising and solving puzzles, and honouring God in systematic works, like the coral insect or the spider; eventually creating a fabric that in its homely intricacy and fullness arrested and moved the heart, the web of it was so vast, and so full of mystery and yearning.

George Santayana, Character and Opinion in the United States

. . . No doubt I must recognize, as even the Ancient Mariner did, that I must tell my story entertainingly if I am to hold the wedding guest spellbound in spite of the siren sounds of the loud bassoon. But "for art's sake" alone I would not face the toil of writing a single sentence. I know that there are men who, having nothing to say and nothing to write, are nevertheless so in love with oratory and with literature that they delight in repeating as much as they can understand of what others have said or written aforetime. I know that the leisurely tricks which their want of conviction leaves them free to play with the diluted and misapprehended message supply them with a pleasant parlor game which they call style. I can pity their dotage and even sympathize with their fancy. But a true original style is never achieved for its own sake: a man may pay from a shilling to a guinea, according to his means, to see, hear, or read another man's act of genius; but he will not pay with his whole life and soul to become a mere virtuoso in literature, exhibiting an accomplishment which will not even make money for him, like fiddle playing. Effectiveness of assertion is the Alpha and Omega of style. He who has nothing to assert has no style and can have none: he who has something to assert will go as far in power of style as its momentousness and his conviction will carry him. Disprove his assertion after it is made, yet its style remains. . . .

George Bernard Shaw, Epistle Dedicatory to "Man and Superman"

Dr. Arnold's energies were by no means exhausted by his duties at Rugby. He became known, not merely as a Headmaster, but as a public man. He held decided opinions upon a large number of topics and he enunciated them— based as they were almost invariably upon general principles—in pamphlets, in prefaces, and in magazine articles, with an impressive self-confidence. He was, as he constantly declared, a Liberal. In his opinion, by the very constitution of human nature, the principles of progress and reform had been those of wisdom and justice in every age of the world—except one: that which had preceded the fall of man from Paradise. Had he lived then, Dr. Arnold would have been a Conservative. As it was, his liberalism was tempered by an "abhorrence of the spirit of 1789, of the American War, of the French Economists, and of the English Whigs of the latter part of the seventeenth century"; and he always entertained a profound respect for the hereditary peerage. It might almost be said, in fact, that he was an orthodox Liberal. He believed in toleration, too, within limits; that is to say, in the toleration of those with whom he agreed. "I would give James Mill as much opportunity for advocating his opinion," he said, "as is consistent with a voyage to Botany Bay." He had become convinced of the duty of sympathising with the lower orders ever since he had made a serious study of the Epistle of St. James; but he perceived clearly that the lower orders fell into two classes, and that it was necessary to distinguish between them. There were the "good poor"— and there were the others. . . .

Lytton Strachey, Eminent Victorians

The bowerbird is another creature that spends so much time courting the female that he never gets any work done. If all the male bowerbirds became nervous wrecks within the next ten or fiteen years, it would not surprise me. The female bowerbird insists that a playground be built for her with a specially constructed bower at the entrance. This bower is much more elaborate than an ordinary nest and is harder to build; it costs a lot more, too. The female will not come to the playground until the male has filled it up with a great many gifts: silvery leaves, red leaves, rose petals, shells, beads, berries, bones, dice, buttons, cigar bands, Christmas seals, and the Lord know what else. When the female finally condescends to visit the playground, she is in a coy and silly mood and has to be chased in and out of the bower and up and down the playground before she will quit giggling and stand still long enough even to shake hands. The male bird is, of course, pretty well done in before the chase starts, because he has worn himself out hunting for eyeglass lenses and begonia blossoms. I imagine that many a bowerbird, after chasing a female for two or three hours, says the hell with it and goes home to bed. Next day, of course, he telephones someone else and the same trying ritual is gone through with again. A male bowerbird is as exhausted as a night-club habitué before he is out of his twenties.

James Thurber, "Courtship Through the Ages".

We spread the blankets inside for a carpet, and eat our dinner in there. We put all the other things handy at the back of the cavern. Pretty soon it darkened up and begun to thunder and lighten; so the birds was right about it. Directly it begun to rain and it rained like all fury, too, and I never see the wind blow so. It was one of these regular summer storms. It would get so dark that it looked all blue-black outside, and lovely; and the rain would thrash along by so thick that the trees off a little ways looked dim and spider-webby; and here would come a blast of wind that would bend the trees down and turn up the pale underside of the leaves; and then a perfect ripper of a gust would follow along and set the branches to tossing their arms as if they was just wild; and next, when it was just about the bluest and blackest —*fst!* it was as bright as glory and you'd have a little glimpse of tree-tops a-plunging about away off yonder in the storm, hundreds of yards further than you could see before; dark as sin again in a second and now you'd hear the thunder let go with an awful crash and then go rumbling, grumbling, tumbling down the sky towards the under side of the world, like rolling empty barrels down-stairs—where it's long stairs and they bounce a good deal, you know.

Mark Twain, Huckleberry Finn

Heart had gone out of these people; health was the principal thing about the faces of the Americans that came crowding through the broken wall to the poorhouse fair. They were just people, members of the race of white animals that had cast its herd over the land of six continents. Highly neural, brachycephalic, uniquely able to oppose their thumbs to the four other digits, they bred within elegant settlements, and both burned and interred their dead. History had passed on beyond them. They remembered its moment and came to the fair to be freshened in the recollection of an older America, the America of Dan Patch and of Senator Beveridge exhorting the Anglo-Saxons to march across the Pacific and save the beautiful weak-minded islands there, an America of stained-glass lampshades, hardshell evangelists, Flag Days, ice men, plug tobacco, China trade, oval windows marking on the exterior of a house a stair landing within, pungent nostrums for catarrhal complaints, opportunism, churchgoing, and well-worded orations in the glare of a cemetery on summer days.

John Updike, The Poorhouse Fair

The American university is not an eleemosynary institution; it does not plead indigence, except in that Pickwickian sense in which indigence may without shame be avowed in polite circles; nor does it put its trust in donations of that sparseness and modesty which the gifts of charity commonly have. Its recourse necessarily is that substantial and dignified class of gifts that are not given thriftily on compunction of charity, but out of the fulness of the purse. These dignified gifts commonly aim to promote the most reputable interests of humanity, rather than the sordid needs of creature comfort, at the same time that they serve to fortify the donor's good name in good company. Donations to university funds have something of the character of an investment in good fame; they are made by gentlemen and gentlewomen, to gentlemen, and the transactions begin and end within the circle of pecuniary respectability. An impeccable respectability, authentic in the pecuniary respect, therefore, affords the only ground on which such a seminary of learning can reasonably claim the sympathetic attention of the only class whose attentions are seriously worth engaging in these premises; and respectability is inseparable from an expensive scale of living, in any community whose scheme of life is conventionally regulated by pecuniary standards.

Thorstein Veblen, The Higher Learning in America

They ain't real, I thought as I walked down the hall, *nary one.* But I knew they were. You come into a strange place, into a town like Mason City, and they don't seem real, but you know they are. You know they went wading in the creek when they were kids, and when they were bigger they used to go out about sunset and lean on the back fence and look across the country at the sky and not know what was happening inside them or whether they were happy or sad, and when they got grown they slept with their wives and tickled their babies to make them laugh and went to work in the morning and didn't know what they wanted but had their reasons for doing things and wanted to do good things, because they always gave good reasons for doing the things they did, and then when they got old they lost their reasons for doing anything and sat on the bench in front of the harness shop and had words for the reasons other people had but had forgotten what the reasons were. And then they will lie in bed some morning just before day and look up at the ceiling they can scarcely see because the lamp is shaded with a pinned-on newspaper and they don't recognize the faces around the bed any more because the room is full of smoke, or fog, and it makes their eyes burn and gets in the throat. Oh, they are real, all right, and it may be the reason they don't seem real to you is that you aren't very real yourself.

Robert Penn Warren, All the King's Men

Today, the language of advertising enjoys an enormous circulation. With its deliberate infractions of grammatical rules and its crossbreeding of the parts of speech, it profoundly influences the tongues and pens of children and adults. Your new kitchen range is so revolutionary it *obsoletes* all other ranges. Your counter top is beautiful because it is *accessorized* with gold-plated faucets. Your cigarette tastes good *like* a cigarette should. And *like the man says,* you will want to try one. You will also, in all probability, want to try writing that way, using that language. You do so at your peril, for it is the language of mutilation.

Advertisers are quite understandably interested in what they call "attention getting." The man photographed must have lost an eye or grown a pink beard, or he must have three arms or be sitting wrong end to on a horse. This technique is proper in its place, which is the world of selling, but the young writer had best not adopt the device of mutilation in ordinary composition, whose purpose is to engage, not paralyze, the reader's senses. . . .

E. B. White, The Elements of Style

The wheeps, beeps, freeps, electronic lulus, Boomerang Modern and Flash Gordon sunbursts soar on through the night over the billowing hernia-hernia sounds and the old babes at the slots—until it is 7:30 A.M. and I am watching five men at a green-topped card table playing poker. They are sliding their Bee-brand cards into their hands and squinting at the pips with a set to the lips like Conrad Veidt in a tunic collar studying a code message from S.S. headquarters. Big Sid Wyman, the old Big-Time gambler from St. Louis, is there, with his eyes looking like two poached eggs engraved with a road map of West Virginia after all night at the poker table. Sixty-year old Chicago Tommy Hargan is there with his topknot of white hair pulled back over his little pink skull and a mountain of chips in front of his old caved-in sternum. Sixty-two-year-old Dallas Maxie Welch is there, fat and phlegmatic as an Indian Ocean potentate. . . . It looks like the perfect vignette of every Big Time back room, "athletic club," snooker house and floating poker game in the history of the guys-and-dolls lumpen-bourgeoisie. . . .

Tom Wolfe, The Kandy-kolored Tangerine-flake Streamline Baby.

Yes, and in that month when Proserpine comes back, and Ceres' dead heart rekindles, when all the woods are a tender smoky blur, and birds no bigger than a budding leaf dart through the singing trees, and when odorous tar comes spongy in the streets, and boys roll balls of it upon their tongues, and they are lumpy with tops and agated marbles; and there is blasting thunder in the night, and the soaking millionfooted rain, and one looks out at morning on a stormy sky, a broken wrack of cloud; and when the mountain boy brings water to his kinsmen laying fence, and as the wind snakes through the grasses hears far in the valley below the long wail of the whistle, and the faint clangor of a bell; and the blue great cup of the hills seem closer, nearer, for he has heard an inarticulate promise: he has been pierced by Spring, that sharp knife.

And life unscales its rusty weathered pelt, and earth wells out in tender exhaustless strength, and the cup of a man's heart runs over with dateless expectancy, tongueless promise, indefinable desire. Something gathers in the throat, something blinds him in the eyes, and faint and valorous horns sound through the earth.

The little girls trot pigtailed primly on their dutiful way to school; but the young gods loiter: they hear the reed, the oaten-stop, the running goat-hoofs in the spongy wood, here, there, everywhere: they dawdle, listen, fleetest when they wait, go vaguely on to their one fixed home, because the earth is full of ancient rumor and they cannot find the way. All of the gods have lost the way.

Thomas Wolfe, Look Homeward Angel

INDEX OF AUTHORS AND TITLES

An asterisk preceding an author's name or a title indicates that the selection is in the Appendix.

SUPPLEMENTARY INDEX

The authors listed below are found in short analyzable passages in the essays themselves.